To
Madalyn
and
William Nicholas

Scrapbooking Plus!

More Than Just Paper

Kathleen Greco & Nick Greco

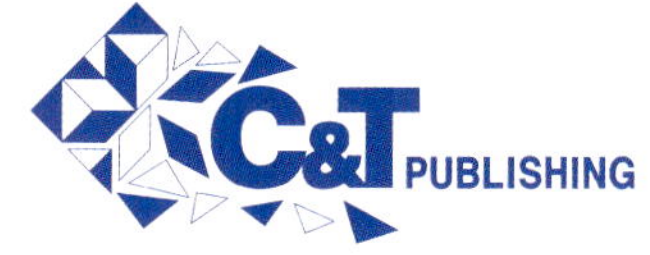

First published in 2005 by
C&T Publishing Inc.,
PO Box 1456
Lafayette, CA 94549
and
Dimensional Illustrators, Inc.
362 Second Street Pike / #112
Southampton, PA 18966
www.3dimillus.com

Attention Teachers: C&T Publishing encourages you to use this book as a text for teaching. Contact us at 800-284-1114 or www.ctpub.com for more information about C&T Teachers Programs.

Library of Congress Cataloging-in-Publication Data

Greco, Kathleen.
Scrapbooking plus! : more than just paper / Kathleen Greco, Nick Greco.
p. cm.
ISBN-13: 978-1-57120-349-6 (paper trade)
ISBN-10: 1-57120-349-4 (paper trade)
ISBN-10: 1-885660-17-0 (paper trade)
1. Photograph albums. 2. Photographs Conservation and restoration. 3. Scrapbooks I. Greco, Nick. II. Title

TR465.G75 2005
745.593--dc22

2005009212

Printed in China 10 9 8 7 6 5 4 3 2 1

Creative Director
Kathleen Greco

Executive Editor
Nick Greco

Design and Typography
Deborah Davis / Deborah Davis Design

Book Photography
Kathleen Greco

We wish to thank all our friends and family for their help and cooperation in compiling all the photographs used in this book. We have enjoyed reminiscing about the past and look forward to creating new memories in the future.

Nick and Kathleen Greco

Contents

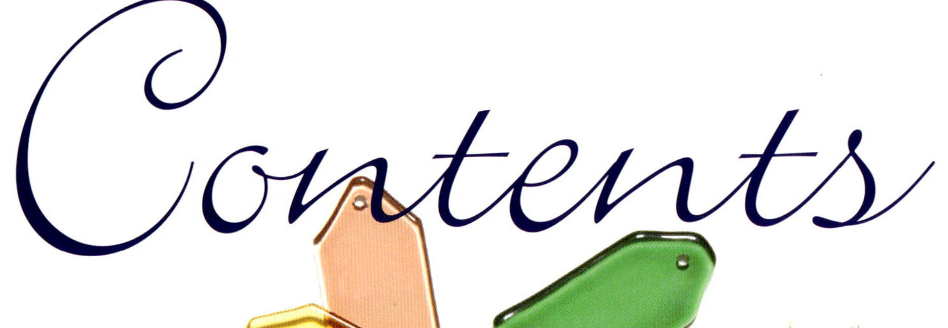

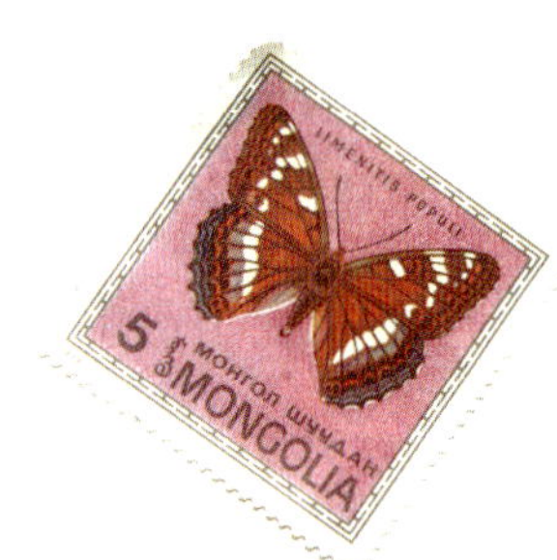

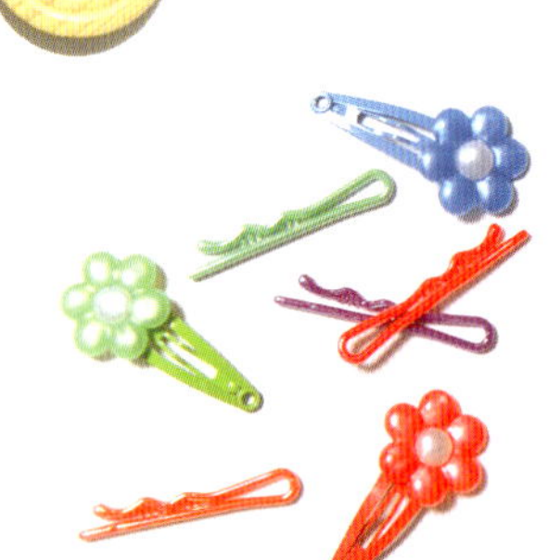

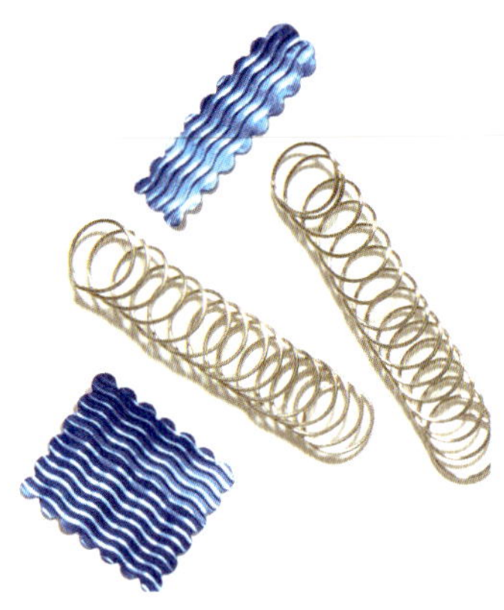

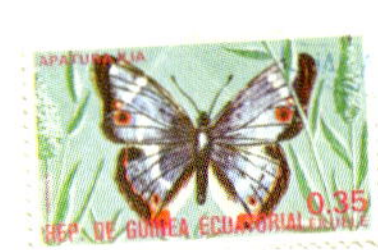

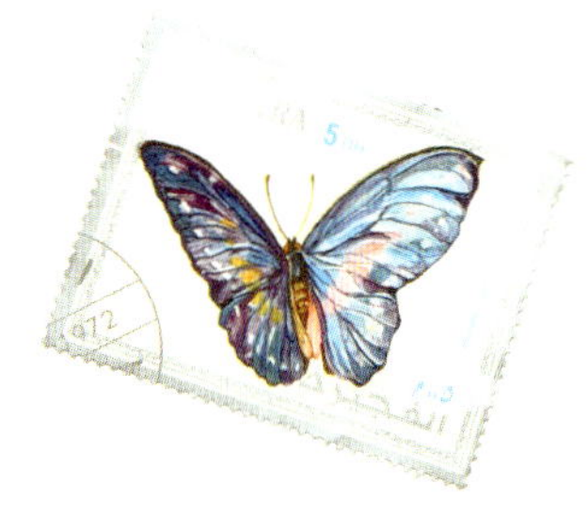

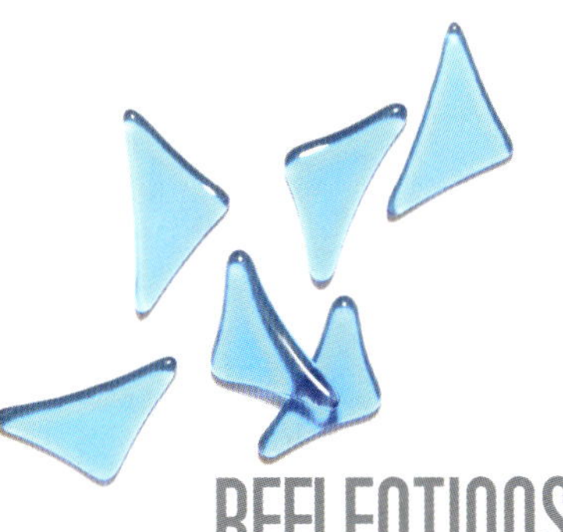

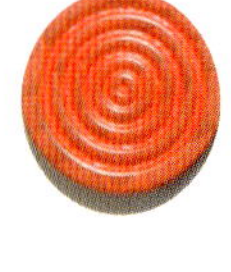

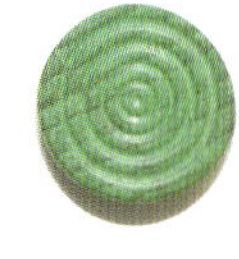

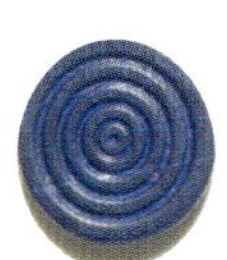

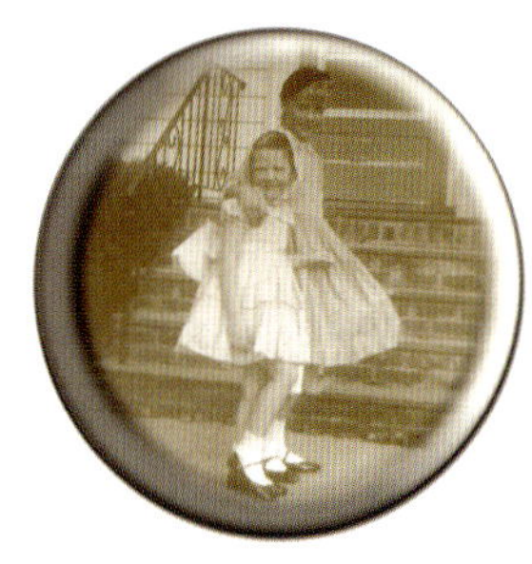

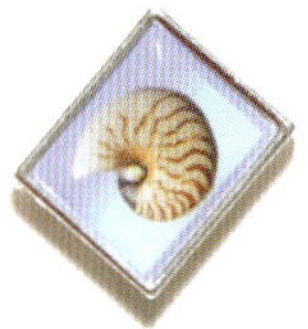

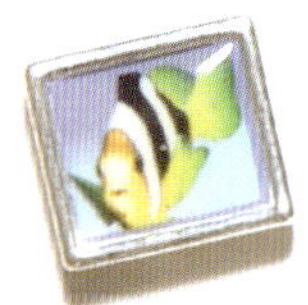

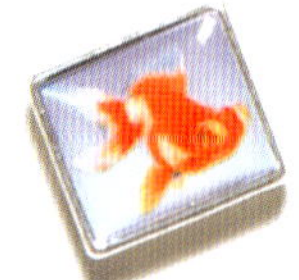

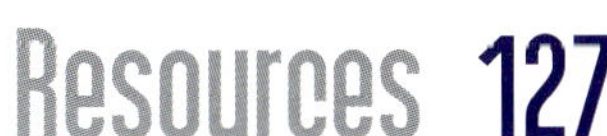

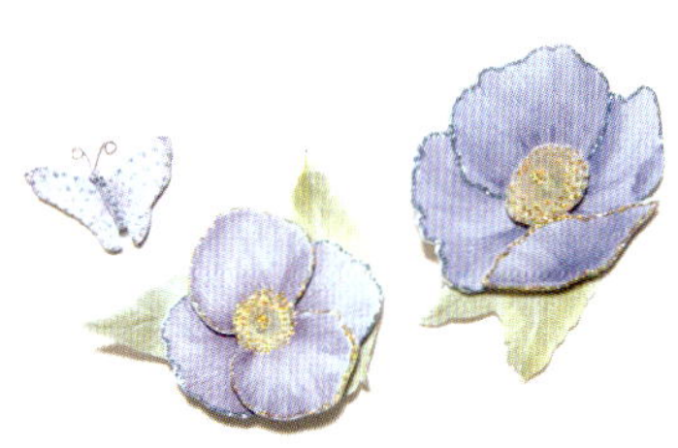

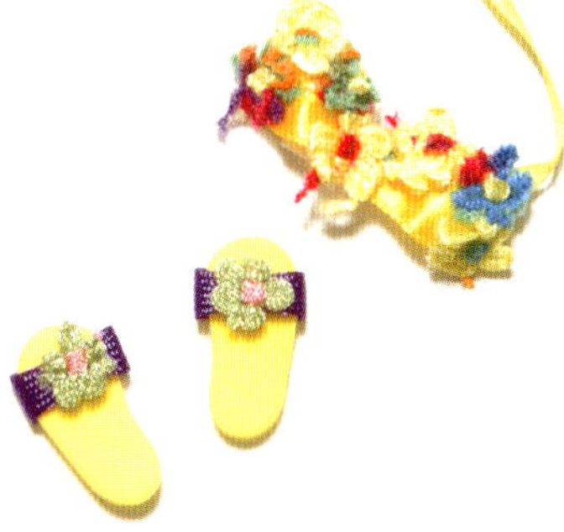

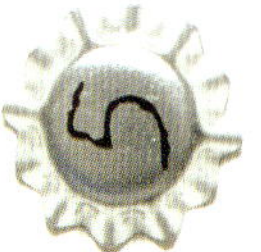

Introduction

In compiling this book, we created scrapbook pages preserving treasured family memories of our life's journey with friends and family. While selecting memorable photos and materials for this premiere edition, we were made privy to upcoming products by some of the foremost manufacturers in the scrapbook industry. As *Scrapbooking Plus! More Than Just Paper* came to fruition, we preserved old memories, and explored new products and design techniques. This book showcases more than sixty-five full-color projects; offers a step-by-step description of each layout, and a detailed color photograph of each product. Technique hints present proven shortcuts to sharpen your scrapbooking skills; get your creativity flowing, and reveal your artistic talents. Our goal is to present fresh ideas using the hottest resources available in craft stores and online.

This indispensable guide provides the inspiration and instructions to produce innovative scrapbook albums using the coolest contemporary materials. Whether you are a novice, intermediate or scrapbook specialist, *Scrapbooking Plus!* provides a fresh dimension in scrapbooking with *more than just paper!*

Nick and Kathleen Greco

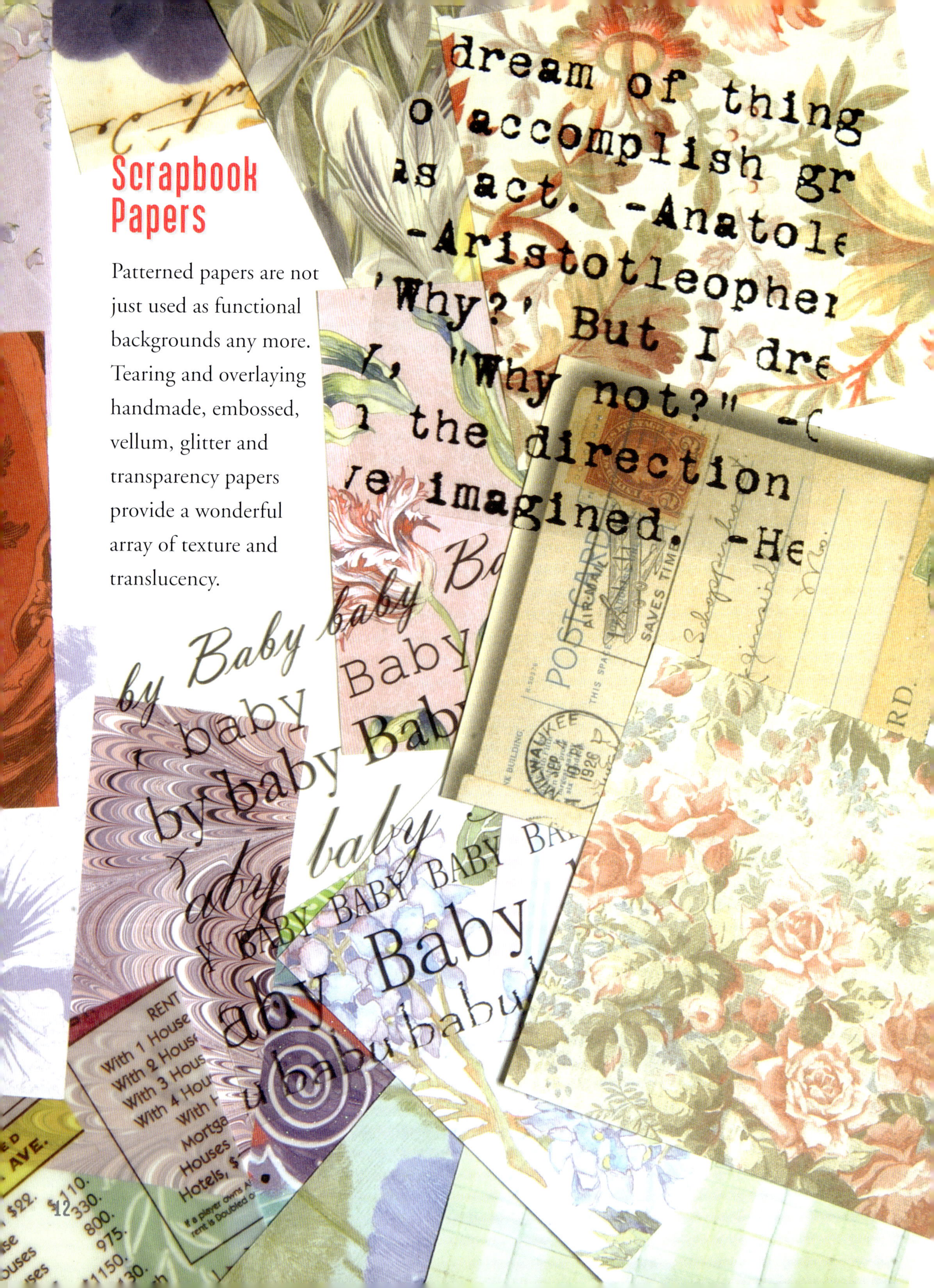

Scrapbook Papers

Patterned papers are not just used as functional backgrounds any more. Tearing and overlaying handmade, embossed, vellum, glitter and transparency papers provide a wonderful array of texture and translucency.

Tags and Pockets

Today, tag art is very hot! Paper, glass, metal, vellum and transparency tags can be collaged, stamped, painted and decorated with yarn or ribbon in a variety of creative themes.

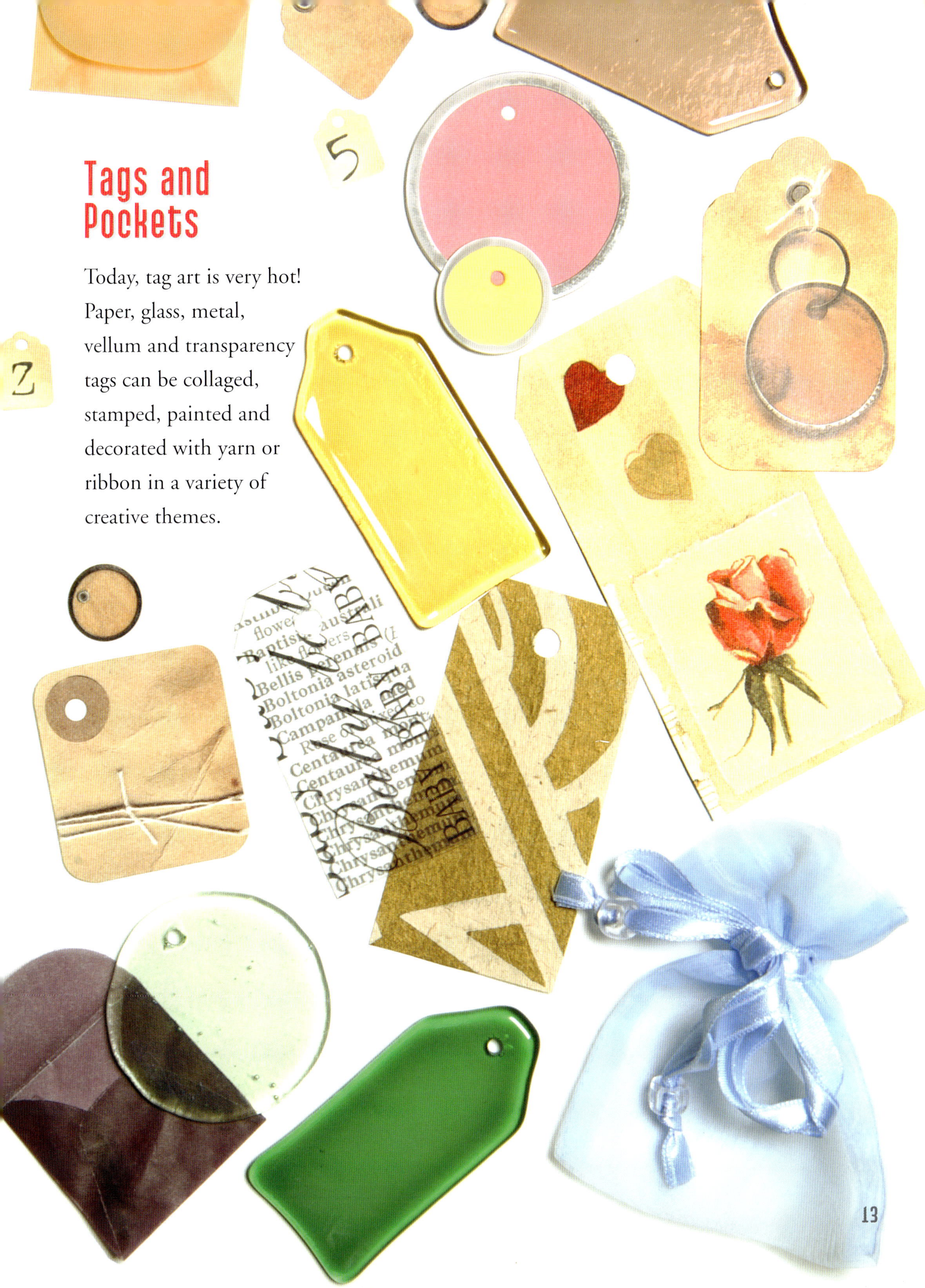

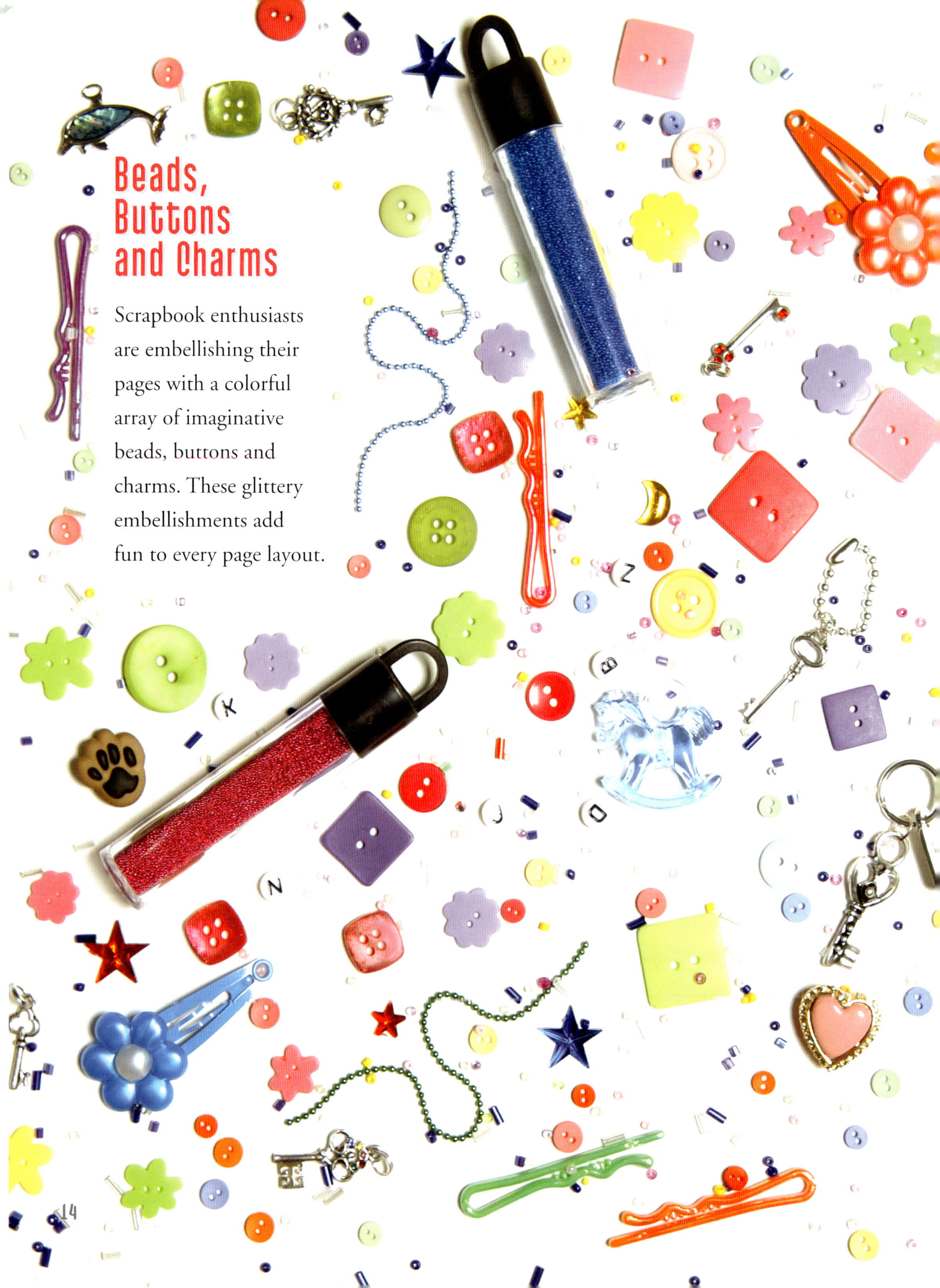

Beads, Buttons and Charms

Scrapbook enthusiasts are embellishing their pages with a colorful array of imaginative beads, buttons and charms. These glittery embellishments add fun to every page layout.

Die Cuts and Dimensional Stickers

Take your cherished scrapbook pages to new heights with dimensional stickers and die cuts. Embellished collage stickers add visual interest to your scrapbook layouts, as well.

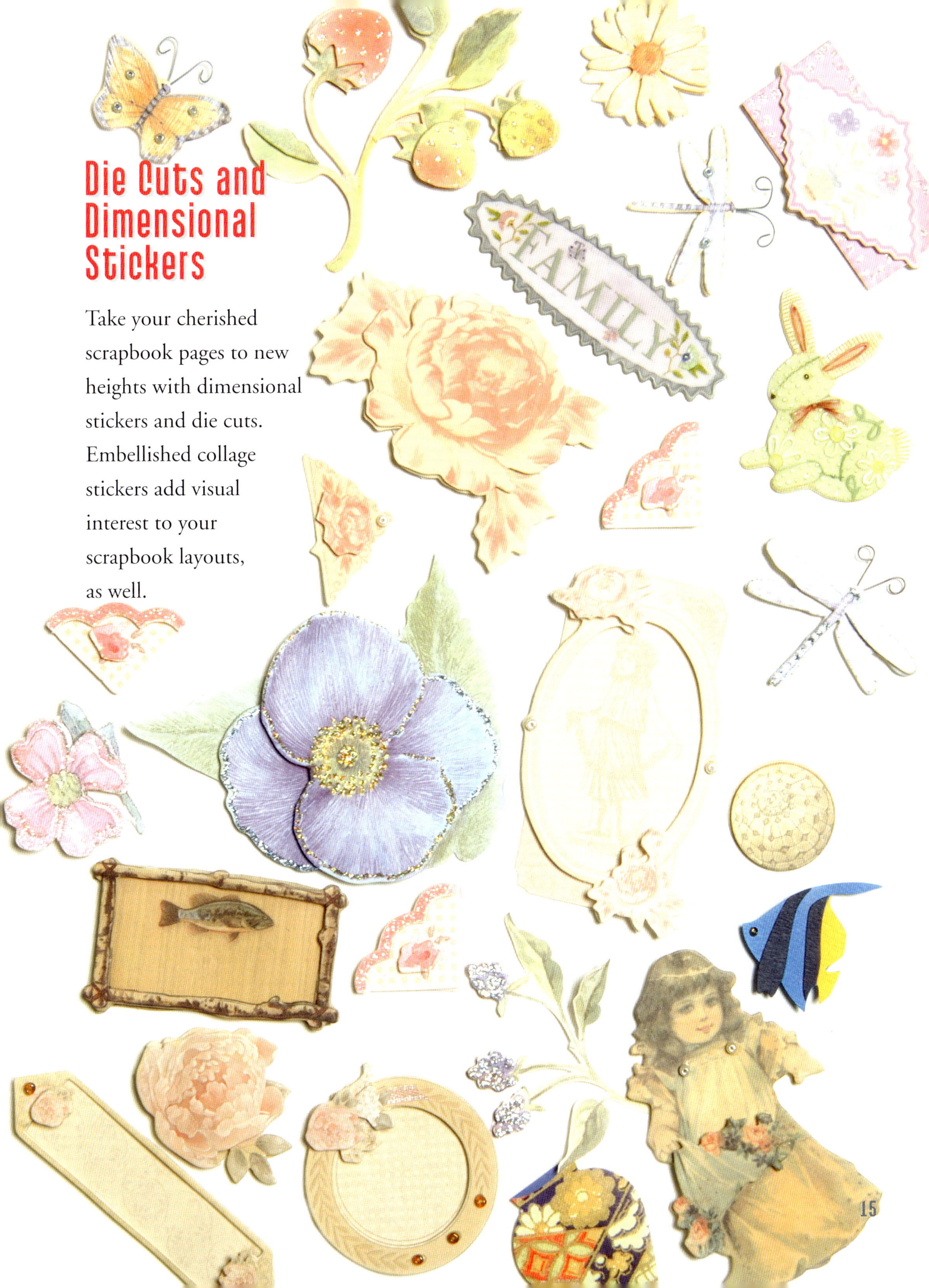

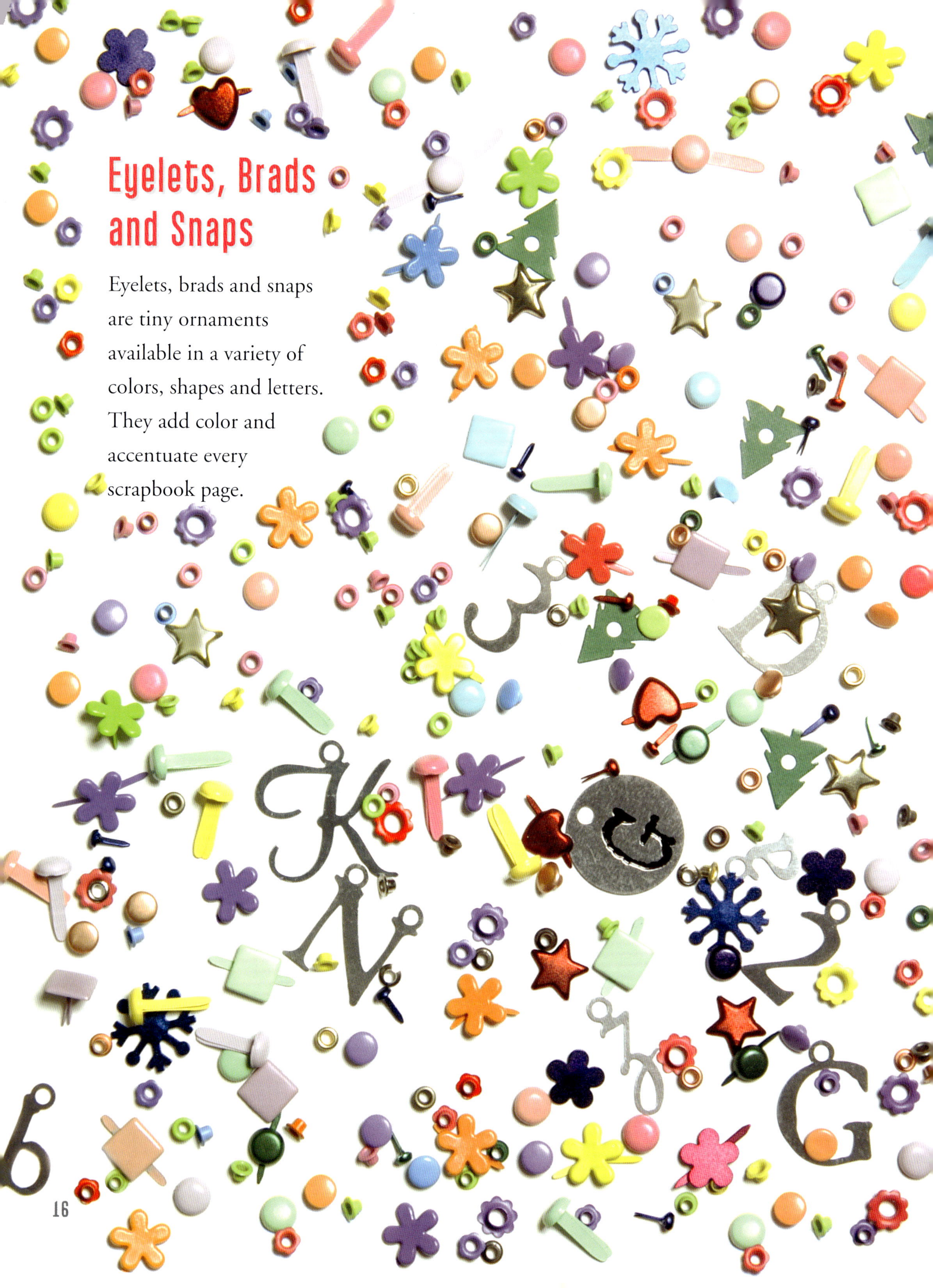

Eyelets, Brads and Snaps

Eyelets, brads and snaps are tiny ornaments available in a variety of colors, shapes and letters. They add color and accentuate every scrapbook page.

Metallic Accents

Add dazzle to your scrapbook pages with metallic accents including micro-thin foil sheets, metal mesh, clips, wire, color staples and gold leaf flakes,—just to mention a few.

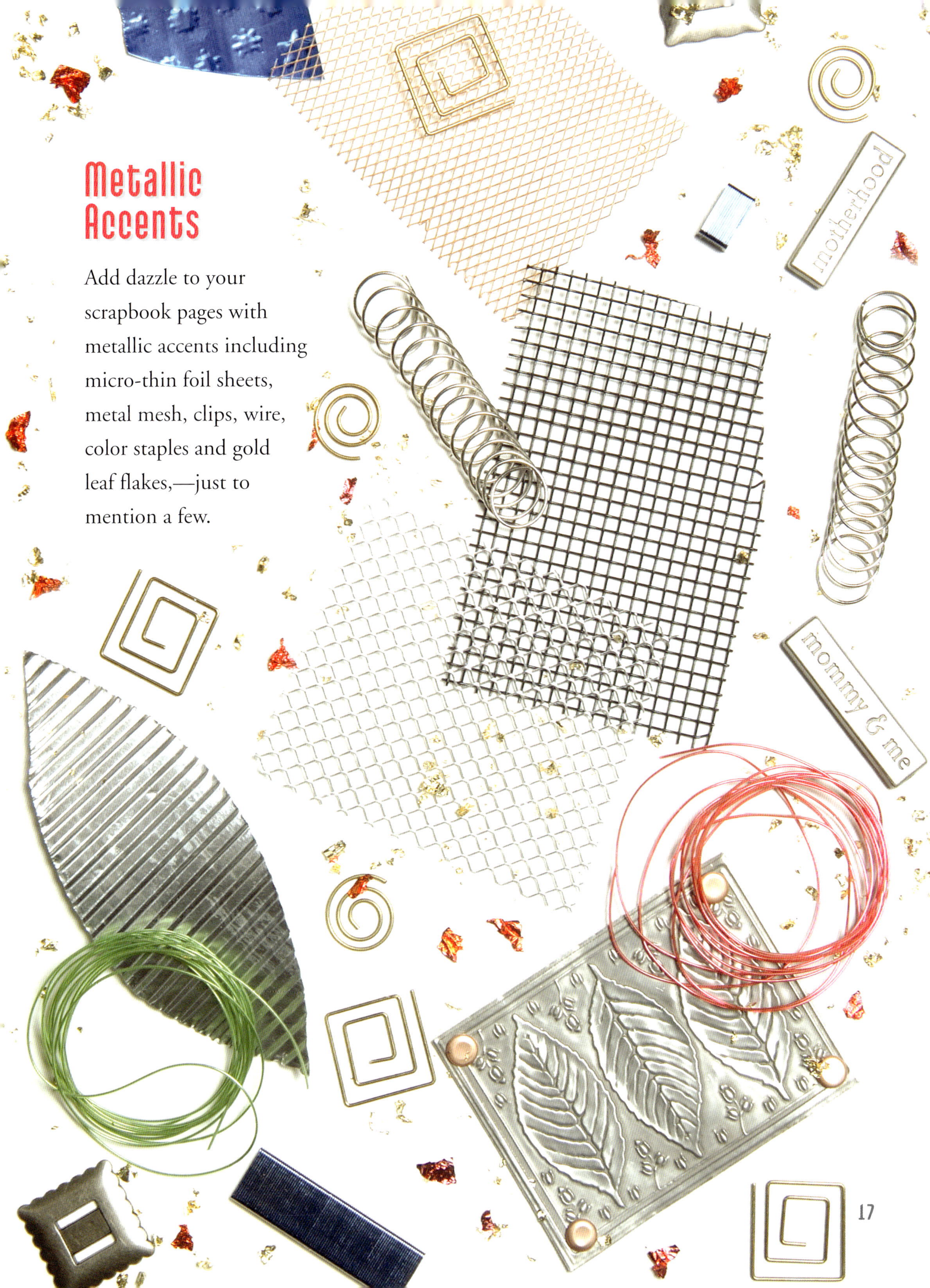

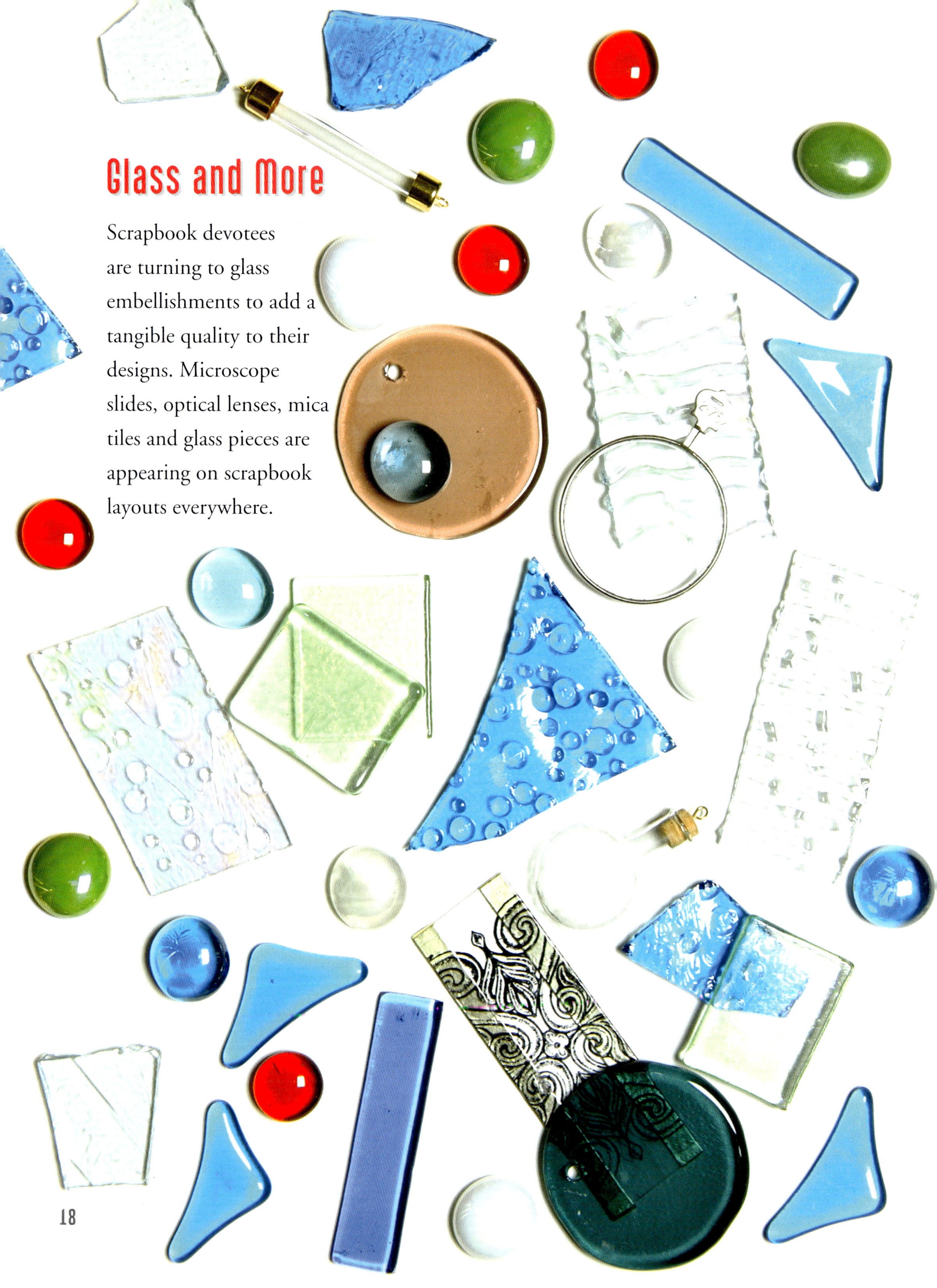

Glass and More

Scrapbook devotees are turning to glass embellishments to add a tangible quality to their designs. Microscope slides, optical lenses, mica tiles and glass pieces are appearing on scrapbook layouts everywhere.

Altered Design

When creating altered scrapbook pages, old is definitely new. Passionate scrapbookers are using everything from zippers, vintage buttons and game pieces, to slide mounts, postage stamps and bottle cap lettering to enhance their pages.

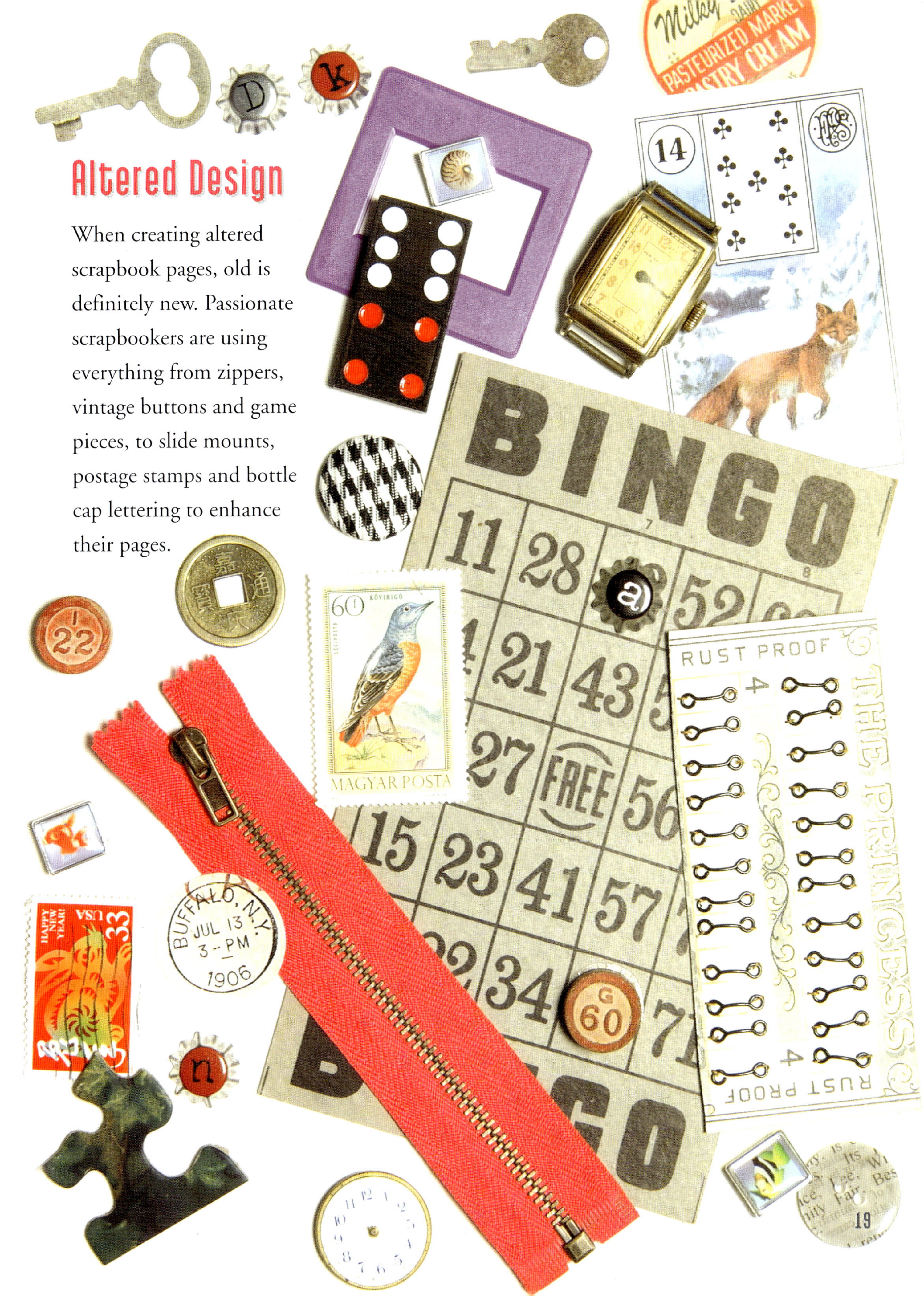

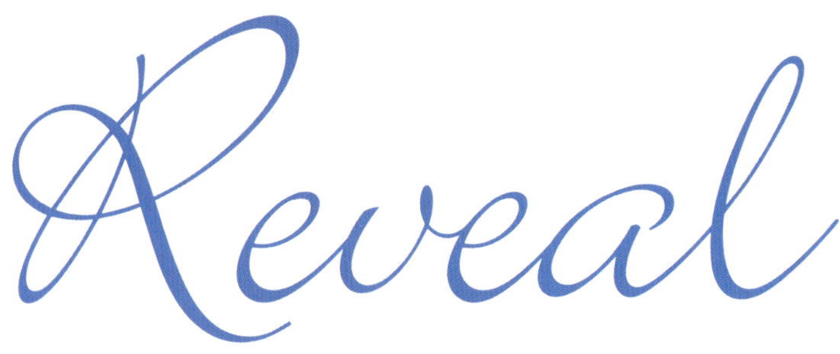

Tags and Pockets

Tag art is one of the hottest scrapbook embellishments. A new class of materials has surpassed plain paper tags. Scrapbook fans are now using tags created from glass, vellum, metal, resin, transparencies and handmade paper. Novel accents including—charms, buttons, die cuts, dimensional stickers, eyelets, snaps, beads and safety pins,—are used to create fresh tag art. Wrap tags in colorful fibers, yarns, ribbons, raffia and colored wire. Use various techniques to decorate tags such as collaging, stamping, embossing, punching or adding metallic powders. Be creative! Design your own tag art with patterned vellum, handmade, mulberry or rice papers. For that treasured keepsake, fill envelopes, pockets and pouches with messages or mementos. Insert your favorite memories in tiny vellum envelopes, paper lace pockets or sheer organza pouches. Tags open a myriad of design possibilities for scrapbook devotees and provide limitless opportunities for designing distinctive scrapbook pages with these inspirational *objets d'art*.

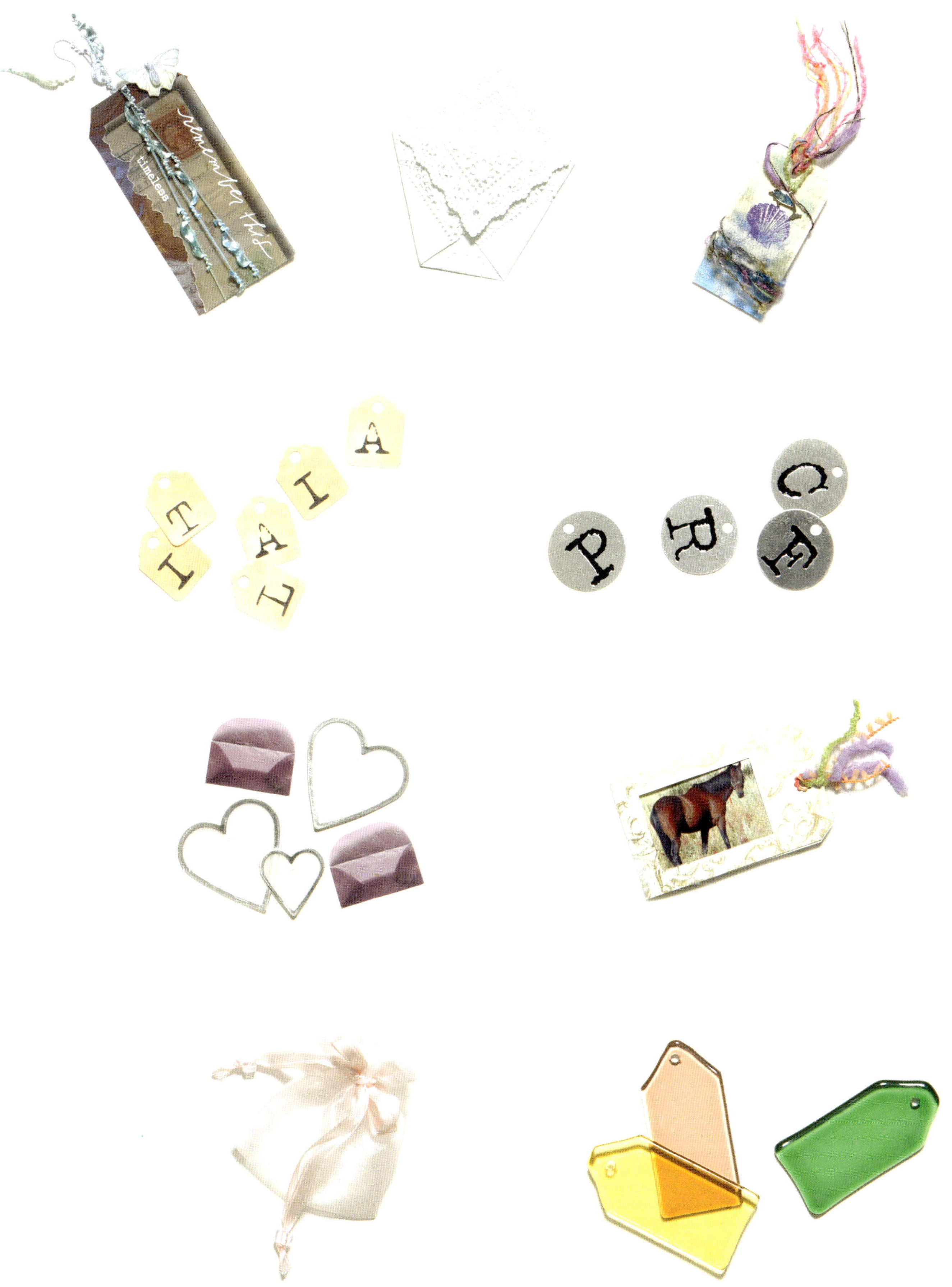
remember this
timeless

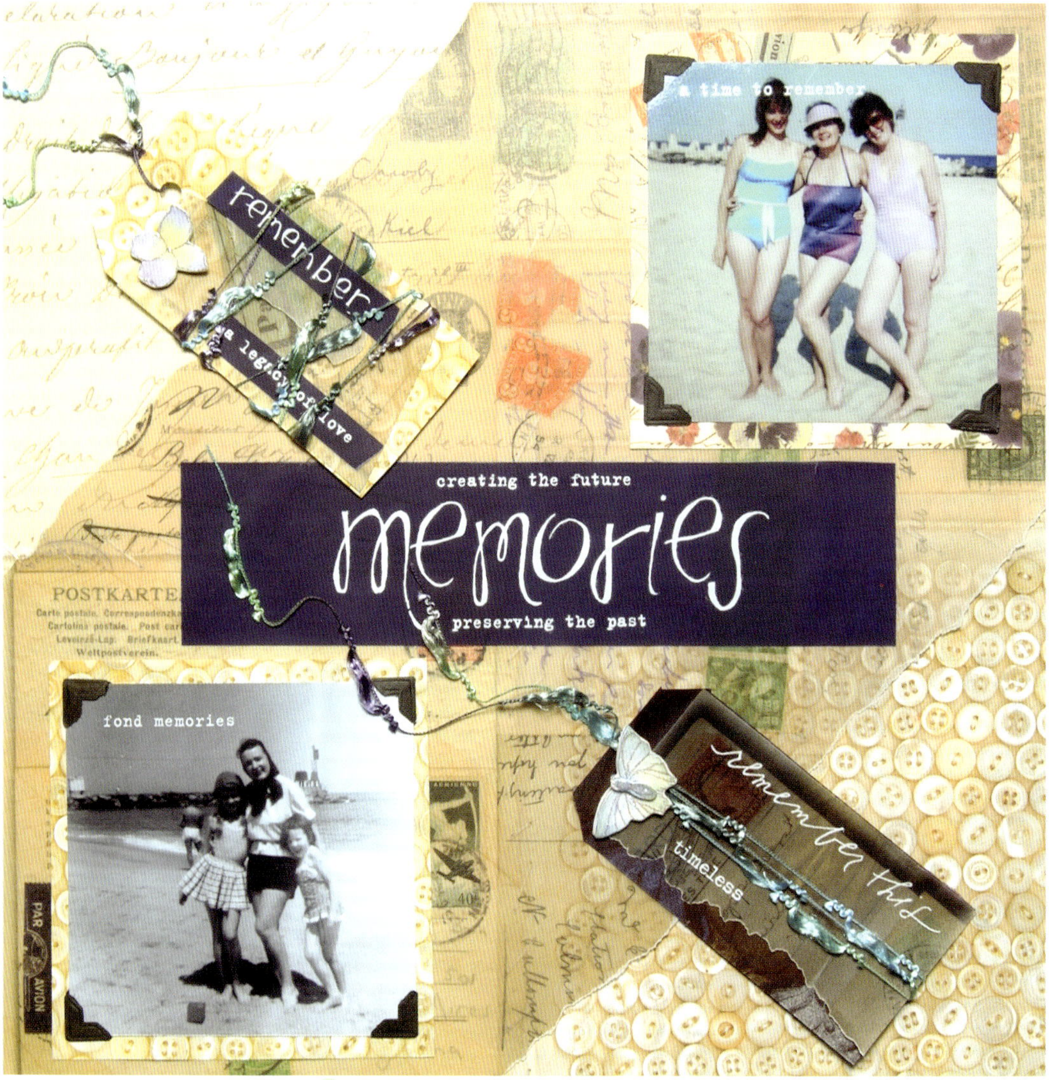

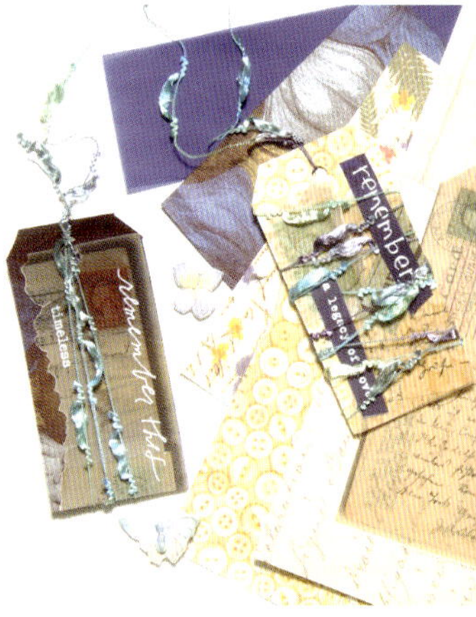

MATERIALS

Solid Vellum *The Paper Company*
Patterned Paper *K&Company*
Patterned Vellum *K&Company*
Dimensional Stickers *K&Company*
Simply Stated Rub-on Words *Making Memories*
Handmade Paper Tags *K&Company*
Photo Corners *Canson*
Candy Yarn *Berroco, Inc.*

TECHNIQUE HINT

When creating handmade tags, position the design with removable glue stick, then adhere permanently with archival glue.

Handmade Collage Tags

I have fond memories of my family on the beach at Point Pleasant, New Jersey. After 30 years, we all returned to the same beach and my Dad photographed us in our favorite spot. Tear patterned vellum on a diagonal and position on patterned paper. Mount photographs with black photo corners on small patterned paper squares leaving a 1/8-inch border. Adhere the photographs in each corner of the patterned vellum paper. Create collage tags from button patterned paper and purple handmade paper. Glue torn strips of vellum to each tag and add dimensional stickers. Apply rub-on lettering and wrap with yarn. For the title, cut a strip of solid blue vellum and apply rub-on lettering. My sister and I often reminisce about the fun-filled days we spent vacationing at the Jersey shore.

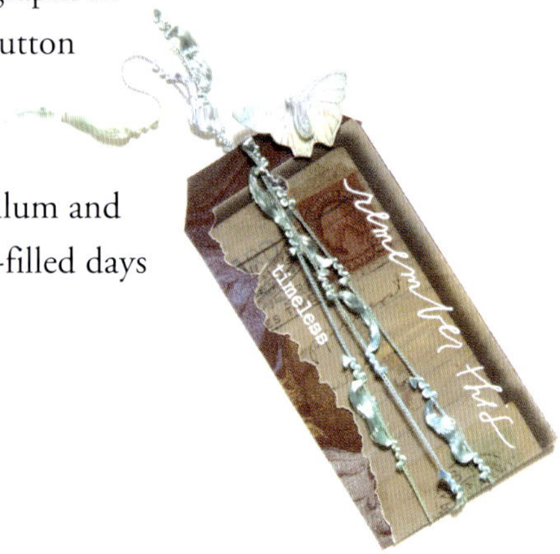

HOW-TO STEPS

handmade collage tags

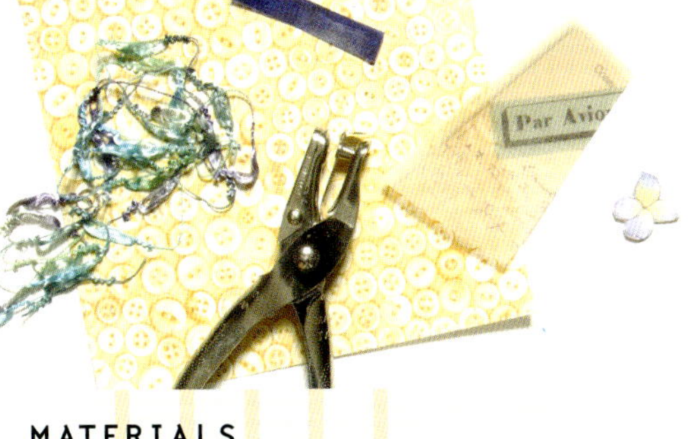

MATERIALS

Button Patterned Paper
Patterned Vellum
Solid Vellum
Dimensional Sticker
Yarn
Hole Punch

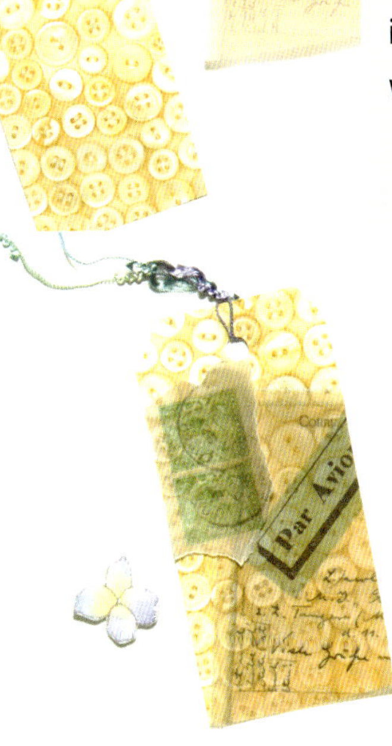

STEP 1
Cut a large tag from a sheet of button paper and punch a hole in the top. Tear interesting parts of vellum into strips.

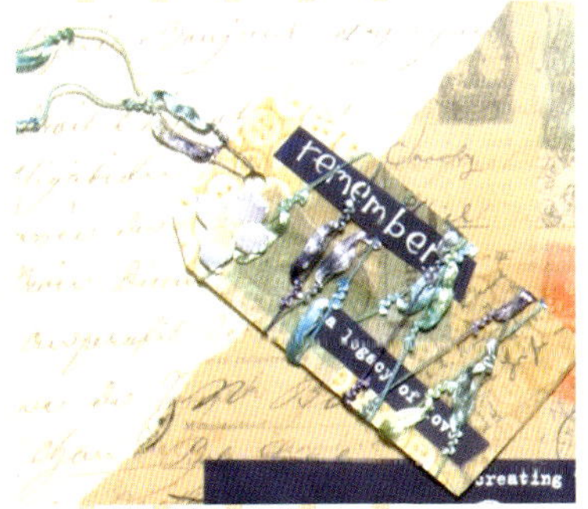

STEP 2
Paste vellum on the tag on an angle. Cut yarn double the required length, fold and loop through the tag hole. Adhere dimensional sticker.

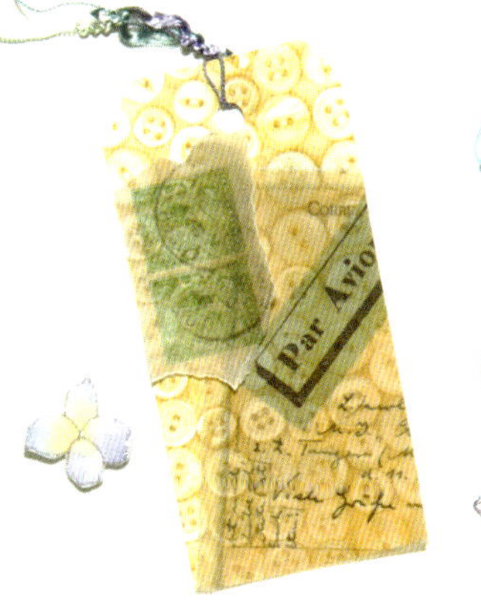

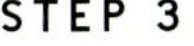

STEP 3
Wrap the yarn around the tags several times on a diagonal. Cut small strips of solid blue vellum and adhere rub-on lettering.

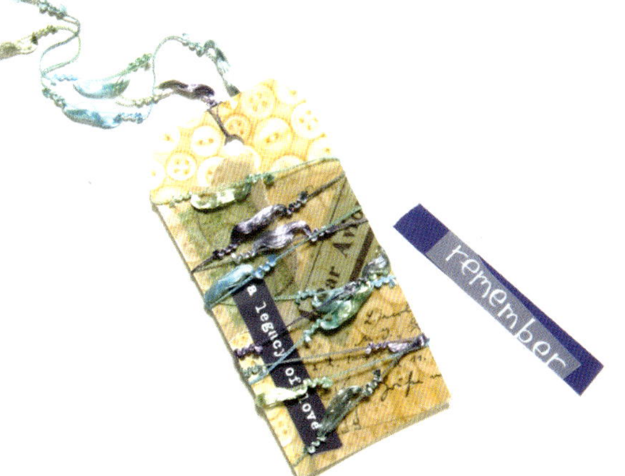

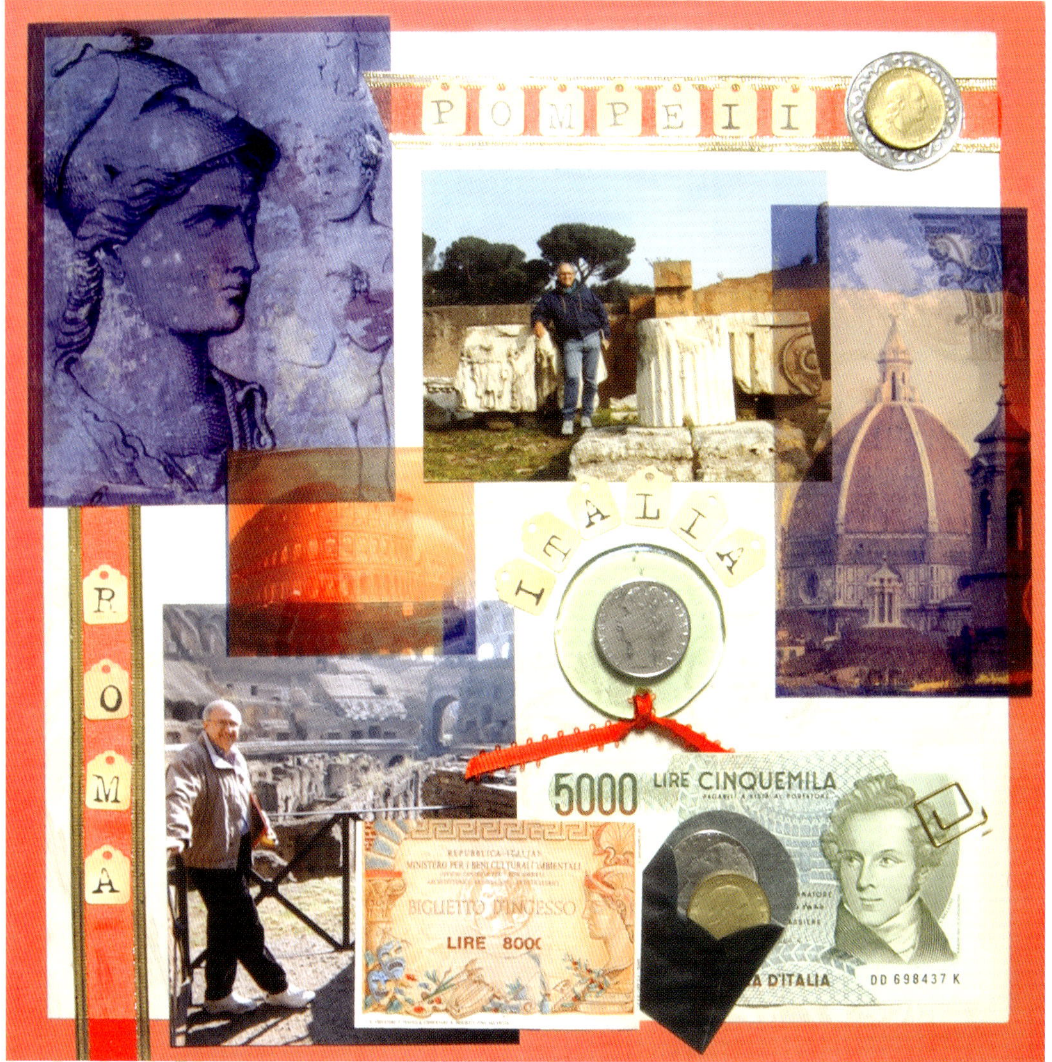

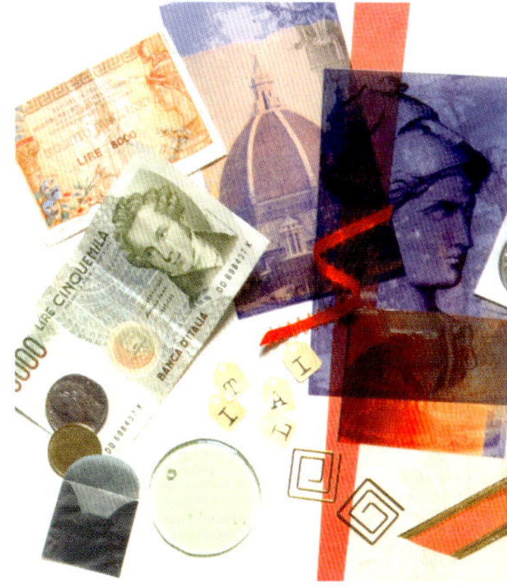

MATERIALS

Solid Paper *Provo Craft*

Patterned Paper *Anna Griffin*

Tea Stained Tag Letters *EK Success*

Transparency Sheet *Available from Stampington & Company*

Glass Tag *Available from Stampington & Company*

Vellum Envelope *The C-Thru Ruler Company*

Italian Currency *Personal Collection*

Ribbon *Offray Ribbon*

Embossed Foil Seal *ANW Crestwood, Inc.*

Shaped Clip *Making Memories*

TECHNIQUE HINT

Self-adhesive tea stained tags are quick and easy. To make your own, stain white tags with a soft sponge dipped in walnut ink.

italia

Tea Stained Tag Letters and Round Glass Tags

Rome and Pompeii are picturesque reminders of the beauty and culture of Italy. Every trip taken to Italy is memorable and worth remembering. To create the border, trim patterned paper 1-inch smaller on two sides and center on red solid paper. Trim photographs and position on the paper. Cut transparencies and place on layout overlapping each photo. Mount photos and glue on transparencies with clear drying glue. Tie red eyelet ribbon to glass tag and glue an Italian coin in the center. Stick tea stained tag letters with the word *Italia* around the glass tag. Cut a 1-inch wide piece of red ribbon and glue down flat. Adhere tea stained tag letters with the words *Roma* and *Pompeii* in position. Stick a silver foil seal in the upper right hand corner and place an Italian coin on top. Adhere vellum envelope with Italian coins. Complete with Italian paper currency, square-shaped clip and museum receipt. The language and culture of the Italian people are constant reminders of the splendid heritage of Italy.

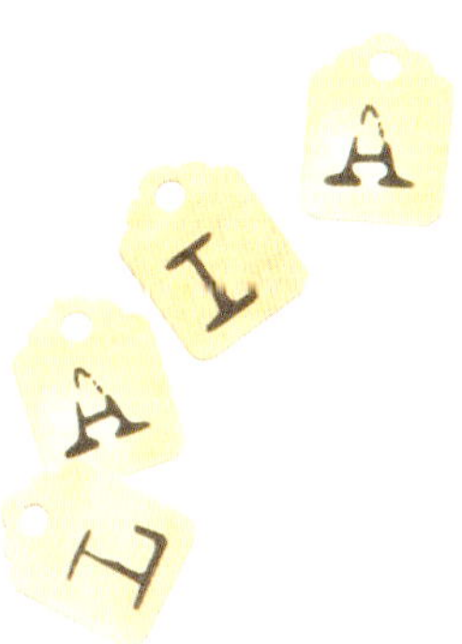

prince Window Tags

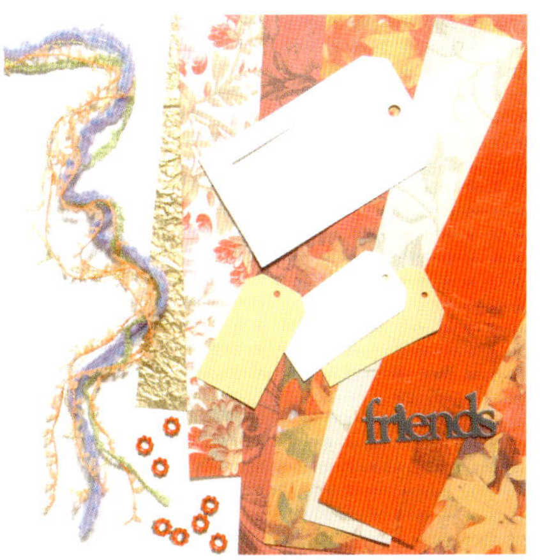

My niece Julia was fortunate to receive a horse for her sixteenth birthday. Her home in Colorado is the ideal setting to exercise her love of riding. Select two 12 x 12-inch pieces of paper, one solid and one patterned. For the left side, trim and mount red patterned paper horizontally leaving a 1/2-inch border. Adhere foam spacers behind photographs. Mount gold mulberry paper on red background paper. Print sentiments on adhesive film using the computer font Swing and mount on green tags. For a shadow effect, glue green and white tags together and set red eyelets. Thread funky fibers through eyelets and glue between the photos and gold paper. To complete the page, mount adhesive postage stamp letters on patterned paper. On the right hand page, mount leaf patterned paper vertically leaving a 1/2-inch border. Mount photo on red paper with a 1/4-inch border. Stamp window tags with gold ink, set with red eyelets and insert photos of Prince. Set red eyelet in large tag and add the metal word "Friends." Thread fibers and mount tags on foam spacers. My niece's ability to communicate with Prince is paramount in understanding the caring and trust they both share.

MATERIALS

- Patterned Paper *Anna Griffin*
- Window Tags *Treasures Memories*
- Fiber Threads *Funky Fibers*
- Metal Words *Making Memories*
- Alphabet Stamp Lettering *Sonnets*
- Eyelets *Making Memories*
- Computer Font *Swing*

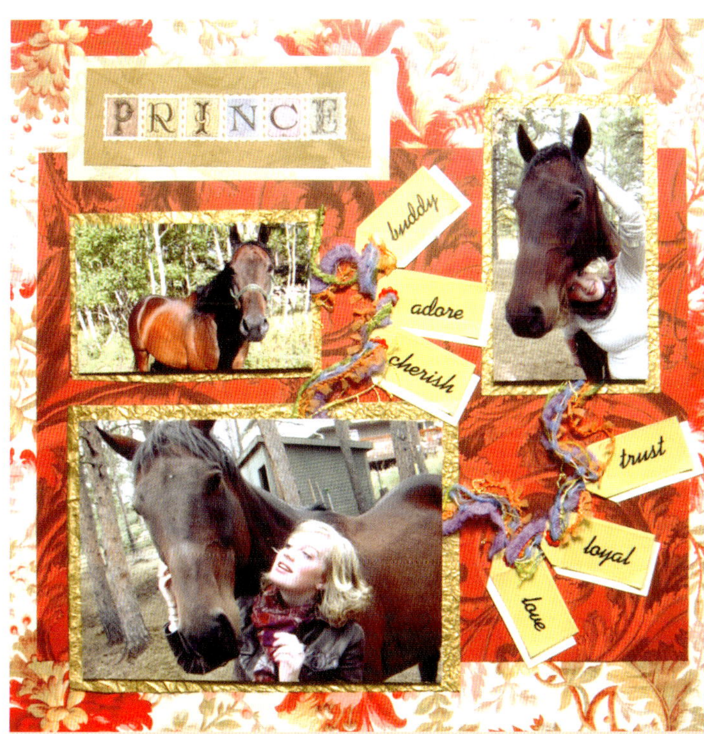

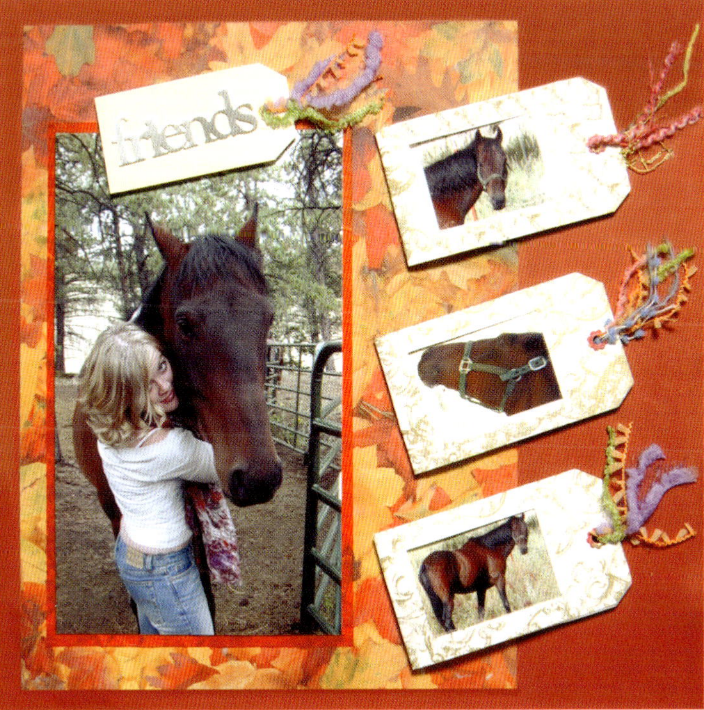

TECHNIQUE HINT

To thread bundles of fiber, use a toothpick or paper clip to push wire through the eyelets.

Handmade Powdered Pigment Tags

Spending a relaxing day at the beach is a pleasant and enjoyable time for both Spencer and his mom. Tear patterned vellum in different widths and mount on textured paper. Mount photographs on green patterned paper leaving a 1/8-inch border. Rubberstamp handmade tags with seashell imprint and emboss in blue. Press metal alphabet letters into gold stamp pad and glue vertically on blue vellum paper. Create collage tags from patterned paper by pressing tag on a watermark stamp pad and rub on powdered pigments. Stamp each tag with a seashell and emboss. Wrap each tag in yarn and fibers and add charms. Playing in the sand with his shovel and bucket is an ideal way for young Spencer to have fun and enjoy the beauty of the seashore.

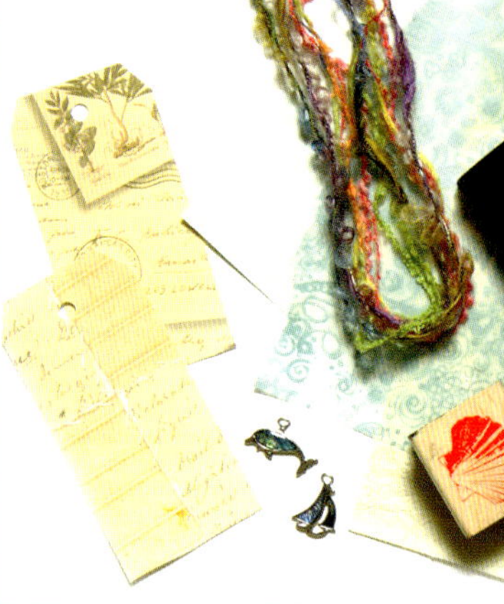

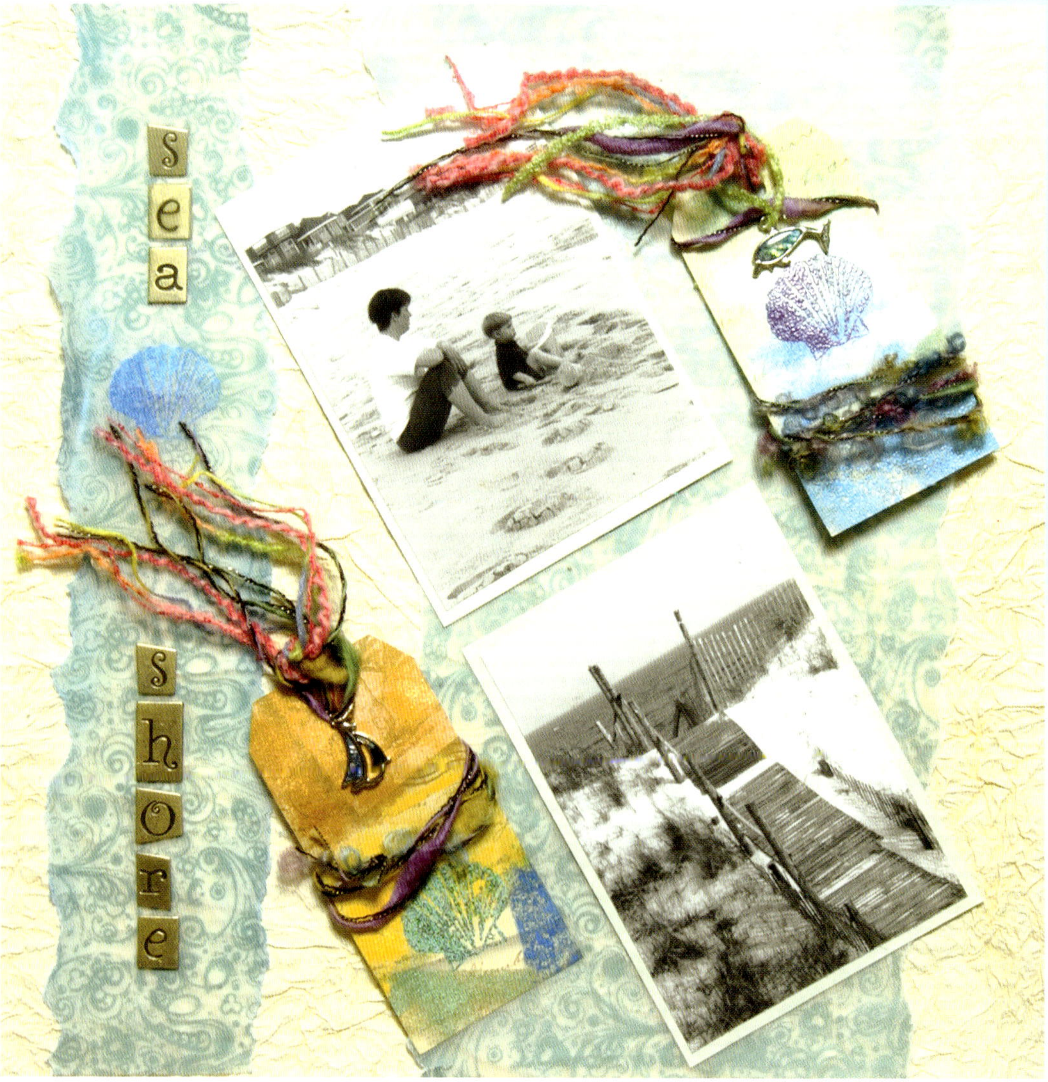

MATERIALS

Textured Paper *Provo Craft*
Vellum Paper *Colorbök*
Patterned Paper *The Paper Company*
Handmade Tags *K&Company*
Shell Rubber Stamp *Inkadinkado*
Metal Alphabet Letters *Making Memories*
Pearl Ex-Powdered Pigment *Jacquard Products*
Watermark Stamp Pad *Versamark™*
Fibers *Making Memories*
Optic Yarn *Berroco, Inc.*
Dolphin and Sailboat Charms *Darice Inc.*
Gold Stamp Pad Ink *StāzOn*

TECHNIQUE HINT

Use a small piece of clay to hold the tiny metal alphabet letters while pressing on the pad. If the letter fills with ink, use a felt tip black marker to outline the letterform.

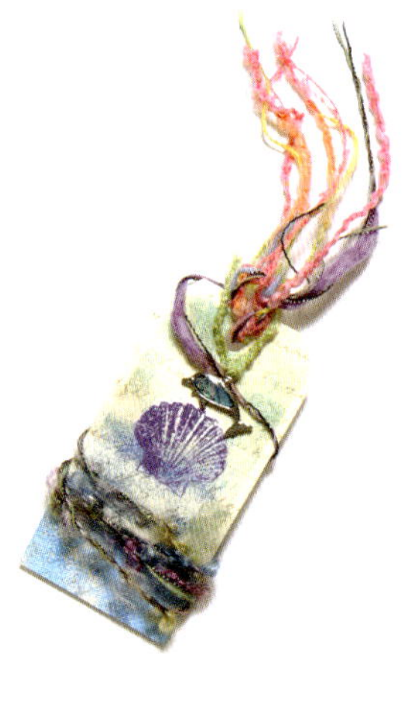

HOW-TO STEPS

seashore handmade powdered pigment tags

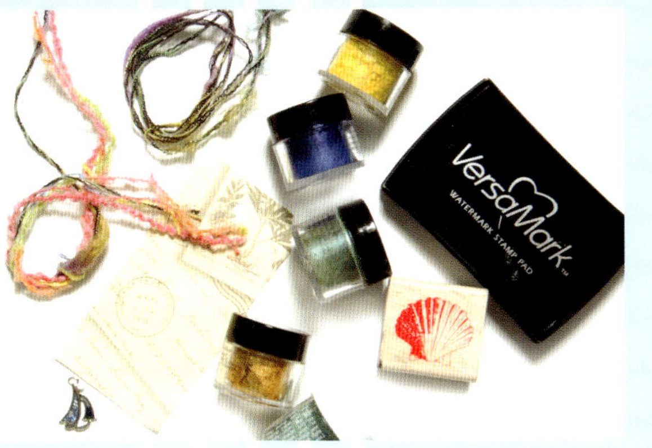

MATERIALS

- Patterned Paper
- Watermark Stamp Pad
- Shell Rubber Stamp
- Powdered Pigments
- Embossing Powder
- Charm
- Fibers
- Yarn
- Hole Punch

STEP 1

Cut a tag from a sheet of paper and punch a hole in the top. Press the top half of the tag into a watermark stamp pad.

STEP 2

Use a soft cotton pad or tissue to rub copper powdered pigment into paper. Repeat process by pressing tag into watermark pad in the lower corners at a right angle. Rub blue and green metallic powdered pigments into stamped area.

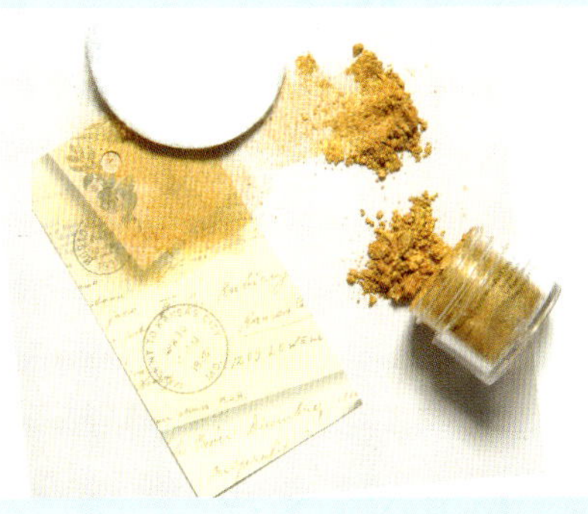

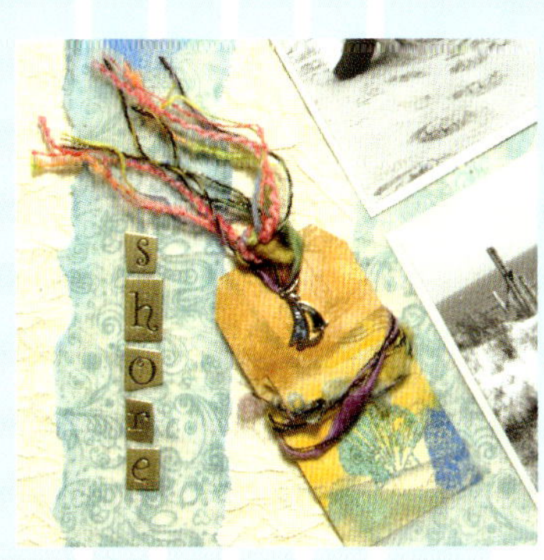

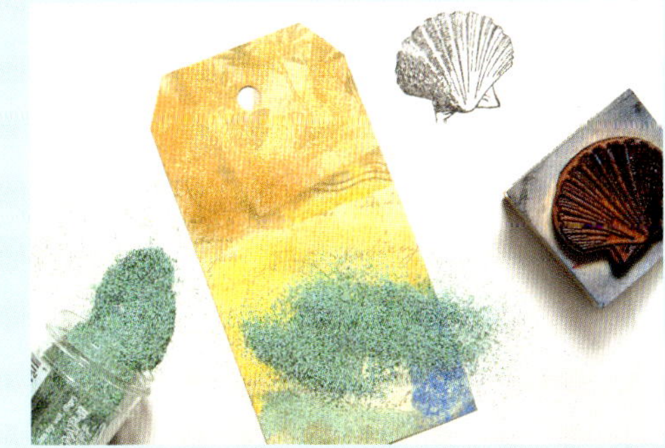

STEP 3

Stamp shell on tag and cover with a generous amount of green embossing powder. Pour off excess and heat emboss.

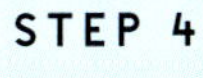

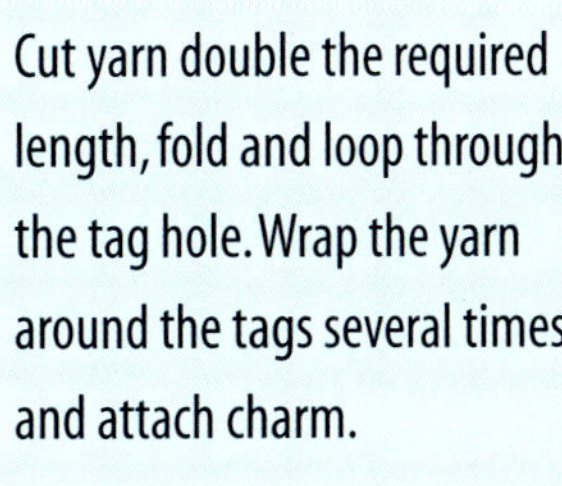

STEP 4

Cut yarn double the required length, fold and loop through the tag hole. Wrap the yarn around the tags several times and attach charm.

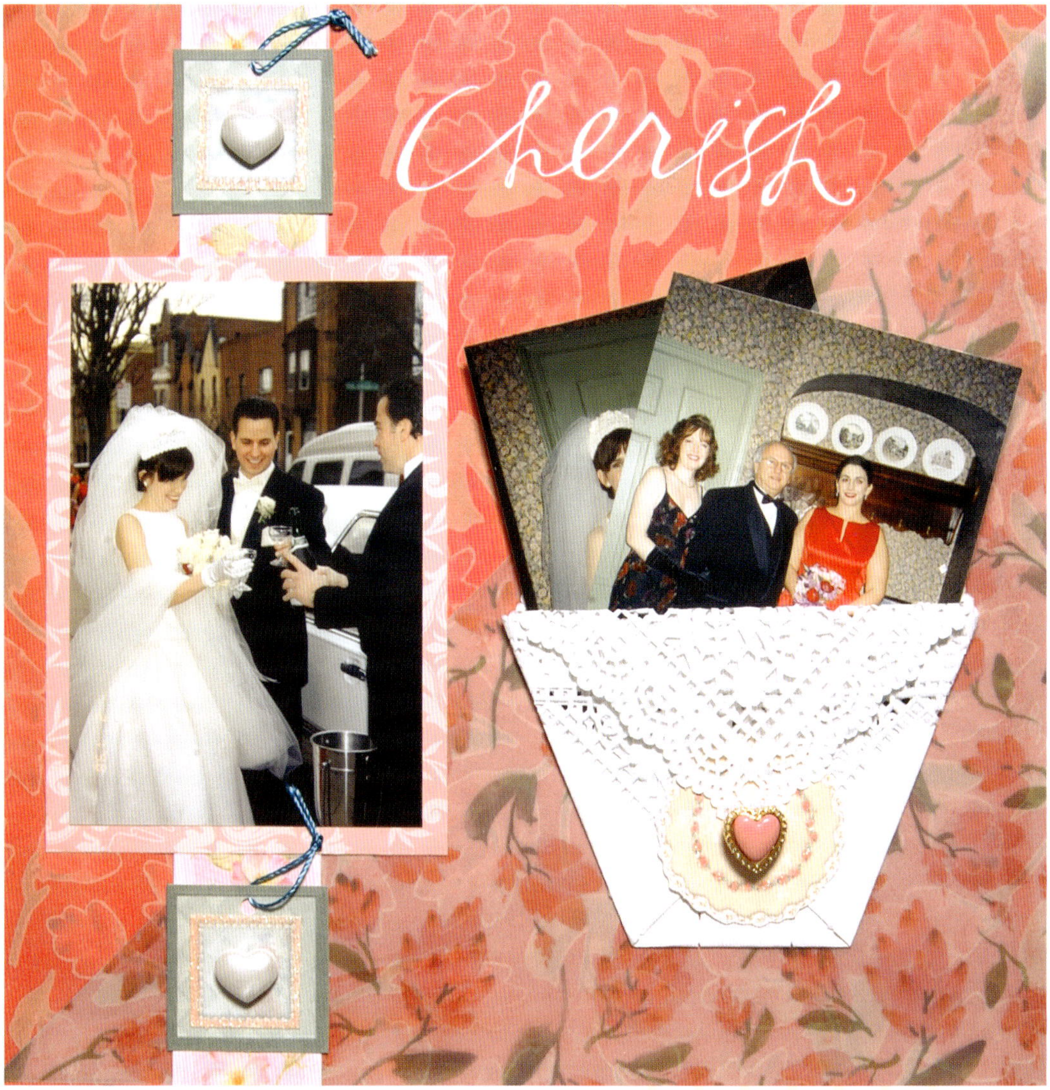

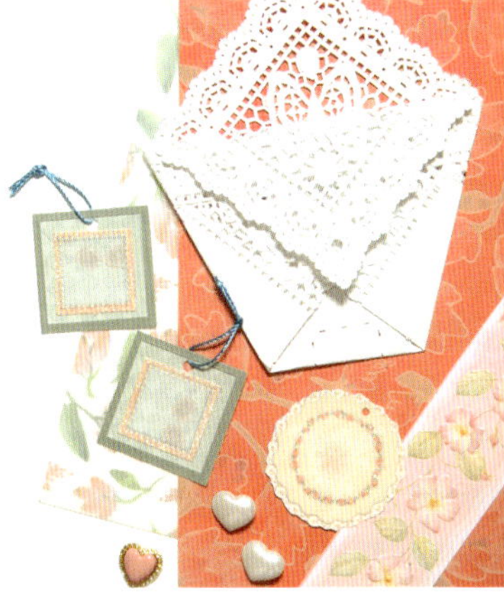

MATERIALS

Patterned Paper *The C-Thru Ruler Company*

Patterned Vellum *The C-Thru Ruler Company*

Glitter Square and Round Frames *The C-Thru Ruler Company*

Embossed Square Tags *The C-Thru Ruler Company*

Paper Lace Pouch *Available from Stampington & Company*

Embossed Borders *K&Company*

Lettering *Making Memories*

Heart Charms *Dress It Up*

Fiber *Thread On The Surface*

TECHNIQUE HINT

Trim the bottom of the photographs to fit in the pocket. Fill pockets with wedding mementos such as seating card, printed napkin, etc.

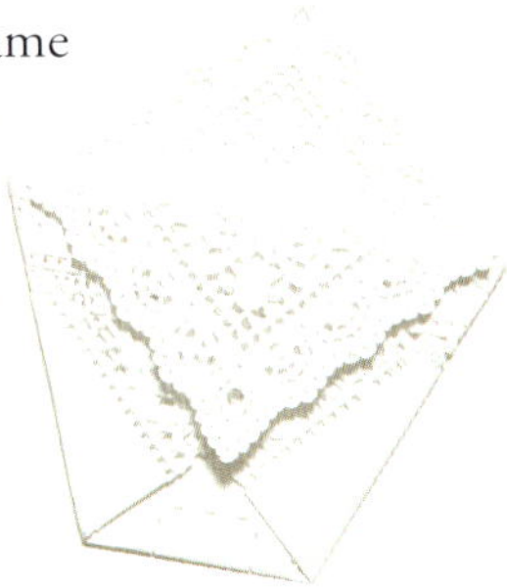

Paper Lace Pouch and Glitter Tags

Treasured wedding photos are a reminder of the love and happiness of a couple's special day. We all wish Michael and Melissa a long, healthy and happily married life together. Slice patterned vellum on a diagonal and mount on patterned paper with transparent drying glue. Mount photograph on pink patterned paper leaving a 1/4-inch border and adhere border strip vertically on page. Tie fibers and mount green embossed square tags on border strip. Glue square glitter frames on top. Snip off the back of the heart buttons and glue on glitter frames. Mount matted photo on border strip and adhere round frame under flap of the paper lace pouch. Glue heart button on point of flap. Apply rub-on lettering "Cherish" to patterned background paper. Mount and fill lace pouch with favorite photos. Michael's loving sister Christa looks beautiful in her red bridesmaid's gown as we all celebrate a special day together.

Handmade Tags, Vellum Tags, Metal Tags and Vellum Envelopes

Love is the nucleus of every successful marriage. As mom and dad complete 50 years of married happiness, we honor their commitment to love and family. Adhere an embossed sticker border across the bottom of a sheet of 12 x 12-inch scrapbook paper. Trim pink patterned paper 1/8-inch larger than photos with Victorian pattern scissors or rotary cutters. Mount photos overlapping on paper. Use the purple tag as a template to cut a second tag. Mount on an angle creating a drop shadow effect and glue torn rice paper pieces on top. Set hearts on tags with pink snaps, add lettering and accent with dimensional glove stickers. Set snaps with metal mom and dad tags on the two smaller vellum hearts. Place snaps on large vellum hearts and apply lettering. Glue two small hearts to larger heart and position glove stickers. On bottom border adhere vellum envelopes with bubble letters and glove stickers. Insert a blank piece of paper in the envelope to simulate a letter. Complete with "Love" wire word. A fiftieth wedding anniversary is a milestone that is both admired and cherished by everyone in the family.

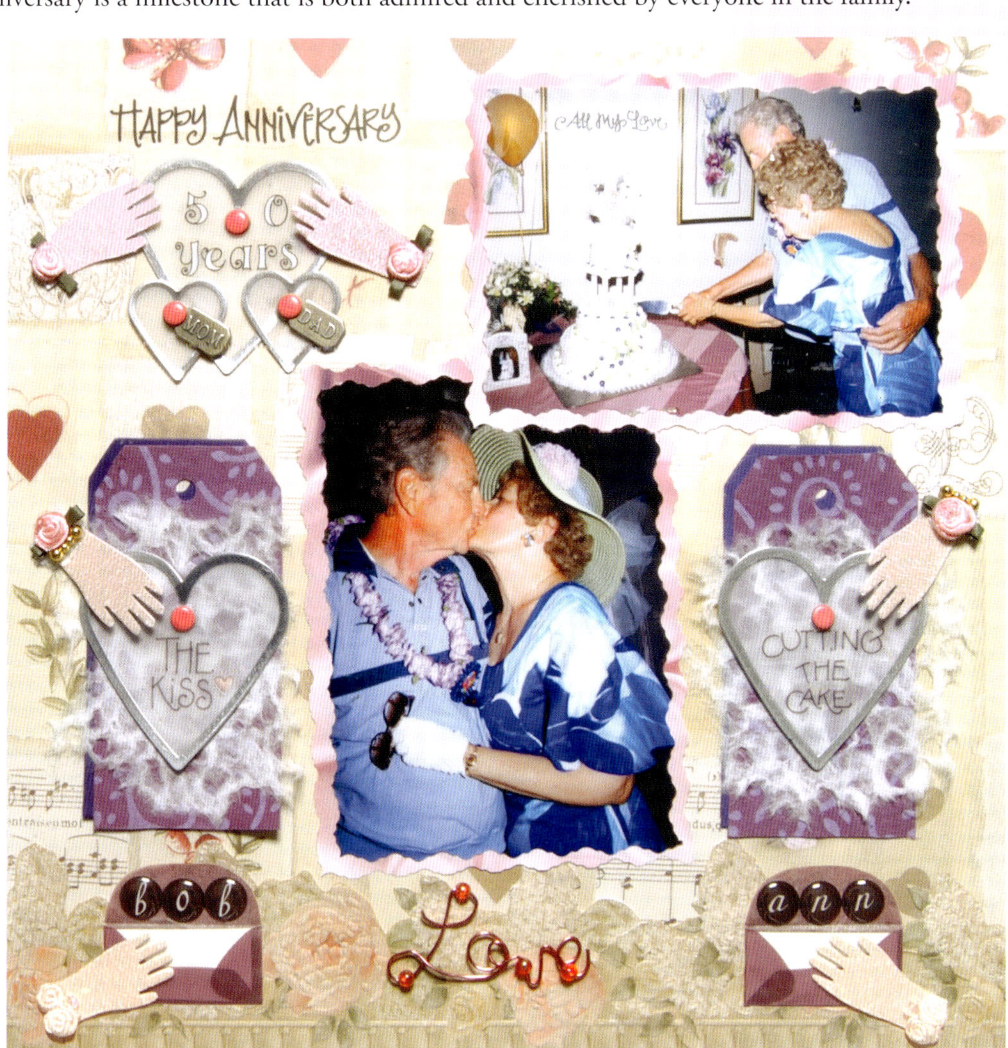

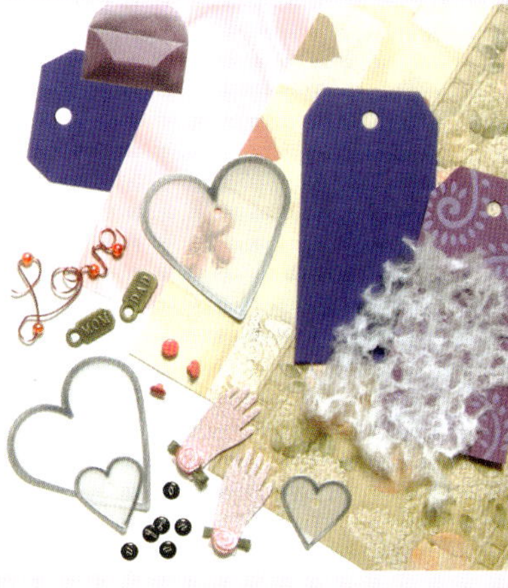

MATERIALS

Patterned Paper *Paper Pizazz/World Win*
Paper Tags *Paper Reflections*
Embossed Sticker Paper *K&Company*
Handmade Tags *Provo Craft*
Vellum Tags *Making Memories*
Vellum Envelopes *The C-Thru Ruler Company*
Metal Tags *K&Company*
Snaps *Making Memories*
Dimensional Glove Stickers *The Card Connection*
Wire Words *The Card Connection*
Bubble Letters *Li'l Davis Designs™*

TECHNIQUE HINT

Be careful when setting snaps through vellum tag, as vellum tears easily.

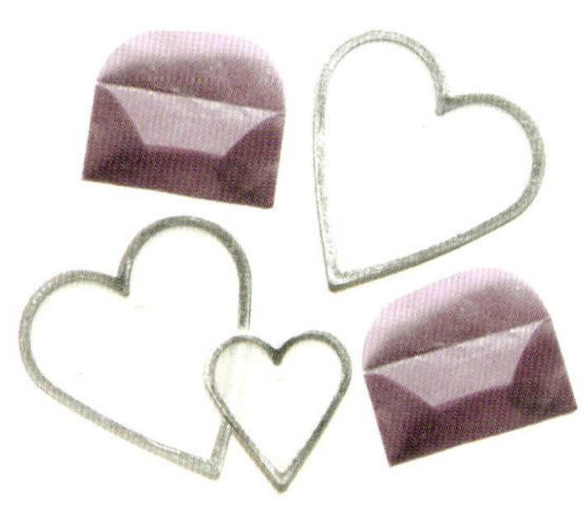

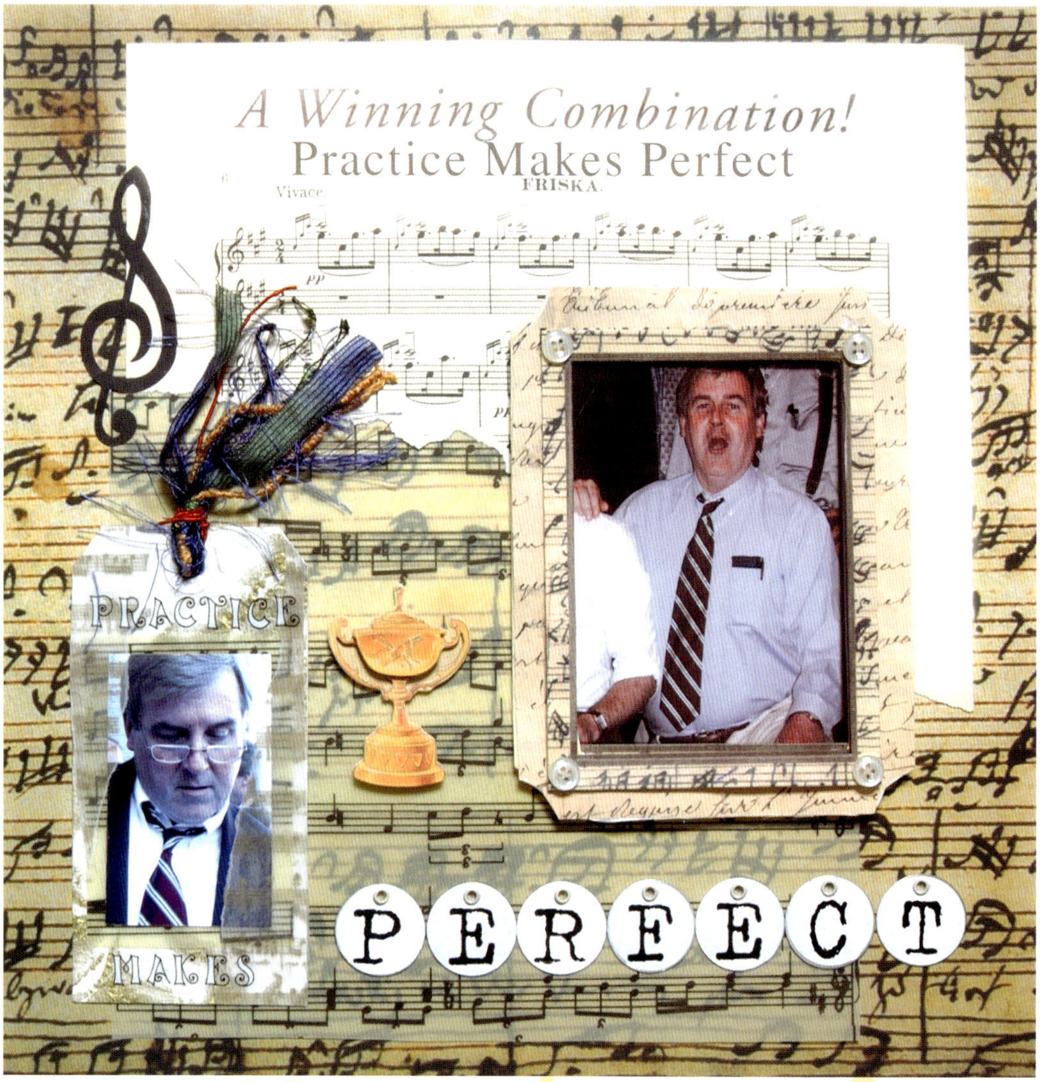

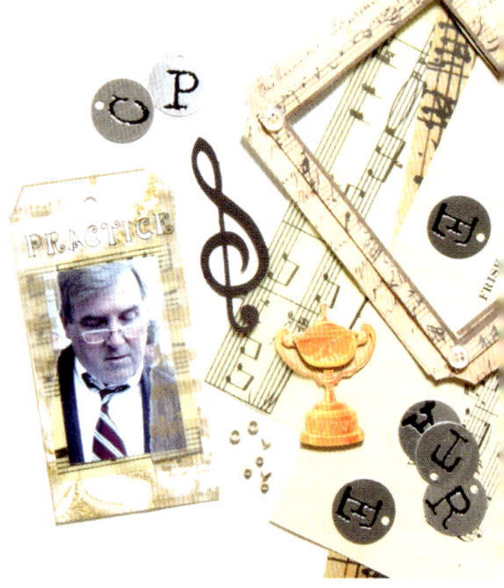

practice makes perfect

Handmade Tag and Metal Tags

Since childhood, singing has played a salient part in the life of my brother-in-law Jon. Competing and winning the grand prize in this year's competition in Wales affirms the maxim that practice really does make perfect. Mount an 8.5 x 11-inch piece of musical notes vellum on 12 x12-inch patterned paper. Print "A Winning Combination" and "Practice Makes Perfect" from the computer on the music sheet. Tear music sheet on an angle and mount on music patterned paper. Trim photograph to fit dimensional frame and adhere. Attach and mount frame on music patterned paper. Set eyelets into metal tags and glue in position. Create handmade tags from vellum and rice paper and embellish with fibers. Place Alphabitties lettering above and below the photo. Paste die cut clef on the music sheet and adhere trophy sticker in the center. The proud Mastersingers continue rehearsing for future competitions, in the hope of repeating their richly deserved first place finish.

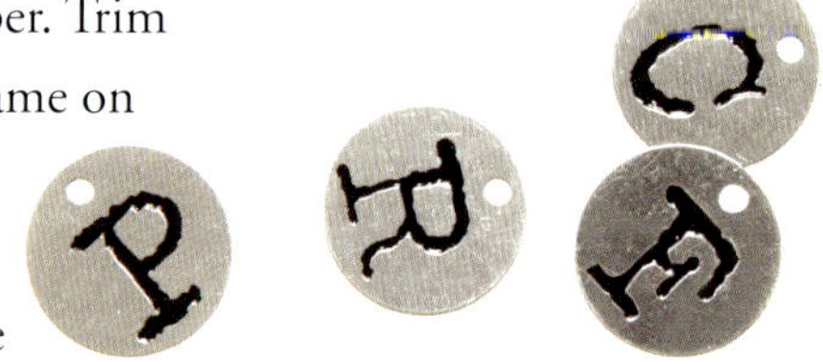

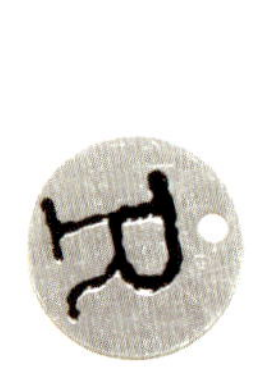

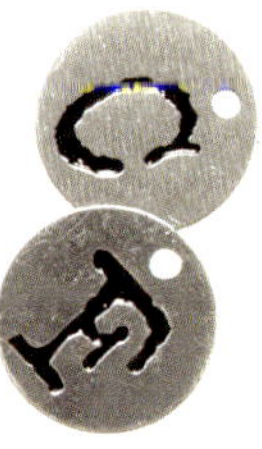

MATERIALS

- Patterned Paper *K&Company*
- Patterned Vellum *DMD*
- Music Paper *Personal Collection*
- Gold Tag Paper *Black Ink*
- Dimensional Frame and Sticker *K&Company*
- Die Cut Clef *Deluxe Laser Border*
- Alphabitties Lettering *Provo Craft*
- Fibers *EK Success*
- Metal Letter Tags *Making Memories*
- Eyelets *The C-Thru Ruler Company*
- Computer Font *Times*

TECHNIQUE HINT

As an alternative to setting eyelets through many layers of paper, set eyelets in metal tags only and glue in position on paper.

HOW-TO STEPS

practice makes perfect

handmade tag

MATERIALS

Large Tag
Gold Rice Paper
Patterned Music Vellum
Fibers
Alphabitties Lettering
Clear Archival Glue
Paper Punch

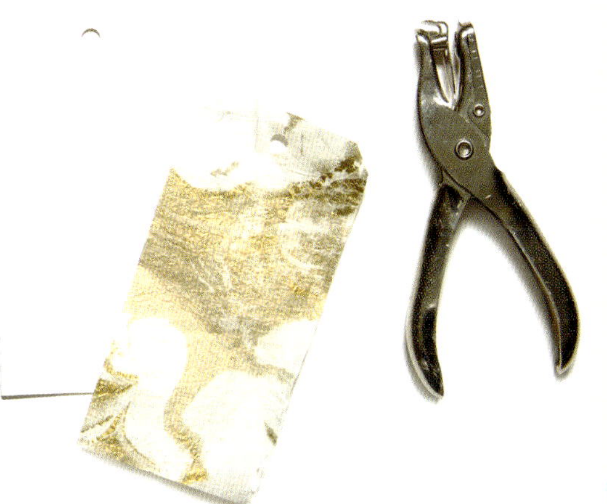

STEP 1

Trim gold rice paper to fit on tag and adhere. Next, trim photograph and music vellum to fit on tag and tear additional strips of music vellum paper.

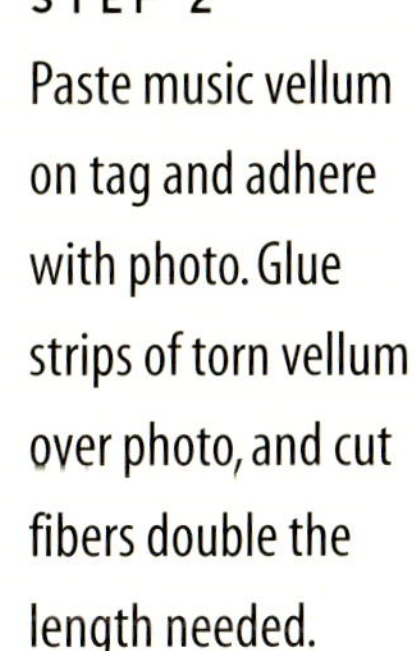

STEP 2

Paste music vellum on tag and adhere with photo. Glue strips of torn vellum over photo, and cut fibers double the length needed.

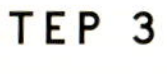

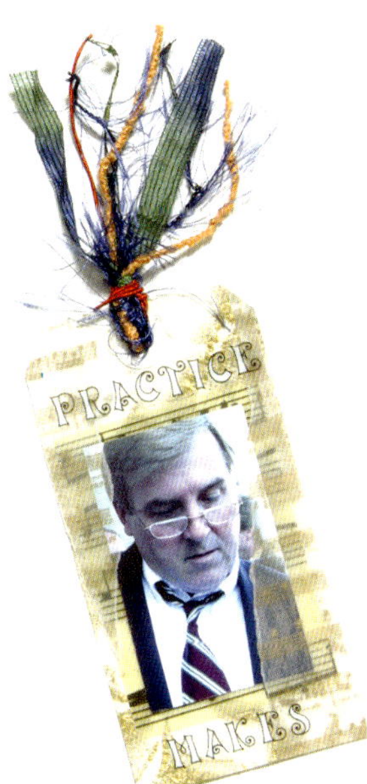

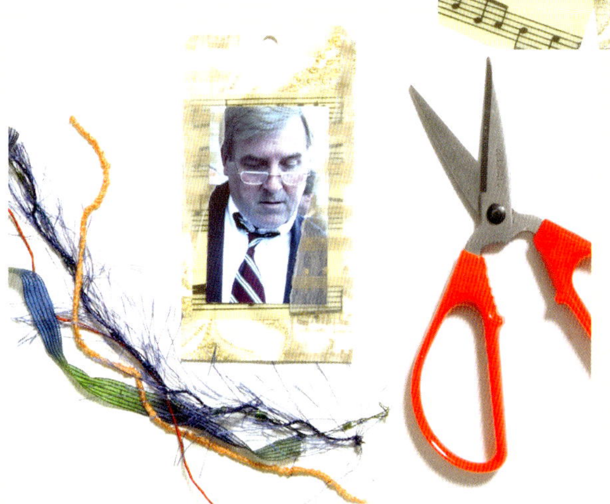

STEP 3

Fold fibers in half and loop through hole in tag. Wrap the red fiber around several times, spread the fibers and mount on page. Add lettering to complete.

Handmade Tags and Sheer Pouches

The baby pictures of Christa and Michael bring back pleasant memories of two special children. Select a piece of 12 x 12-inch glitter patterned paper as a background. Rubberstamp baby feet on top of tags; pink for girl and blue for boy. Trim and mount photos in center and add button stickers. Push pink and blue satin ribbons through holes in the tags, attach pink and blue baby bear charms and make bows. Trim ends of ribbon on a diagonal. Add "Baby Girl" and "Baby Boy" stickers on bottom of tag. Insert plastic charms in sheer pouch and tie into a bow. Add oval page pebble on each pouch and attach initial sticker. Mount to paper with transparent drying glue. Glue purple satin ribbon on top to complete the page. Spell out the word "Love" in bubble letters. As infants, both Christa and Michael were happy, fun-loving bundles of joy.

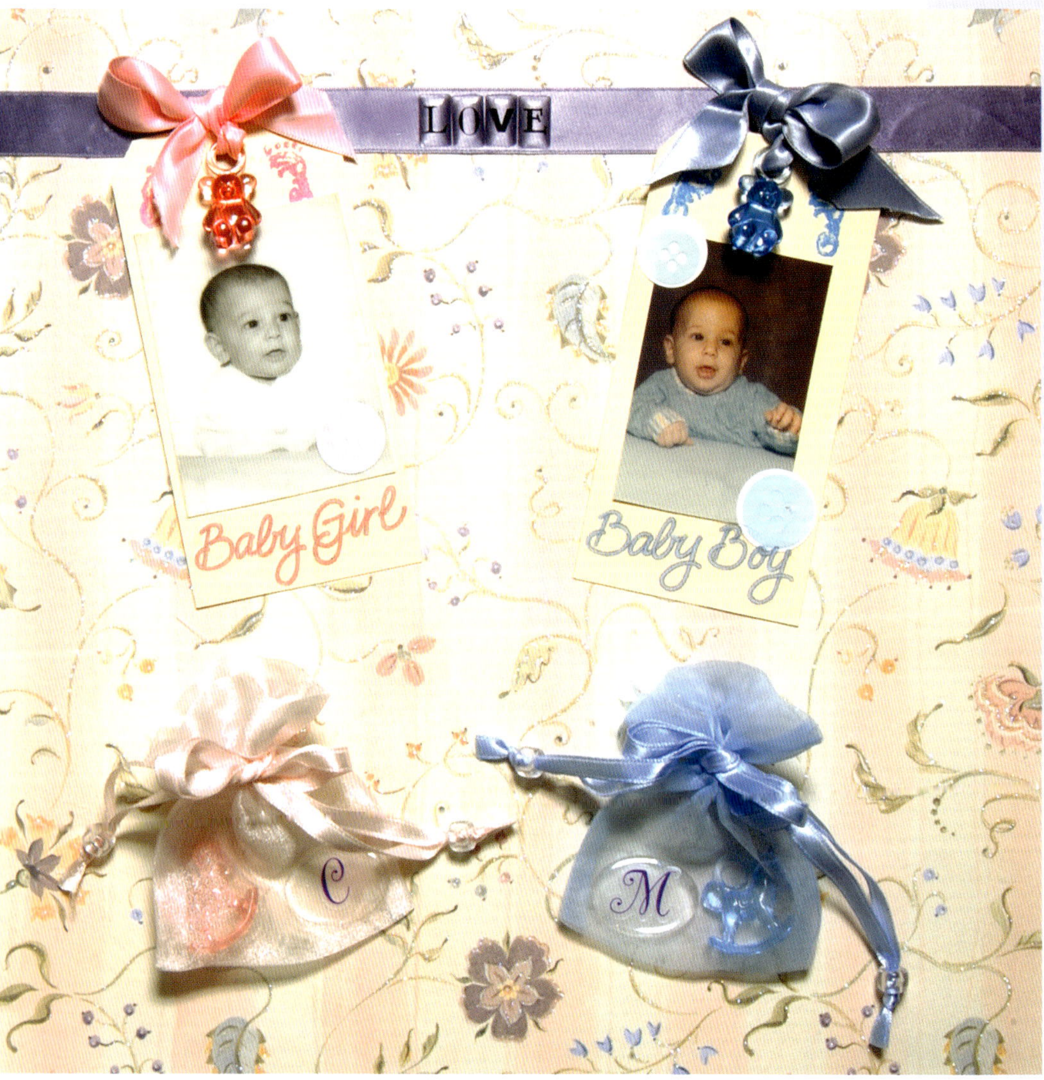

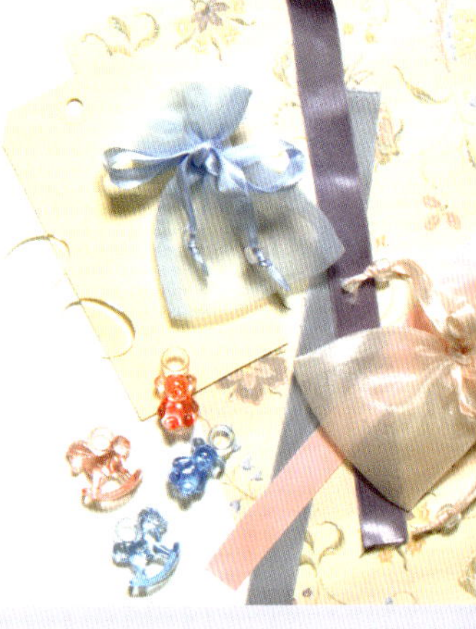

MATERIALS

Glitter Patterned Paper *K&Company*
Manila Large Tags *Creative Tags*
Feet Rubberstamp *Inkadinkado*
Pink and Blue Ink Pad *Color Box*
Button Stickers *K&Company*
Satin Ribbon *Anna Griffin*
Baby Charms *Hirschberg Schutz & Co., Inc.*
Sticker Lettering *Me & My Big Ideas*
Oval Page Pebble *Making Memories*
Letter Stickers *Sandy Lion*
Bubble Letters *K&Company*

TECHNIQUE HINT

Add mementos to sheer pouches including locket of hair from first haircut or baby charms.

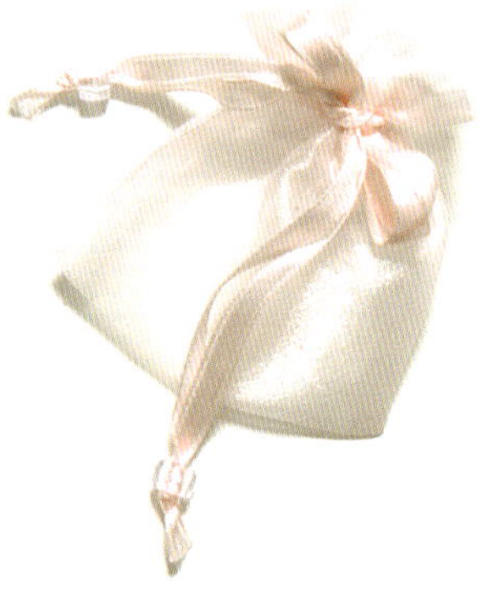

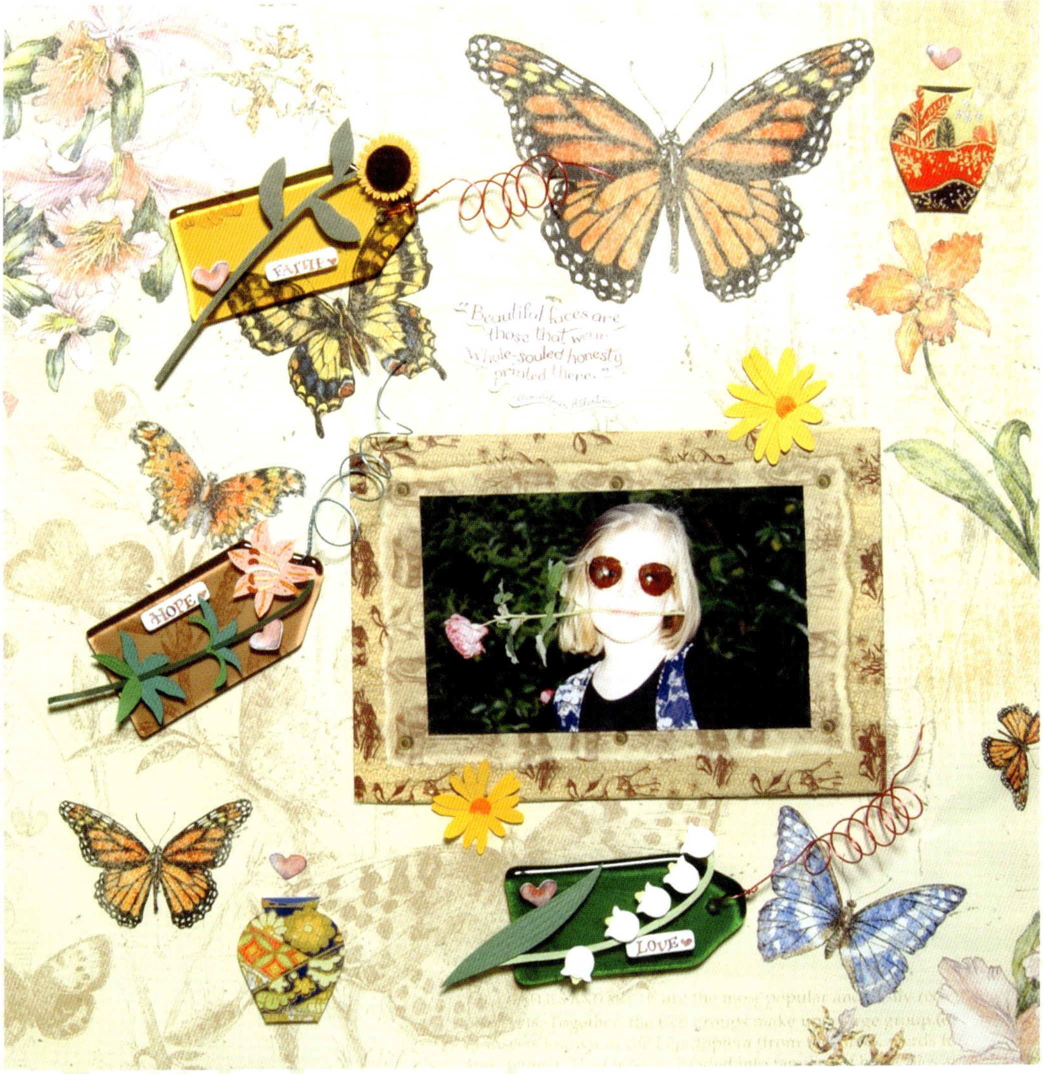

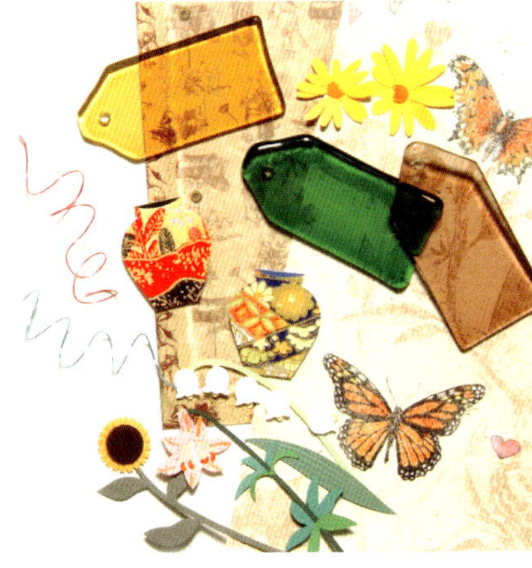

MATERIALS

Patterned Paper *PSX Papers for Creativity*

Designer Block Quickit™ *Provo Craft*

Die Cut Flowers and Vases *Jolee's By You*

Glass Tags *Available from Stampington & Company*

24 Gauge Jewelry Wire *Nicole*

Sticker Words *Susan Branch*

TECHNIQUE HINT

Position glass tags over interesting parts of the patterned paper.

Faith hope love

Glass Tags

The hopes and expectations of my young niece demonstrate the infinite possibilities that lie in her future. Begin with a sheet of 12 x 12-inch patterned butterfly paper. Trim photo to fit into the designer block paper. Position photo in an empty space on the patterned paper. Remove the stems from yellow die cut flowers and glue on to the edges of the designer block. Twist jewelry wire around the opening of the glass tags. To create a spiral, wrap wire around a pencil or knitting needle. Glue die cut flowers on tags and sticker words. Accent with vase jars and place heart stickers on top. Faith, hope and love are three words that inspire a young girl to dream above and beyond her expectations.

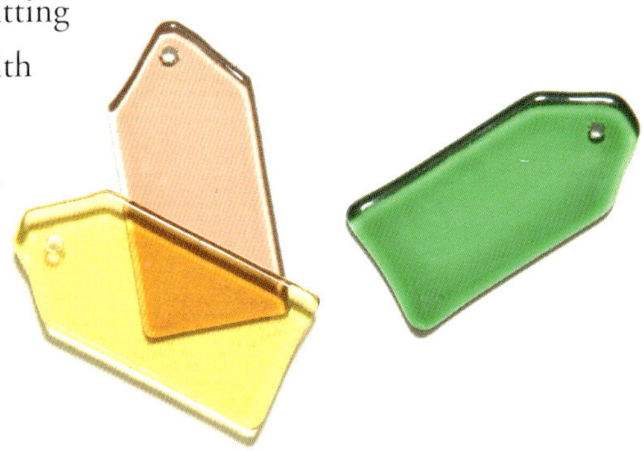

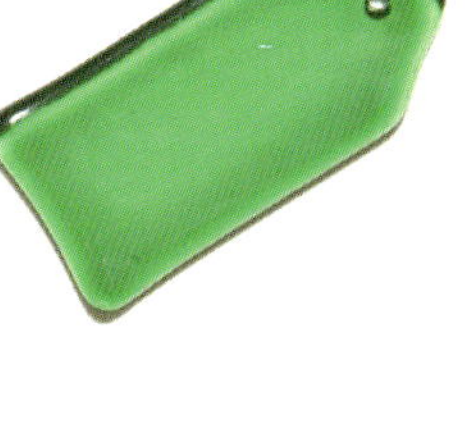

Embellish

Beads, Buttons and Charms

Add sparkle, style and adornments to your scrapbook page with beads, buttons and charms. Use scrapbooking beads to accentuate themes or enhance color schemes. Micro and glass beads are solid, miniature marbles made of glass or plastic in clear, colored and metallic colors. Create beaded borders, shapes and frames with pre-cut double adhesive shapes to achieve smooth surface textures. Metallic scrapbooking bead chains are the latest bead craze. Connect photos and story lines using these new colorful links. Beautify your treasured memories with glittery bead embellishments.

Buttons are charming additions to take your pages to the next level of creativity. Vintage buttons convey a classic style, while scrapbook buttons are chic. Utilize antique buttons to characterize a theme or highlight a generation. Choose from an assortment of contemporary scrapbook button shapes and colors from warm pastels to hot, sparkling hues. Sewn or glued, buttons are versatile notions that are always fashionable.

From amulets to ornaments, charms are enchanting elements to decorate any scrapbook page. Enhance your themes with plastic, paper, metal or resin miniature mementos. These endearing curios evoke a smile, generate a sentiment or savor a memory. The hottest charms in scrapbooking today are hair accessories. Try using colorful bobby pins, barrettes and clips to highlight cute photos and charming subjects. Charms are the perfect embellishments for accentuating scrapbook themes and motifs. Add excitement to your pages with buttons, beads and charms—they're easy and fun to use.

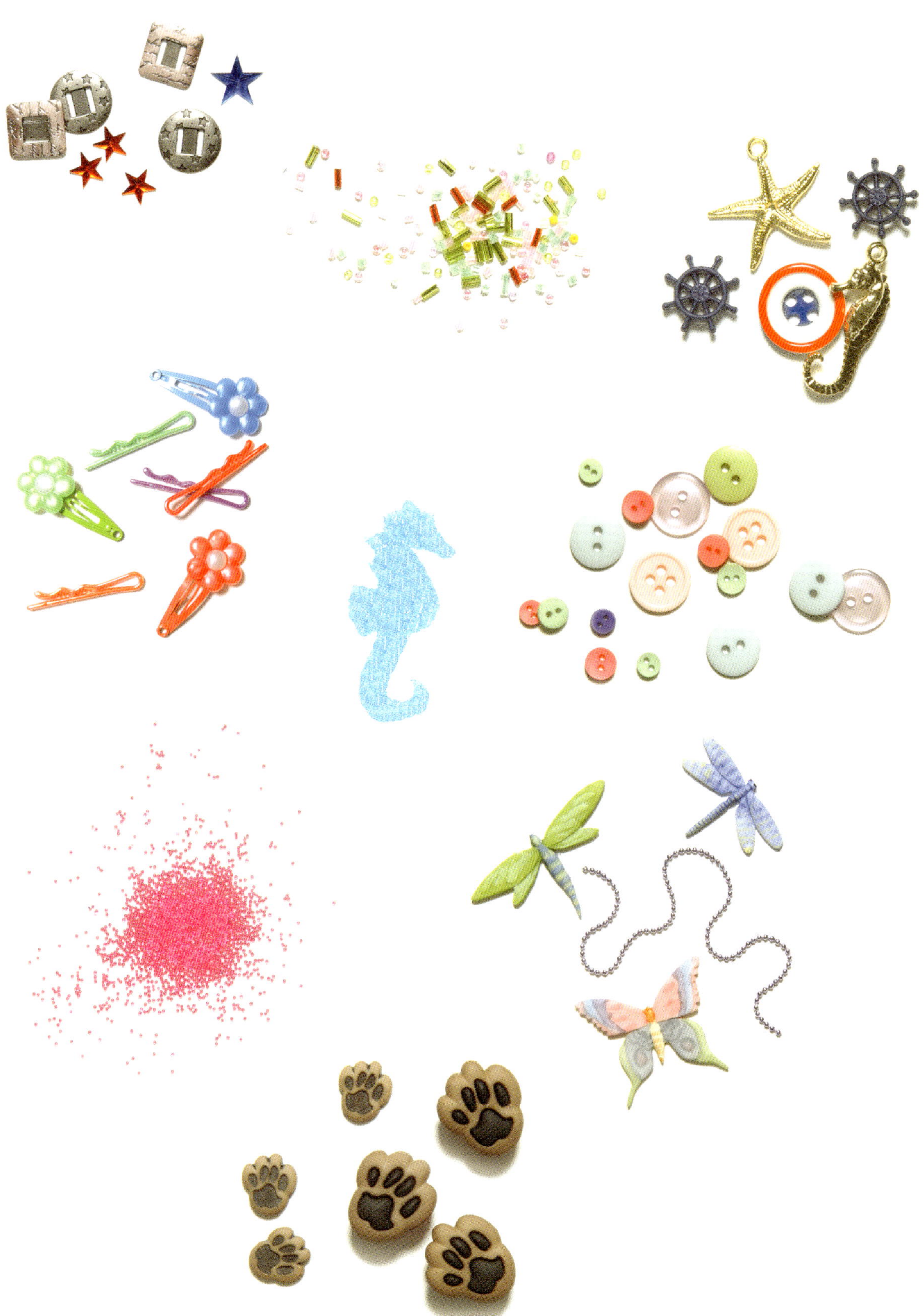

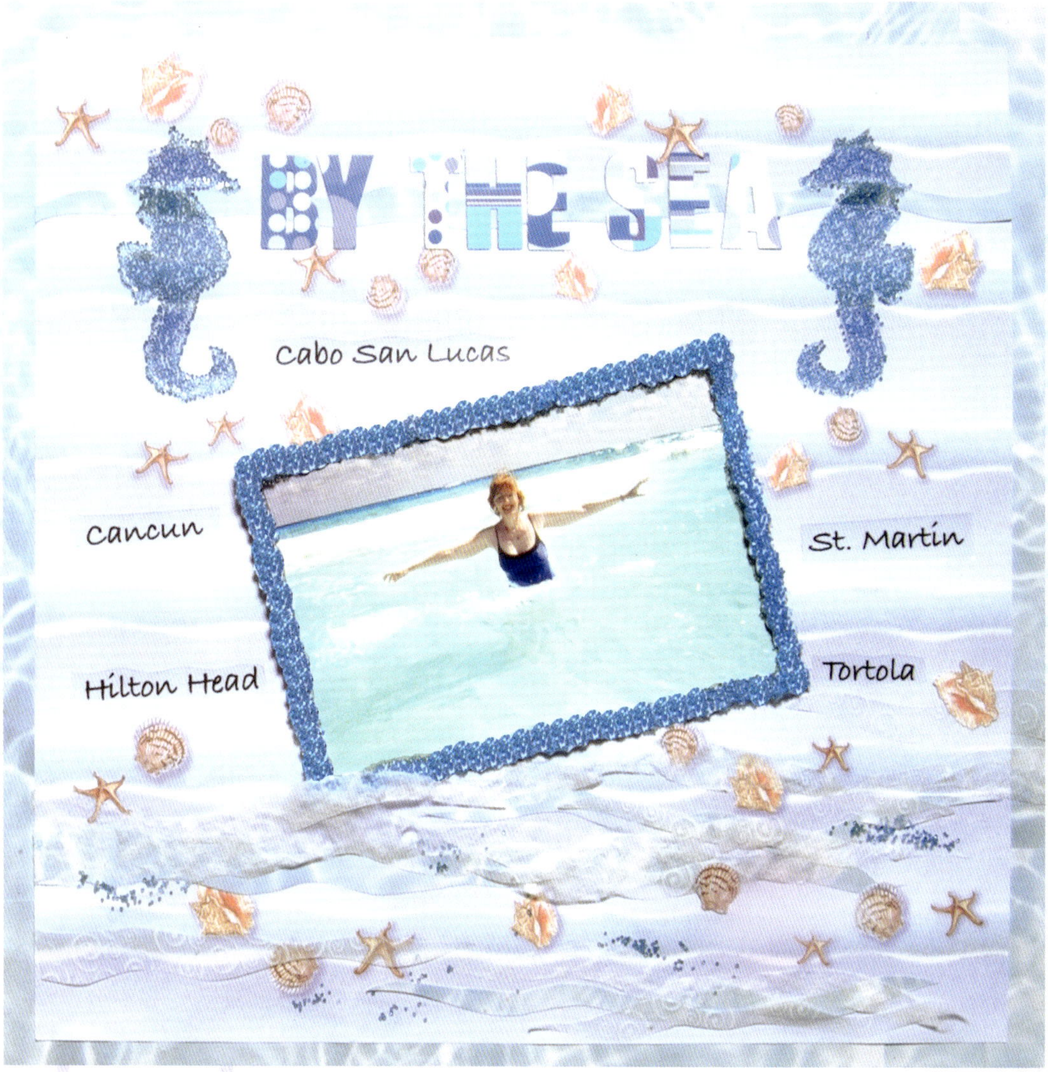

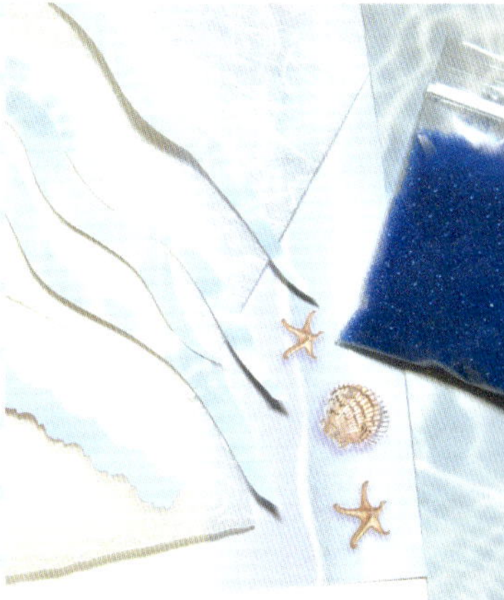

MATERIALS

Patterned Paper *PSX Papers for Creativity*

Spiral Patterned Vellum *Paper Pizazz*

Tiny Glass Beads *Treasured Memories*

Rice Paper *Black Ink*

Double Stick Adhesive Sea Horse Shapes *Treasured Memories*

Lettering *Simple Sets*

TECHNIQUE HINT

Apply a mound of micro glass beads and press in place with your fingertips to achieve an even surface texture. Gently pour off excess beads.

Glass Bead Shapes and Frame

My fascination with the sea dates from my early family excursions to the Jersey shore. Over time, I have been fortunate to visit many pristine beaches throughout the world. For this page, double mount a 12 x 12-inch sheet of water patterned paper as a background. To create the ocean foam, cut rice paper, spiral patterned vellum and water patterned paper into wavy strips. An adhesive sea horse shape is mounted to the paper and coated with tiny glass beads. Frame the photograph with a paper border; apply glue, and sprinkle with additional glass beads. Paper lettering completes the title. Swabs of glue are wiped on the waves and dotted with glass beads for a sea green effect. Today, the sea continues to attract and captivate me with its awe and splendor.

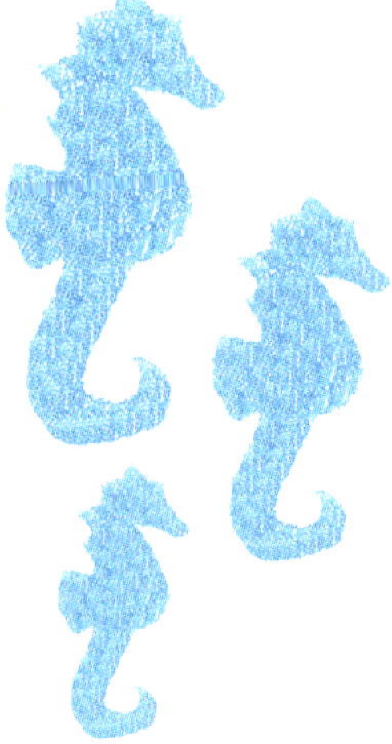

dancin' lady

Vintage Buttons, Bead Chains and Charms

Our boat, Dancin' Lady, named for mom, has been the source of many relaxing hours of enjoyment along the Jersey shore. Trim blue water patterned paper 1/2-inch on two sides and center on the blue dotted paper. Print text with Garamond computer font on white paper. Punch medium sized rounded corners on photos and print on vellum. Mount together leaving a thin border and adhere to water paper. Put a thin line of clear glue on the edge of each picture and lay bead chain around the perimeter. String seahorse and starfish buttons with alpha charm lettering on bead chain. Secure with adhesive under vintage nautical buttons in upper corners. Glue nautical ship wheel charms on top of red and white vintage nautical buttons and fasten. My dad is always ready to teach everyone the finer points of navigation as we cruise each summer on the beautiful waters of Barnegat Bay.

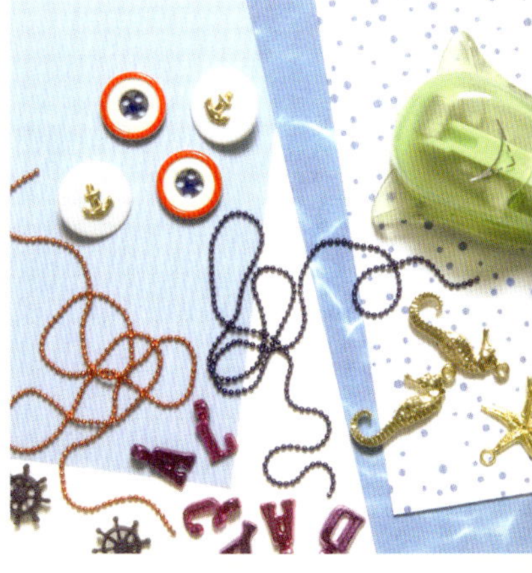

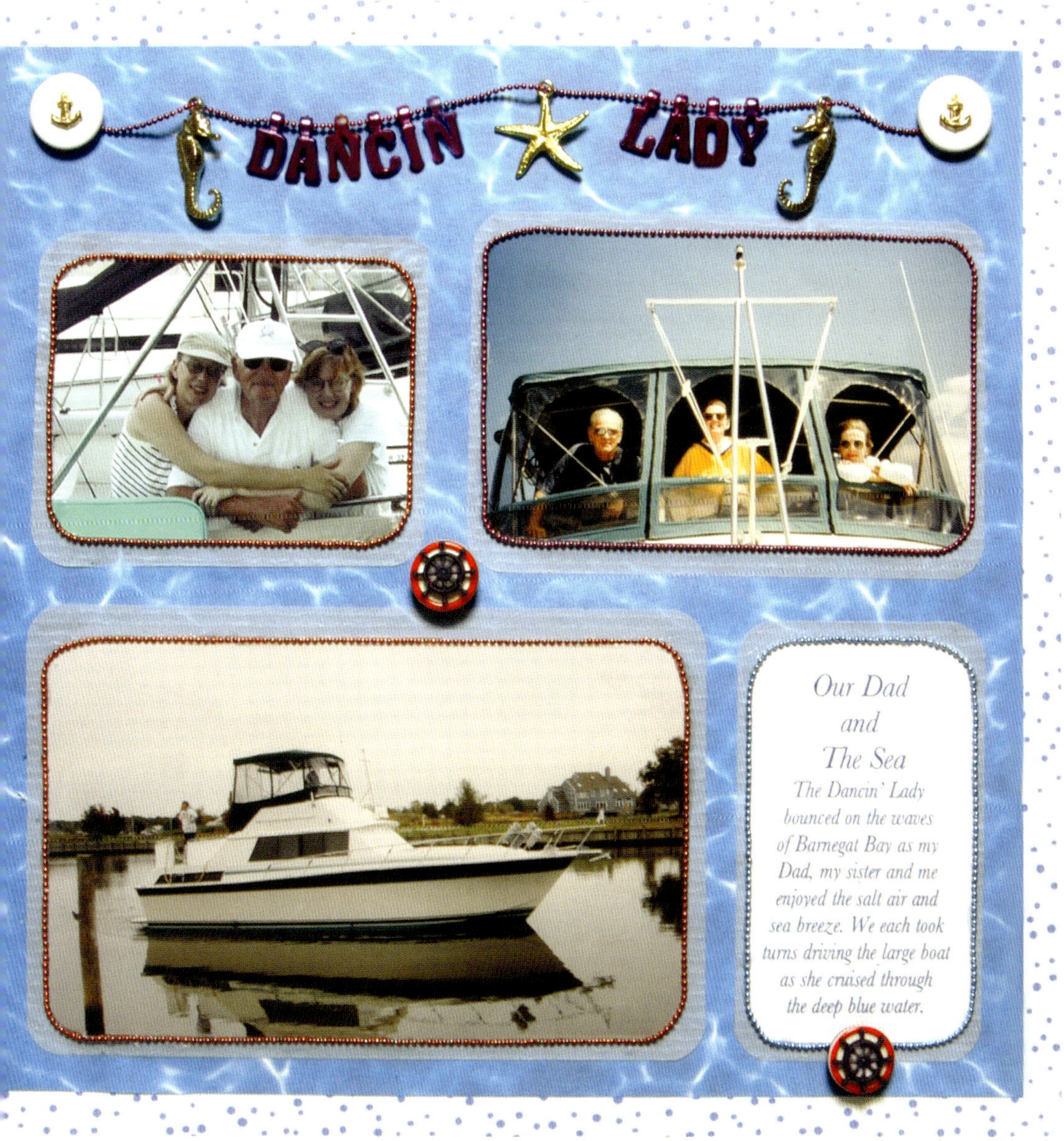

DANCIN LADY

Our Dad and The Sea

The Dancin' Lady bounced on the waves of Barnegat Bay as my Dad, my sister and me enjoyed the salt air and sea breeze. We each took turns driving the large boat as she cruised through the deep blue water.

MATERIALS

Patterned Paper *Paper Pizazz*

Vellum *The Paper Company*

Bead Chain *Making Memories*

Medium Corner Punch *EK Success*

Alpha Charms *Jewelry & Craft Essentials*

Nautical Charms *Dress It Up*

Nautical Vintage Buttons *Antique Shop*

Seahorse and Starfish Buttons *Dress It Up*

Computer Font *Garamond*

TECHNIQUE HINT

Position alpha charms on bead chain and glue letters on paper to hold in place.

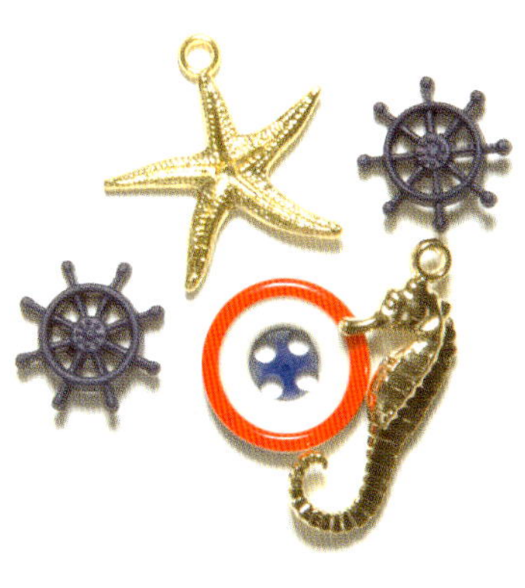

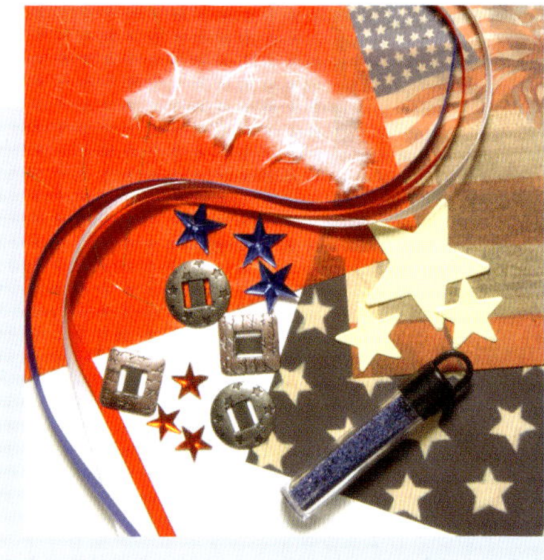

Ribbon Charms and Micro Glass Bead Shapes

Mom captured these photographs representing the true spirit of all that is America. Begin with two sheets of ghosted patriotic patterned paper. Trim photos with deckle rotary cutter or deckle scissors. Mount photos on red rice paper with a 1/4-inch border. Adhere photos on patriotic paper and print a copy of America the Beautiful (download from the internet) with Baskerville font in blue type on blue vellum. Make computer print of America the Beautiful in red Edwardian Script on matte adhesive. Tear and adhere metallic script vellum with red words on top and bottom. Glue red, white and blue ribbons with square and round ribbon charms; dot i's with red plastic star charms. Use double stick adhesive stars and sprinkle blue micro glass beads in place. America the Beautiful is a powerful reminder of the liberties treasured by all Americans throughout our great history.

MATERIALS

- Patterned Paper *K&Company*
- Metallic Script Vellum *Colorbök*
- Blue Vellum *The Paper Company*
- Rice Paper *Black Ink*
- Plastic Star Charms *Jewelry & Craft Essentials*
- Matte Adhesive *Chartpak*
- Ribbon *Offray Ribbon*
- Round and Square Ribbon Charms *Making Memories*
- Micro Glass Beads *Treasured Memories*
- Double Stick Adhesive Stars *Treasured Memories*
- Decoliner Metallic Red Marker *Marvy Uchida*
- Computer Fonts *Baskerville and Edwardian Script*

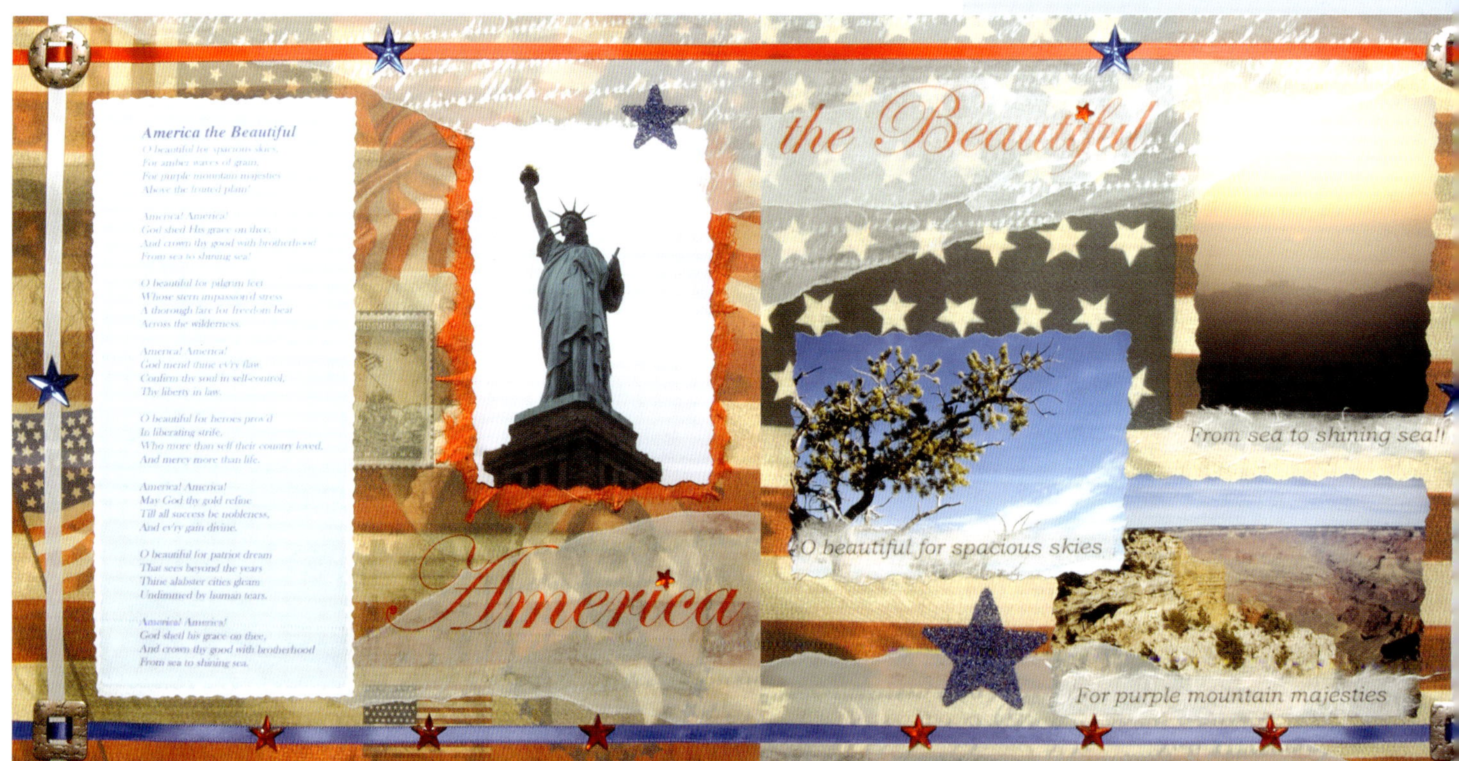

TECHNIQUE HINT

To create the illusion of a white ribbon woven into the corner charms, snip a small piece of white ribbon and glue it under the top ribbon of each charm.

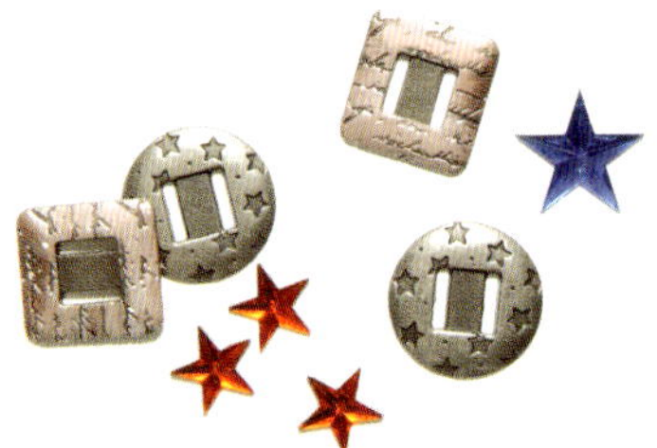

HOW-TO STEPS

america the beautiful ribbon charms

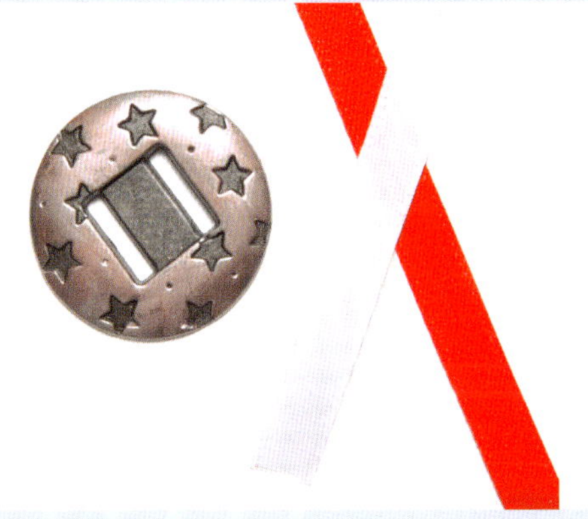

MATERIALS

Round and Square Ribbon Charms

Ribbon

Craft Knife

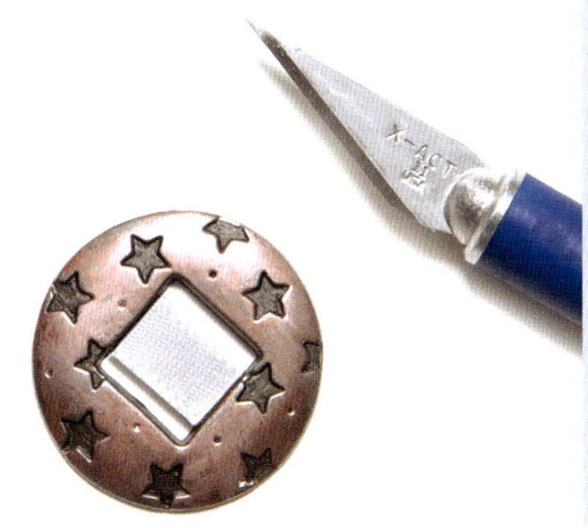

STEP 1

Trim and glue white ribbon to fit perfectly inside ribbon charm.

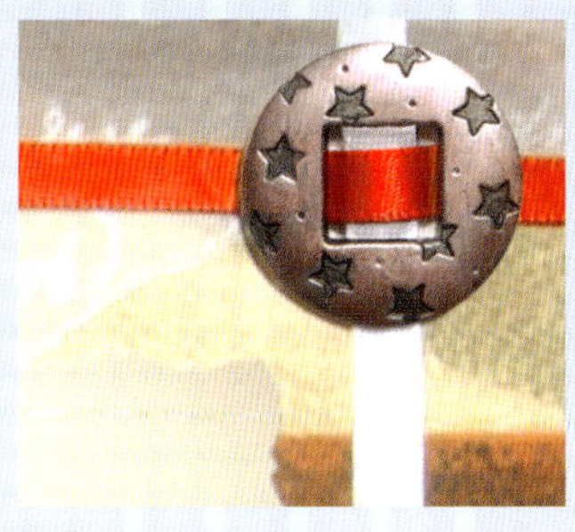

STEP 2

Loop red ribbon under and over white ribbon.

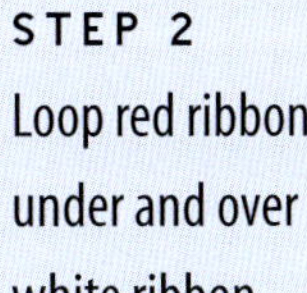

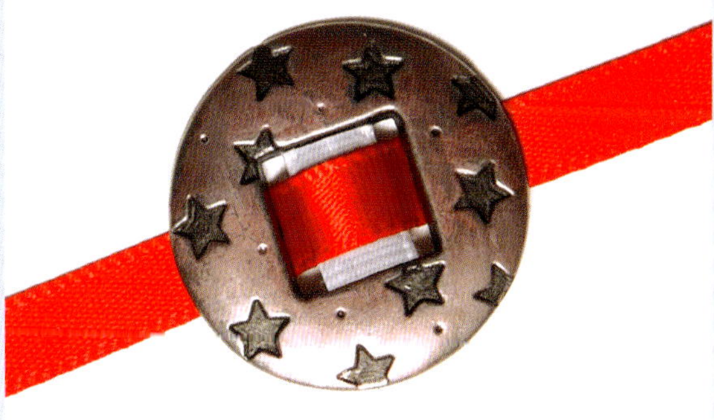

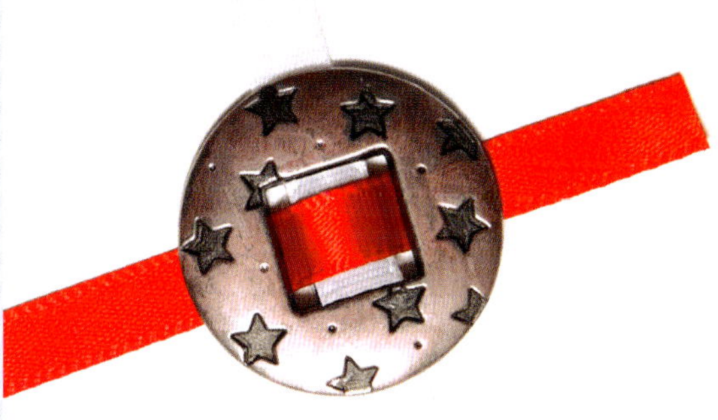

STEP 3

Lay ribbon charm on top of white ribbon. Make sure the inside white ribbon is aligned with the outside white ribbon.

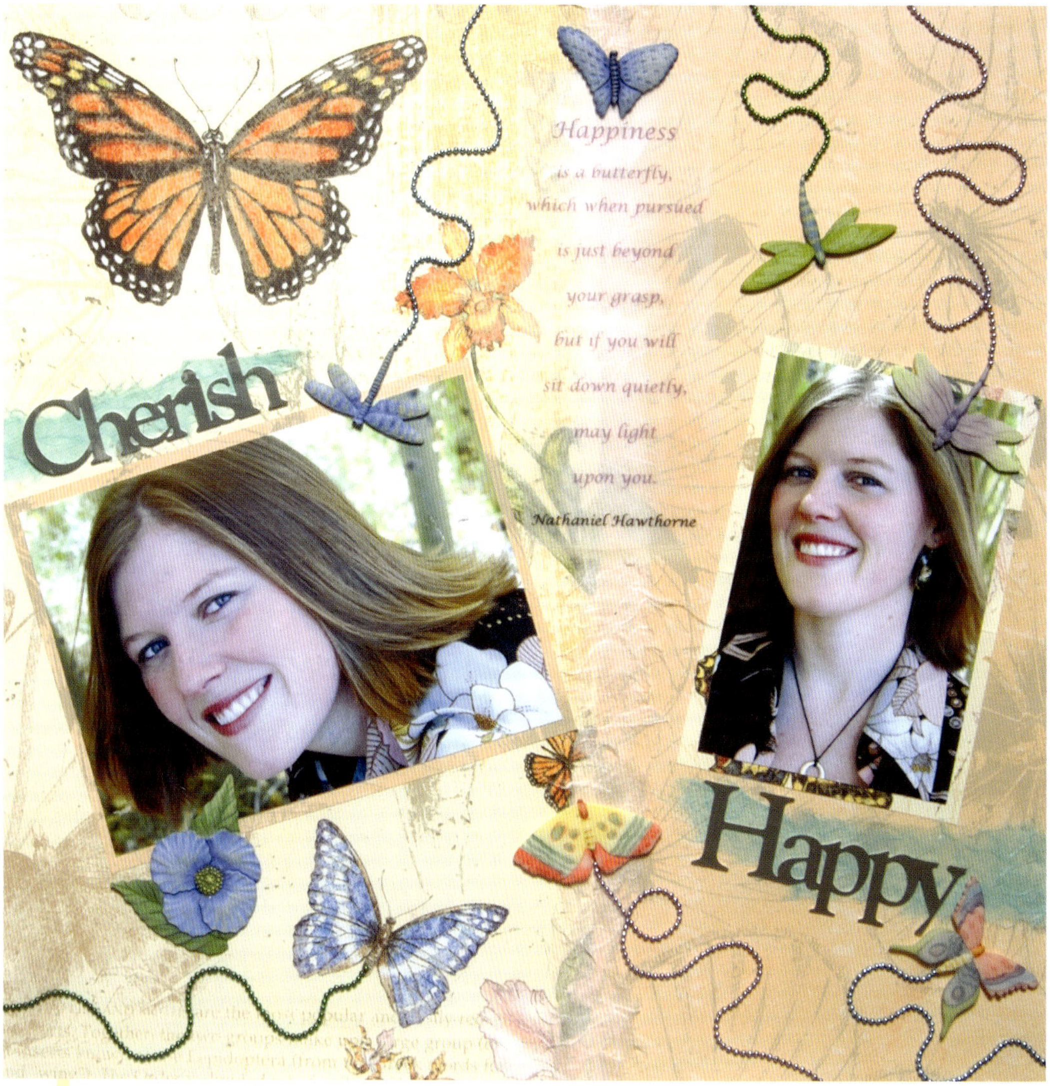

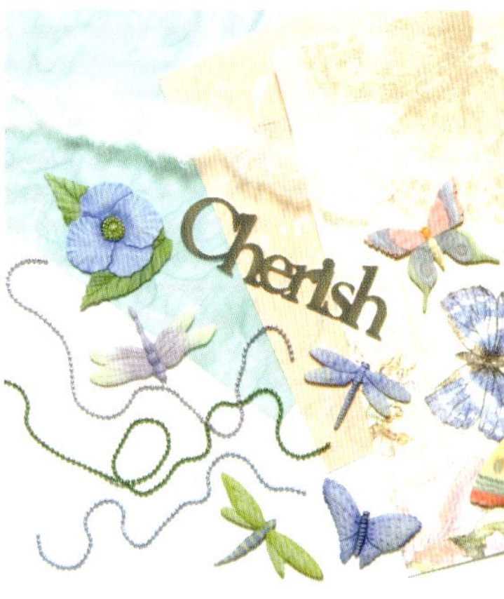

MATERIALS

Patterned Paper *PSX Papers for Creativity*

Rice Paper *Black Ink*

Butterfly, Dragonfly and Flower Resin Charms *K&Company*

Bead Chain *Making Memories*

Metal Words *Making Memories*

Matte Adhesive *Chartpak*

TECHNIQUE HINT

To eliminate the seam, glue a thin strip of light rice paper along the line.

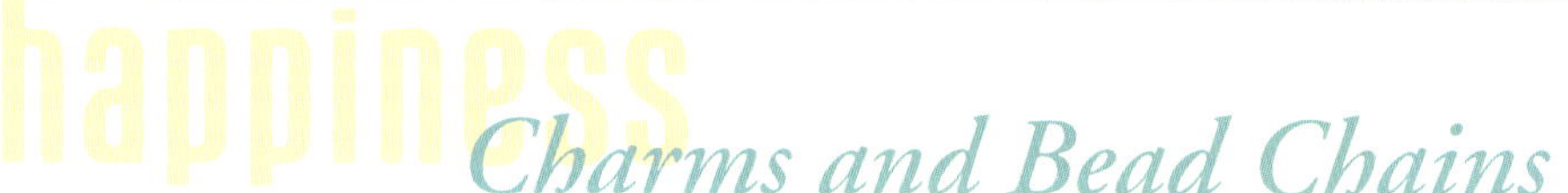

happiness Charms and Bead Chains

The free spirit of the butterfly and the loving nature of my niece Catherine are beautifully captured on the page titled, Happiness. To create the page design, join two matching pieces of patterned butterfly paper. Trim the left hand paper 7-inches wide and the right hand paper 5-inches wide. To blend the papers, glue a thin strip of white rice paper over the seam. Mount photos on patterned paper and trim leaving a thin border. Position metal words on green rice paper and glue in place. Add bead chains with butterfly and dragonfly resin charms to symbolize a sporadic pattern of flight. Use a pencil and trace the bead chain design. Using clear glue, trace a line over the pencil pattern. Gently place bead chain along the pattern line. To complete, glue butterflies, dragonflies and flower charms in place. The joy of youth and the beauty of nature are constant reminders of the precious gifts that abound around us.

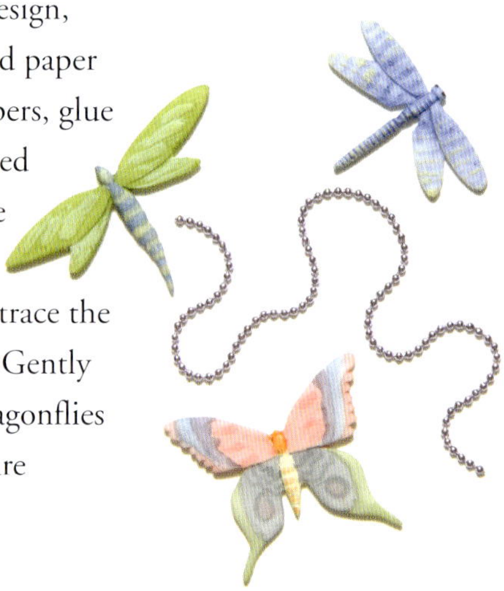

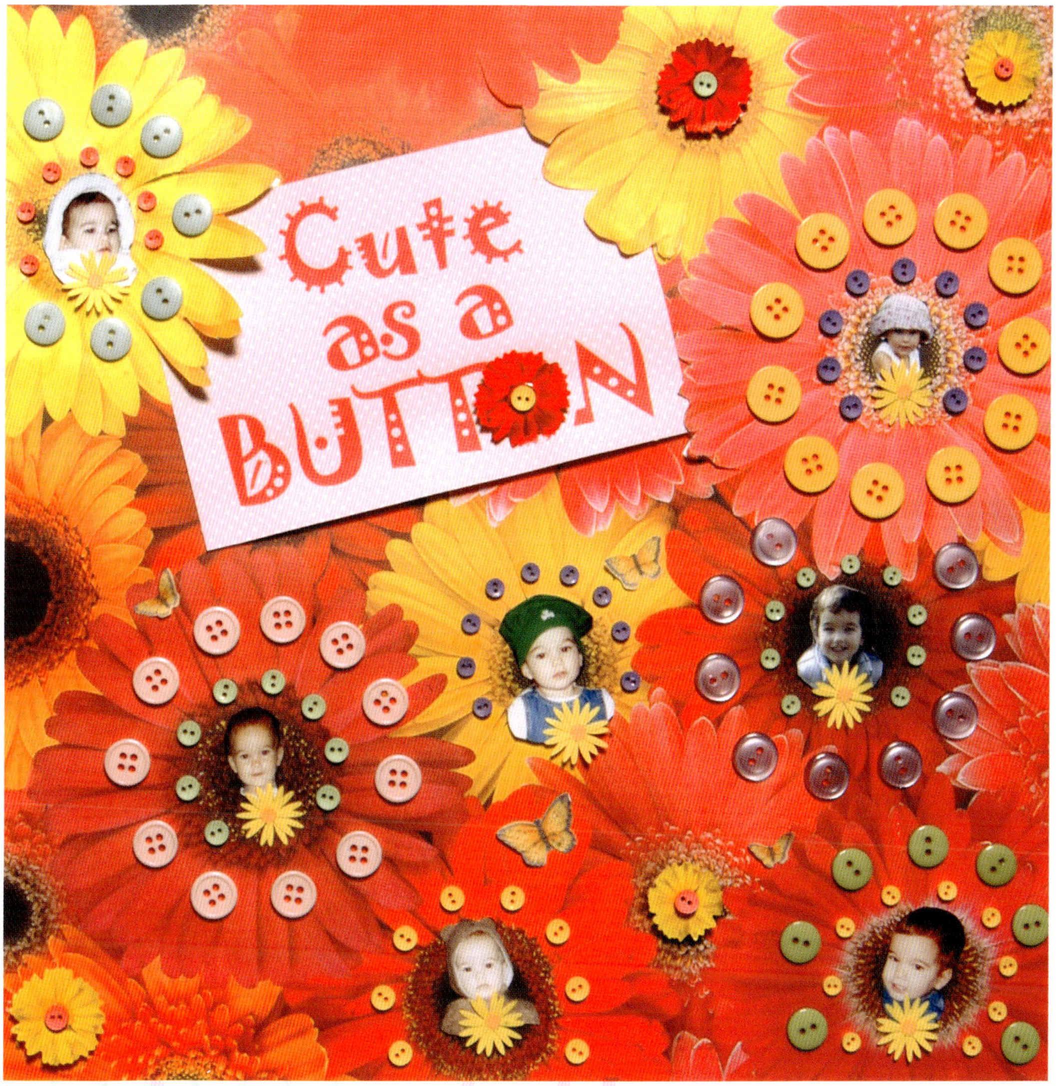

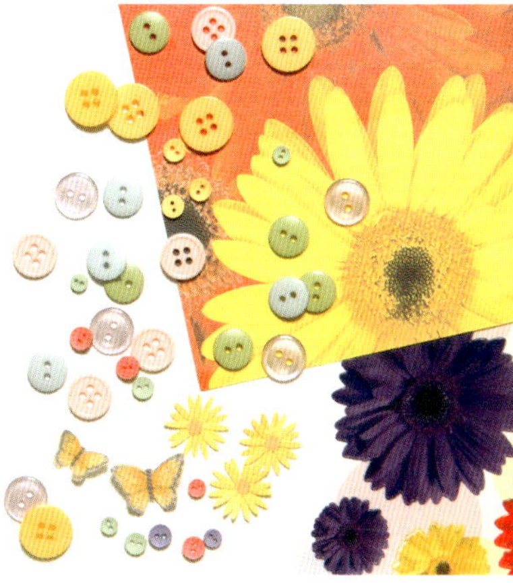

MATERIALS

Patterned Paper *Rainbow World*

Scrapbook Buttons *Making Memories*

Die Cut Daisies *Jolee's By You*

Flower and Butterfly Stickers *Frances Meyer, Inc.*

Computer Font *Jokerman*

TECHNIQUE HINT

Display titles on a scrapbook page by cutting around the daisy petals and sliding the paper underneath. Curl the petals with your fingertips.

cute as a button

Scrapbook Buttons

Nothing gives more credence to the phrase "Cute as a Button," as the smiling headshots of baby Madalyn. Gerbera daisies are the inspiration for this page showing the many expressions of Madalyn from ages one to three. Cut candid portrait photographs wearing cute hats, a hooded Halloween costume and happy smiles; paste in the center of the patterned flower paper. Space tiny scrapbook and large colorful buttons around each photo and attach with clear glue. To accentuate the face, glue die cut daisies and attach flower and butterfly stickers on foam spacers. Print the title with the Jokerman font on dotted patterned paper. This page captures the joy and innocence of the sweetest little girl in the world.

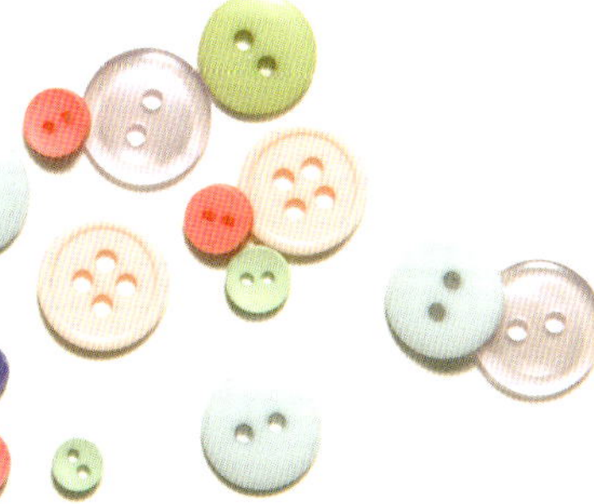

Glass Bead Borders

Maddy's first meeting with the Easter bunny is both exciting and rewarding. Use a combination of embossed and vellum patterned papers for this double scrapbook page. Cut three openings in the vellum, trim photographs slightly smaller and center. Print title and journaling marking the special day on striped pattern paper from the computer using the Bradley Hand font. Hand cut pansy flowers from translucent paper and mount with foam spacers. A laser cut Easter egg border is mounted with a double adhesive backing. Sprinkle alternating tiny red glass beads and blue micro glass beads in the openings to create a decorated egg effect. Finally, apply small vellum egg stickers to accentuate the theme. Hunting for Easter eggs with a new friend proves to be a memorable experience.

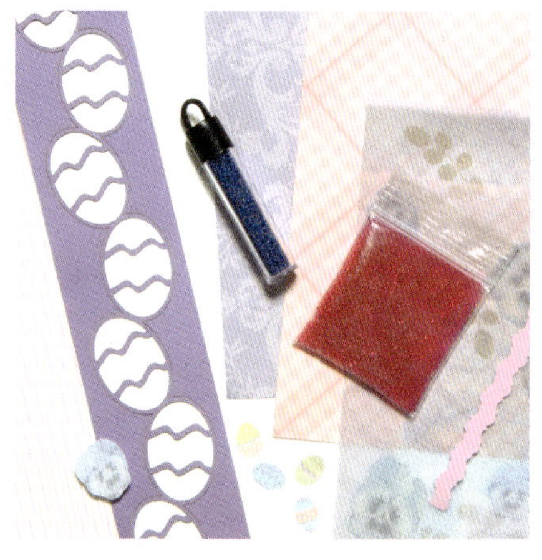

MATERIALS

Patterned Paper *PSX Papers for Creativity*
Patterned Translucent Vellum *World Win*
Micro Glass Beads *Halcraft*
Tiny Glass Beads *Treasured Memories*
Egg Border Deluxe *Laser Border*
Double Adhesive Paper *ScottiCrafts*
Vellum Egg Stickers *Mrs. Grossmans*
Computer Font *Bradley Hand*

TECHNIQUE HINT

Apply micro glass beads to the adhesive on the die cut border, and attach to scrapbooking page.

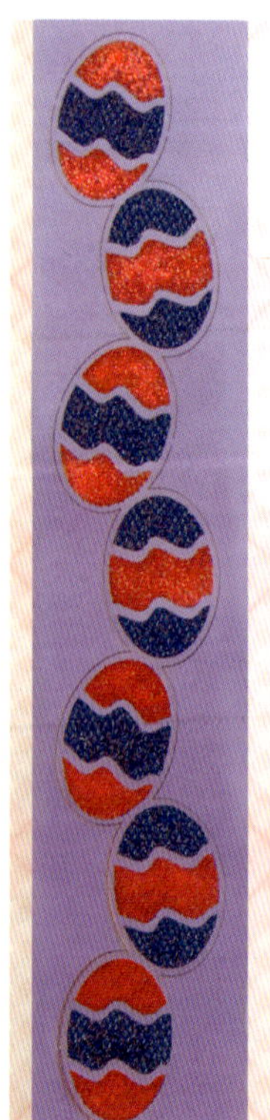

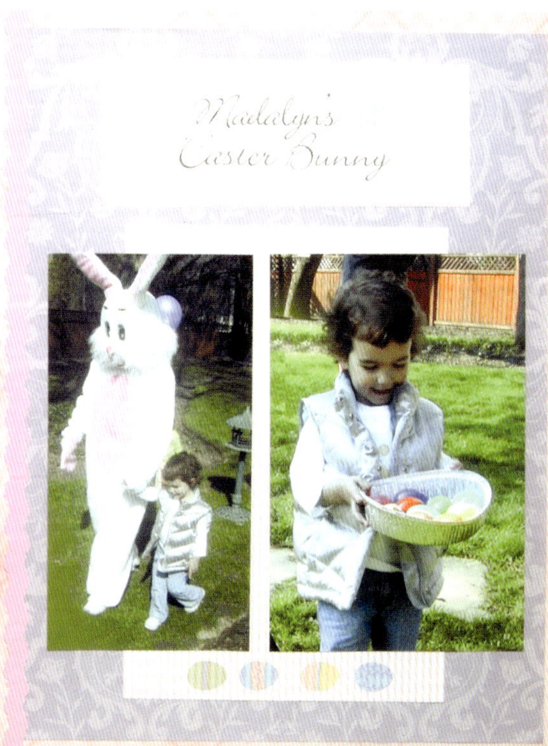

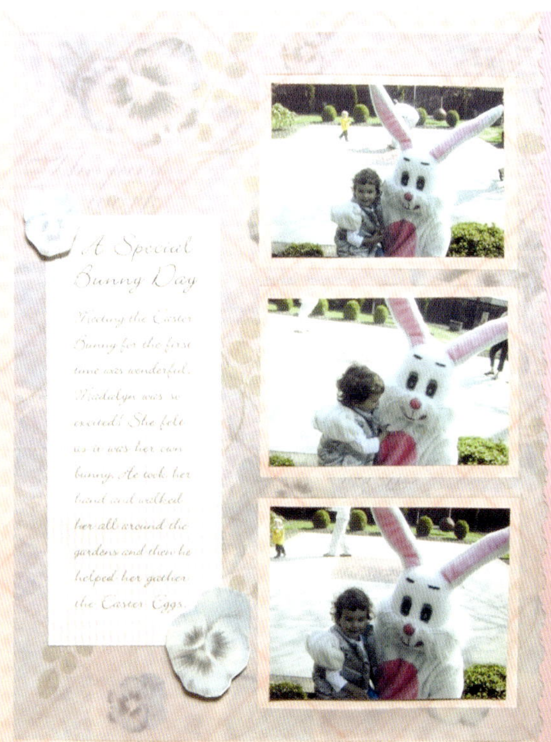

HOW-TO STEPS

easter bunny glass bead borders

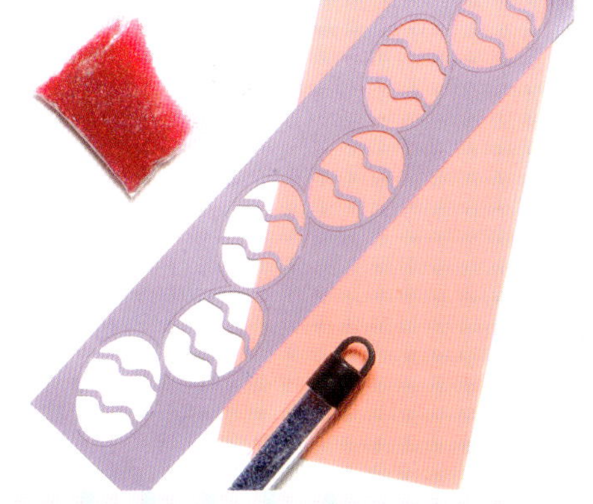

MATERIALS

Egg Border
Double Adhesive
Micro Glass Beads
Tiny Glass Beads

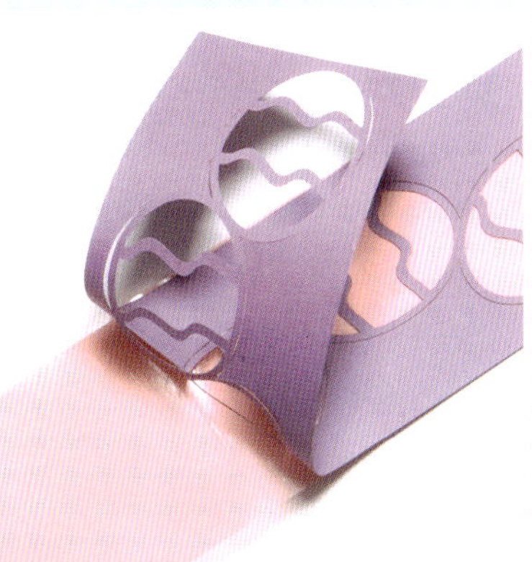

STEP 1

Trim double adhesive paper to width of egg border. Peel backing and adhere.

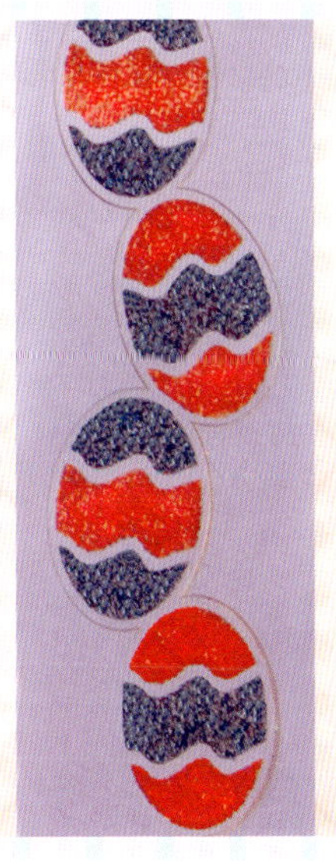

STEP 2

Cut pieces of the adhesive backing and cover the top and bottom bands of the egg pattern. Gently pour micro glass beads on the center band. Push in place with fingertips.

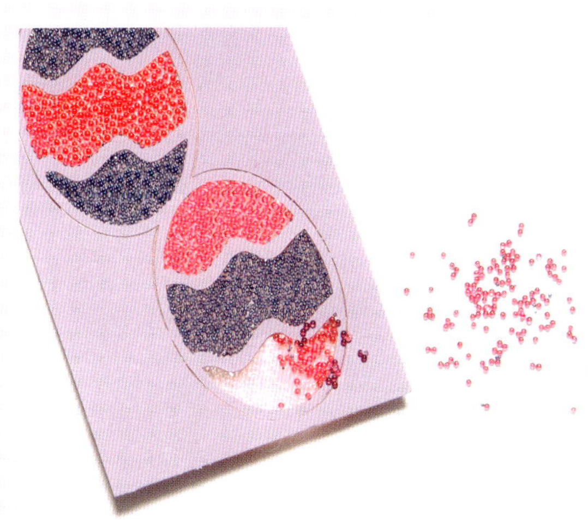

STEP 3

Remove paper backing and gently pour tiny glass beads on top and bottom bands of the egg.

little irish girl

Seed Beads

The Irish proudly display their national emblem, the shamrock. This past St. Patrick's day, Maddy honors half of her heritage by donning her festive green cap. Select shamrock patterned paper for the background. Next, glue a wide strip of patterned blue vellum on a diagonal and mount photos on solid red paper with a thin vellum strip on top. Set yellow and green snaps in the corners and wrap green fiber around each photo; cut large and small solid green paper squares with a deckle edge blade. Glue shamrock stickers to page pebbles and adhere on the green paper squares. The large green square is mounted on red paper on top of the blue and red fibers. Place adhesive strips in position and pour seed beads on the surface. Print "Little Irish Girl" in Goudy font on matte adhesive. Finally, position clear alphabet words "cute" and "pixie" vertically on the photo. Our little Irish lass proudly displays a great smile for all to see.

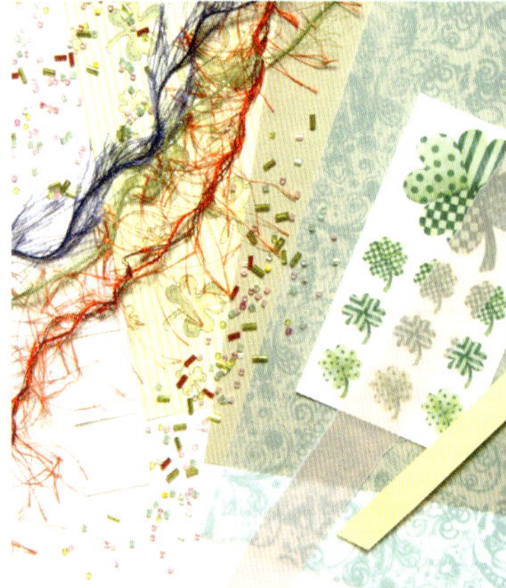

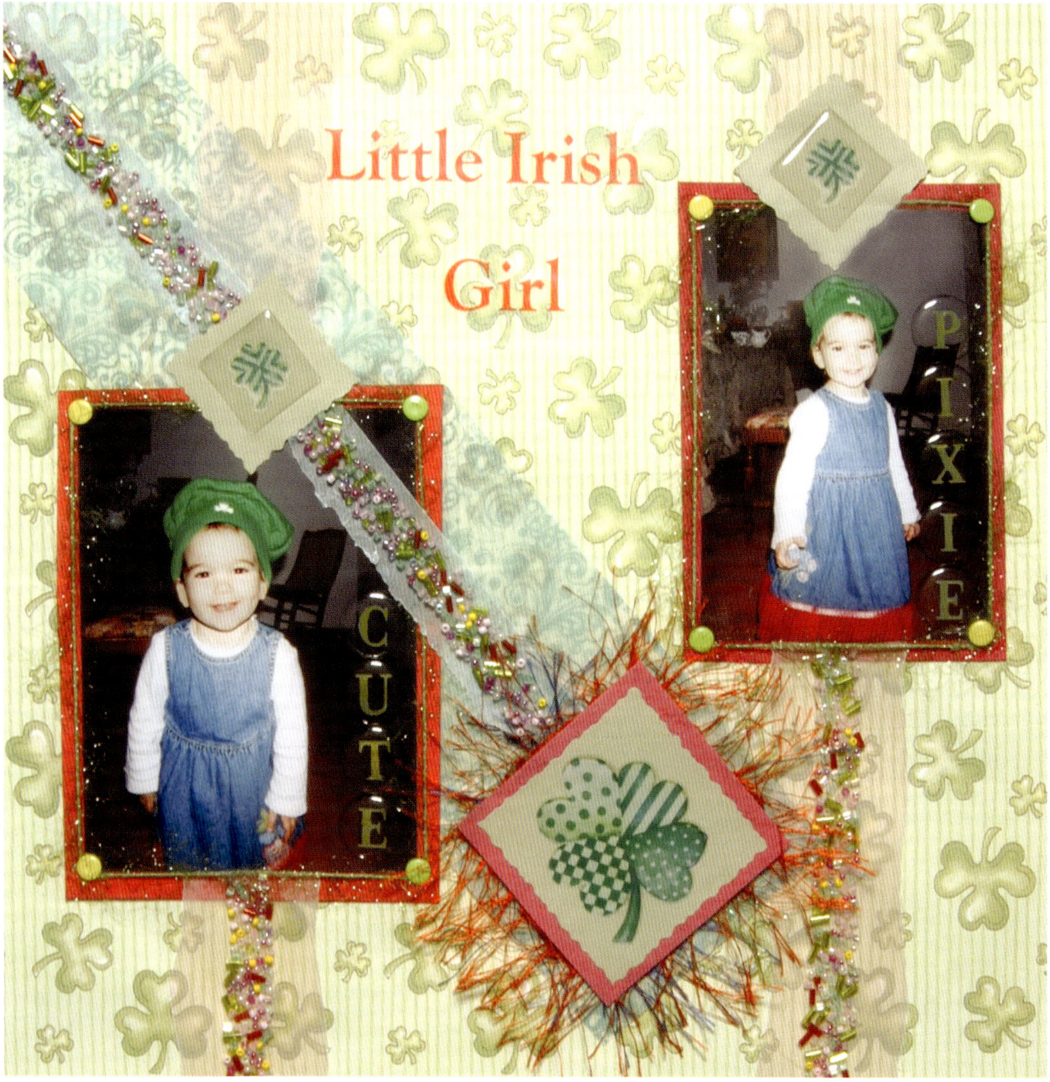

MATERIALS

Patterned Paper *Provo Craft*
Solid Red and Green Paper *Anna Griffin*
Patterned Vellum *Colorbök*
Shamrock Stickers *Frances Meyer, Inc.*
Fibers *EK Success*
Adhesive Strip *Treasured Memories*
Square Page Pebbles *Making Memories*
Seed Bead Mix *Treasured Memories*
Yellow and Green Snaps *Making Memories*
Clearly Yours Alphabet *K&Company*
Matte Adhesive *Chartpak*
Computer Font *Goudy Oldstyle*

TECHNIQUE HINT

After seed beads are poured on adhesive tape, use tiny glass beads or micro beads to fill the empty spaces.

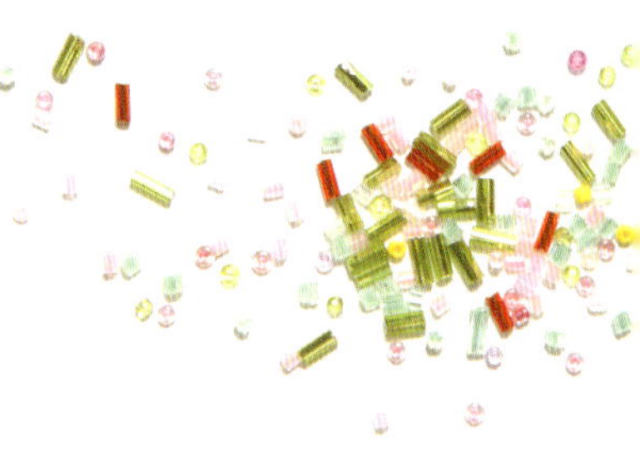

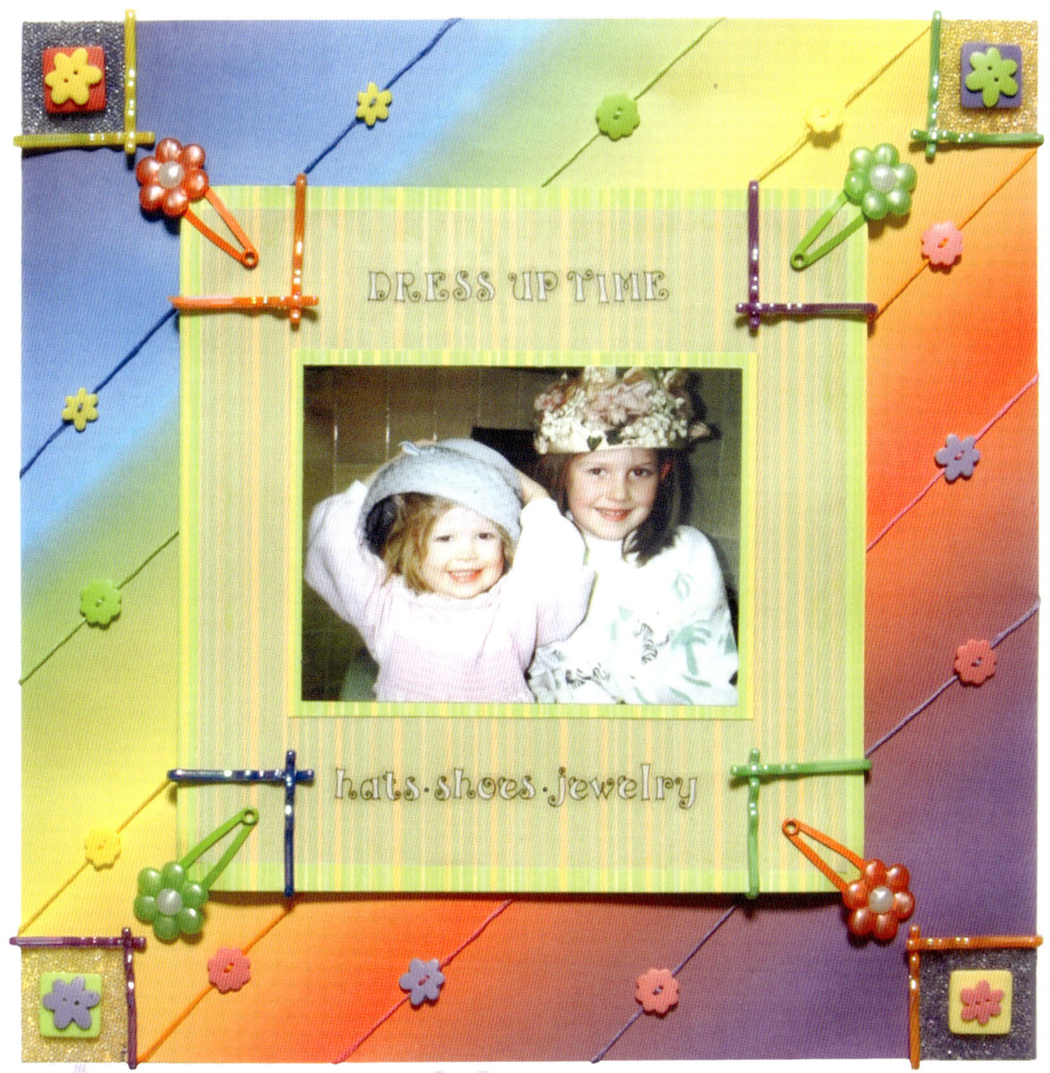

MATERIALS

Patterned Paper *Amscan Memory Kit*

Two-Sided Cardstock *Making Memories*

Vellum *The Paper Company*

Scrapbook Square and Flower Buttons *Making Memories*

Scrapbook Stitches Floss *Making Memories*

Bobby Pins and Barrettes *Goody*

Bead Sheet *Craftware*

Alphabitties *Provo Craft*

TECHNIQUE HINT

When using bead sheet, let cool before decorating.

dress up time

Bobby Pins, Barrettes and Bead Sheets

Little Catherine and Julia never miss an opportunity to put on mom's best shoes, jewelry and hats. Trim 1-inch square pieces of bead sheet and heat melt in each corner of the rainbow scrapbook paper. Interlock bobby pins at a 90-degree angle around the melted bead sheets. Glue square and flower buttons in each corner. Thread flower buttons on colored floss and position evenly on paper. Match floss to paper color and tape in position. Glue photo on striped cardstock and mount on larger square cardstock with vellum. Adhere to rainbow paper, slide bobby pins in each corner and add a barrette. Wearing mom's clothing and pretending to be all grown-up are rites of passage enjoyed by all little girls throughout the ages.

Theme Buttons and Photo Flip Hinges

With his playful exuberance and steadfast devotion, Gatsby, Deanna's lovable Boston terrier, is one of the most cherished members of the family. Choose two sheets of two-sided cardstock and trim the striped side in the shape of a house; glue in position on top of the blue paper. Trim dog photos with scallop scissors and mat on red patterned paper. Place hinges on either side to create an open door effect and cover inside of doors with striped cardstock. For the inside, trim two equal size photos and punch rounded corners. Mount with strip of red patterned paper. Print words on matte adhesive using the Harrington font. Glue the words "Playful" and "Pensive" on the inside of the doors and place, "The Great Gatsby," above the doors. Cut triangle from blue paper and mount words, "A House is Not a Home Without a Dog." Glue red ribbon and embellish with doggie paw print buttons, red vintage buttons and bones. Complete with Boston terrier rubber stamp and accent with tiny paw print buttons. Our playful friend Gatsby makes a welcome companion for little Spencer.

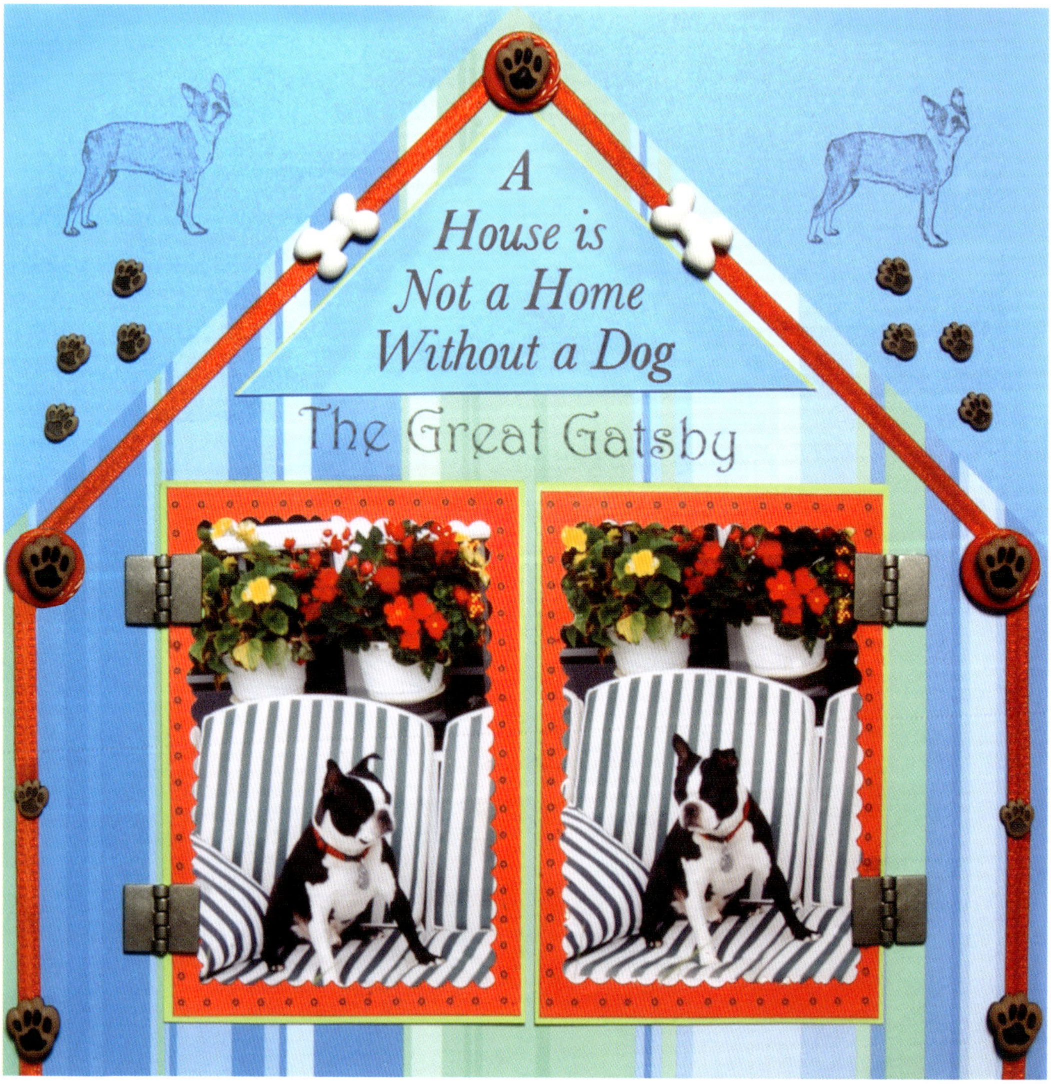

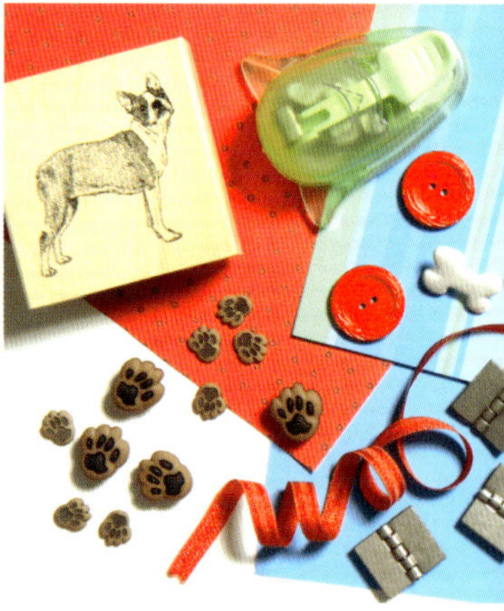

MATERIALS

Two-Sided Cardstock *Making Memories*
Patterned Paper *Paper Pizazz*
Medium Round Punch *EK Success*
Matte Adhesive *Chartpak*
Ribbon *Making Memories*
Photo Flip Hinges *Making Memories*
Fido Collection Buttons *Dress It Up*
Red Vintage Buttons *Antique Shop*
Rubber Stamp *Stamp Gallery*
Computer Font *Harrington*

TECHNIQUE HINT

Snip off buttonhole loop on back of button and lay flat on page.

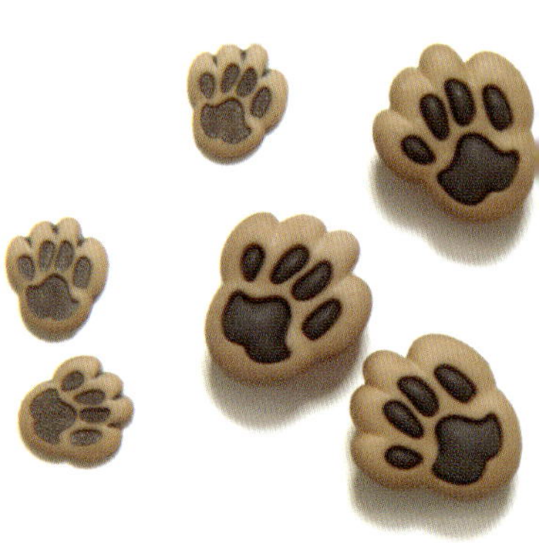

HOW-TO STEPS

photo flip hinges

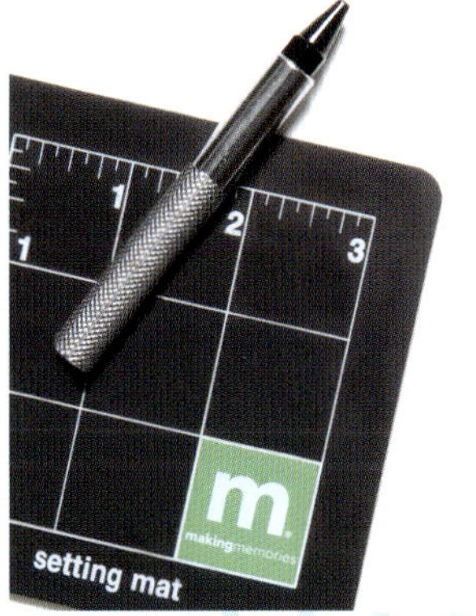

MATERIALS

Setting Mat
Medium Round Punch and Set Tool
Photo Flip Hinges
Hammer

STEP 1

Use a medium round punch to make two holes on the side of the mounted photo.

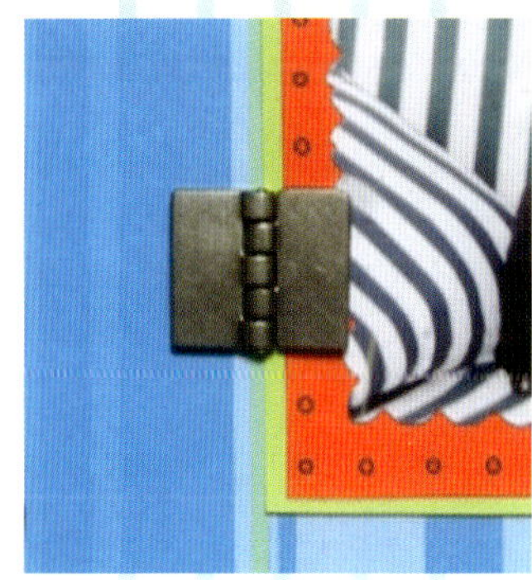

STEP 2

Use the setting tool to attach the hinge to the paper, and hammer to flatten completely. Cover opening by mounting another piece of paper on top.

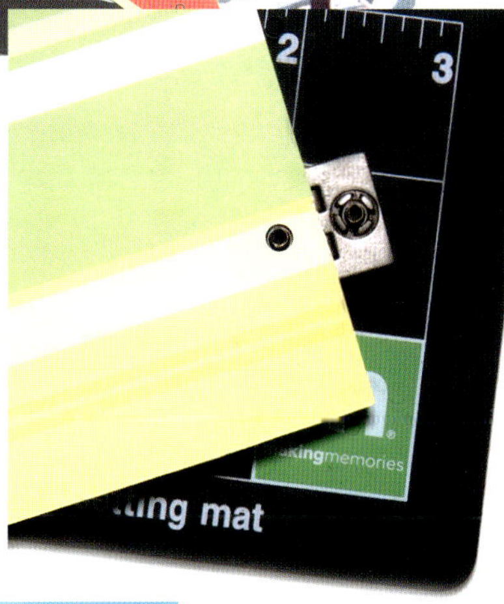

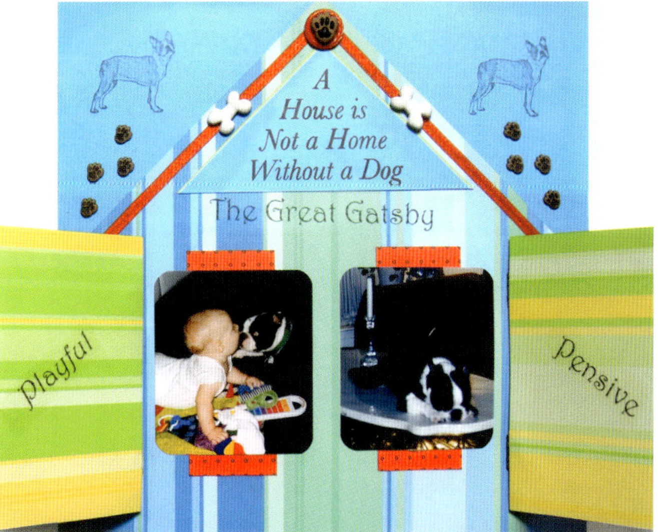

STEP 3

Punch and set hinges to the back of the scrapbook page.

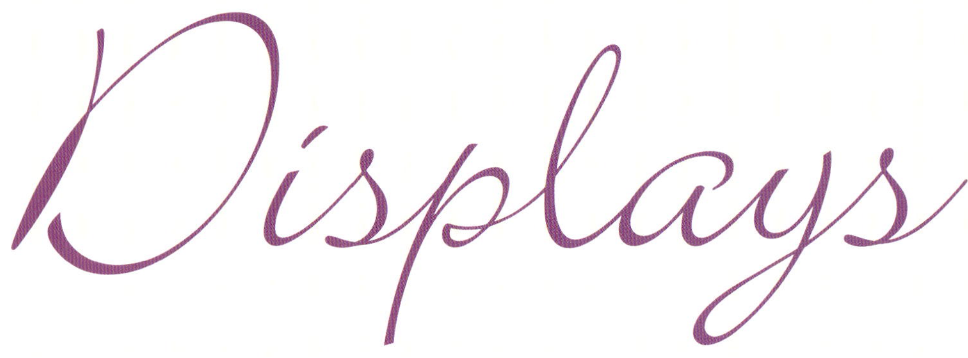

Die Cuts and Dimensional Stickers

Die cuts and dimensional stickers have significantly enhanced scrapbook layout designs. Stickers are available in a variety of everyday themes including—travel, holidays, sports, baby, birthdays, weddings,—and more. Today, miniature paper illustrations provide an excellent medium for showing details, highlighting a theme or telling a story. Die cuts are typically stamped out or laser cut from flat paper. The shapes stand alone or are decorated for added dimension. For a personal touch, use a craft knife to create your own handmade custom die cuts. Dimensional stickers are thin, printed-layers, separated by spacers and embellished with glitter, beads, wire, pearls, sequins and foil. They are available in a wide range of shapes, photo frames, borders and photo corners. Embossed stickers have textures for added dimension. Use dimensional stickers to accentuate your next scrapbook page and you will experience a new level of reality. These nouveau stickers are small enough to fit in your scrapbook, yet large enough to make a big impression.

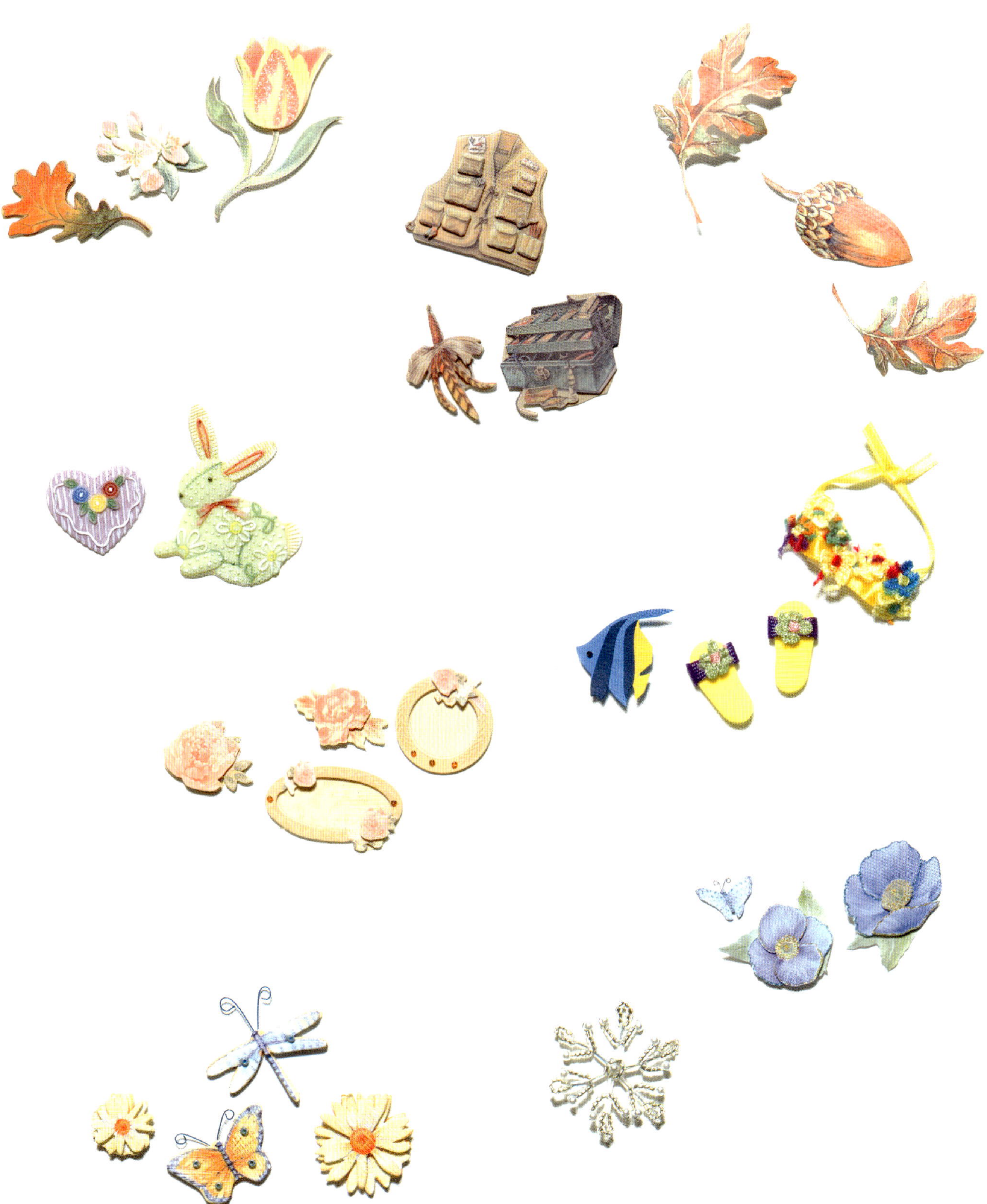

Fly-fishing
Dimensional Embossed Stickers

Fly-fishing is a passion shared by thousands throughout the world. There is no better way to experience the excitement of the catch than by a father teaching his daughter the nuances and techniques of the sport. Three embossed patterned papers are chosen to reflect fly-fishing: trout fish, fly lures and green lake motif. The trout fish paper is the main background on the left hand page. Tear strips of fly lure and green lake motif paper and glue on top.

For the right hand page, strips of torn trout fish and green lake paper are glued along the top and bottom. For the top layer, tear vellum to resemble water. Trim photographs to fit and anchor the design with dimensional fishing stickers. Plastic charmers and paper embossed fish stickers complete the page. "Fly-Fishing" is printed on vellum from the computer using the Jokerman font. The thrill of catching her first fish with dad is a memorable experience in the life of this young angler.

TECHNIQUE HINT

Tear paper away from you on an angle to create a dramatic white edge effect.

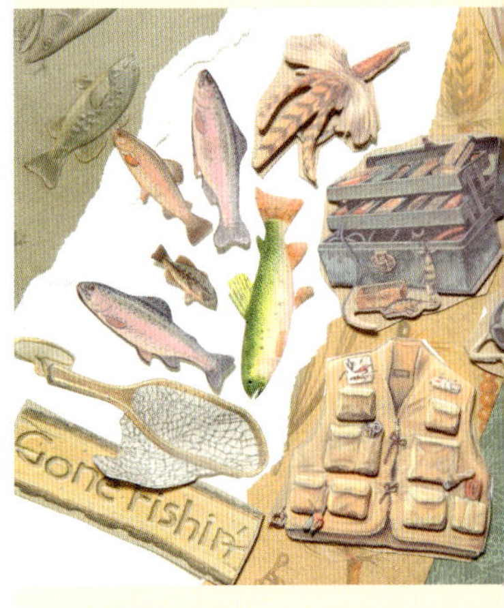

MATERIALS

Patterned Paper *K&Company*

Vellum *PSX Papers for Creativity*

Fishing Charmers *K&Company*

Dimensional Stickers Fishing Gear *K&Company*

Embossed Stickers Fishing Images *K&Company*

Computer Font *Jokerman*

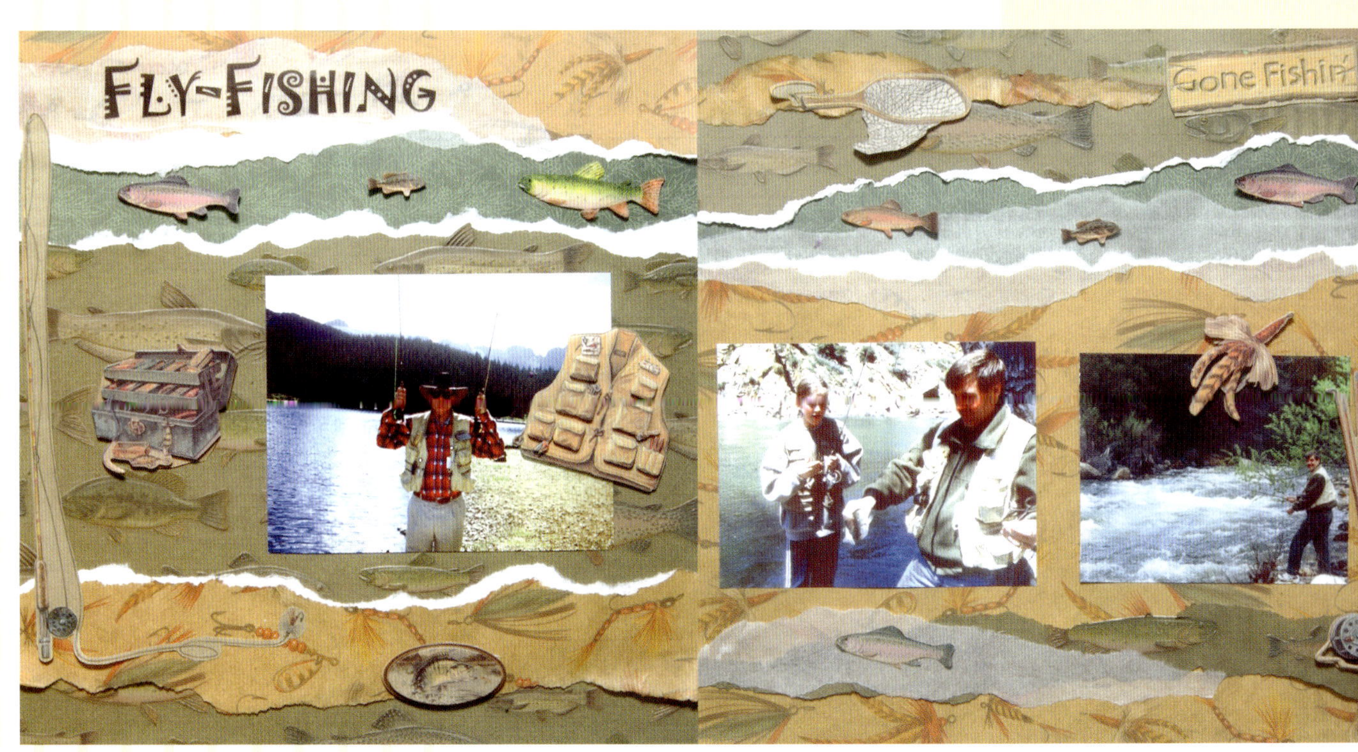

the four seasons

Dimensional Borders and Stickers

These four seasons embossed stickers inspired me to create a scrapbook page to celebrate the one-year anniversary of our new home. For the background, trim two pieces of mauve Canson paper 12-inches square. Trim 1/2-inch off each side of the square patterned pansy and monochromatic garden paper and glue in position over the mauve paper. Trim photographs the same size and use mauve Canson paper strips as a border.

Adhere the four seasons embossed stickers on top of the botanical embossed stickers. Use floral dimensional stickers for spring and summer. Leaf, acorn and pinecone dimensional stickers are used for fall; create a winter snowflake with a punch and collage sticker. Use white dimensional border flowers for spring and summer. Mauve dimensional borders complete the fall and winter scenes. The beauty of our home is remembered throughout the year by this seasonal scrapbook page.

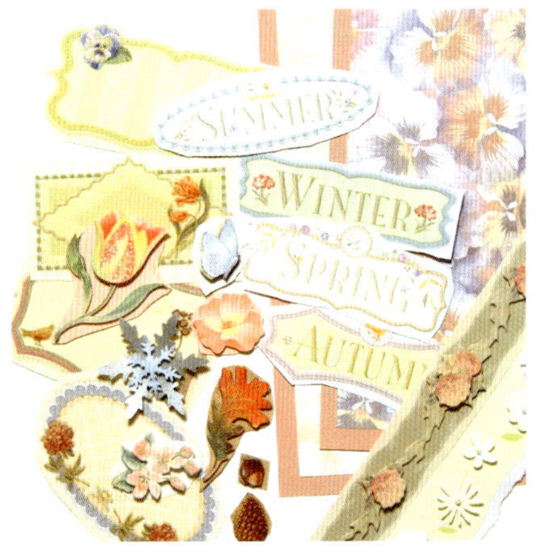

MATERIALS

- Patterned Paper *PSX Papers for Creativity*
- Canson Paper *Canson*
- Botanical Journal Tags *K&Company*
- Seasons Embossed Stickers *K&Company*
- Dimensional Stickers and Borders *K&Company*
- Snowflake Collage Sticker *Jolee's Boutique*
- Snowflake Punch *Marvy Uchida*

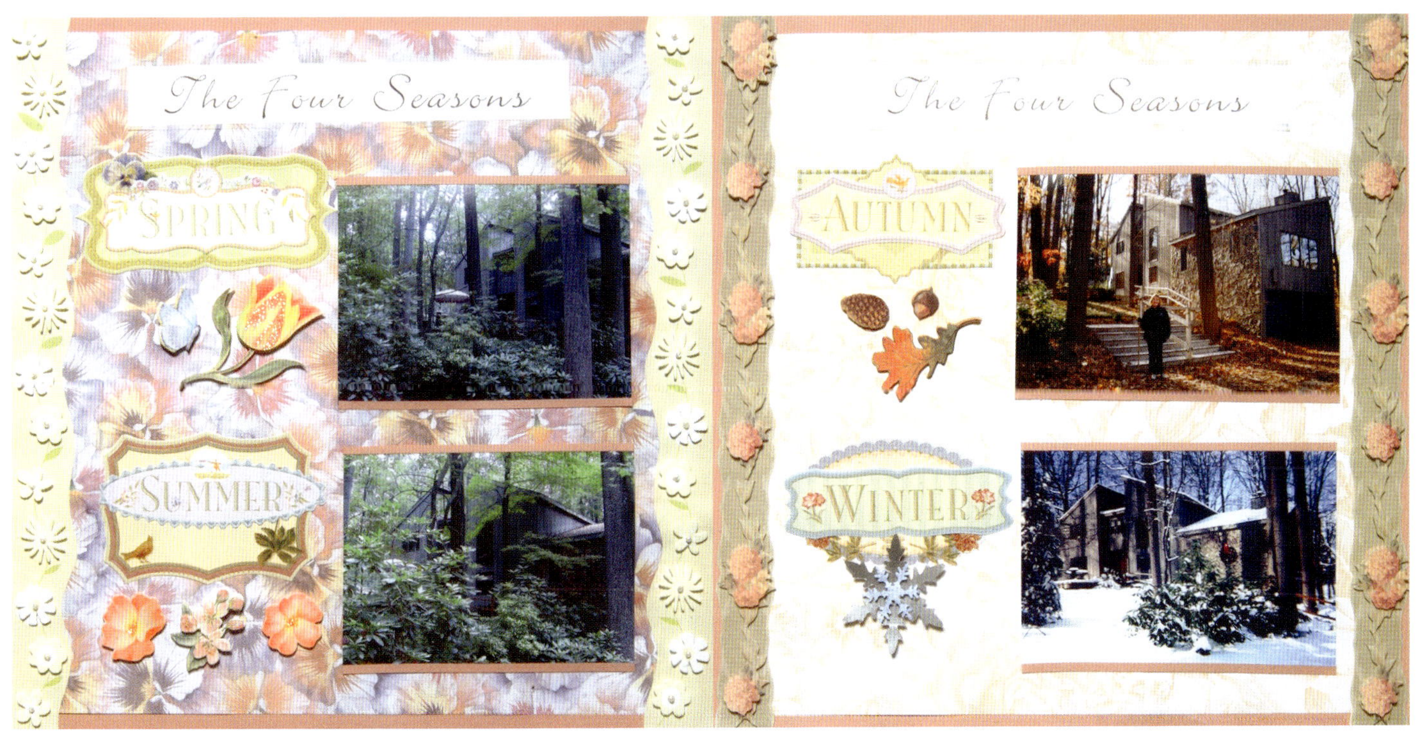

TECHNIQUE HINT

To frame each photograph, cut an opening in the patterned paper 1/4-inch larger than the photograph and glue to background.

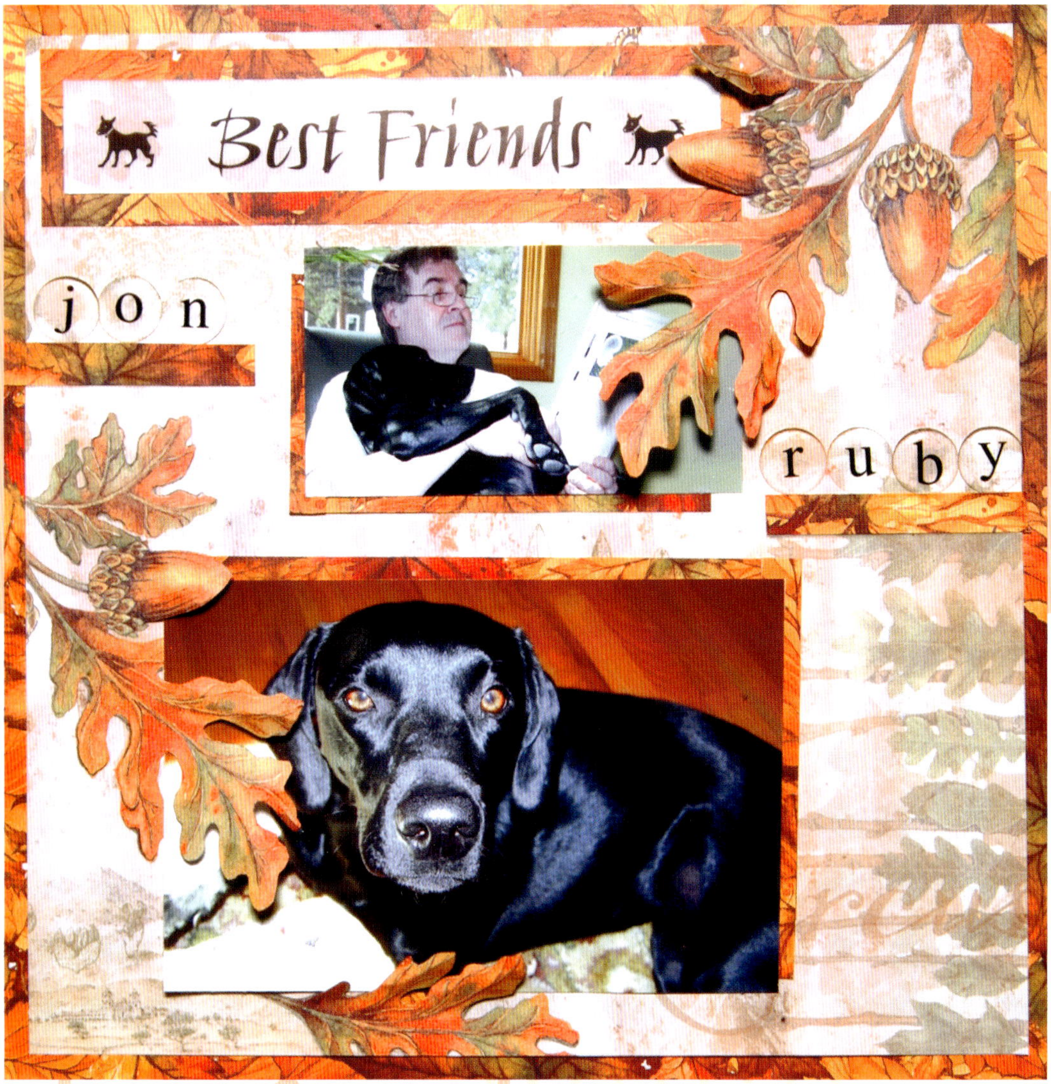

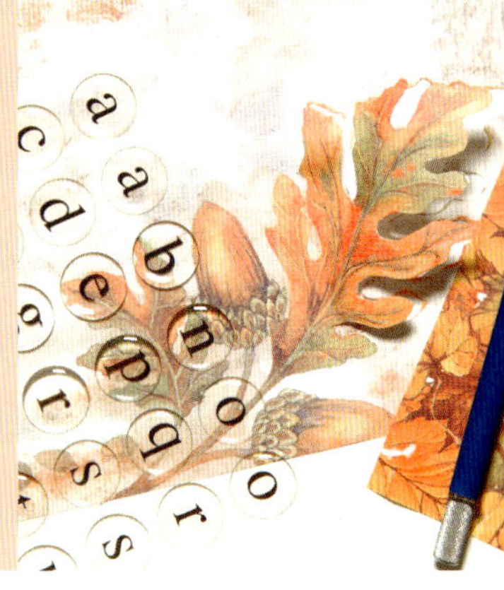

best friends

Handmade Die Cuts

Man's best friend is no more evident than in this photo of my brother-in-law Jon and his reliable Labrador retriever, Ruby. Select two pieces of autumn leaf patterned paper for the base and photo border. Place a piece of oak leaf paper on top. To create the border, trim a 1/4-inch strip off the oak leaf paper and center. Use a sharp craft knife to cut out the three oak leaves.

Position photographs under the leaves to create a die cut *trompe l'oeil* effect. To add dimension, curl the edges of the leaves. Place pieces of the autumn paper behind the photos to create a drop shadow and glue additional strips for the title borders. Print "Best Friends" using the computer font Humana Script on adhesive film and use page pebbles for the names. The loving image of Jon and Ruby is a priceless photo of two best friends.

MATERIALS

Patterned Paper *PSX Papers for Creativity & Provo Craft*

Page Pebbles *Making Memories*

Adhesive Film *Chartpak*

Computer Font *Humana Script*

TECHNIQUE HINT

To create the dimensional leaf, use a new knife blade and cut halfway around the edge of the leaf on a self-healing mat. For a more dimensional effect, slide the edge of the photo under the cut portion of the leaf and curl the edges.

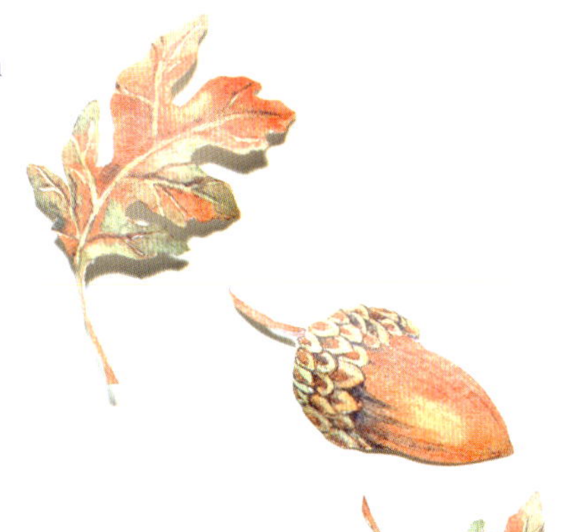

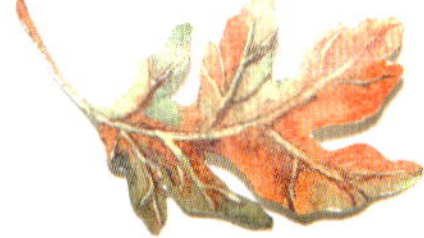

HOW-TO STEPS

best friends handmade die cut

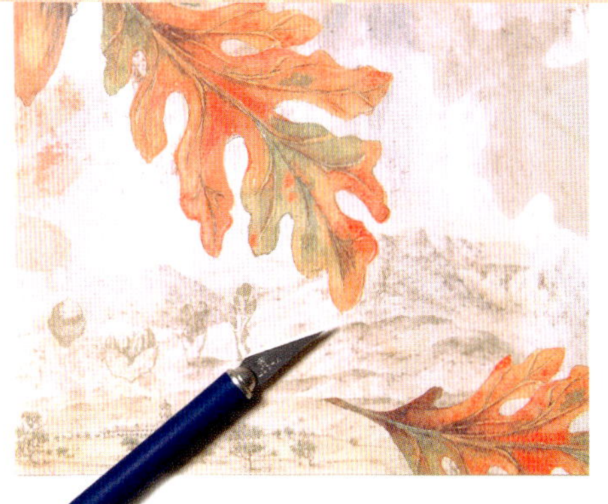

MATERIALS

Patterned Paper

Craft Knife

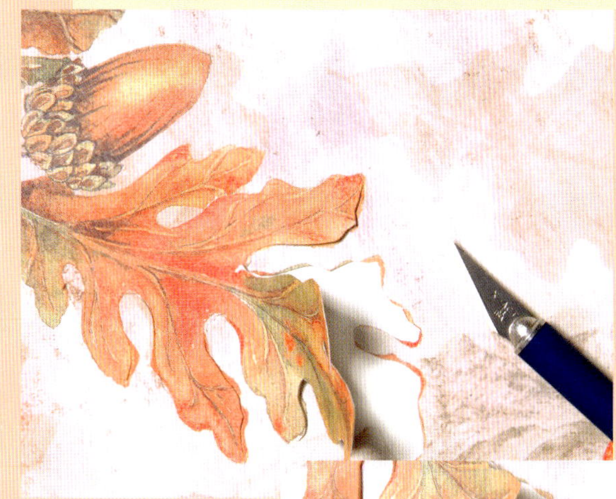

STEP 1

Use a craft knife with a new blade and carefully cut around the tip of the large oak leaf leaving the remaining leaf attached to the paper.

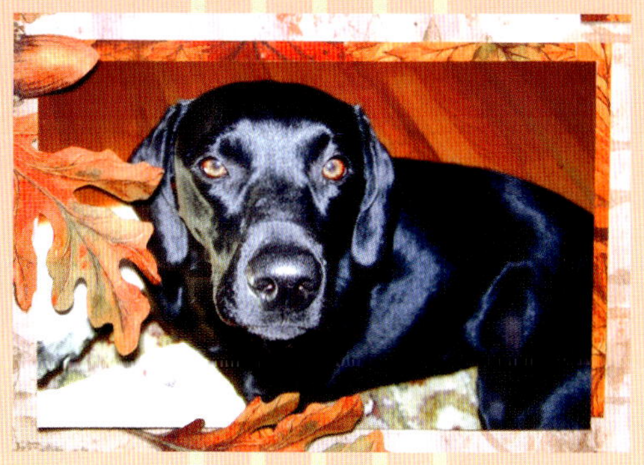

STEP 2

Carefully cut around the side of the small oak leaf leaving the remaining leaf attached to the paper.

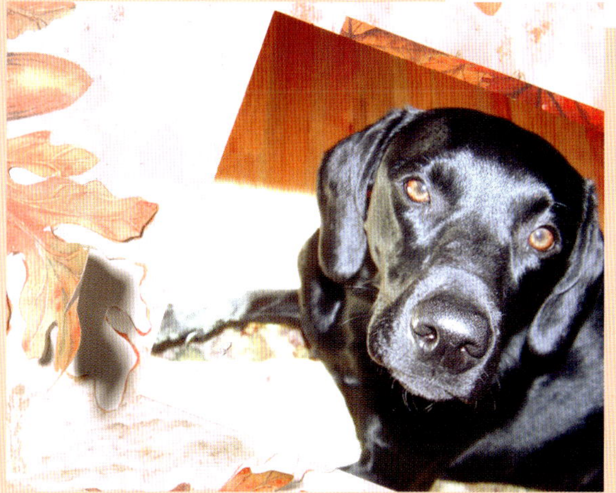

STEP 3

Curve the cut edges and slide mounted photograph under the hand-cut edges.

my first computer

Dimensional Borders and Corners

Maddy's ability to navigate the technical complexities of the computer demonstrates the educational future of children in school today. Her favorite site, www.nickjr.com, affords her the opportunity to have fun and teaches her to use the mouse. Cuddly stuffed animal patterned paper is chosen for the background. Next, mount dimensional border stickers on each side and adhere photographs with borders and corner stickers. Print journaling and title with Bradley Hand computer font on vellum paper; secure with border and corner stickers. Embellish with charmers and embossed animal stickers. A child's inherent curiosity is evident as we document Maddy's magical journey through cyberspace.

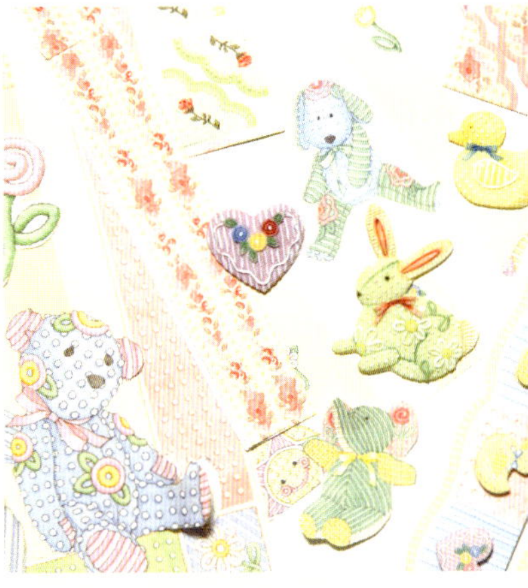

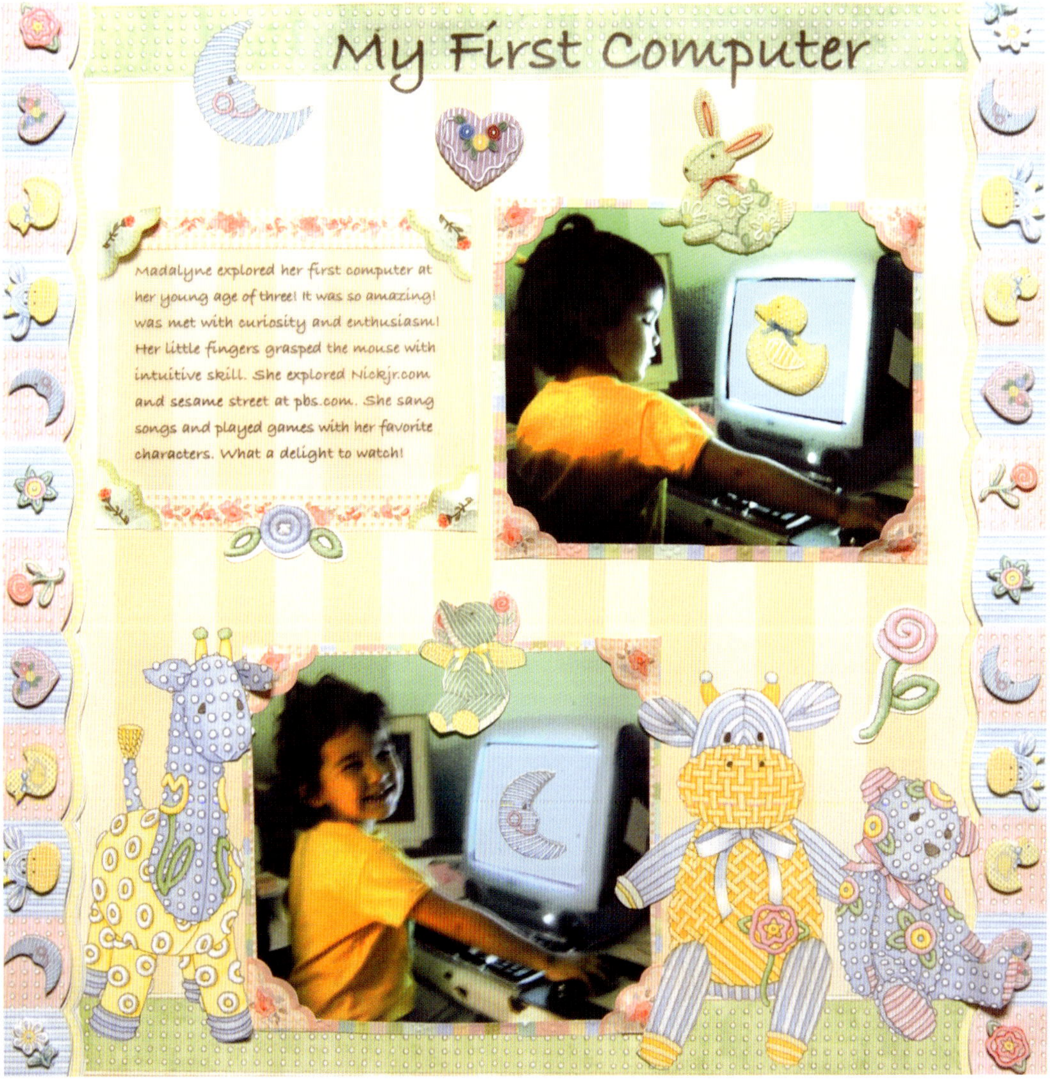

My First Computer

Madalyne explored her first computer at her young age of three! It was so amazing! was met with curiosity and enthusiasm! Her little fingers grasped the mouse with intuitive skill. She explored Nickjr.com and sesame street at pbs.com. She sang songs and played games with her favorite characters. What a delight to watch!

MATERIALS

Cuddly Friends Patterned Paper *K&Company*

Vellum *K&Company*

Charmers *K&Company*

Garden Party Borders and Corners *K&Company*

Cuddly Friends Embossed Stickers *K&Company*

Computer Font *Bradley Hand*

TECHNIQUE HINT

To create a dimensional effect, lift edge of animal sticker over photographs and borders.

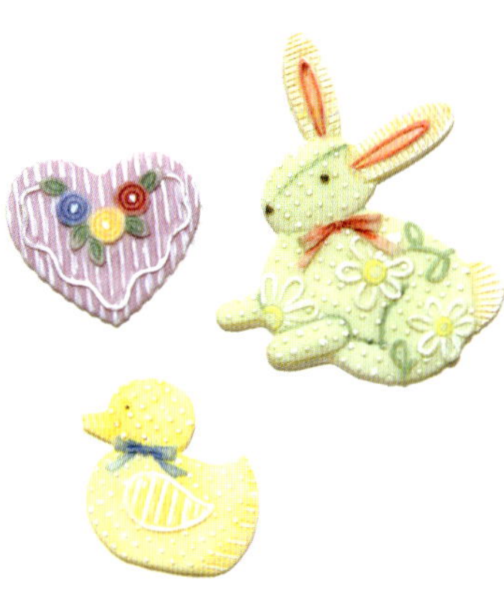

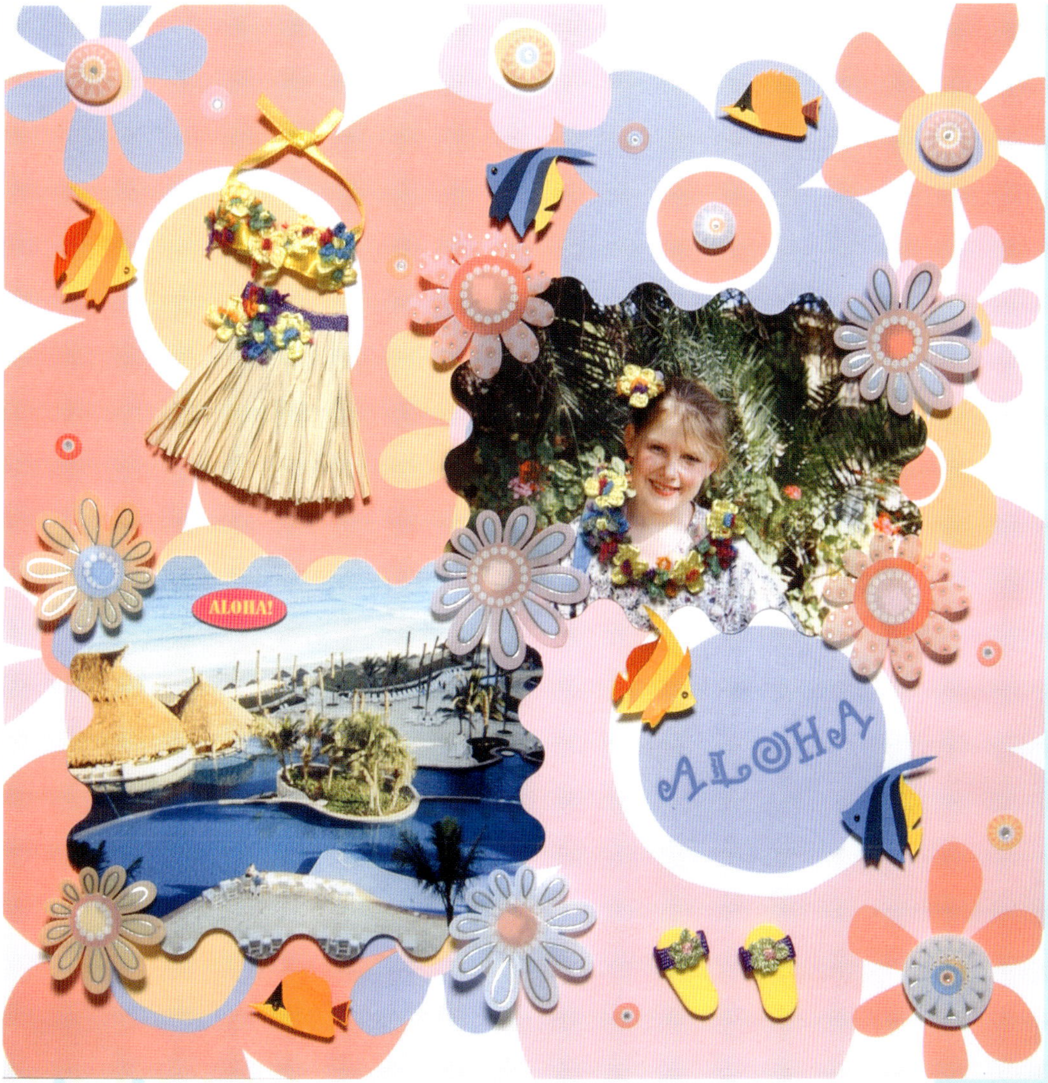

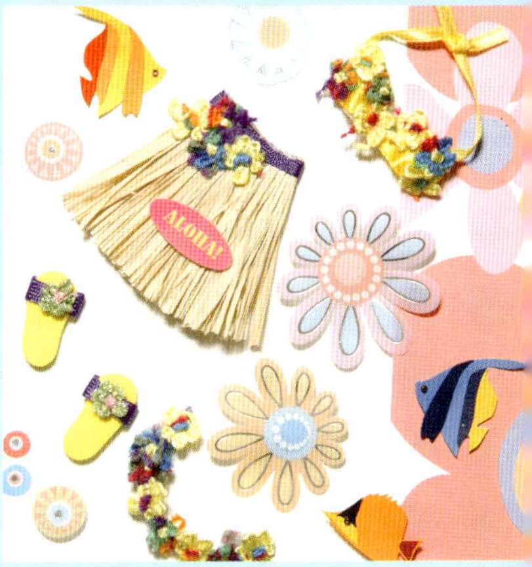

MATERIALS

Patterned Paper *Frances Meyer, Inc.*

Creative Letters *Making Memories*

Die Cut Tropical Fish *Jolee's By You*

Vellum Stickers *Stickopotamus*

Dimensional Collage Stickers *The Card Connection*

Scallop Scissors *Making Memories*

TECHNIQUE HINT

Vellum stickers are translucent. They look best on a light background.

aloha

Dimensional Collage Stickers

The sun, sand and surf make Hawaii the ideal place to enjoy the pristine beaches and magnificent island paradise of the South Pacific. Patterned paper with large flowers set the theme for "Aloha." Cut photographs with large scallop scissors to reflect the ocean waves. Place vellum flower petal stickers in each corner and in the center of the flowers on the background paper. Dimensional collage stickers of a lei and flower, glued on to the photograph, complete the theme. Angelfish die cuts compliment the page. This colorful tropical paradise will long be remembered as the perfect place to relax and enjoy the warm sun and cool ocean breeze.

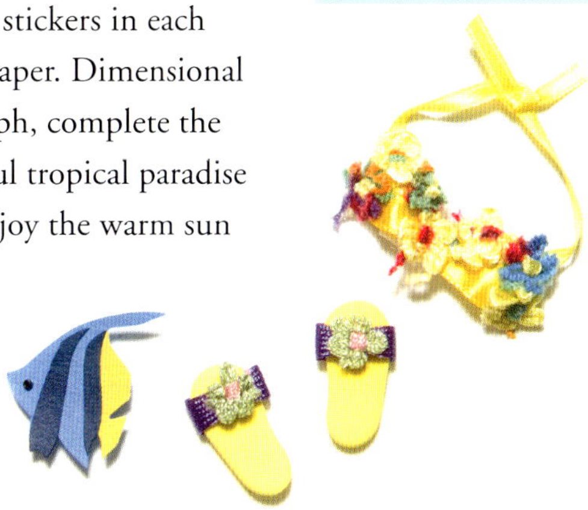

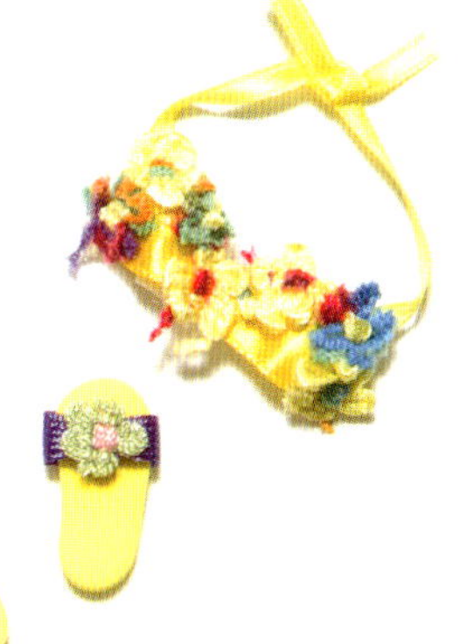

tea time

Die Cut Frames and Dimensional Stickers

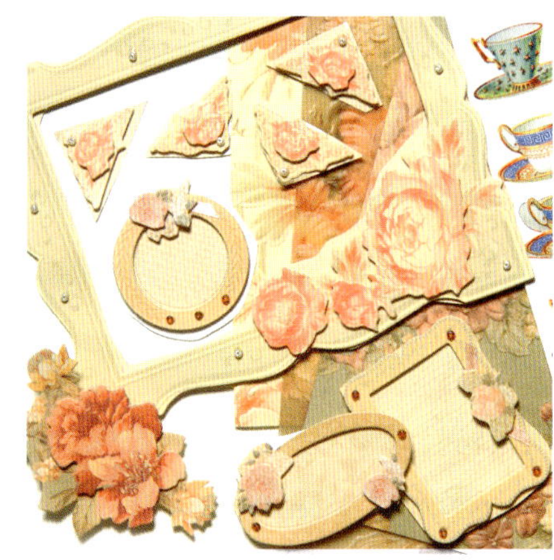

Two days prior to my wedding, I celebrated the big event at the Four Seasons hotel with my mother and bridesmaids. To create the background, tear embossed and vellum papers and place on top of the patterned paper. On the first page, insert a photograph of the memorable day in a die cut frame; place teacup stickers in die cut frames and position around the photograph. Use floral block stickers for the title "Tea Time" and attach with foam spacers.

On the facing page, frame two pictures with die cut photo corners on foam spacers. Journaling is created from the computer font Bradley Hand printed on vellum and anchored with dimensional roses. Use a punch for the corners and embellishment details. Celebrating a happy occasion with family adds to the excitement of a bride's special day.

MATERIALS

Patterned Paper *K&Company*
Embossed Vellum *K&Company*
Die Cut Frames *K&Company*
Dimensional Stickers *K&Company*
Garden Alphabet Stickers *K&Company*
Tea Stickers *The Gifted Line*
Computer Font *Bradley Hand*

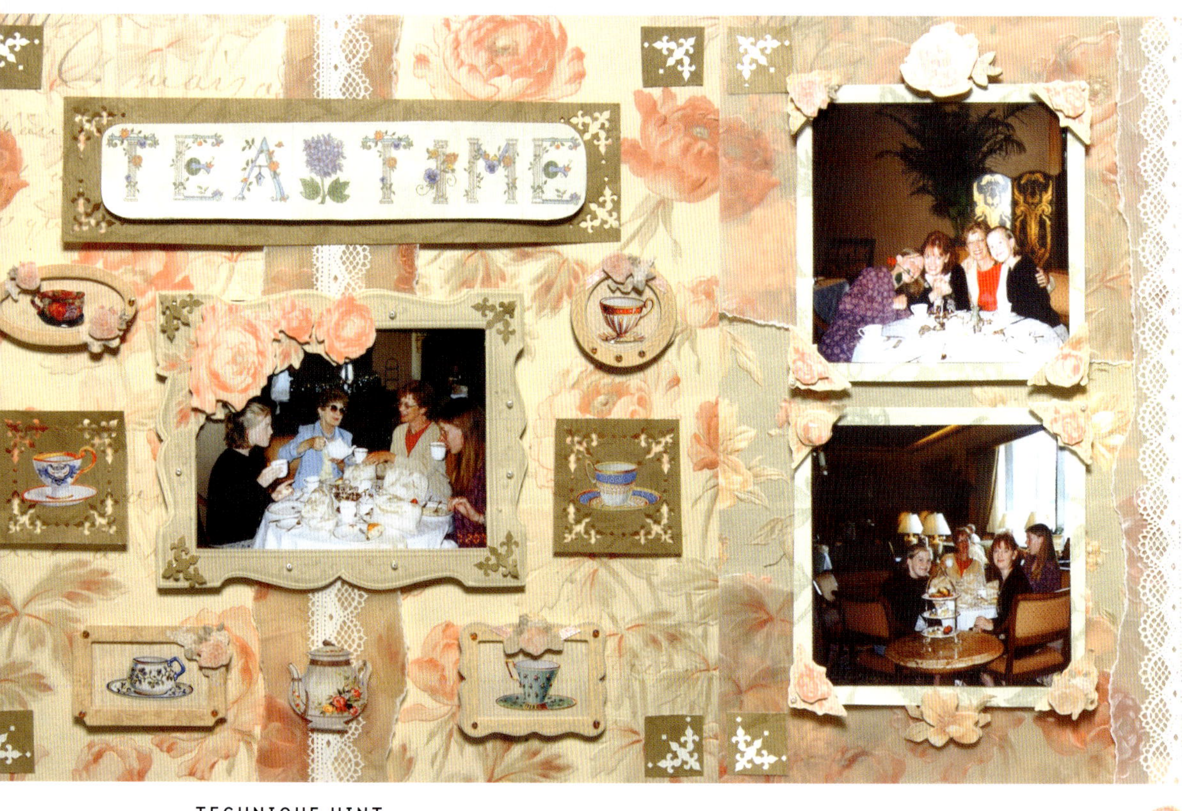

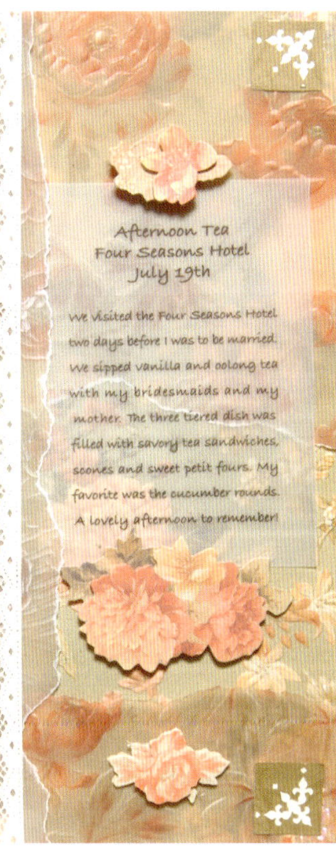

TECHNIQUE HINT

Prior to adhering die cut stickers and frames to the paper background, cut out and place in the desired position. When the layout is complete, peel and stick in place.

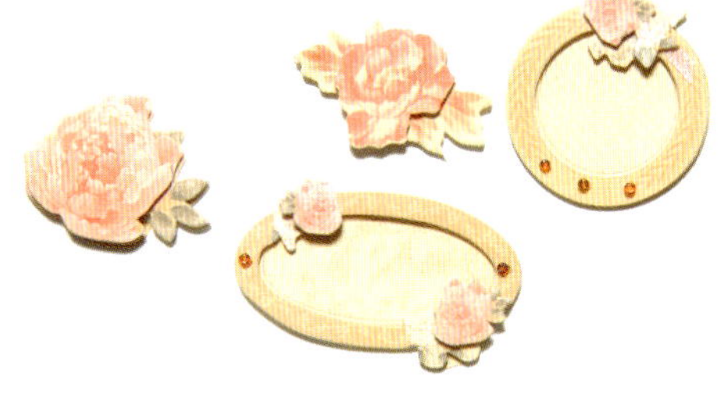

HOW-TO STEPS

tea time dimensional stickers

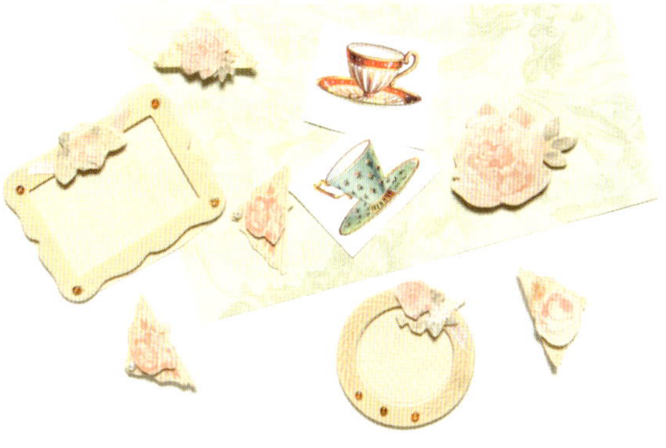

MATERIALS

Patterned Paper
Die Cut Frames
Dimensional Stickers
Tea Stickers

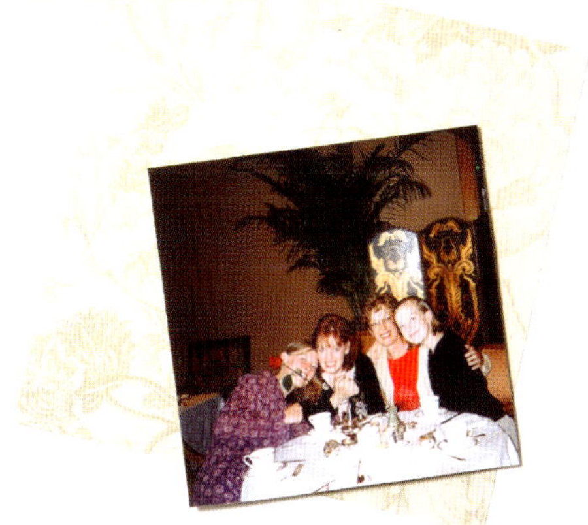

STEP 1

Trim and mount patterned paper and photograph leaving a 1/4-inch border.

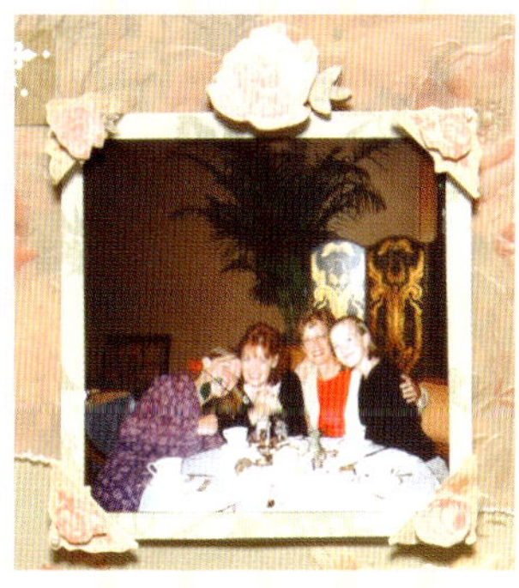

STEP 2

Attach dimensional stickers to each corner of the mounted photograph.

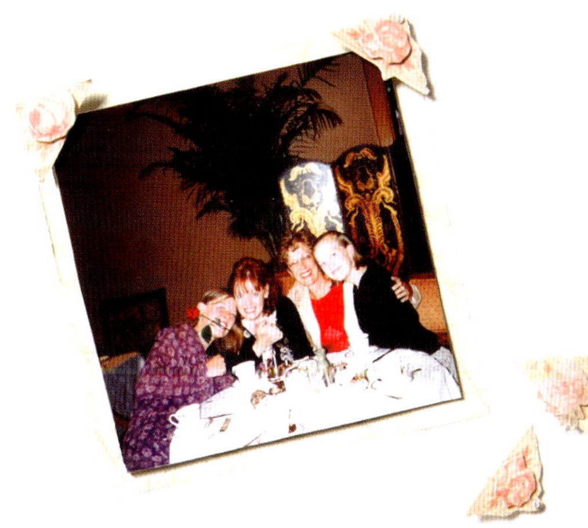

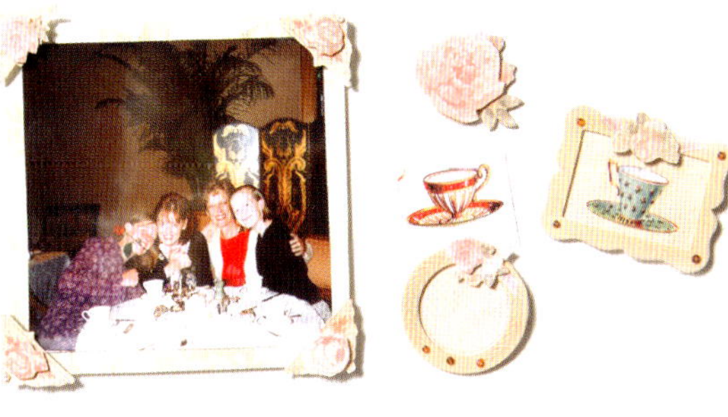

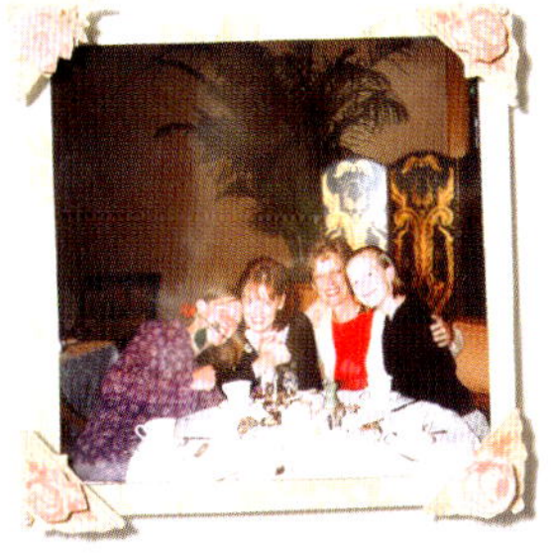

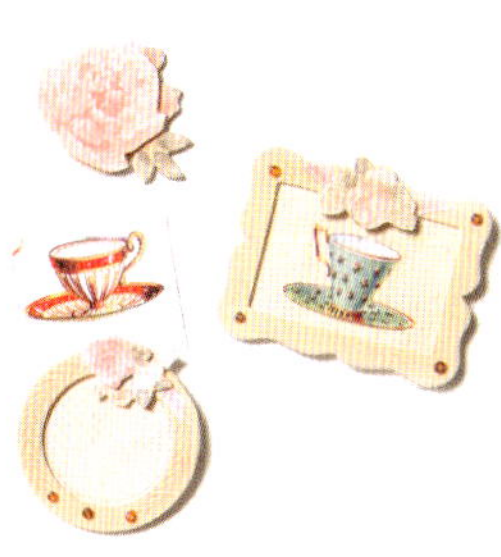

STEP 3

Peel and stick tea sticker in the center of the die cut frames.

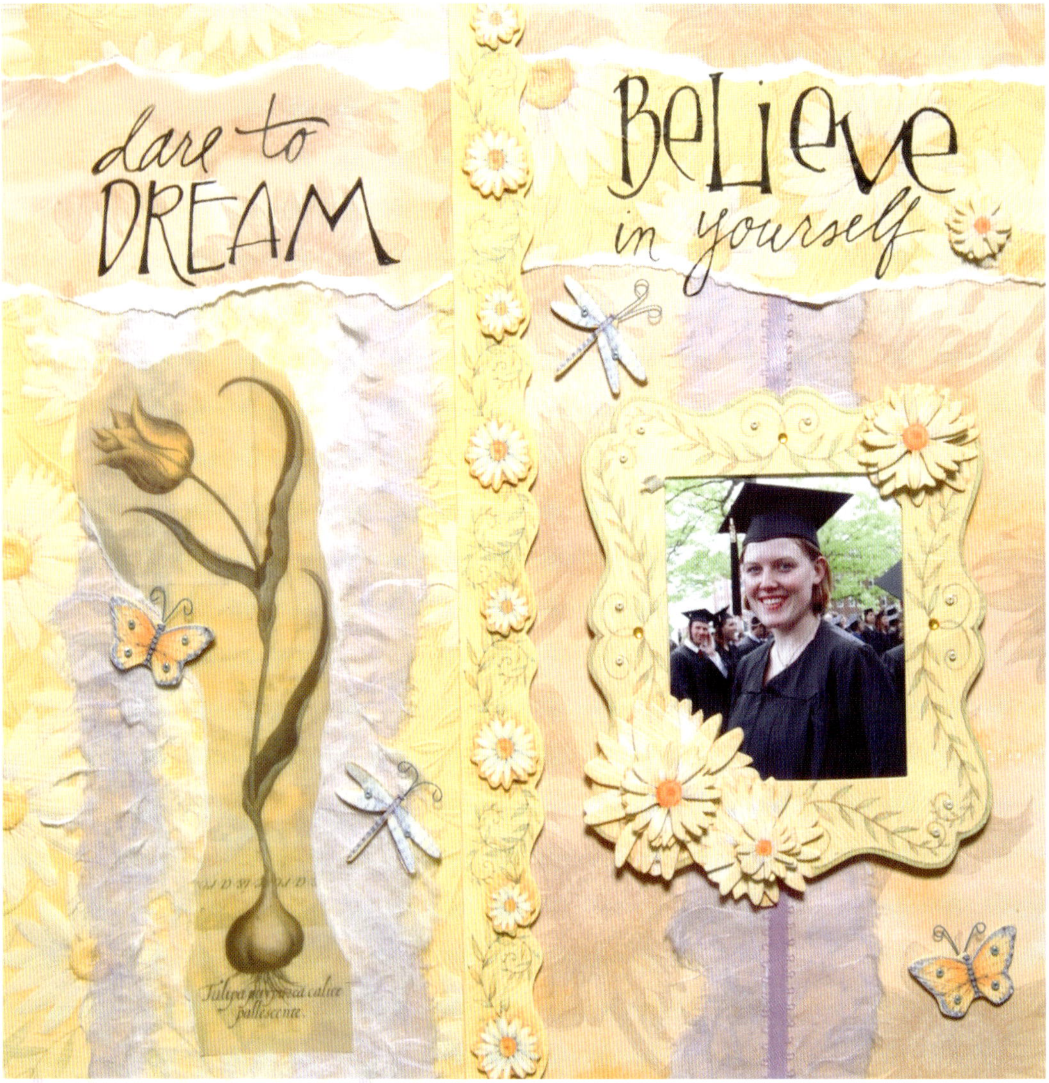

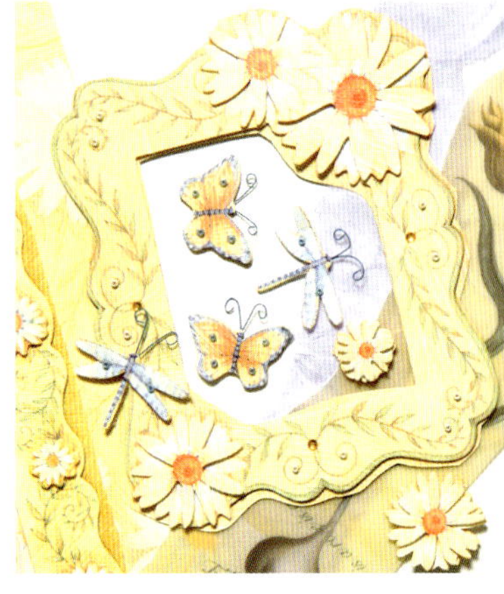

MATERIALS

Patterned Papers *K&Company*

Die Cut Frame, Border and Shapes *K&Company*

Transfer Type *Making Memories*

Translucent Vellum *World Win*

Rice Papers *Black Ink*

TECHNIQUE HINT

When tearing rice paper, use a ruler as a guide. Tear along the grain for straighter results. If a piece of paper will not tear, snip the spot with scissors. Permanent archival glue is best for thin rice paper.

dare to dream: believe in yourself

Die Cut Frame and Border

This page commemorates my niece Catherine's graduation from Amherst College in 2003. Create the unique background with two different embossed patterned papers. The opposite background paper is torn and used for the title borders. Apply rub down type and work over the torn edge. Tear mulberry lavender and rice papers in vertical strips and glue on both sides. Paste a flower torn from botanical translucent vellum paper over the rice papers. Glue a purple ribbon, representing Amherst's school colors, over the lavender rice paper strip. Catherine's graduation photo is matted in a die cut frame and mounted. A die cut butterfly, dragonfly and daisy border strip complete the page. The smiling graduate seems well prepared to face the many challenges that lie ahead.

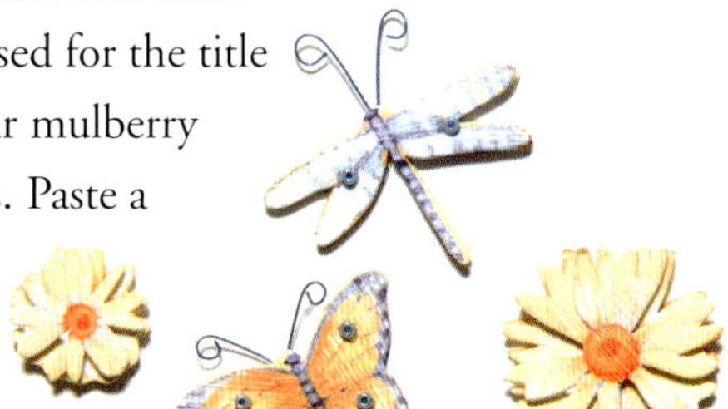

prom girls

Dimensional Glitter Stickers

My niece Julia and her girlfriend Kakie look radiant as they prepare to celebrate their senior prom. Begin by gluing vertical lavender eyelet ribbons on glitter patterned paper. Accent with matching vellum glitter paper and adhere embossed border stickers on top and bottom of vellum strips. Frame photographs with thin strips of embossed borders and mount on foam spacers. Decorate corners with dimensional poppy stickers and dimensional photo corners. Create the title with clear, pebble lettering and accent with a dimensional butterfly sticker. The "Memories" and "Friends" word charms accentuate the page. Spending a memorable night with a special friend is an ideal way for Julia to celebrate an important milestone in her life.

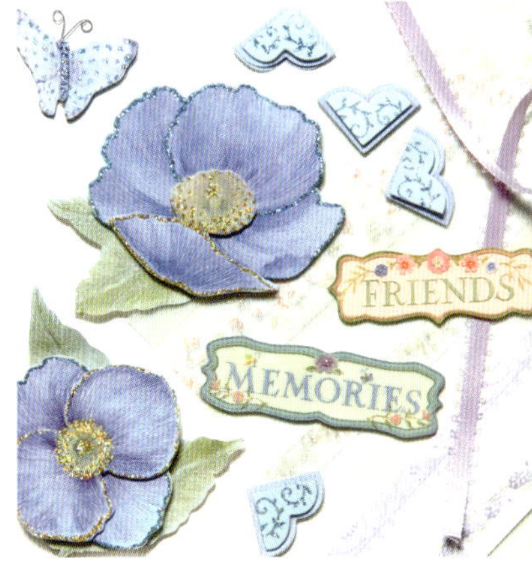

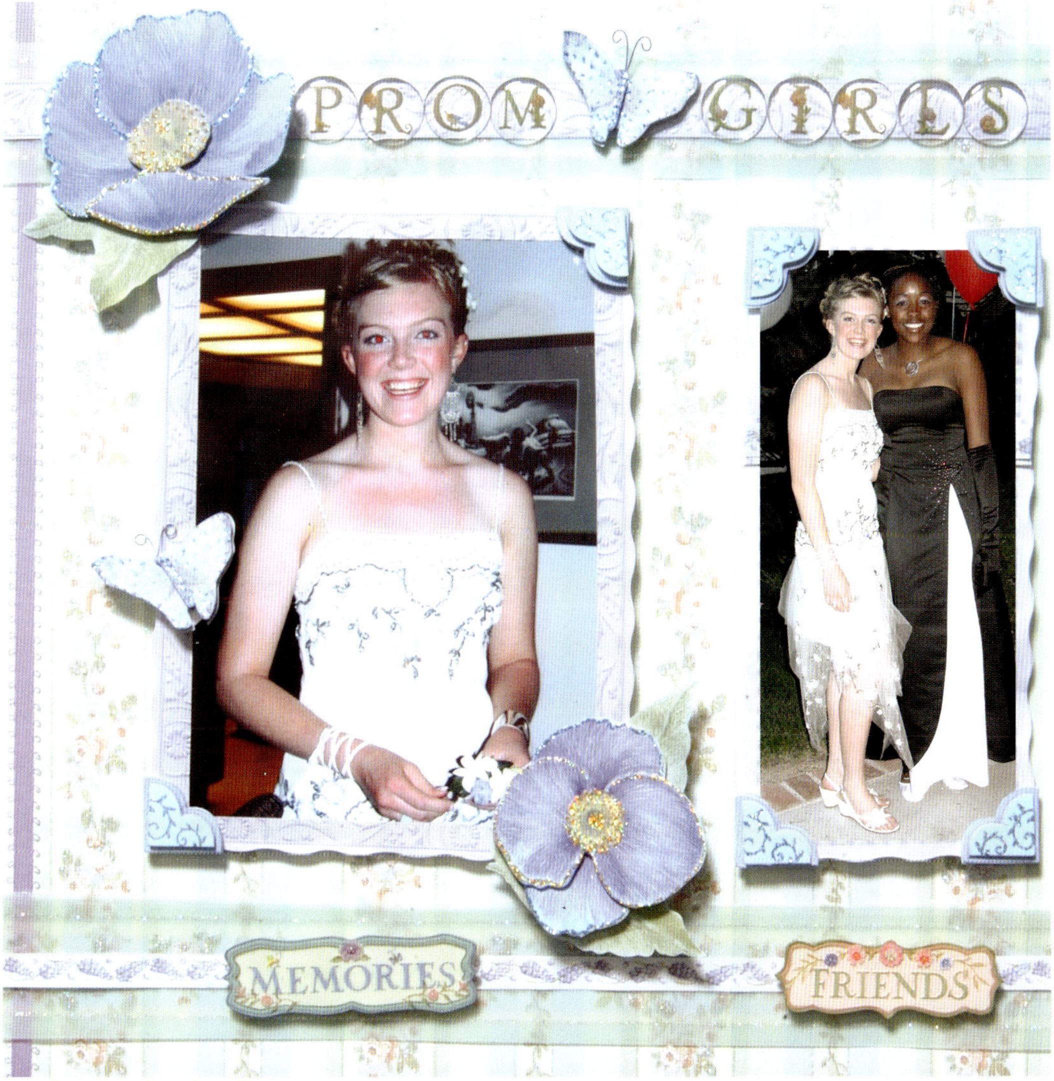

PROM GIRLS

MEMORIES

FRIENDS

MATERIALS

Glitter Paper and Glitter Vellum *K&Company*

Embossed Borders and Stickers *K&Company*

Eyelet Ribbon *Offray Ribbon*

Charmers *K&Company*

Poppy Pop-Ups Dimensional Glitter Stickers *K&Company*

Bella Alphabet Letters *K&Company*

TECHNIQUE HINT

To get exact spacing and positioning when using clear pebble lettering, cut individual letters with backing and align. Cover word with a strip of clear tape; remove backing, position and glue in place.

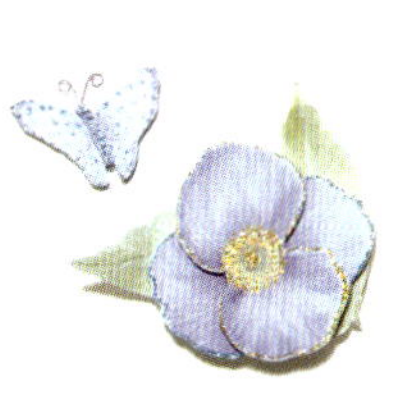

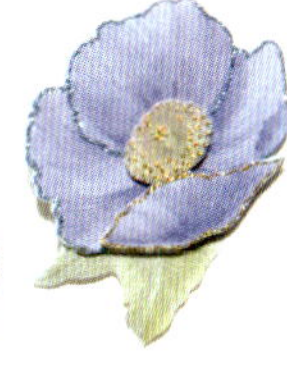

Die Cuts and Collage Stickers

Winter is my favorite season. The splendor of nature is captured beautifully in this picturesque, snow-filled photograph of our home in Bucks County. Mount the photo on snowflake patterned paper and compose the title, "Winter Wonderland" on the computer using the Sparkly free font. Print on a clear self-adhesive. Cut and place each letter on curved white paper. Use two snowflake punches to create gold and silver flakes in different sizes. Stick on glitter snowflake collage stickers and paper die cuts to create larger dimensional flakes. Cut various lengths of mohair yarn and adhere snowflakes in position with white glue. While winter snow will surely melt, this pristine landscape is a constant reminder of a perfect winter wonderland.

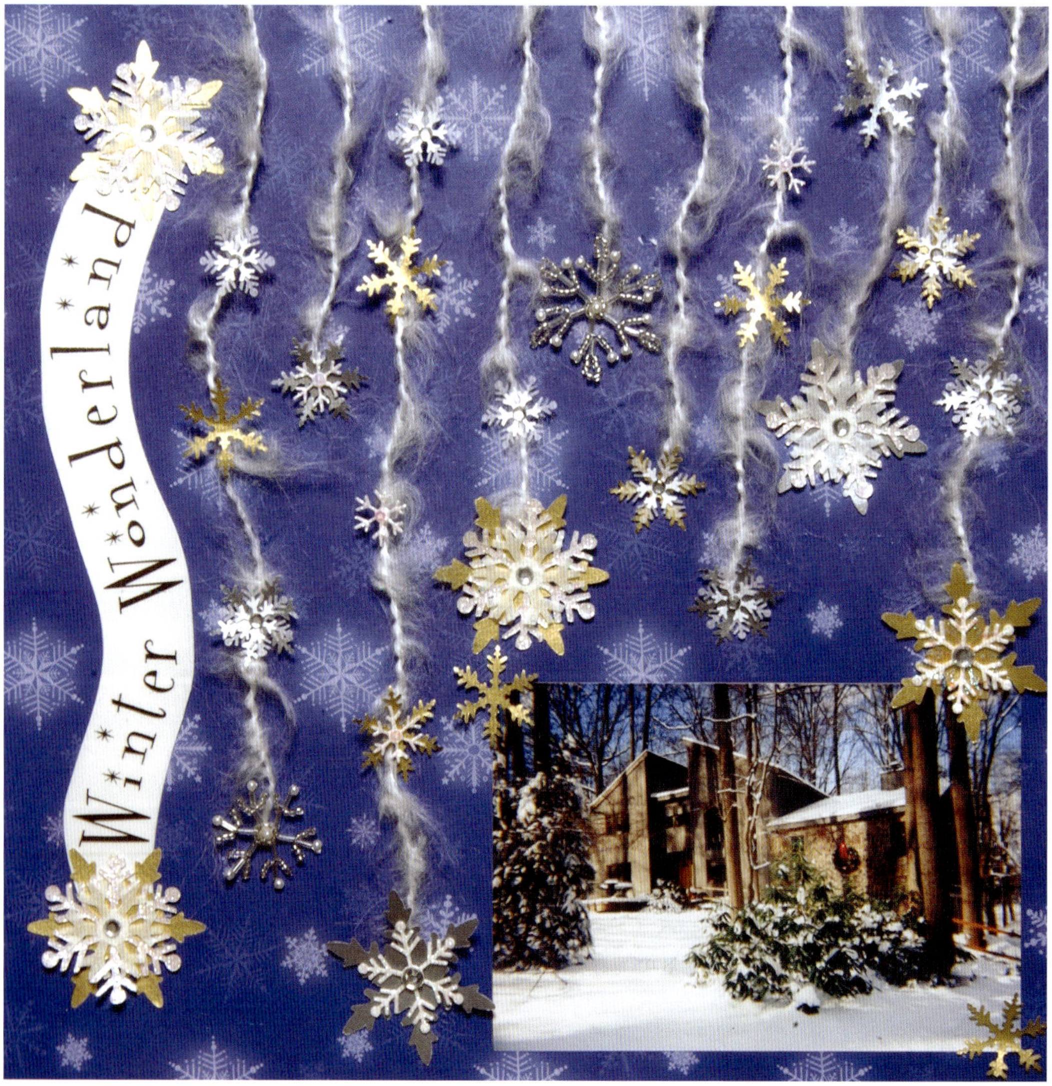

MATERIALS

Patterned Paper *PSX Papers for Creativity*
Adhesive Film *Chartpak*
Mohair Yarn *Patons*
Snowflake Punch *EK Success*
Mega Punch *Nankong Enterprises*
Snowflake Sticker Collage *Jolee's Boutique*
Snowflake Die Cut *Jolee's By You*
Computer Free Font *Sparkly.com*

TECHNIQUE HINT

To keep yarn in place, secure mohair with tape and adhere with dots of transparent glue.

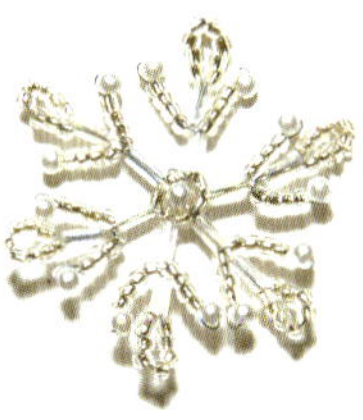

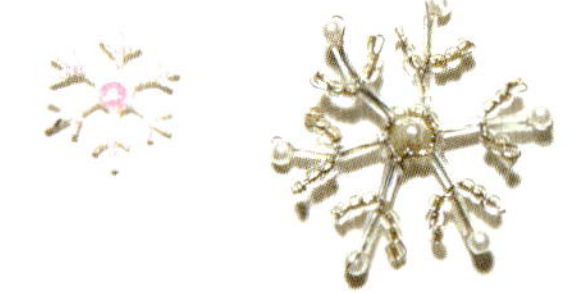

HOW-TO STEPS

winter wonderland
die cuts and collage stickers

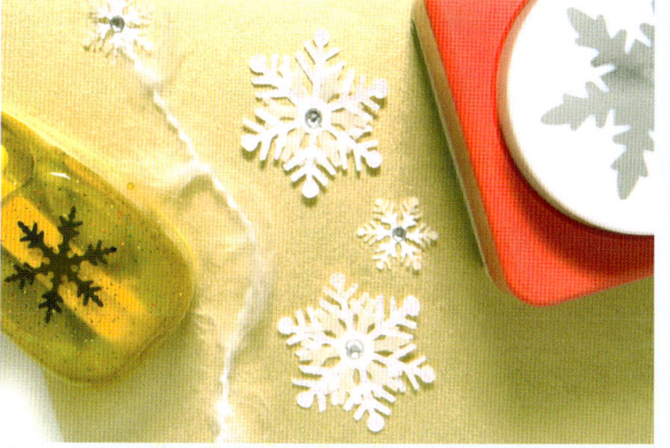

MATERIALS

Gold Paper	Snowflake Mega Punch
Small Snowflake Punch	Snowflake Sticker Collage

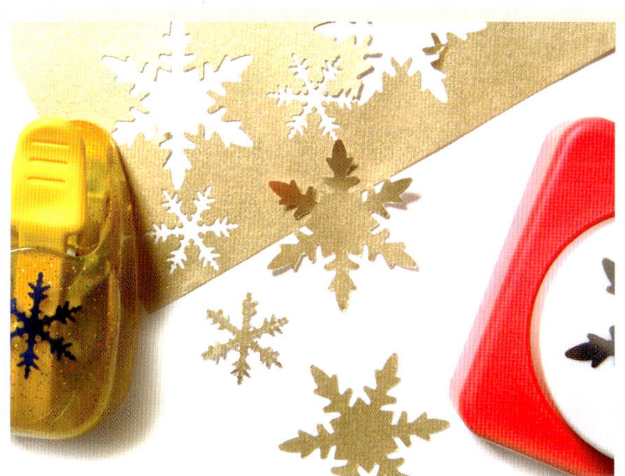

STEP 1

Use a punch to create large and small snowflake die cuts out of gold paper.

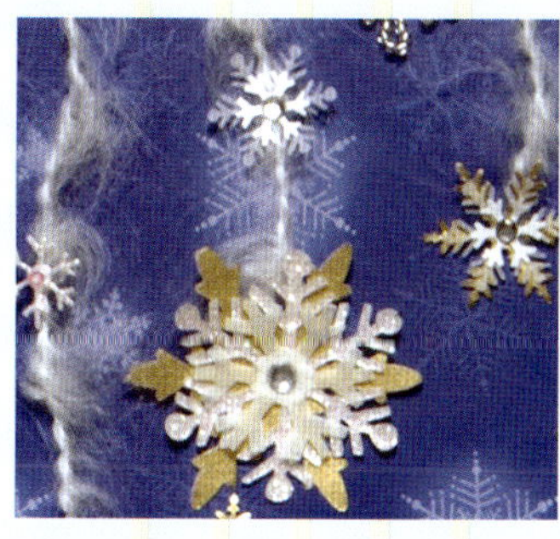

STEP 2

Glue the collage stickers to the gold snowflakes.

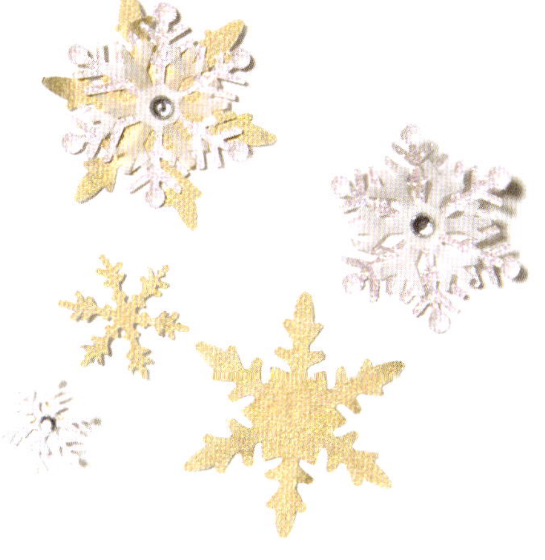

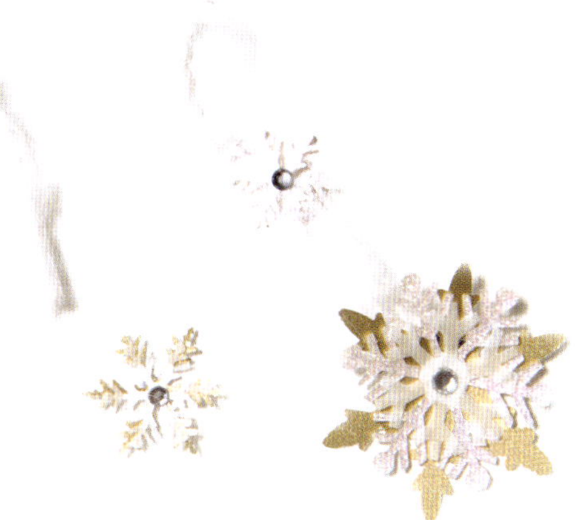

STEP 3

Attach the end of the yarn to the large snowflake assemblage and glue small snowflake stickers on the fibers.

Attachments

Eyelets, Brads and Snaps

Eyelets, brads and snaps offer scrapbook enthusiasts a myriad of colorful attachments designed to accent and enhance every page layout. These tiny ornaments are available in a rainbow of colors and shapes including—circles, squares, stars, hearts, flowers, letters, words, holiday designs,—and more. Eyelets have circular or square openings and come in small, medium and large sizes. Snaps are solid pieces and are available in various shapes. To secure eyelets and snaps in position properly, punch a hole through the paper with a punch tool, turn the paper over and use a setting tool to attach the eyelet to the paper. To attach brads, punch a hole through the paper with a punch tool, turn the paper over and bend the tabs to secure them in place. Eyelets, brads and snaps provide scrapbook artists the opportunity to accentuate their scrapbook page layout with shinning elements designed to add color and dimension.

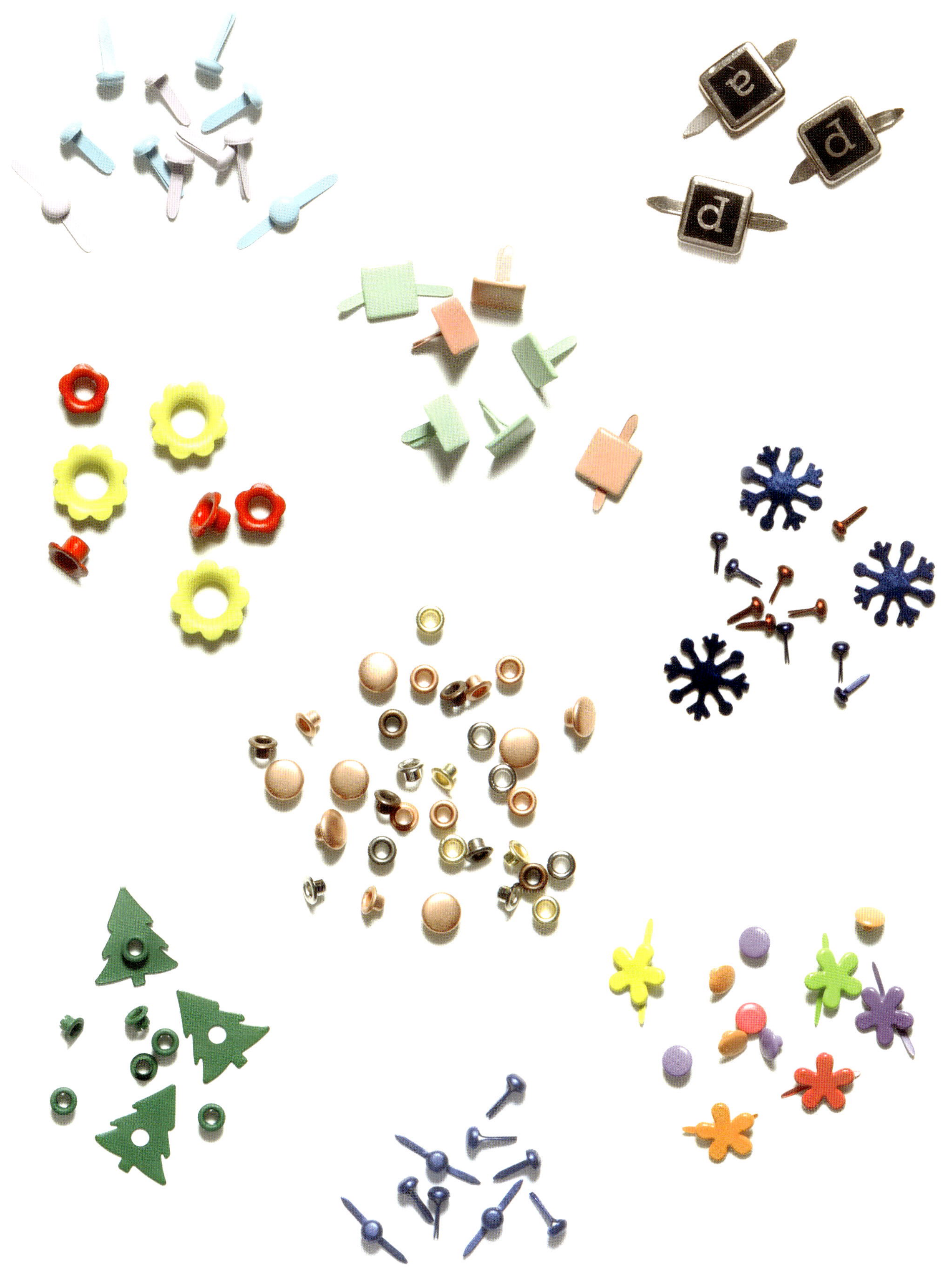

a star is born

Pastel Round Brads

The birth of baby William is a welcome addition to a rapidly growing family. Trim embossed star patterned paper 1/2-inch on two sides and position in the center of the gold paper. Crop photos to fit under paper frames and fasten blue and lavender brads. Embellish with foam star and moon charms. Adhere to star paper with "Cherish" ribbon running underneath. Create name, date and weight using the computer font Zapfino, print on blue vellum and trim. Embellish with large and small plastic star and moon charms. Center "A Star Is Born" sticker on top of the page and complete with decorative plastic stars. This memorable photo, commemorating the birth of a precious little boy, is a cherished reminder that everyone loves William, especially Mom-Mom and Pop-Pop.

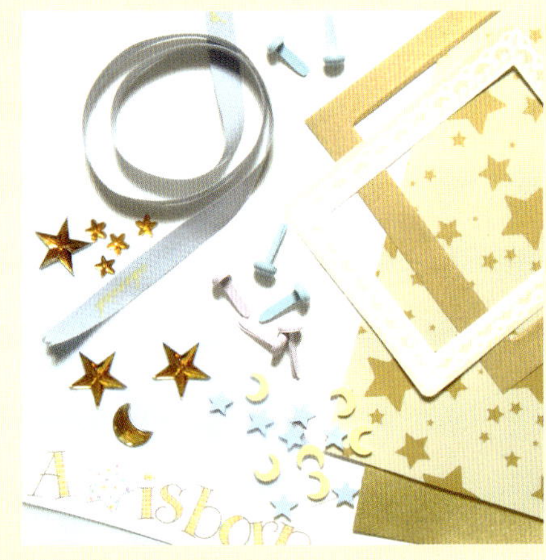

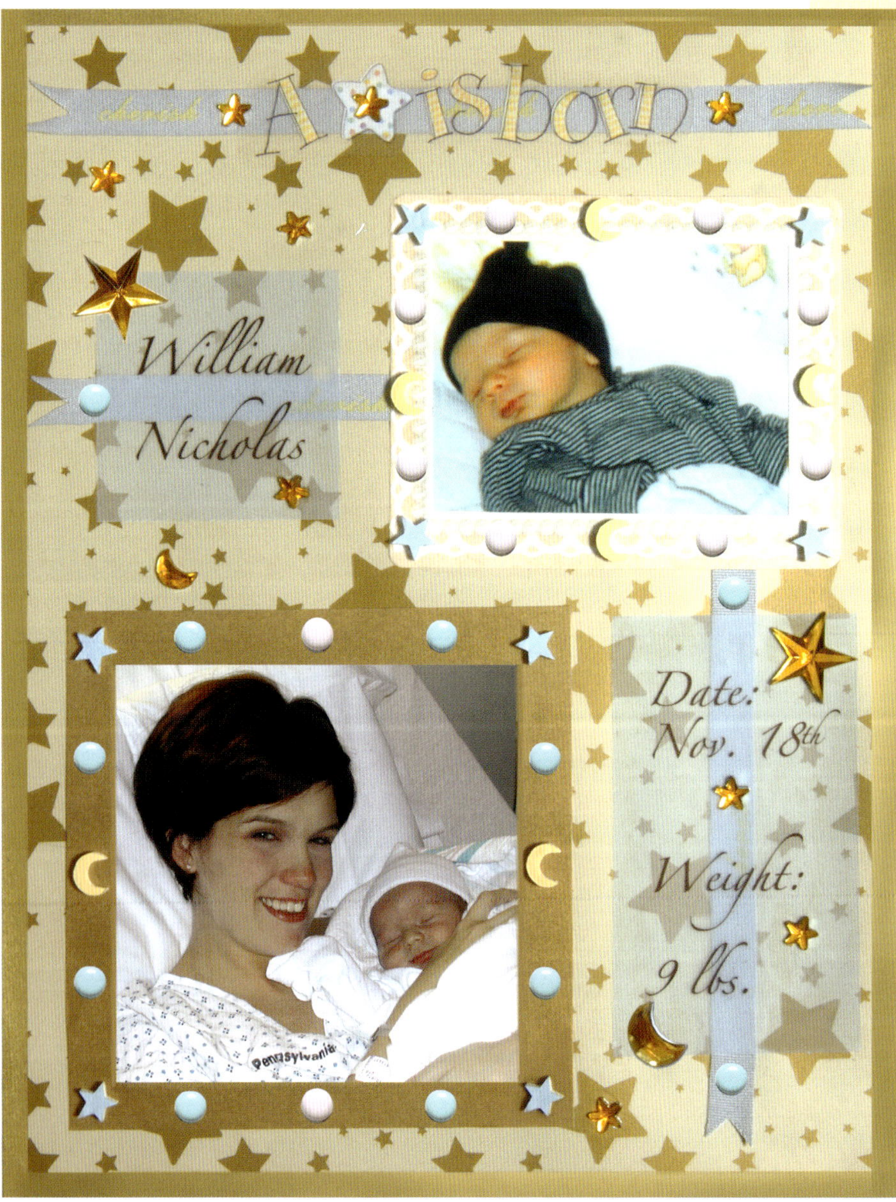

MATERIALS

Patterned Paper *Making Memories*
Gold Paper *The Paper Company*
Paper Frames *Amscan Memory Kit*
Vellum *The Paper Company*
Pastel Round Brads *Making Memories*
Foam Star and Moon Charms *Wilton Enterprises*
Plastic Star and Moon Charms *Jewelry & Craft Essentials*
Baby Sayings Sticker *Me & My Big Ideas*
Ribbon Words *Making Memories*
Computer Font *Zapfino*

TECHNIQUE HINT

When printing on vellum in the computer, allow ink to dry a few minutes before handling.

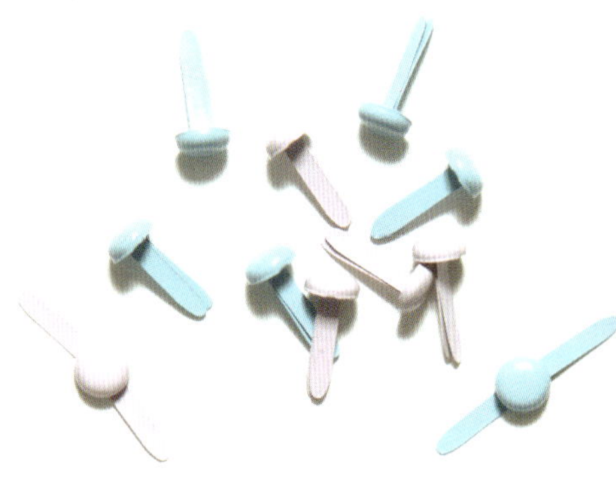

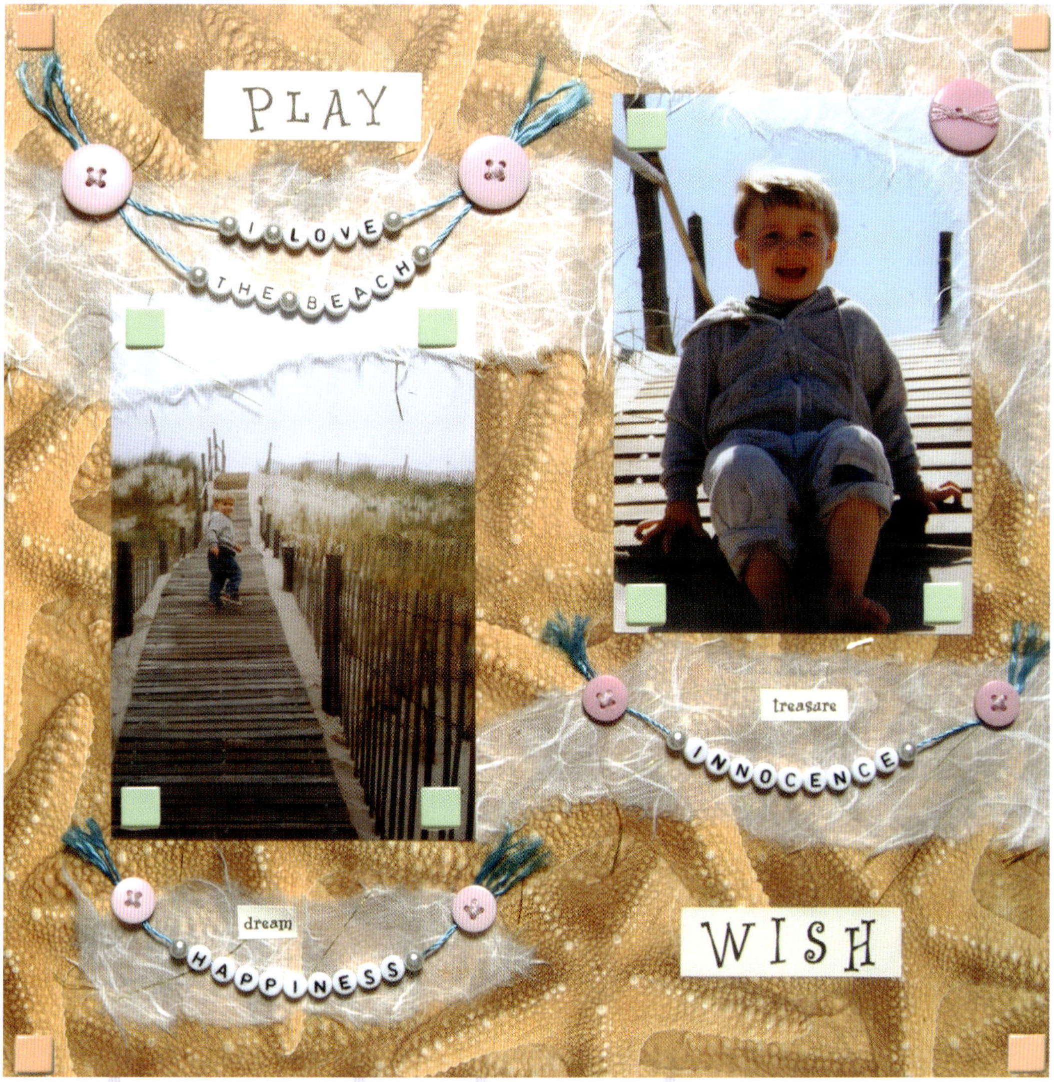

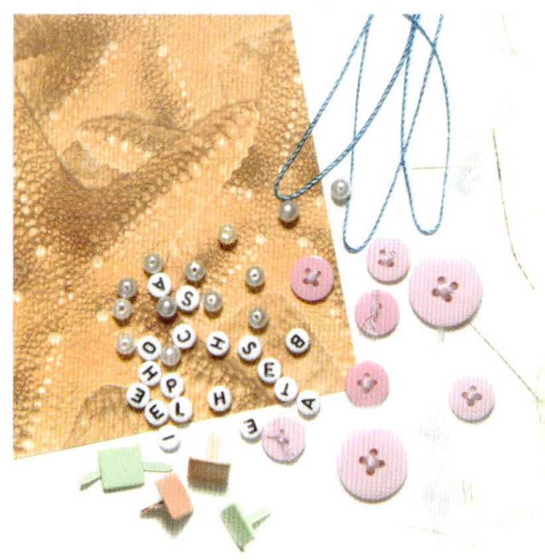

MATERIALS

Patterned Paper *Frances Meyer, Inc.*

Rice Paper *Black Ink*

Square Brads *Making Memories*

Scrapbook Buttons *Sticko Buttons Ups*

Fiber Thread *On The Surface*

6 mm Beads *Jewelry & Craft Essentials*

Alpha Beads *Jewelry & Craft Essentials*

Paper Words Defined *Making Memories*

TECHNIQUE HINT

To thread beads and pearls easily, trim fiber, rub glue stick on the end and twist threads together tightly. To flatten fiber, iron or pull through curling iron or hair straightener.

i love the beach

Square Brads

Little Spencer loves the beach and takes every opportunity to run in the surf and play in the sand. Giant starfish patterned paper is one of my favorites for a beach background. Tear rice paper in strips for the upper right corner and middle pieces. Mount photographs and rice paper in layers. Fasten square brads to photos and background paper. Thread alpha bead words on turquoise fiber and separate words with 6mm beads. Accentuate ends with adhesive scrapbook buttons. To complete the page, fray fiber ends and add adhesive "Play" and "Wish" titles. Spending a fun-filled day at the shore building sand castles and swimming in the ocean is an ideal way for a child to experience the joys of nature firsthand.

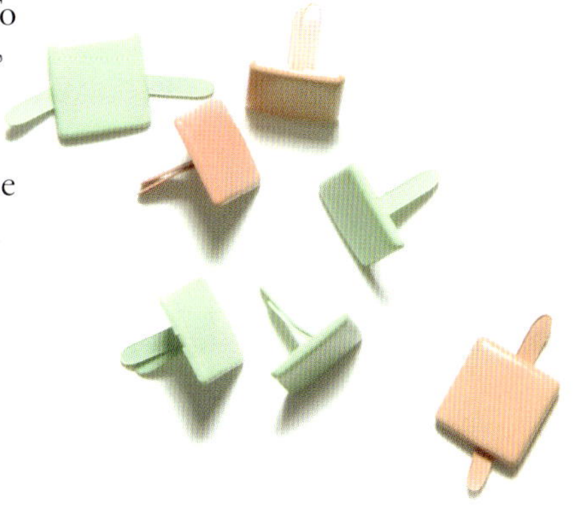

halloween babies

Round Brads

Babies are always cute, especially at Halloween. All dressed up in their favorite characters, these festive toddlers epitomize the fun and joy of Halloween. Select 12 x 12–inch spider web Halloween patterned paper and matching solid orange cover paper. Trim orange paper and mount photographs of the children in their costumes. Leave a 1/8-inch border on all sides. Create titles with the computer font Curlz, print on white paper and trim. Mount name and costume titles on black rice paper and glue scrapbook title page on orange paper leaving a thin border. Push out spider web from die cut border and mount on double adhesive paper. Cut around web shape with a sharp craft knife. Sprinkle orange glitter on adhesive and tap off excess. Remove backing and adhere on both sides of title. For the bottom of the page, mount web border on double adhesive; sprinkle orange glitter, remove backing and adhere to bottom of page. To complete the page, punch a hole in the center of each spider web and insert a round brad. Halloween affords children the opportunity to dress up and fantasize while enjoying the sweet rewards of trick or treating.

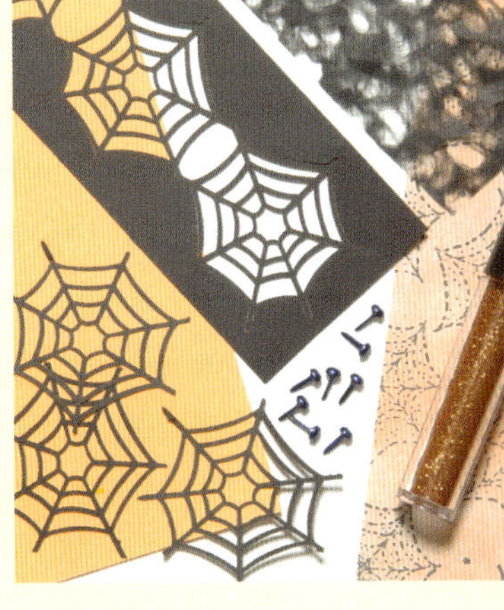

MATERIALS

Patterned Paper *Design Originals*

Solid Orange Cover Paper *The Paper Company*

Rice Paper *Black Ink*

Spider Web Border *Deluxe Laser Border*

Glitter *Treasured Memories*

Round Brads *Treasured Memories*

Computer Font *Curlz*

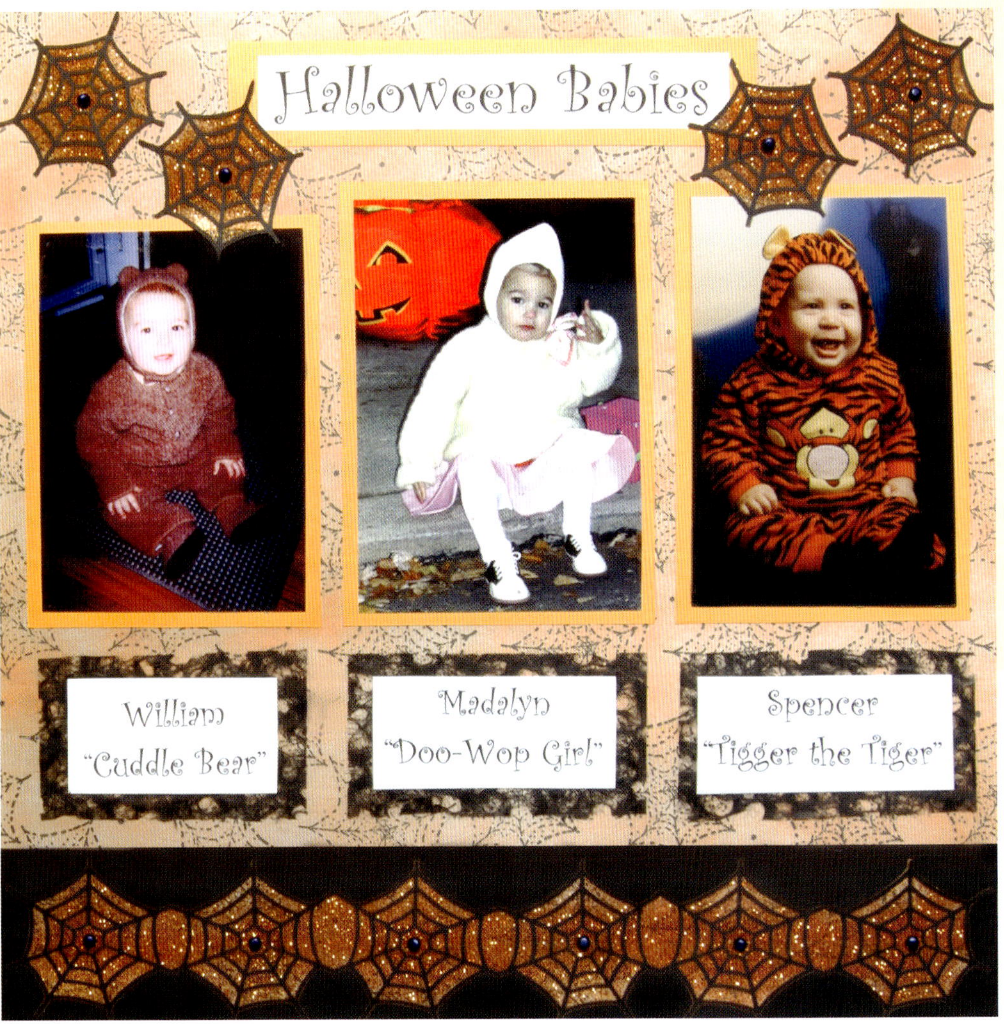

TECHNIQUE HINT

For more control, apply glitter with a cotton swab. For a dimensional effect, place more glitter in the center of the web.

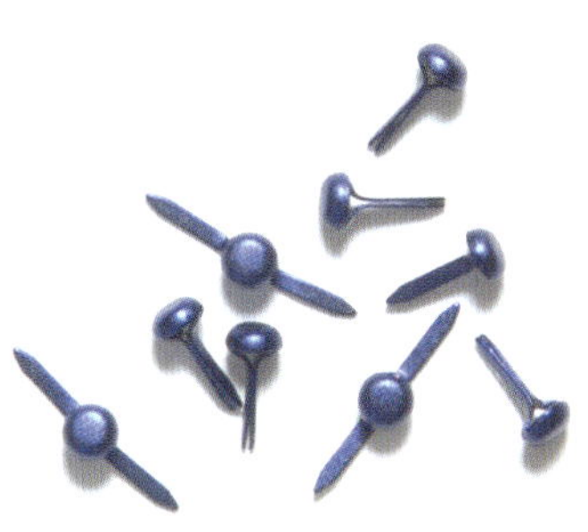

HOW-TO STEPS

halloween babies

round brads

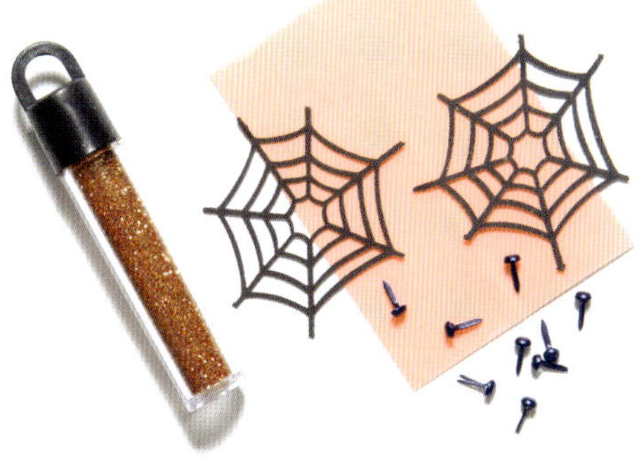

MATERIALS

Round Brads
Glitter
Double Adhesive
Spider Web

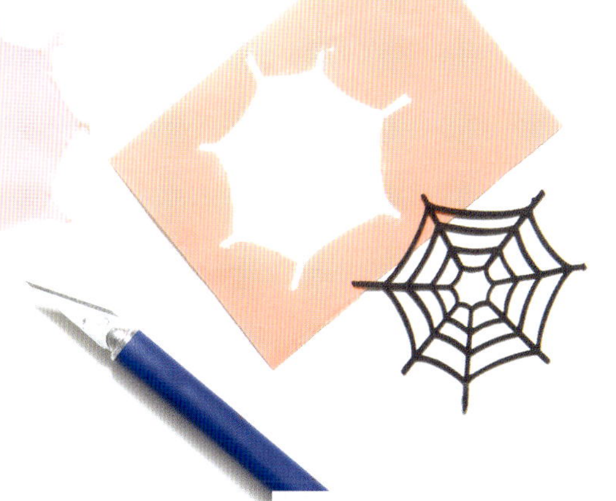

STEP 1

Lightly tack spider web on double adhesive. Cut around web with a sharp craft knife. Peel off top layer of double adhesive.

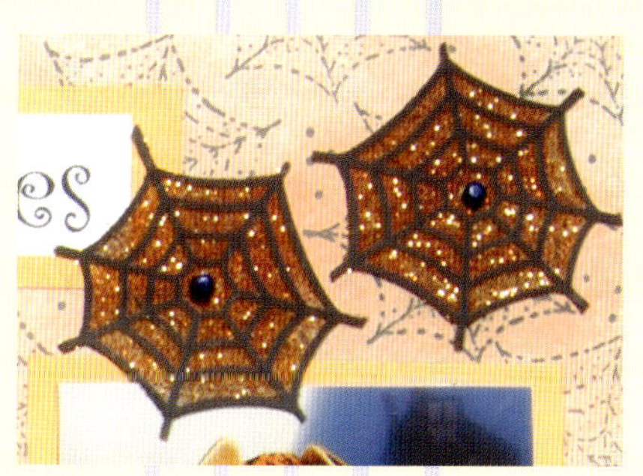

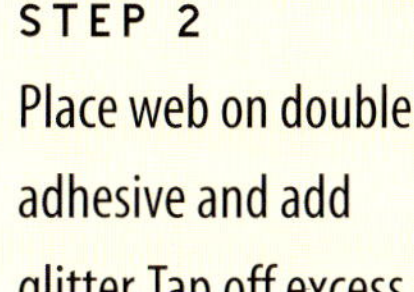

STEP 2

Place web on double adhesive and add glitter. Tap off excess.

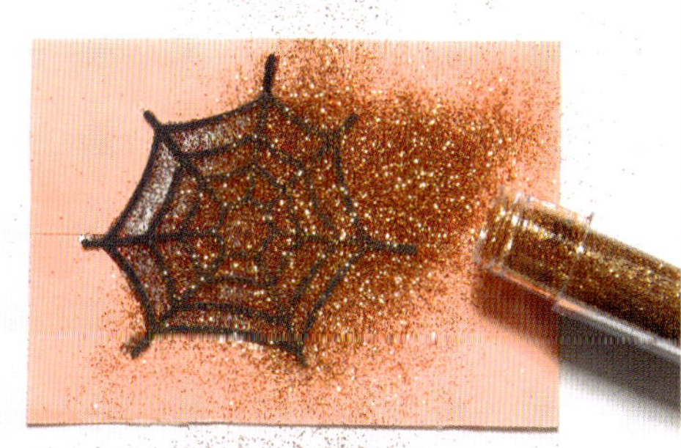

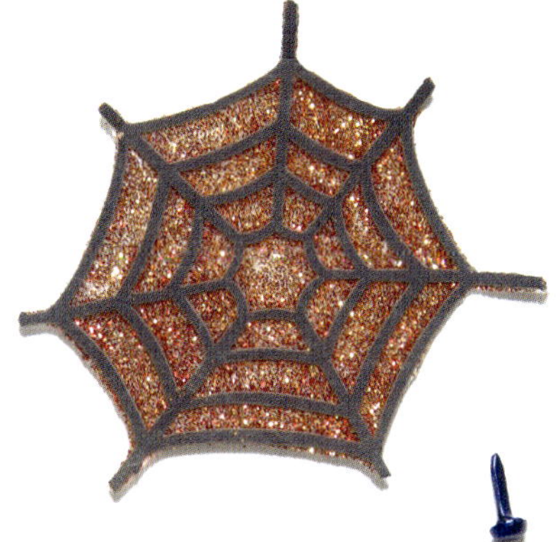

STEP 3

Cut out glitter spider web and insert brad. Peel off backing and adhere to paper.

my dad my hero

Alphabet Brads and Metal Eyelet Letters

My sister Deborah, in this tribute, beautifully portrays a daughter's special love for her dad, her hero. To begin, double mat a vintage black and white photograph and current photograph with silver mulberry and patterned paper. Place a vertical portrait photo of dad on patterned paper. Mount all three photos with foam spacers on 12 x 12-inch plaid embossed patterned paper. Tear metallic script vellum, glue strips on top and bottom and insert fiber through metal hang tags. Attach the words, "My Dad, My Hero" with metal eyelet letters and alphabet brads. "Then" and "Now" tags are designed with typewriter and numbered tea stained tag stickers. My Dad, My Hero reflects the bond of love and affection between a father and a daughter over the past forty years.

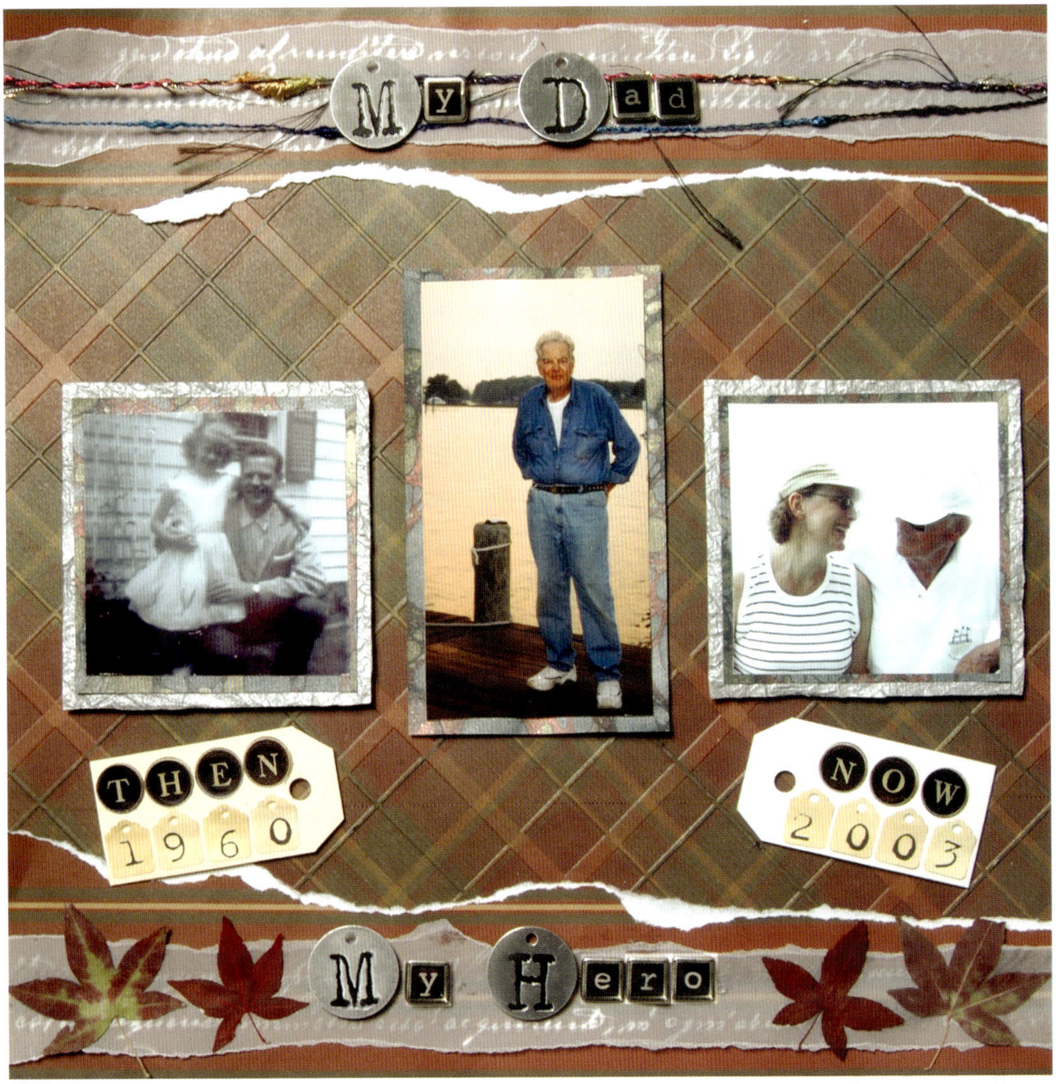

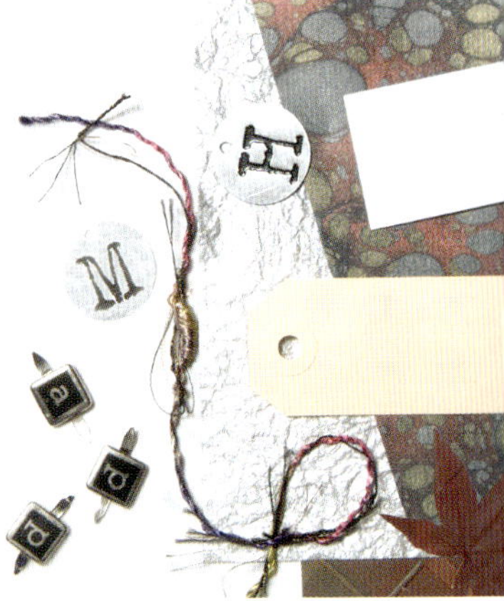

MATERIALS

Silver Metallic Mulberry Paper *Black Ink*

Embossed Pattern Paper *K&Company*

Metallic Vellum *Paper Pizazz*

Alphabet Brads *JoAnn Essentials*

Metal Eyelet Letters *Making Memories*

Paper Tags *Paper Reflections*

Pressed Leaves *Pressed Petals*

Funky Fibers *Making Memories*

Tea Stained Tag Numbers *EK Success*

Nostalgiques™ Typewriter Lettering *Sticko*

TECHNIQUE HINT

To create a dramatic edge on the patterned paper, tear paper away from, instead of towards you. Tear on an angle for a thicker white edge.

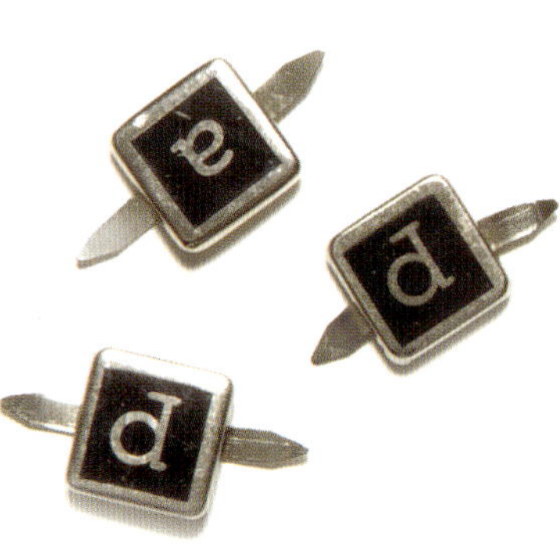

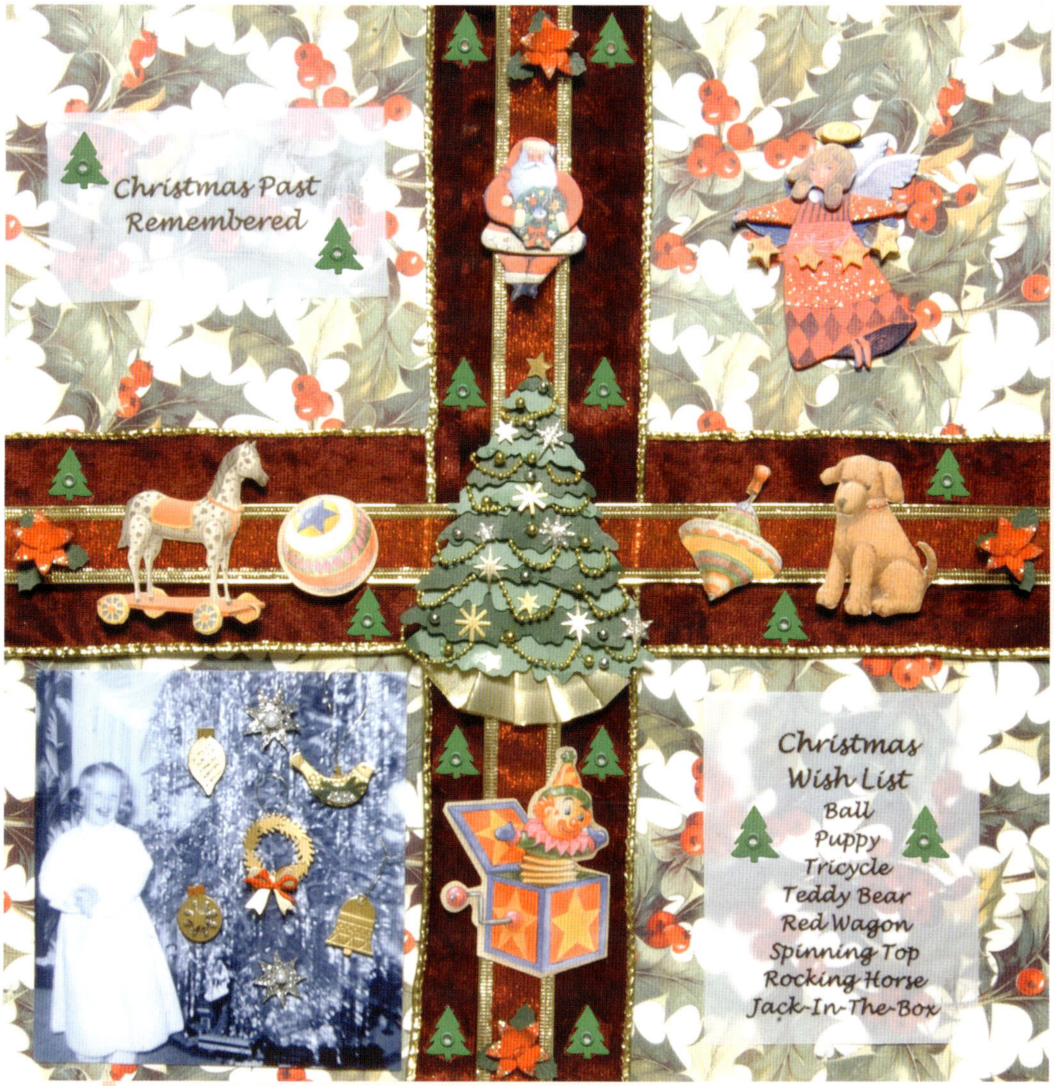

Christmas Past Remembered

Christmas Wish List
Ball
Puppy
Tricycle
Teddy Bear
Red Wagon
Spinning Top
Rocking Horse
Jack-In-The-Box

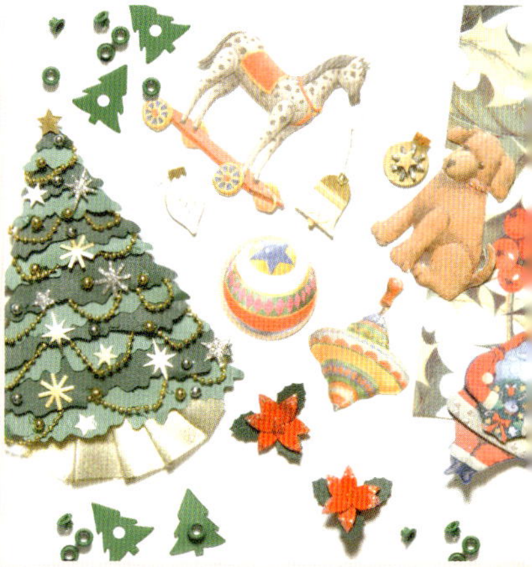

MATERIALS

Patterned Paper *Anna Griffin and Provo Craft*
Vellum *K&Company*
Tree Eyelets *Making Memories*
Red Ribbon *Offray Ribbon*
Dimensional Stickers Christmas *K&Company*
Embossed Stickers Christmas *K&Company*
Sticker Collage *Jolee's Boutique*
Computer Font *Bradley Hand*

TECHNIQUE HINT

To preserve old black and white photos, scan images and print on photo paper.

christmas past remembered

Tree Eyelets

The true joy of Christmas is reflected on my sister's face, age five, standing next to an old fashion tinsel-draped tree. To set the theme, choose 12 x 12-inch square Christmas holly patterned paper. Place a black and white scanned photo in lower corner and decorate with sticker collage ornaments. Print title and Christmas wish list on vellum paper. Mount velvet ribbon on page, attach collage Christmas tree and embossed stickers. Punch and set tree eyelets on the ribbon and vellum. Embossed sticker toys float around the page evoking the wonder and joy of the season. This holiday photograph of Christmas past captures my sister's fondest memories.

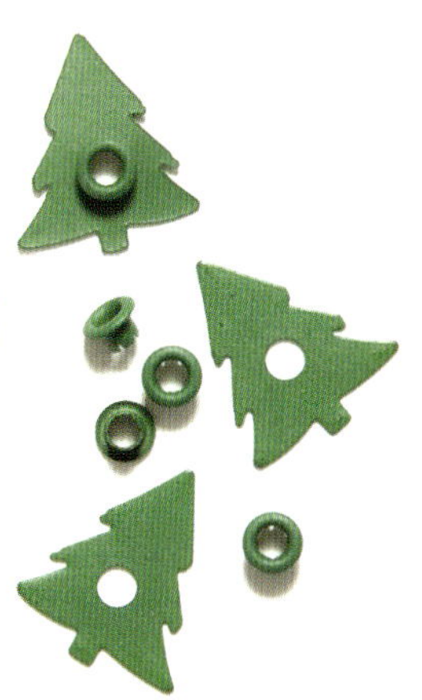

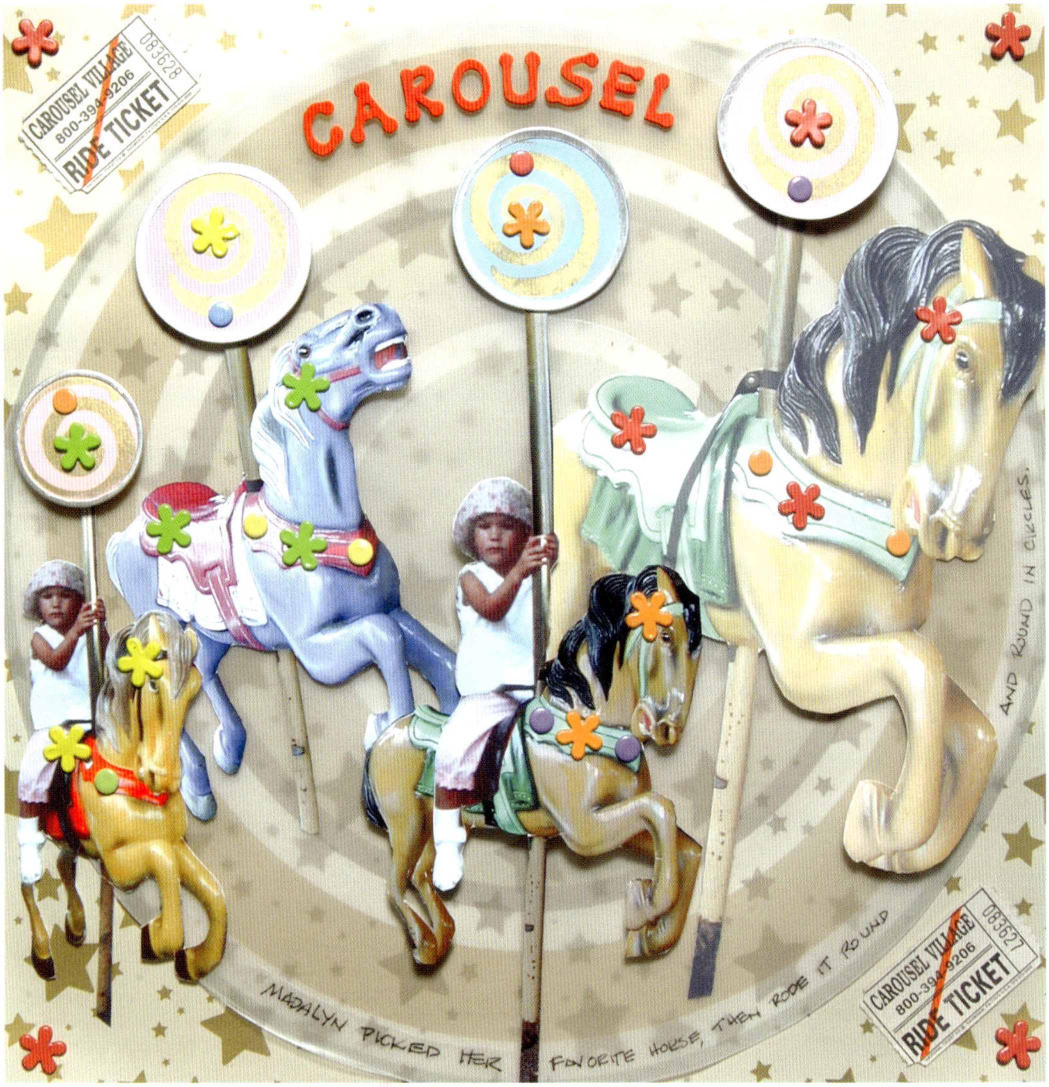

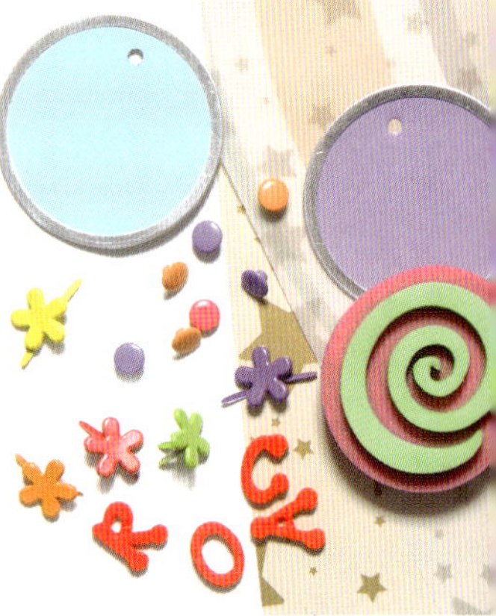

MATERIALS

Patterned Paper *Making Memories*
Vellum Circles *Simple Sets*
Flower Brads *Making Memories*
Colorful Round Snaps *Making Memories*
Metal Rim Tags *Treasured Memories*
Swirl Rubber Stamp *Inkadinkado*
Foamies Letters *MSI*

TECHNIQUE HINT

Use a new craft blade to cut out each horse. Follow outline of the horse carefully and trim excess for a smooth edge.

carousel

Snaps and Flower Brads

Carousel Village is four-year old Madalyn's favorite places to visit. It has one of the best-preserved carousels complete with magical horses and music of a vintage era. For this labor of love, cut vellum in a large circle and mount on 12 x 12-inch star patterned paper. Enlarge various size digital photographs of the carousel horses on the computer, print on photographic paper and cut out each horse. Decorate horses with colorful brads and snaps and mount in layers with foam spacers. Stamp metal rim tags with a gold spiral and attach with a brad and snap. Use foam letters to create the word "Carousel" and place flower brads and ride tickets in each corner. Madalyn's adventure at Carousel Village is a childhood memory that will be remembered and cherished by a sweet little girl on her magical horse.

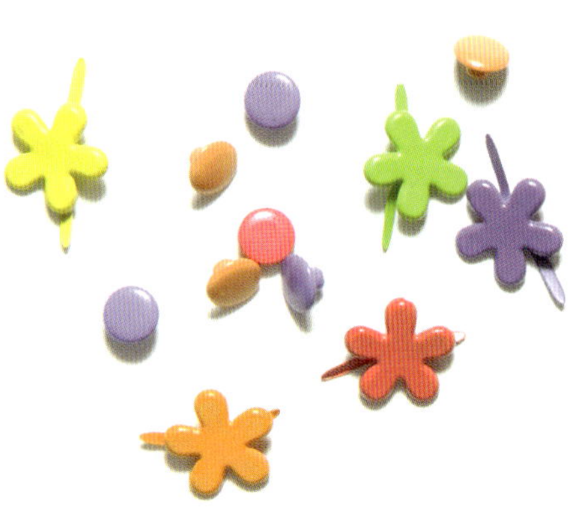

HOW-TO STEPS

carousel

brads and snaps

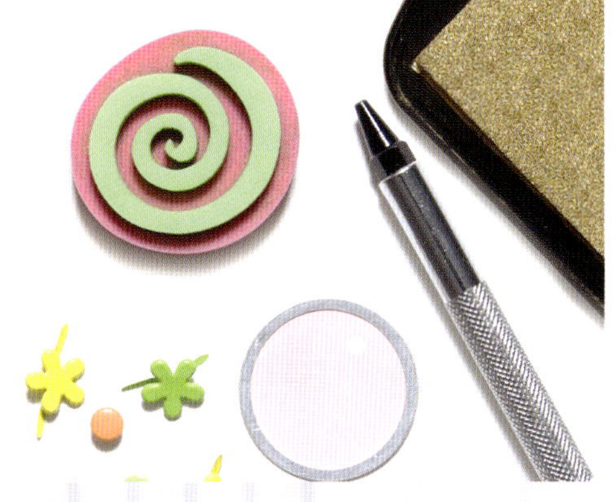

MATERIALS

Flower Brads	Gold Ink Pad
Colorful Round Snaps	Metal Rim Tags
Swirl Rubber Stamp	Punch

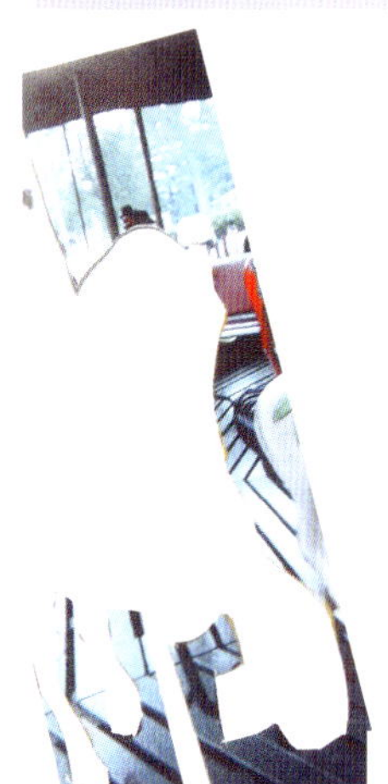

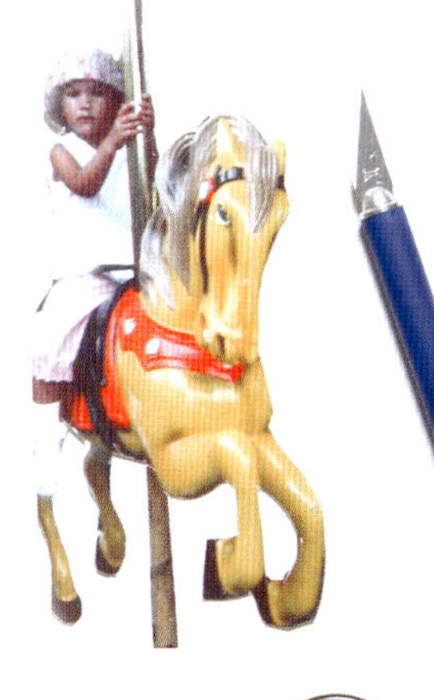

STEP 1

Use a sharp craft knife to cut carousel horse from photograph.

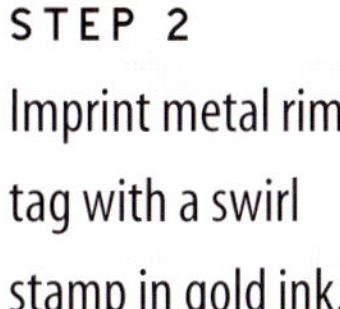

STEP 2

Imprint metal rim tag with a swirl stamp in gold ink.

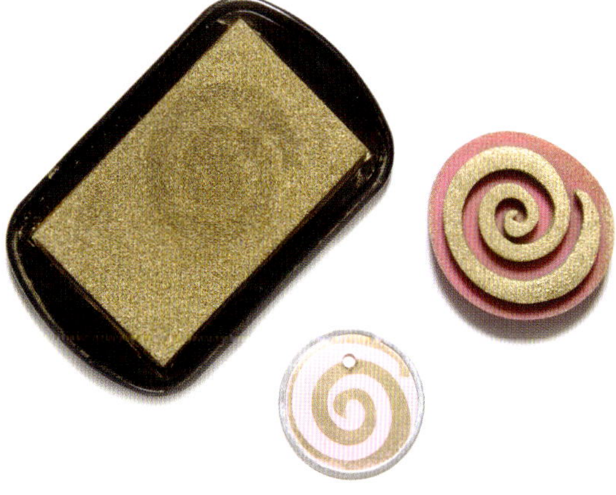

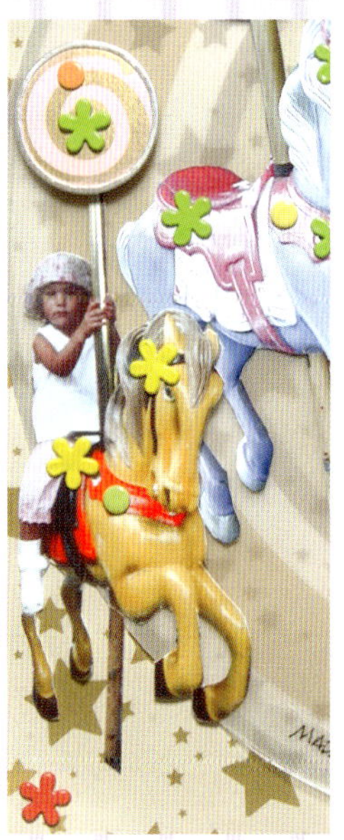

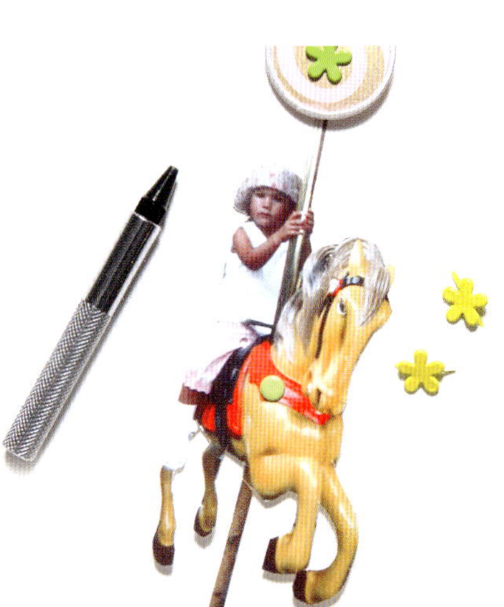

STEP 3

Punch holes in horse and tag. Attach snaps and brads.

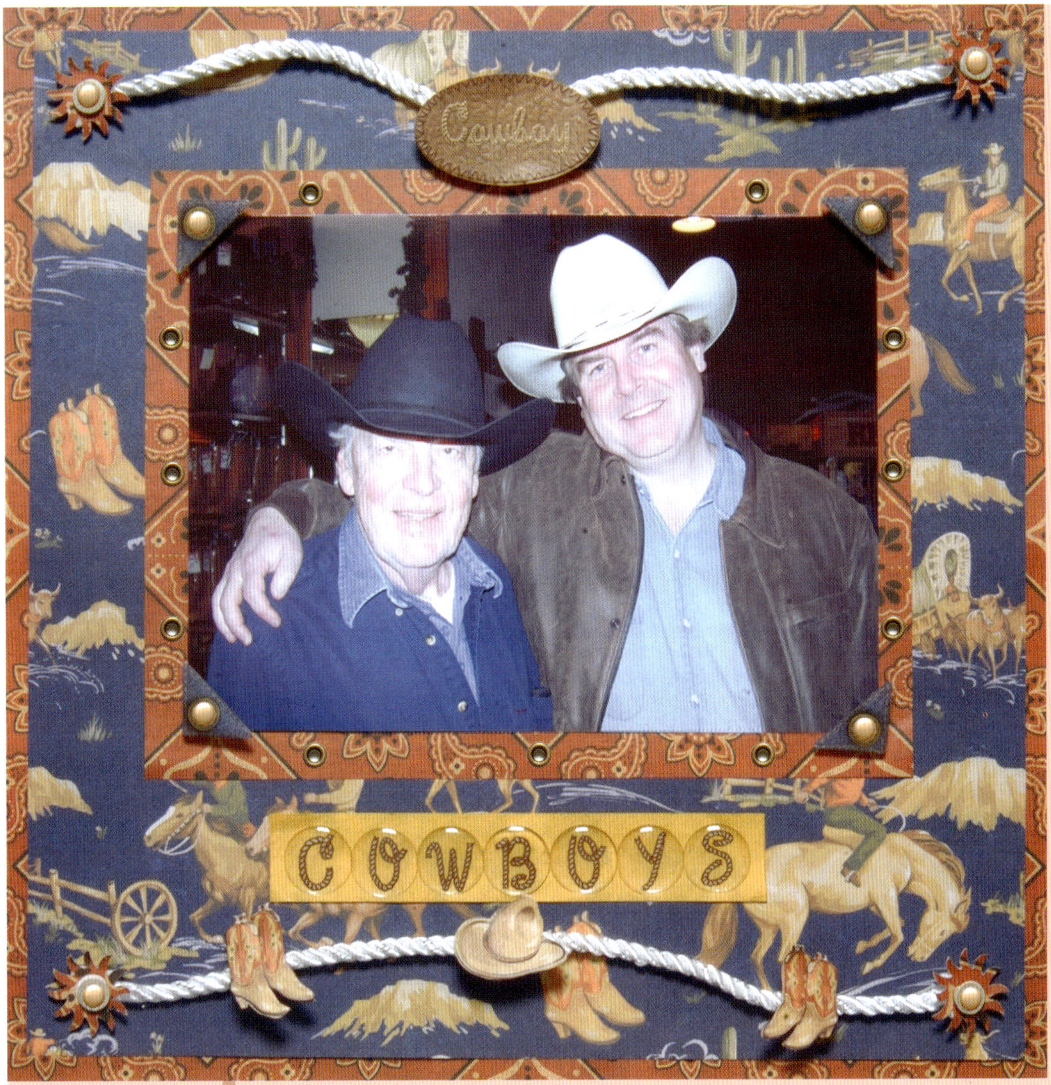

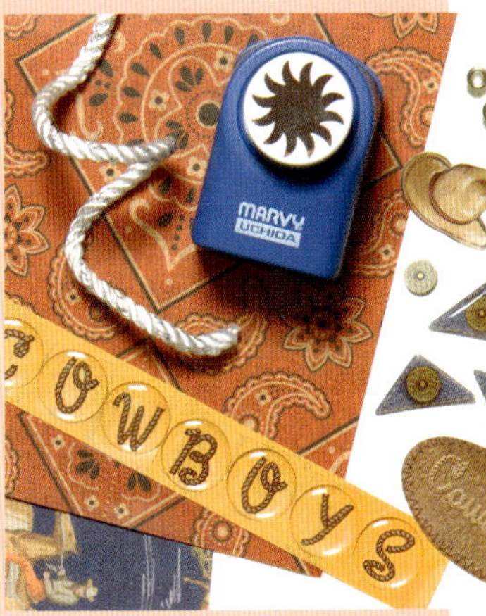

MATERIALS

Patterned Paper Embossed Stickers *K&Company*

Metallic Eyelets and Snaps *Making Memories*

Cowboy Frames and Corners *K&Company*

Jumbo Letters Clearly Yours *K&Company*

Sun Punch *Marvy Uchida*

Cord *Craft or Fabric Store*

TECHNIQUE HINT

Purchase a thin cord or roping trim in a craft or fabric store. Use a real bandana for the red patterned paper, starch and iron to size.

cowboys

Metallic Eyelets and Snaps

The Wild West has never seen a more fearsome duo than my dad and brother-in-law Jon. For the background, select a red bandana patterned paper; trim a piece of cowboy paper 1/2-inch around and adhere to background. Attach photograph to a second piece of bandana paper, center and decorate with cowboy photo corners, eyelets and snaps. Decorate top and bottom with a rope cord. Using a sun die cut punch, create four shapes for each corner of the paper to simulate cowboy spurs and glue on snaps. Trim a 1-inch piece of paper for the title, glue "Cowboy" pebble rope lettering on top and adhere to cowboy paper. Butch Cassidy and the Sundance Kid have very little to fear from these lovable *bandidos*.

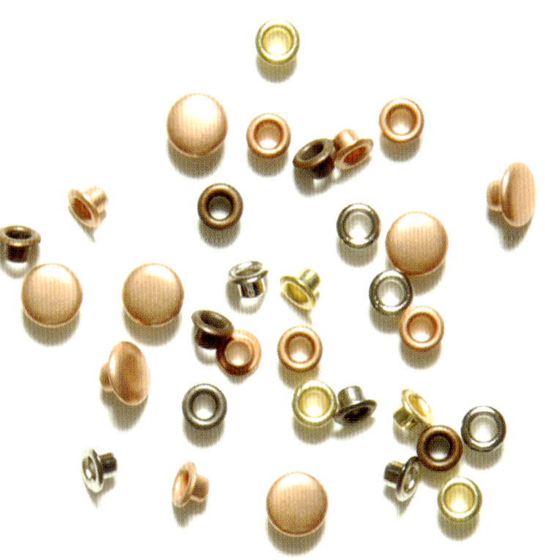

retire in style *Flower Eyelets*

Sharing retirement with family members is a special milestone to be enjoyed and cherished forever. Select a sheet of 12-inch square tropical patterned paper as a base. Trim photo and mount on blue patterned paper leaving a 1/4-inch border. Attach red flower eyelets in each corner. To secure eyelets, punch a hole through the paper with the punch tool, turn the paper over and use a setting tool to attach the eyelet to the paper. Trim a sheet of vellum paper 4 x 5-inches using a deckle rotary cutter or scissors. Align the metal words, "Retire in Style" on blue vellum paper; punch holes for each letter, and attach eyelets and metal letters with the setting tool. Position vellum above photograph and set 1/8-inch yellow eyelets in place. Accent with dimensional sandal stickers. Spending quality time with our family is the true meaning of retiring in style.

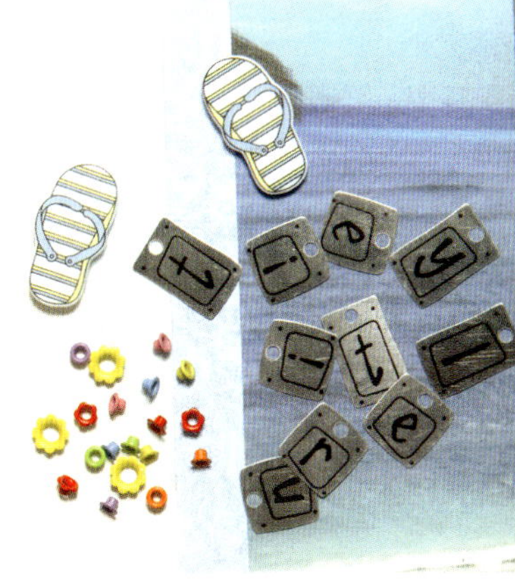

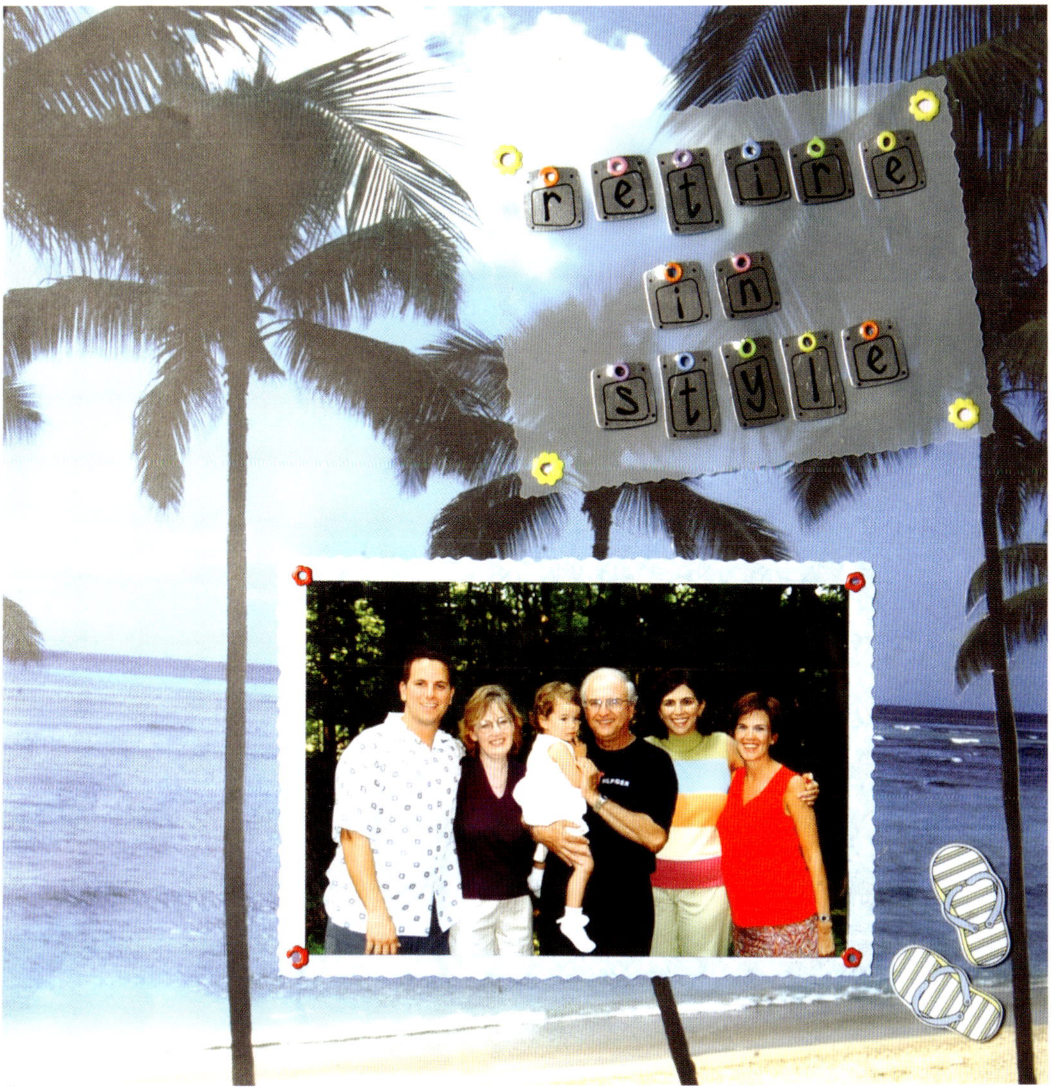

MATERIALS

Patterned Paper *Rainbow World*

Blue Patterned Paper *The Paper Company*

Vellum T*he Paper Company*

Flower Eyelets *Making Memories*

Alphabet Tagz *Provo Craft and Art Accents, Inc.*

Dimensional Sandal Stickers *Hirschberg Schutz & Co., Inc.*

TECHNIQUE HINT

Once alphabet letters are attached, put a small dot of glue under letter to prevent movement.

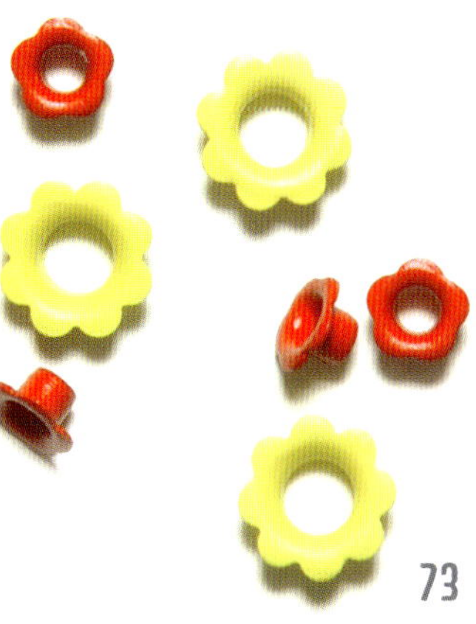

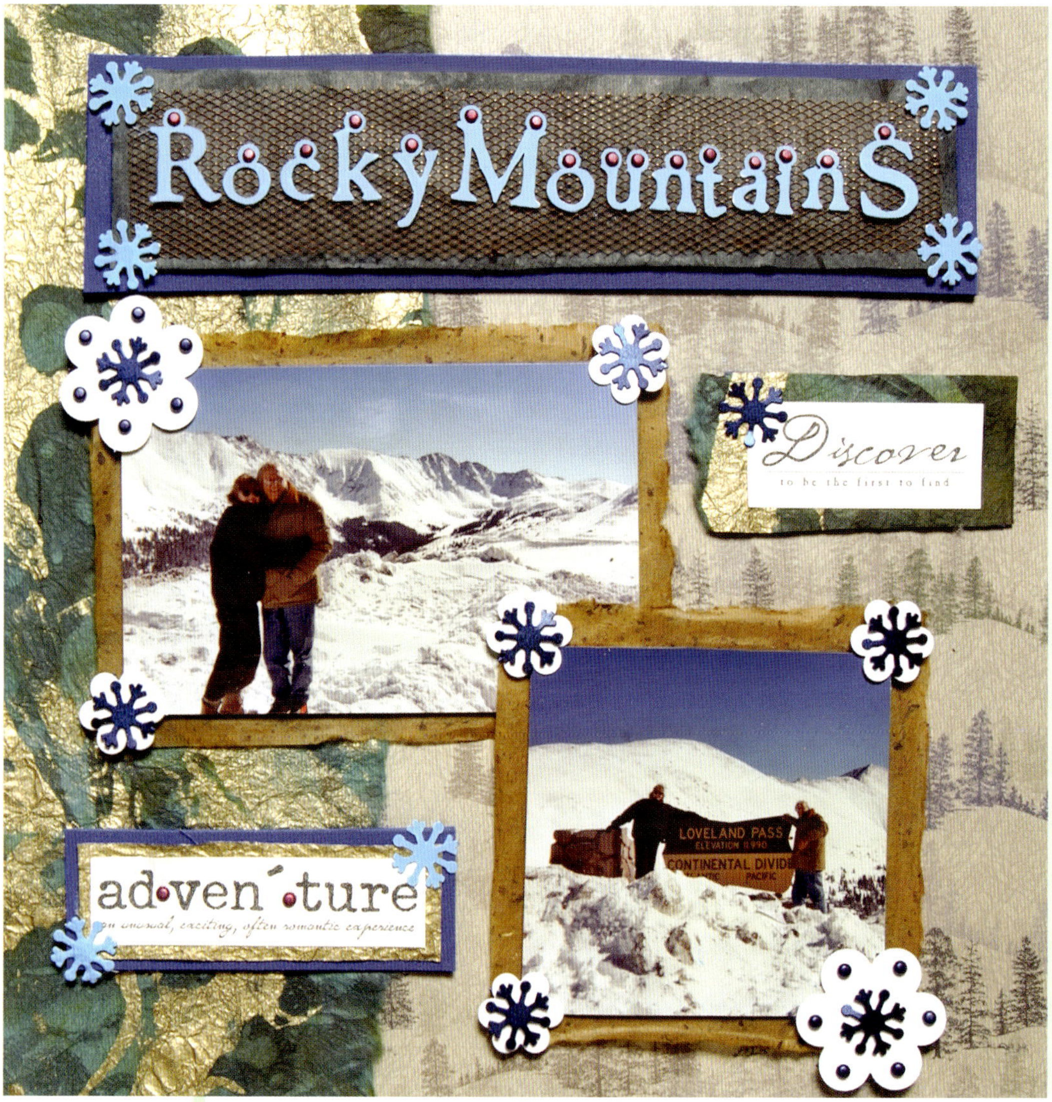

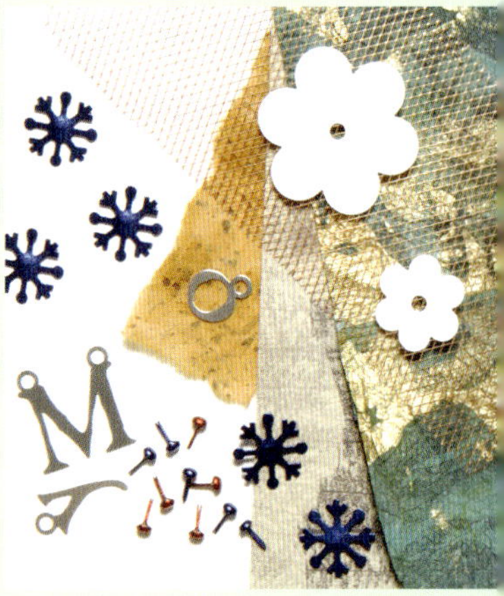

MATERIALS

Patterned Paper *PSX Papers for Creativity*
Rice Paper *Black Ink*
Snowflake and Round Brads *Treasured Memories*
Spinner Tags *Creative Tags*
Copper Mesh *Paragona*
Metal Eyelet Letters *Making Memories*
Watermark Stamp Pad *Versamark™*
Aqua Embossing Powder *Stamp-n Stuff*
Paper Words Defined *Making Memories*
Foam Sheet *Flexi Foam*

rocky mountains

Eyelet Letters and Snowflake Brads

At an elevation of 11, 990 feet, the Continental Divide evokes feelings of awe and adventure. To construct the page, insert spinner paper tags with dark blue snowflake brads and position around the edge of each photograph. Rounded blue brads complete the corner snowflake design. To create embossed brads and title, press metal eyelet letters and brads in stamp pad and heat emboss with aqua powder. Anchor the letters with red brads on layers of copper mesh and green rice paper. Glue the assemblage to a foam blue mat. To add dimension, lay torn marbled paper over patterned paper to reflect the mountain landscape. Glue photographs and adhesive words to mat board mounted on brown rice paper. The wintry scene instinctively captures the majestic beauty and grandeur of the Colorado Rockies.

TECHNIQUE HINT

Metal eyelet letters become extremely hot when embossed with a heat gun. Allow sufficient time for metal to cool before touching.

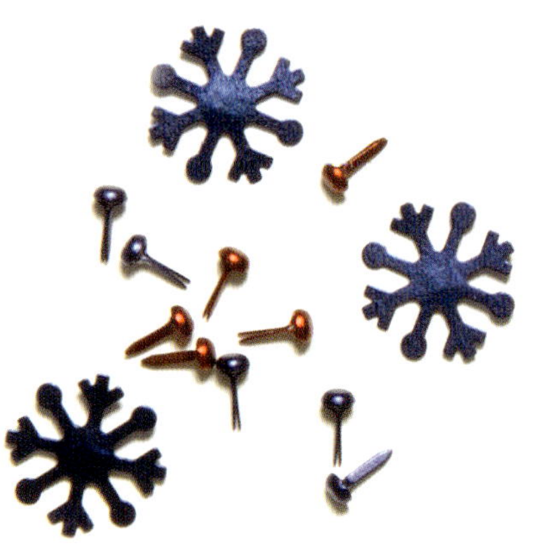

HOW-TO STEPS

rocky mountains

embossed eyelet letters

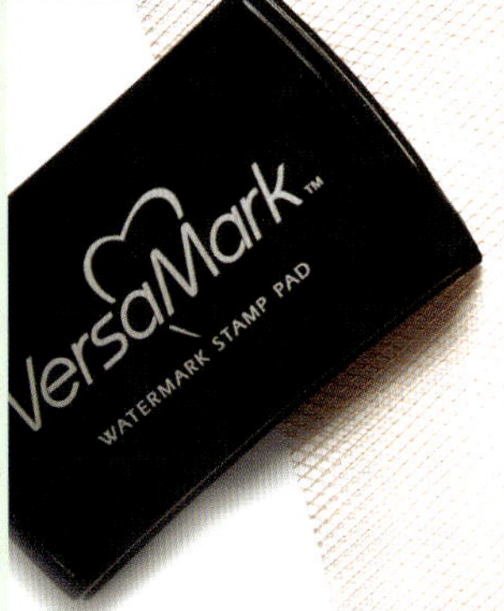

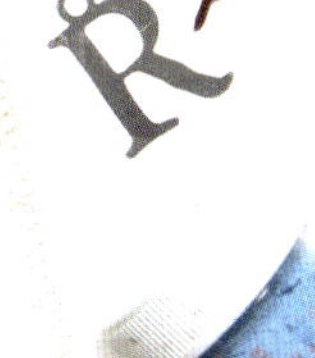

MATERIALS

Metal Mesh	Embossing Powder
Watermark Stamp Pad	Heat Gun
Metal Eyelet Letters	Metal Cutting Scissors

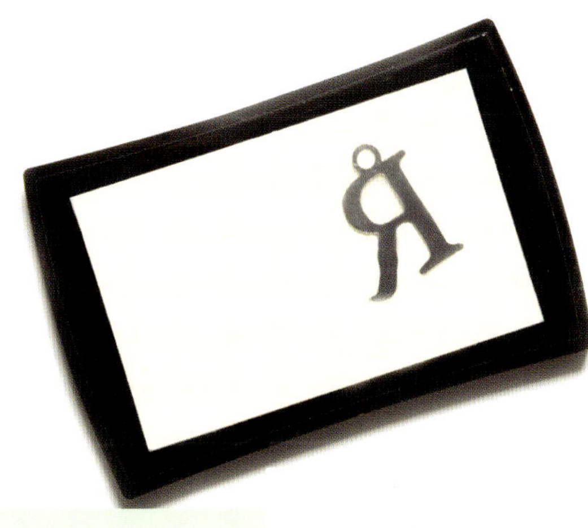

STEP 1

Press letter face down into the watermark stamp pad.

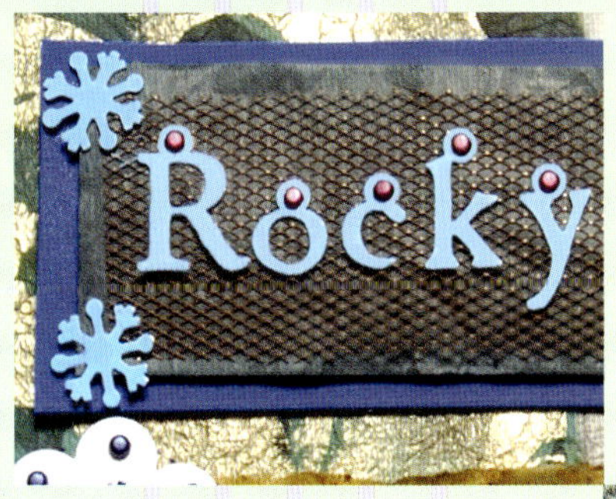

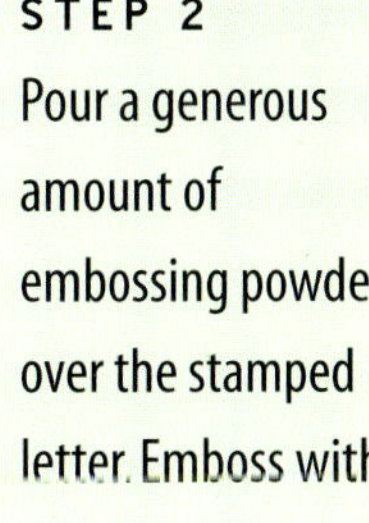

STEP 2

Pour a generous amount of embossing powder over the stamped letter. Emboss with heat gun.

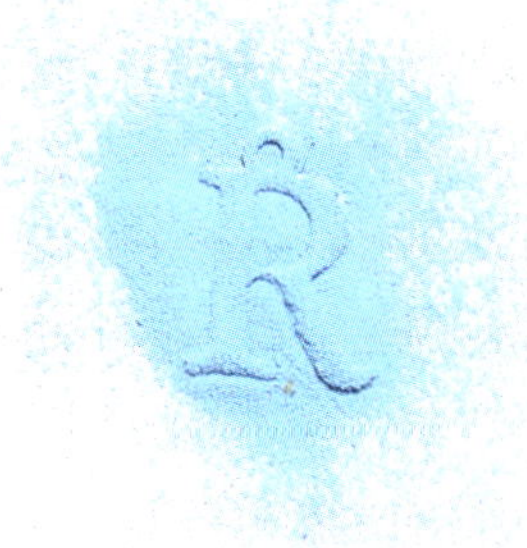
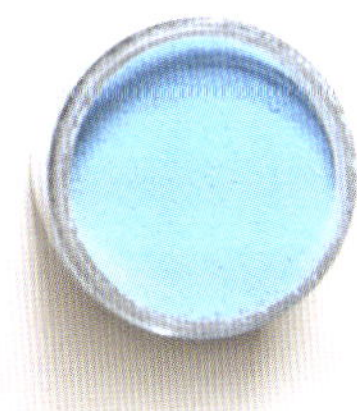

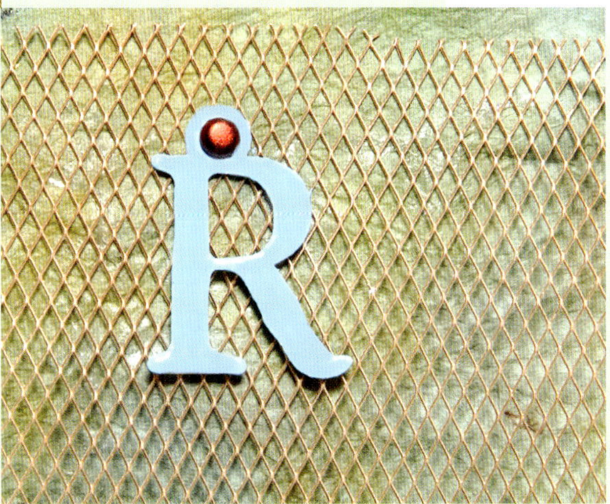

STEP 3

Let cool, then insert red brad in eyelet and fasten through mesh and paper.

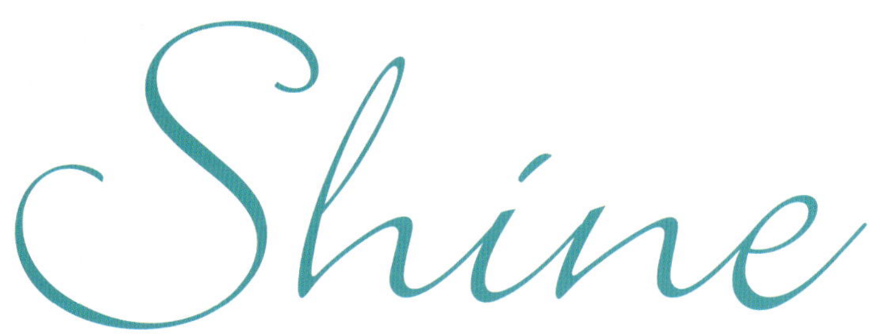

Metallic Accents

Metallic accents are the latest rage in scrapbooking. In addition to gold, silver, copper and bronze, a shimmering range of cool metallic colors are available. New products including metal stickers, mesh, sheets, foils and frames add sparkle to your scrapbooking pages. Incorporate thin miniature frames to highlight a special person or theme. Add color or texture by stamping, embossing, painting or covering with metal flakes. Choose a variety of metal mesh materials to stamp, emboss or paint. Are you looking for added luster? Sheet metal is a versatile new product that is shaped, embossed, stamped or burnished.

Innovative applications incorporate metal leafing flakes, metallic pens, markers, ink pads and powdered pigments. Gilding has never been easier. Add glimmer and shine to your page with metal leafing flakes. These delicate flakes are available in new metallic colors including red, purple and blue. For added sparkle, rub on colorful metallic powdered pigments. Lettering, metallic pens, markers and ink pads highlight photographs and accentuate themes. For a fresh approach, accentuate your pages with metal spirals, clips, wire or staples. Color staples add a fresh, new look to your scrapbooking pages. Staple photos and mats to create colorful tactile patterns. Metallic accents offer new products, new applications and new possibilities to all scrapbook *aficionados* who are willing to experiment with new scrapbooking materials and techniques.

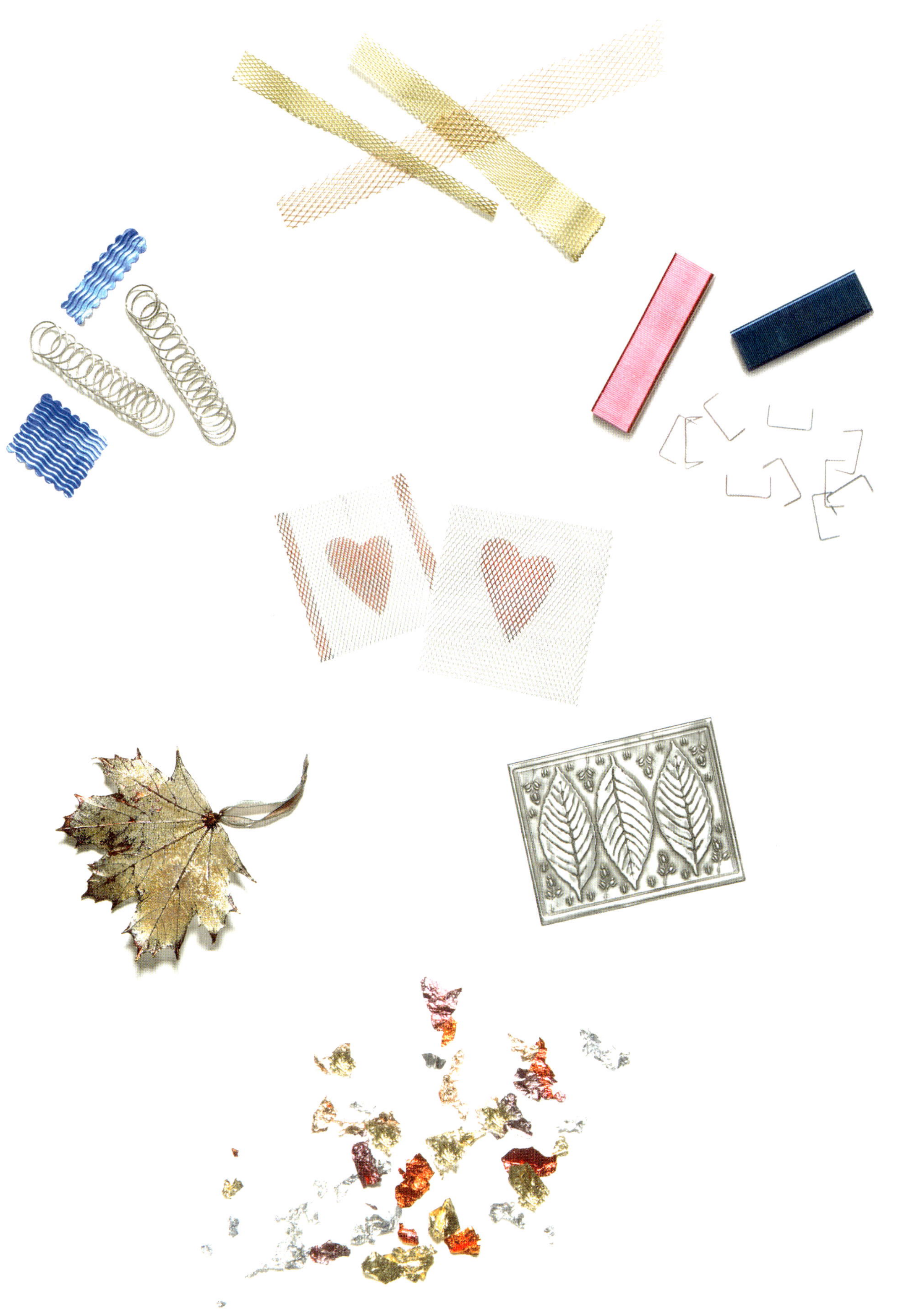

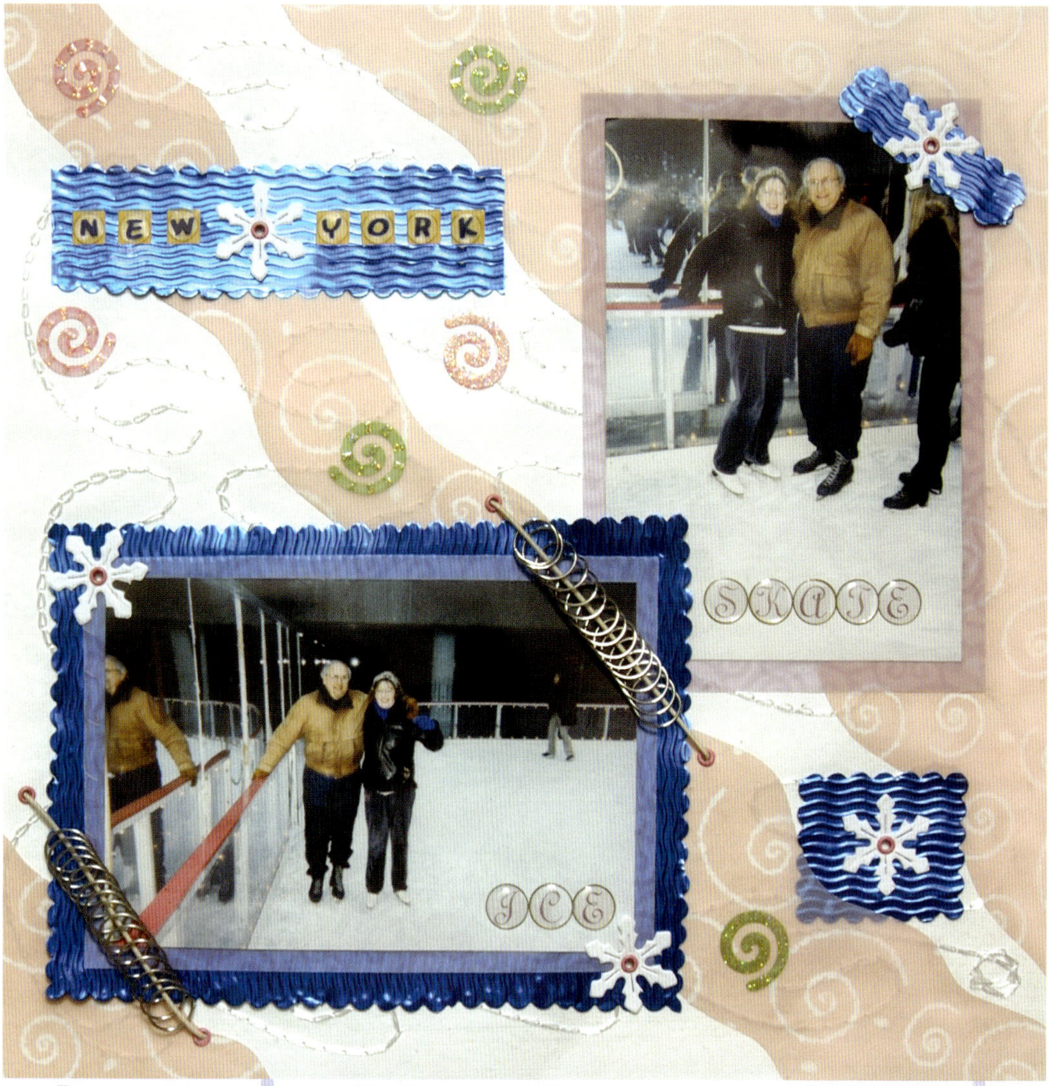

ice-skating in new york

Embossed Foil and Metal Spirals

Each year during the Christmas holidays, we enjoy ice-skating at Rockefeller Plaza and shopping in the Big Apple. Using a craft knife, cut pink patterned vellum into wavy strips and mount on stitched paper. Glue photographs on lavender patterned vellum leaving a 1/4-inch border. Emboss two large blue foil pieces on wave texture plate. Using scallop scissors, trim foil 1/4-inch larger than the photographs, mount and adhere to scrapbook page. Punch holes through foil and set eyelets with paper snowflakes. Punch holes 1/4-inch from mounted foil photograph and set eyelets. Thread elastic through metal spirals and connect through eyelet holes. Trim the smaller blue embossed foil accents with scallop scissors, punch and set eyelets with snowflakes. For the title, trim a 5 x 1-inch piece of embossed blue foil, punch and set eyelets with snowflake. Add orange mosaic stickers with bubble dome letters and accent with spiral stickers. Ice-skating in New York during Christmas is our time-honored way of opening the holiday season.

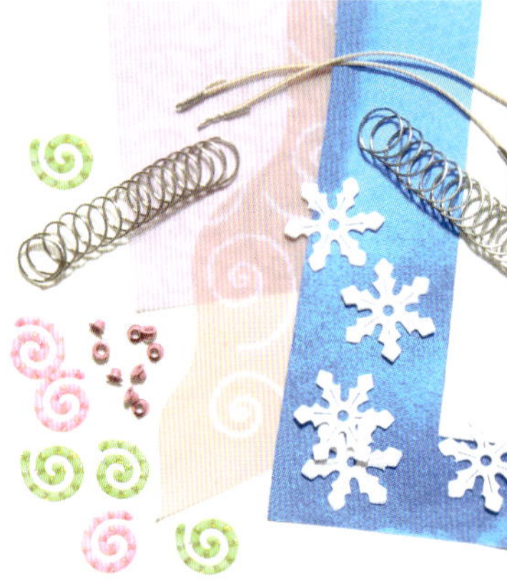

MATERIALS

- Stitched Paper *Provo Craft*
- Patterned Vellum *World Win/Colorbök*
- Blue Foil *Paragona*
- Wave Texture Plate *Fiskars*
- Eyelets *Making Memories*
- Snowflake Paper Cuts *Nicole*
- Metal Spiral *Available from Stampington & Company*
- Elastics *Available from Stampington & Company*
- Spiral Stickers *Sticko*
- Mosaic Stickers *Sticko*
- Treasure Domes *Brenda Walter*
- Bubble Alphabet *Mark Richards*
- Scallop Scissors *Making Memories*

TECHNIQUE HINT

When using elastics with eyelets, make sure the metal clamp fits the opening before setting eyelet in place.

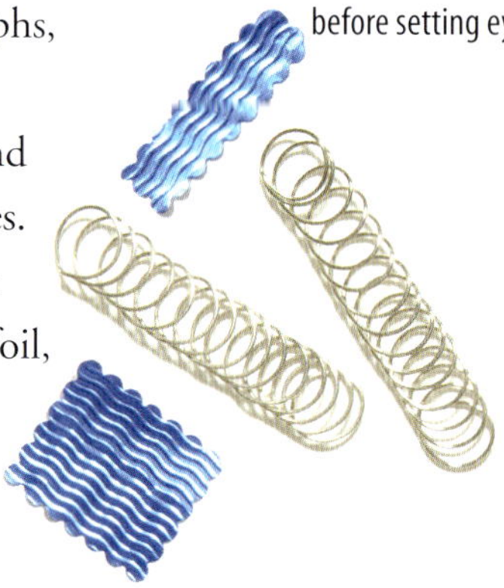

HOW-TO STEPS

ice-skating in new york

embossed foil

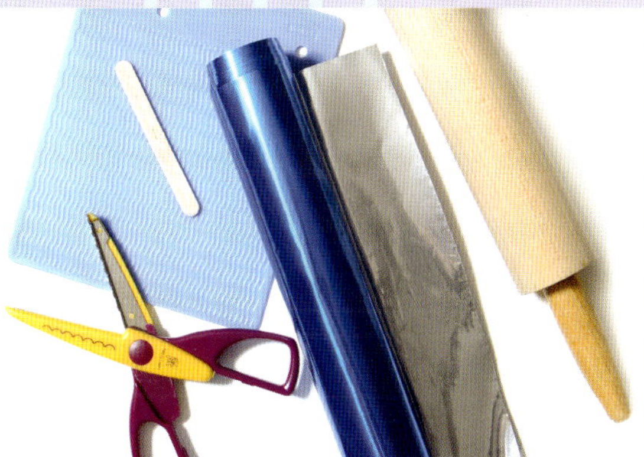

MATERIALS

Blue Foil
Waves Texture Plate
Rolling Pin
Embossing Tool
Scallop Scissors

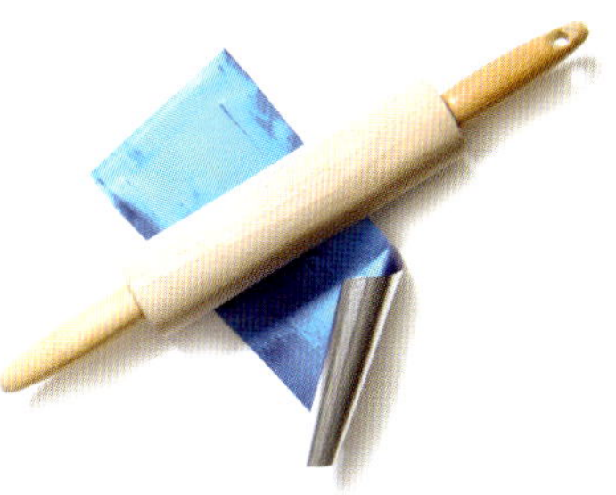

STEP 1

Trim a piece of foil longer than the desired length. Roll foil flat with rolling pin on smooth, even surface.

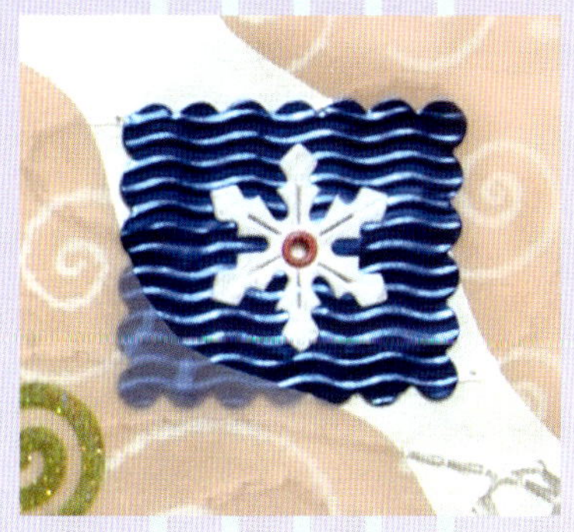

STEP 2

Trim a small section and place flattened foil on embossing plate. Use the embossing tool to form the pattern.

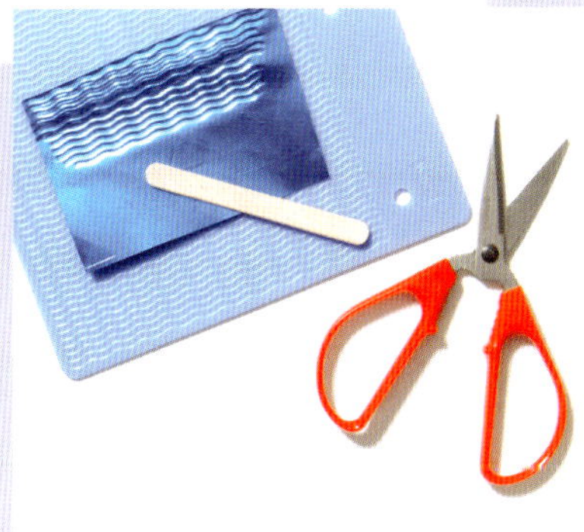

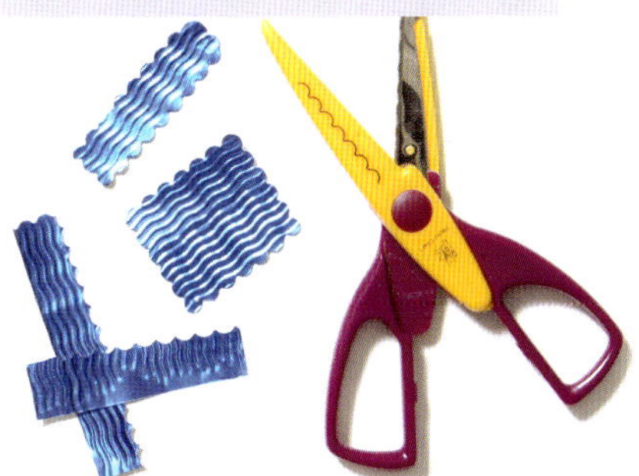

STEP 3

Trim foil pieces to exact size with scallop scissors. To keep embossed texture intact, keep flat and handle carefully.

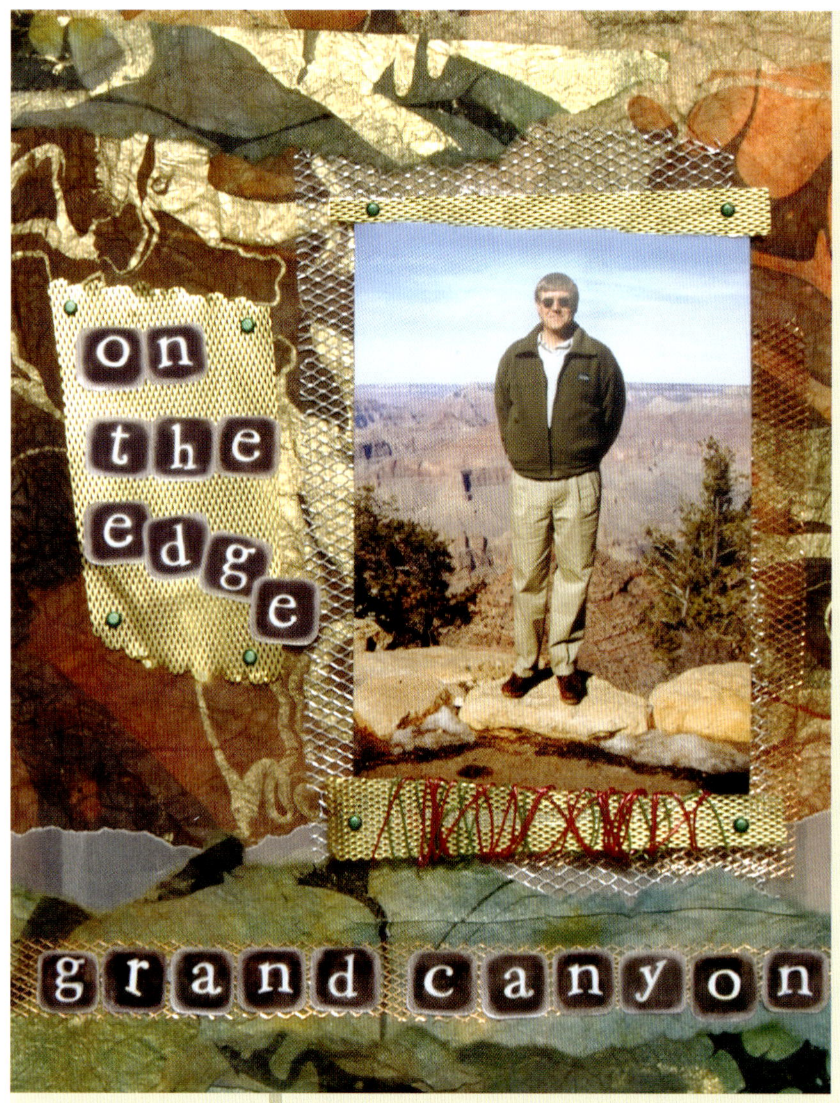

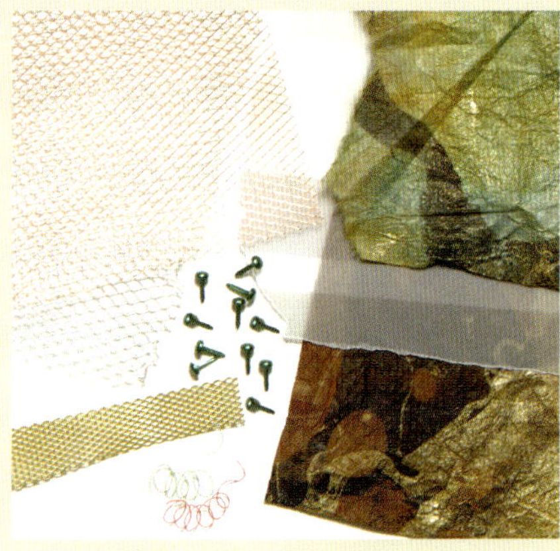

MATERIALS

Handmade Paper *Black Ink*
Vellum *Simple Sets*
Silver, Copper and Brass Wire Mesh *Paragona*
Brads *Treasured Memories*
24 Gauge Jewelry Wire *Nicole*
Sonnets Scrapbook Letters *Creative Imaginations, Inc.*

TECHNIQUE HINT

Take great care when cutting metal mesh. Edges are sharp and can easily pierce skin or hook onto clothing.

grand canyon
Metal Mesh

The Grand Canyon is one of nature's most spectacular natural phenomena. As a lover of the outdoors, Jon has spent many happy hours hiking in the Arizona landmark. Create the base with one piece of 8.5 x 11-inch brown handmade paper. Tear strips of green handmade paper and adhere along the top edge of the base paper. For the bottom, tear strips of vellum and green handmade paper and mount. Place scrapbook letters on copper mesh and glue along the bottom. Glue photograph to silver wire mesh and attach a thin brass strip along the top edge of the photo. Wind jewelry wire around a brass strip and glue on bottom edge of photo. Snip the tabs off of green brads and glue in each corner. Cut a rectangular piece of brass mesh, attach "on the edge" letters and glue green brads in each corner. Thousands of tourists from around the world enjoy Arizona's most scenic gorge, Jon included.

lovin' nature

Color Staples and Foil Stickers

Children love to climb trees. These three young siblings are no exception. Tear large and small corners from textured paper and place in position over patterned striped paper. Use red staples and fasten along torn edges of the textured paper. In the upper left hand corner, leave a 1-inch gap without staples. Mount photos on blue patterned paper and staple along the sides. Adhere photos to paper and slip the left corner of the top photo under the textured paper. Attach green brads in each corner. Place oak leaf stickers and accent with green staples. Glue *Scrabble*® letters around the photo and complete with laser cut leaves. Summertime is the ideal season for children to experience the awesome beauty of nature.

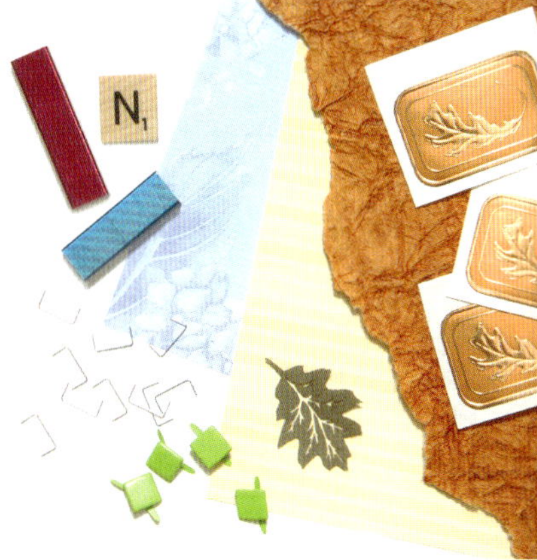

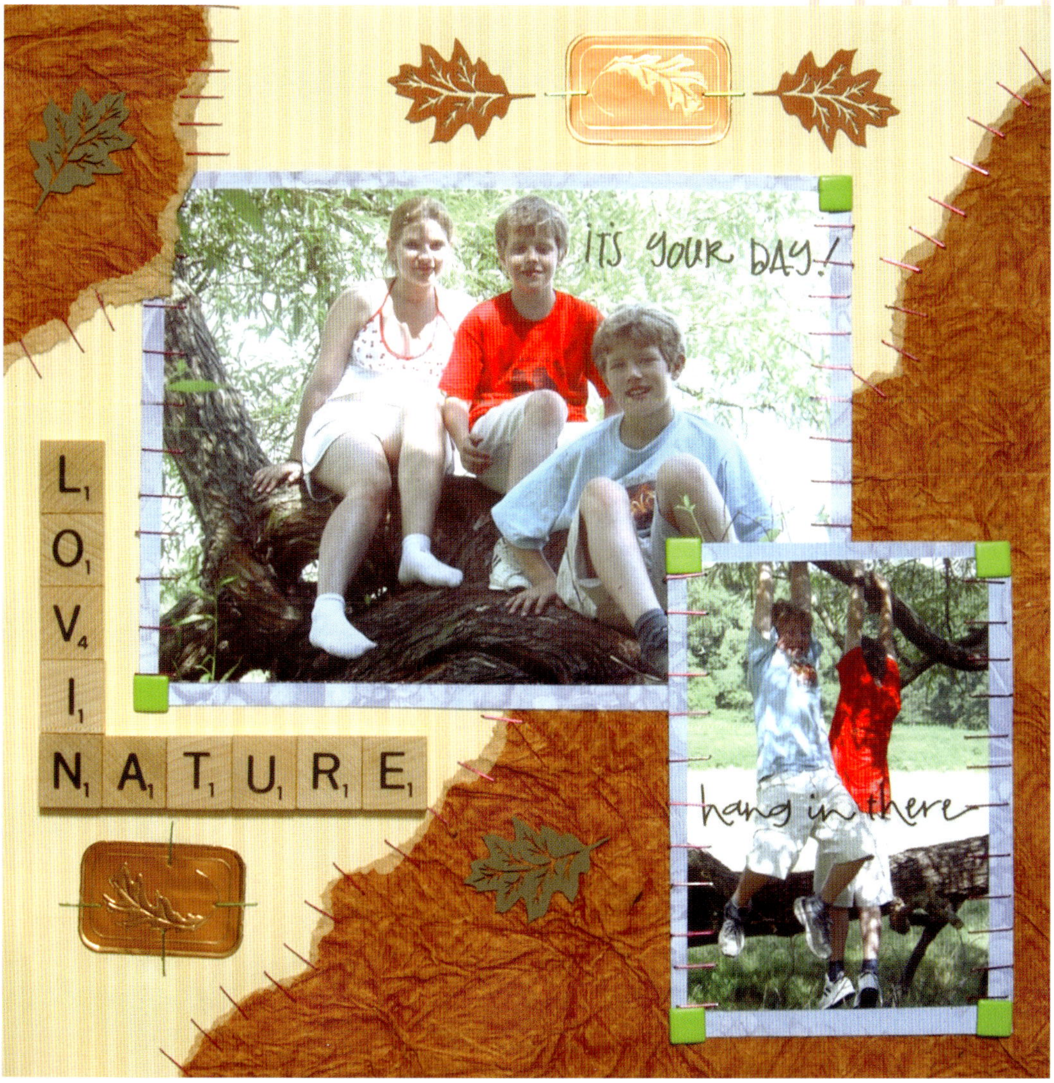

MATERIALS

Textured Paper *Provo Craft*

Patterned Paper *PSX Papers for Creativity / K&Company*

Color Staples *Making Memories*

Brads *Making Memories*

Oak Leaf Foil Stickers *Available from Stampington & Company*

Laser Cut Leaves *Die Cuts With A View*

Wood Letters *Scrabble*®

TECHNIQUE HINT

A stapler is not long enough to reach the inside edge of the torn paper. Open the stapler flat and staple on a hard surface.

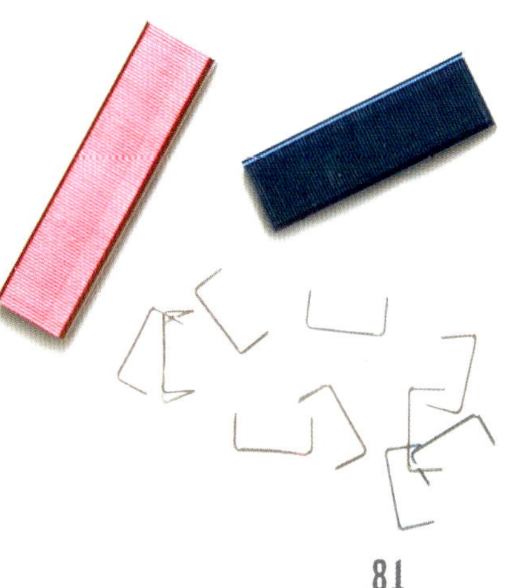

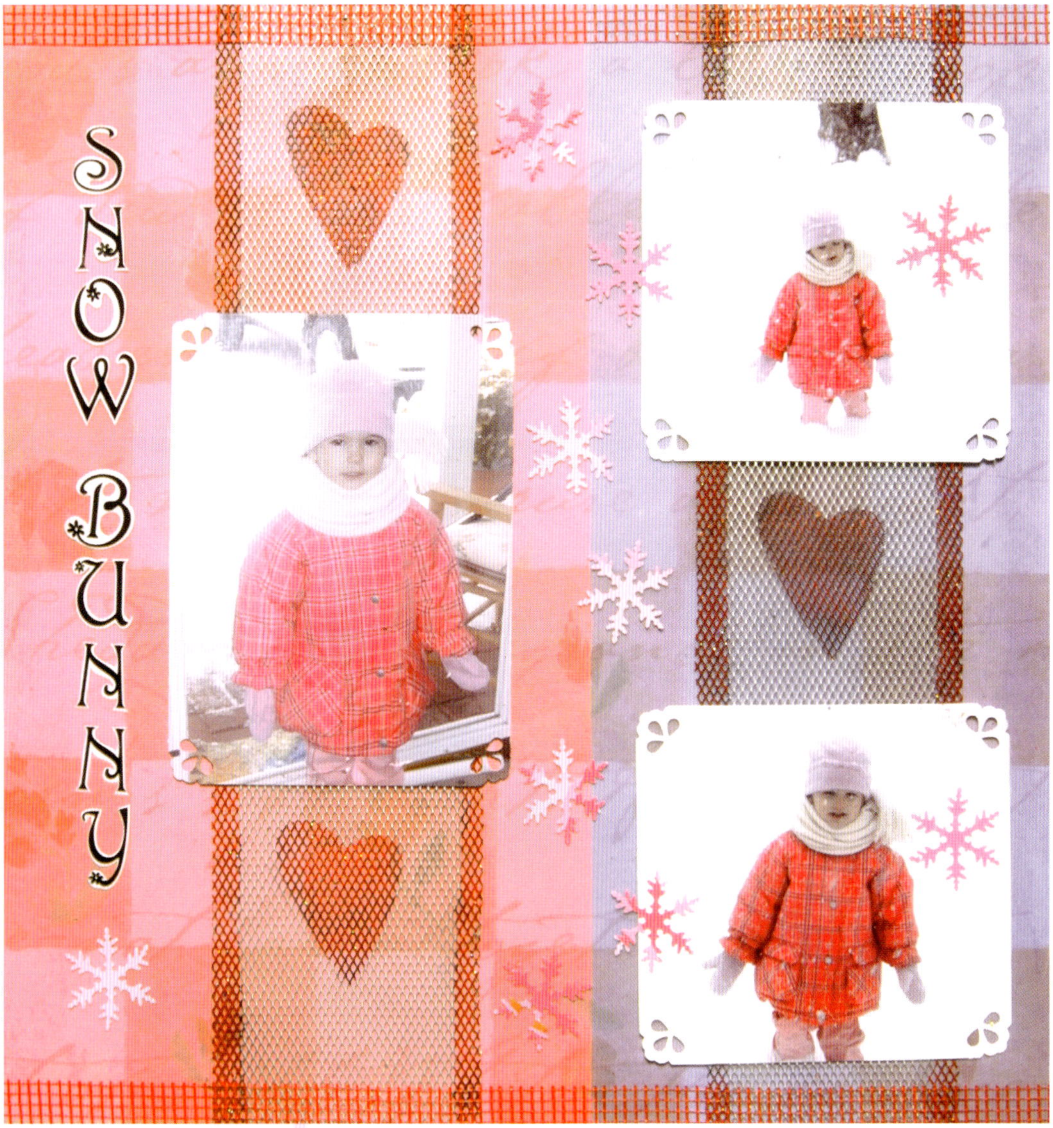

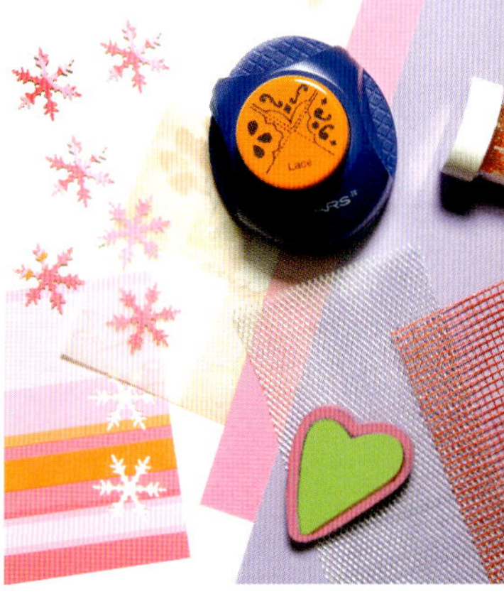

MATERIALS

Two-Sided Cardstock *Making Memories*
Patterned Vellum *The C-Thru Ruler Company*
Metal Mesh *Making Memories*
Sticky Mesh *Making Memories*
Snowflake Punch *EK Success*
Lace Corner Punch *Fiskars*
Black Solvent Ink Pad *StāzOn*
Heart Rubber Stamp *Rubber Stampede*
Red Embossing Powder *Mark Enterprises*
Lettering *Colorbök*

snow bunny

Rubber Stamped Metal Mesh

All children love playing in the snow. Wintertime affords them the opportunity to enjoy many happy hours sledding and making snowmen. Trim a sheet of magenta cardstock 7-inches wide and purple cardstock 5-inches wide. Mount 12-inch square patterned vellum on top. Trim two pieces of metal mesh 3 x 12-inches. Rubber stamp heart and edges in red ink and emboss. Adhere metal mesh pieces on page. Trim photographs to fit mesh, punch corner lace designs and glue in place. Wrap 1/2-inch red plastic mesh around top and bottom edges of the page. Adhere title, "Snow Bunny" with sticker letters and glue on snowflakes to complete the page. Children never tire playing in the snow, and our granddaughter is no exception.

TECHNIQUE HINT

Solvent ink adheres to non-porous surfaces and will stain clothing and skin.

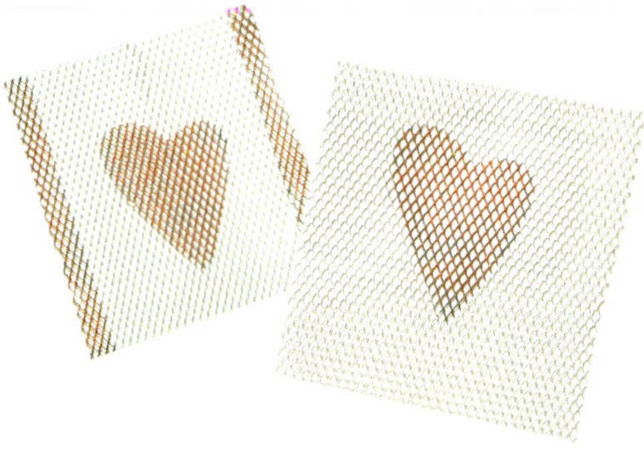

HOW-TO STEPS

rubber stamped metal mesh

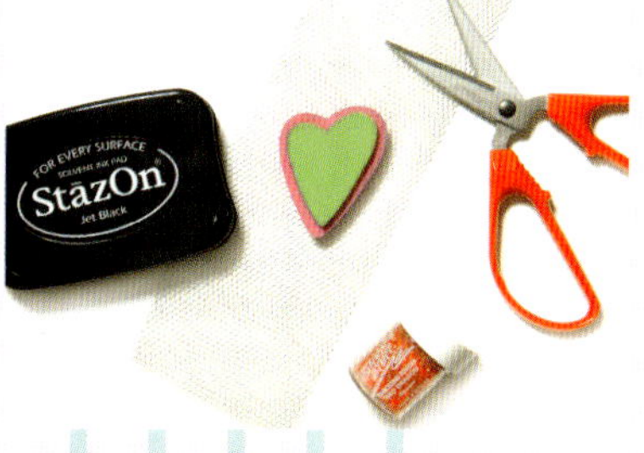

MATERIALS

Metal Mesh
Black Solvent Ink Pad
Heart Rubber Stamp
Heat Gun
Embossing Powder
Metal Cutting Scissors

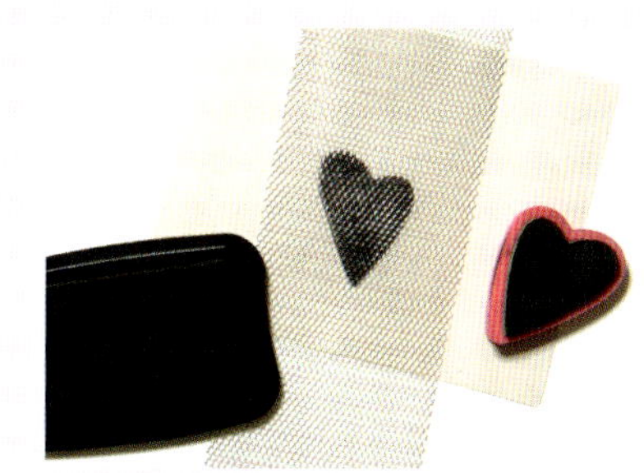

STEP 1

Place paper behind metal mesh and rubber stamp a heart in solvent ink.

STEP 2

Replace paper behind metal mesh and sprinkle red embossing powder.

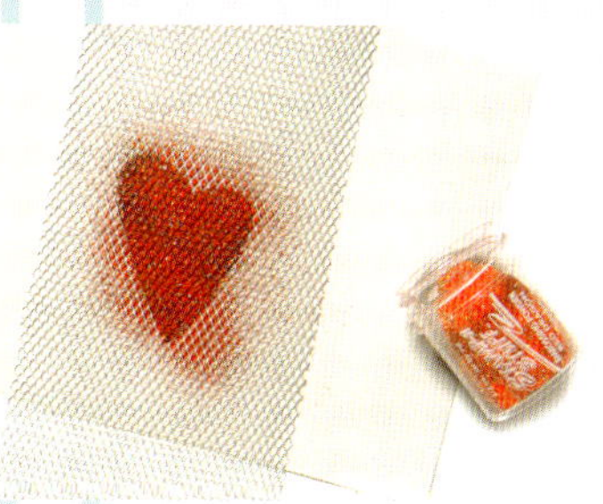

STEP 3

Tap away excess powder and heat gently. Do not position heat gun too close, as red embossing powder will turn black.

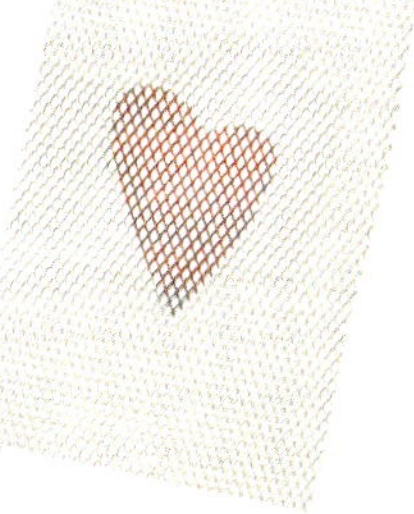

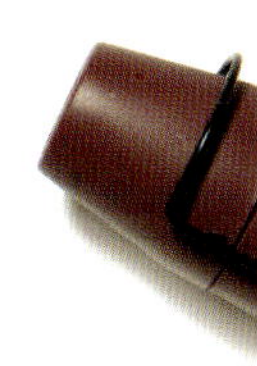

STEP 4

To create rubber stamp embossed sides on mesh, place tape 1/2-inch from edges. Gently press mesh into inkpad. To prevent staining your hands, place a piece of paper over the mesh.

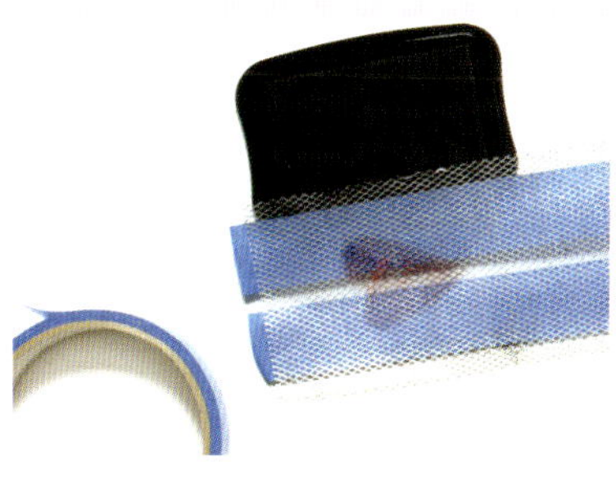

STEP 5

Place paper behind metal mesh and sprinkle red embossing powder along edges.

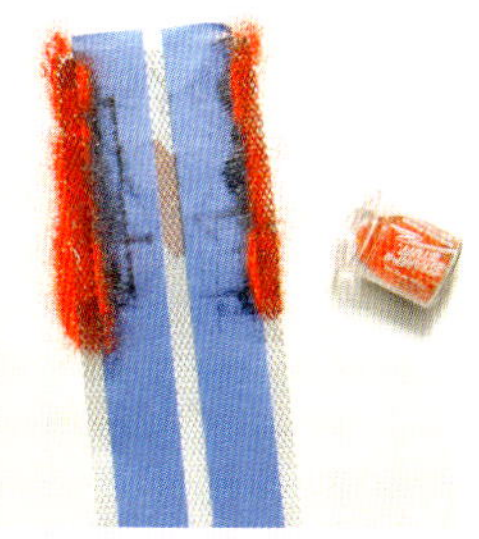

STEP 6

Tap away excess powder, remove tape and gently emboss with a heat gun.

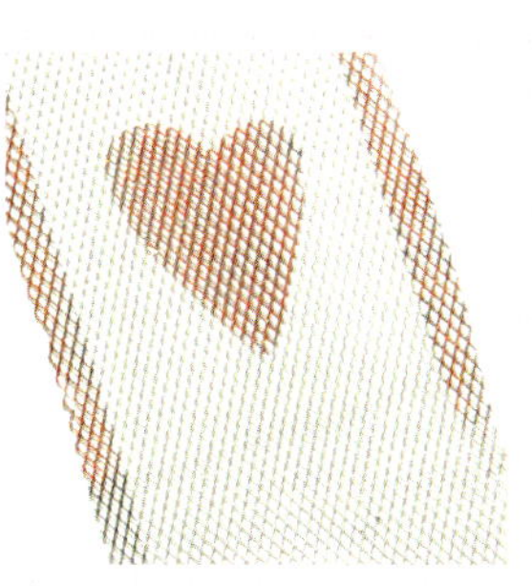

Metal Leaves

Fifty years of married bliss is a milestone envied by all married couples. Create the title text on the computer and print on vellum. Trim the solid purple paper 1/4-inch larger than the title paper and mount. Punch fleur-de-lis design in each corner and remount title on blue patterned paper. For the metal words section, punch fleur-de-lis design on blue patterned paper, mount on purple paper leaving a 1/4-inch border and apply rub-on gold leaves. Adhere metal art words with copper snaps. Mount photo on purple paper leaving a 1/4-inch border. Punch fleur-de-lis design on photograph and remount on blue patterned paper. Use the gold marker to make a thin gold line inside each mat. Apply rub-on gold leaves on the background paper and mount metal dipped leaf to page. Mom and Dad continue to share a wonderfully married life together.

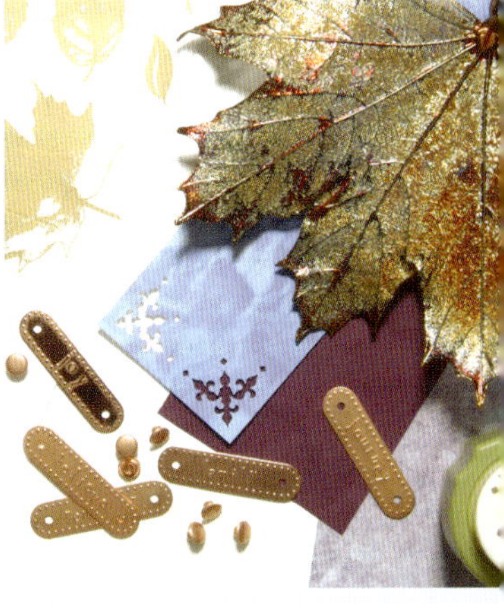

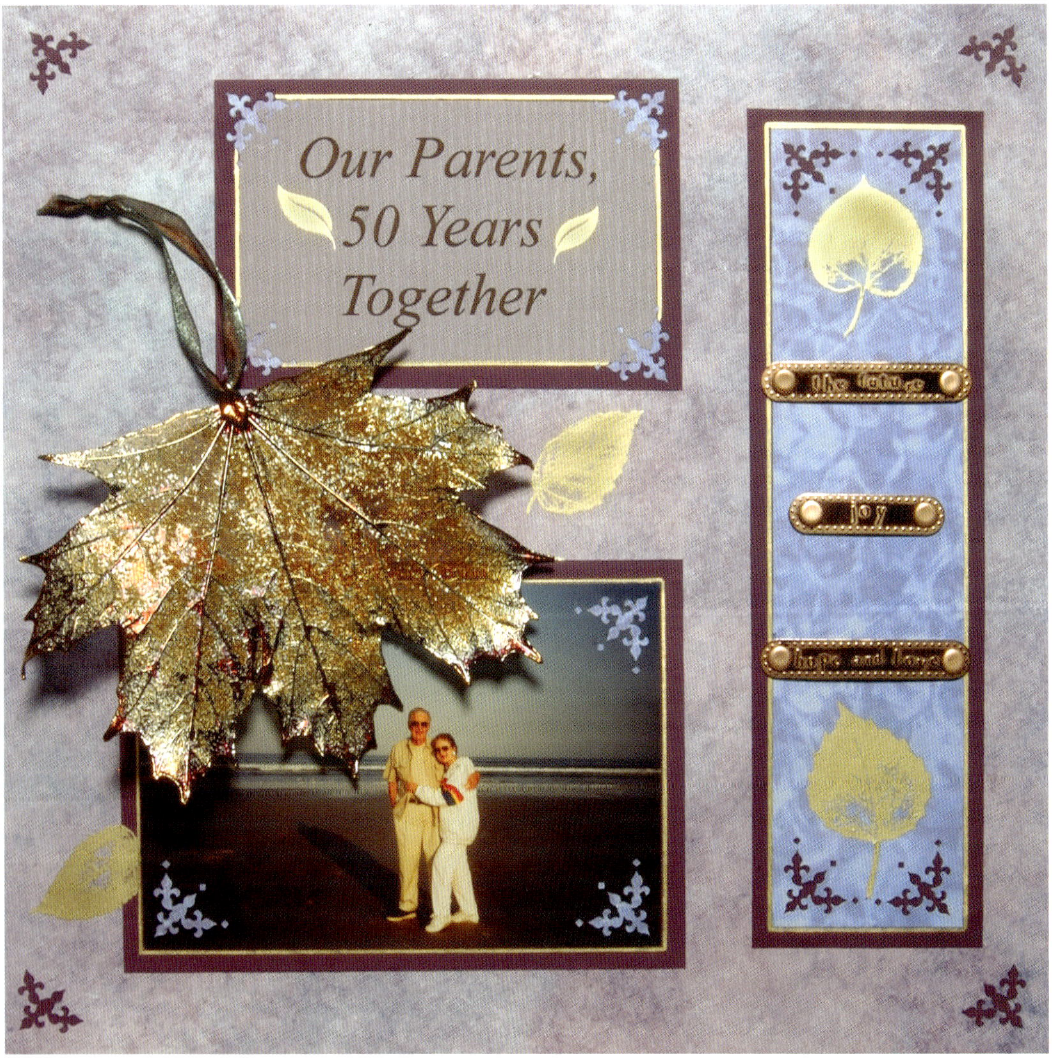

MATERIALS

Patterned Paper *Paper Pizazz*
Vellum *The Paper Company*
Solid Paper *Black Ink*
Fleur-de-lis Punch *Anna Griffin*
Copper Snaps *Making Memories*
Precious Metal Rub-on Leaves *Chartpak*
Metal Art Words *K&Company*
Zig Gold Marker *EK Success*
Metal Dipped Leaf *Takashimaya New York, Inc.*

TECHNIQUE HINT

To simulate a metal leaf, spray a dried pressed leaf with gold paint.

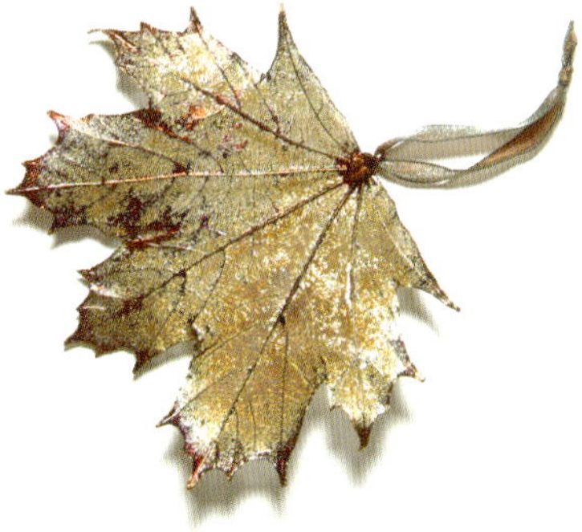

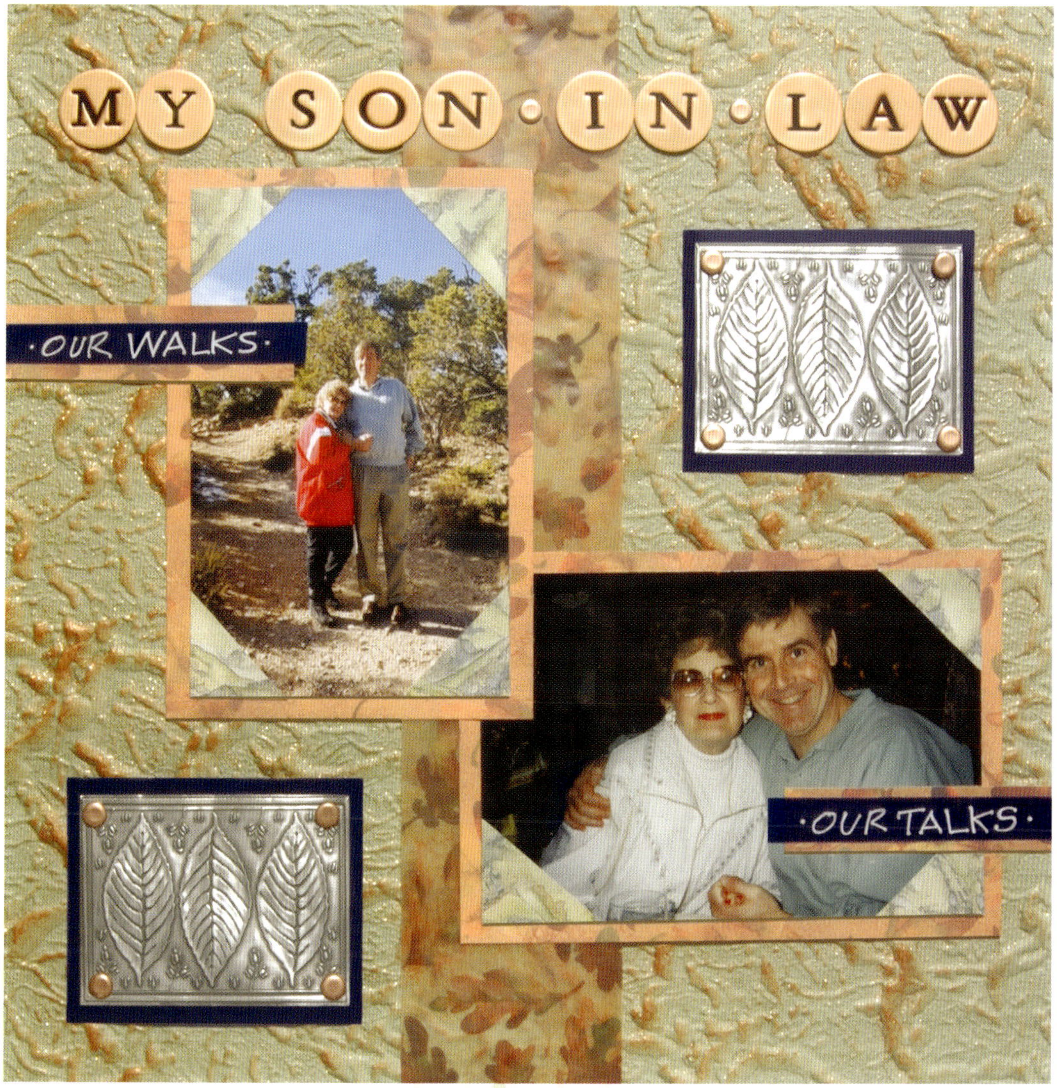

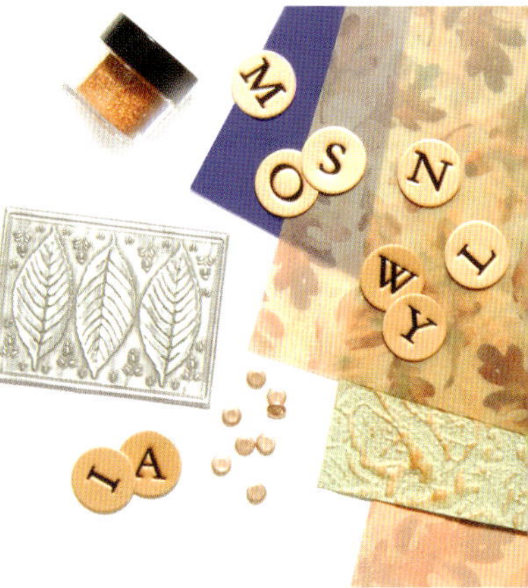

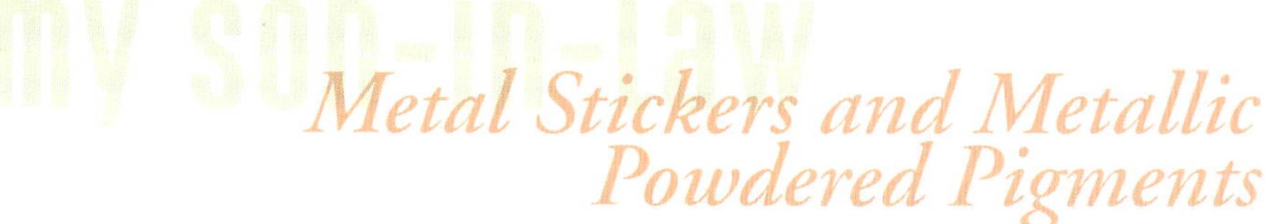

Metal Stickers and Metallic Powdered Pigments

Mutual respect is the basis of a true and lasting relationship. Jon and his Mother-In-Law share a deep, mutual admiration for each other. Stamp textured paper with watermark stamp pad. Use a cotton ball to dab powdered pigment over the surface of the textured paper. Trim a strip of patterned vellum and mount down the center of the copper textured paper. Mount photographs on leaf patterned paper and leave a 1/4-inch border. Trim triangular shapes from green patterned paper and mount in corners. Adhere pewter metal stickers on trimmed solid vellum. Flatten copper snaps with a hammer and glue in corners. Cut stripes of leaf patterned and blue vellum paper and use a silver gel pen for the journaling. Complete title with metal sticker letters. Over the years, Jon and Ann's friendship has blossomed into a true mother and son relationship.

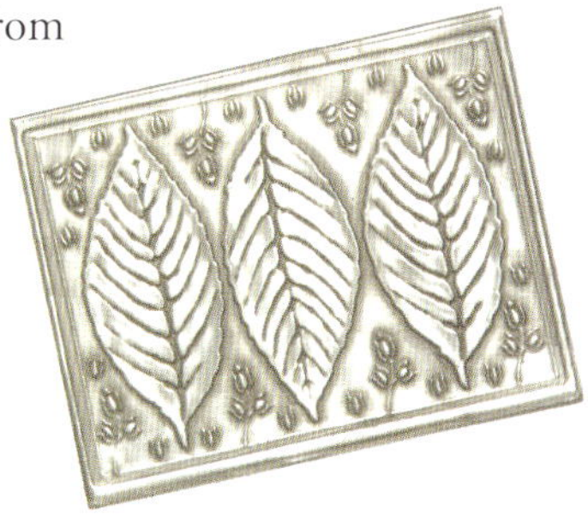

MATERIALS

Patterned Paper *The C-Thru Ruler Company*

Patterned Vellum *The C-Thru Ruler Company*

Solid Vellum *The Paper Company*

Textured Paper *Provo Craft*

Pewter Stickers *Available from Stampington & Company*

Silver Gel Pen *Uniball*

Watermark Stamp Pad *Versamark™*

Pearl Ex-Metallic Powdered Pigment *Jacquard Products*

Copper Snaps *Making Memories*

Metal Sticker Letters *EK Success*

TECHNIQUE HINT

Cut extra strips of paper and practice writing with the gel pen. Allow journaling words to dry completely before adhering to scrapbook page.

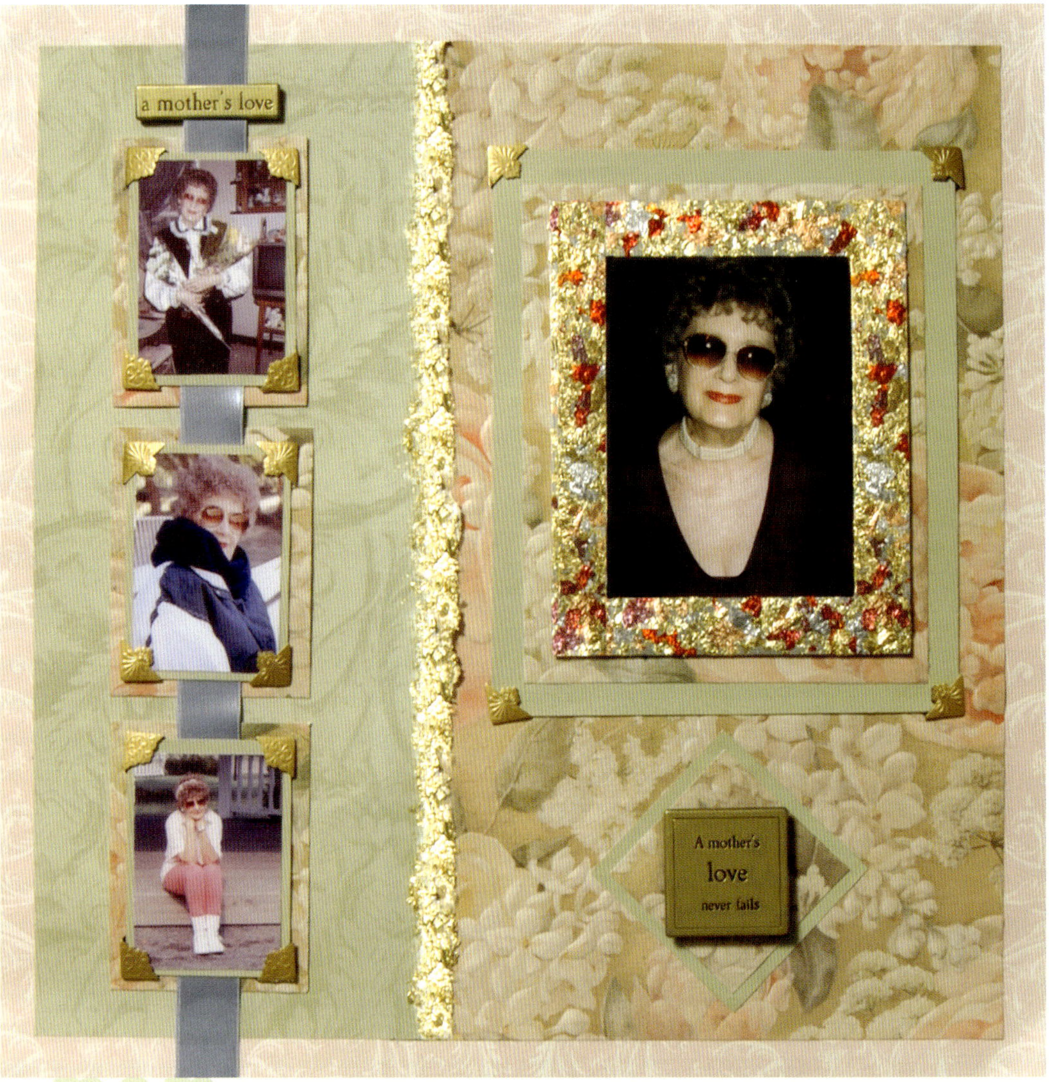

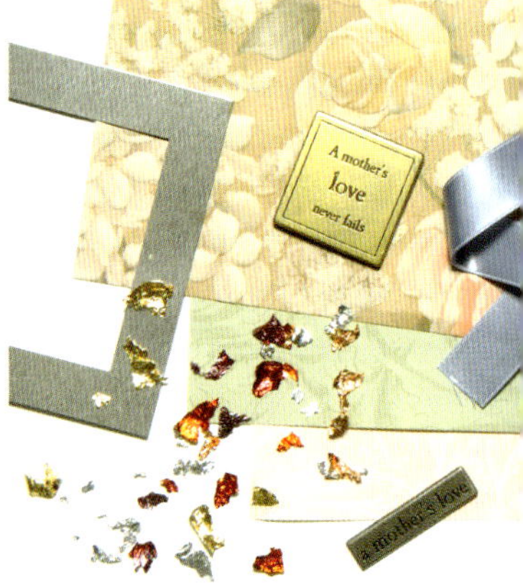

MATERIALS

Patterned Paper *Anna Griffin*
Embossed Paper *K&Company*
Metal Frame *Making Memories*
Metallic Gilding Leaf *US Art Quest, Inc.*
Metal Quotations and Phrases *Making Memories*
Embossed Gold Photo Corners *Jolee's Boutique*
Satin Ribbon *Anna Griffin*

TECHNIQUE HINT

Use gold inkpad for metal quotations. Press quotation on surface of inkpad, let dry and fill in letters with black marker.

mom Metal Leaf Flakes

A mother's unconditional love is cherished and nurtured all the days of our life. Choose three matching pieces of 12-inch square patterned paper; embossed flowers, patterned green and lavender. To make the left side, trim the green paper 11.5-inches high and tear the paper 5-inches wide creating a ragged edge. Position on lavender paper, apply clear glue along the torn edge and sprinkle with gold leaf flakes. Press in place with fingertips and tap off excess. Use the remaining embossed flower paper to trim three mats for the smaller pictures. For the inner mat, trim green solid paper smaller and stack photos with satin ribbon underneath. Accent with embossed gold photo corners and metal quotation. To create the right side, trim the embossed paper 7-inches by 11.5-inches. Apply a thin layer of white glue on the metal frame, sprinkle on metallic gilding leaf and press in place with fingertip. Double mat the metal leaf frame and metal quotation with embossed and solid green papers. Accent with embossed gold photo corners. Each photo reflects the caring moments of a dear mother who is loved by everyone in the family.

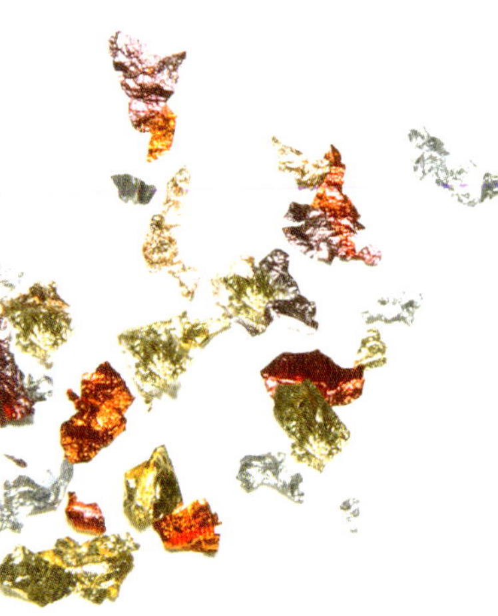

HOW-TO STEPS

metal leaf flakes

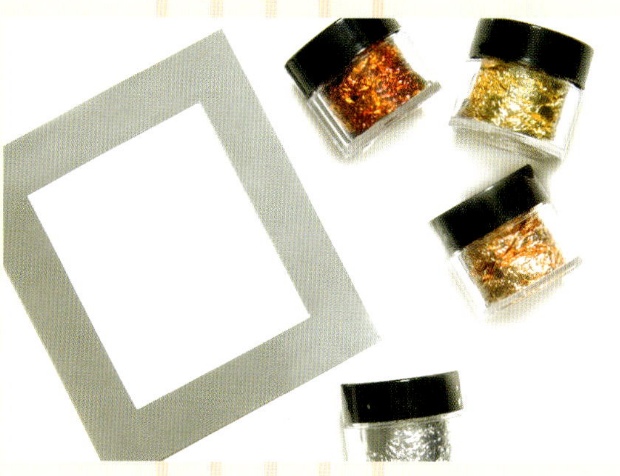

MATERIALS

Metal Frame
Metallic Gilding Leaf
Clear Archival Glue

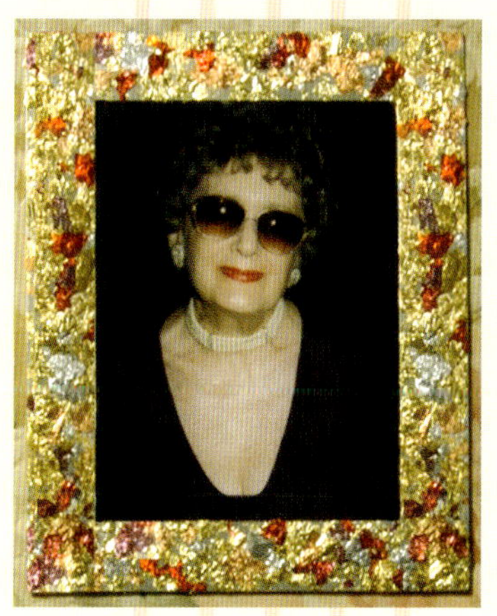

STEP 1

Place the metal gilding leaf pieces and colors on a clean surface. Apply a thin layer of glue to one side of the metal frame.

STEP 2

Gently adhere leafing layers one color at a time to one side of the frame. Next, apply gold and silver on the bottom layer, and top with copper and red flakes.

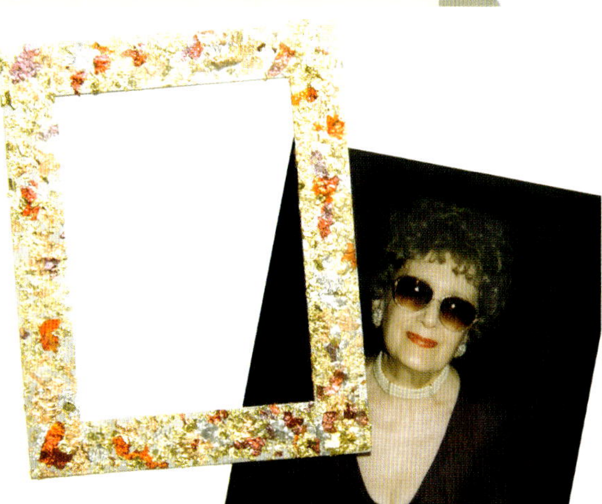

STEP 3

When completed, place clean paper on top and rub with hand or brayer to flatten flakes in position. Fold excess leaf pieces around the edge of the frame. Attach photograph from the back.

Reflections

Glass and More

Everything glass and more is the motto for this chapter. The popularity of glass in scrapbook design has surpassed everyone's expectations. The color, texture and translucency of glass make it an attractive element for accenting scrapbook layouts. Today's scrapbookers are using glass elements to add cutting-edge visual interest and subtle variety. Choose clear or iridescent glass pieces that have surface texture imbedded in the glass such as lines, air bubbles or shapes. Glass embellishments include—color marbles, optical lenses, capsules, microscope slides, tags, mica tiles, stained glass pieces, glass photo corners and mosaic pieces,—to name just some of the most popular items. The hottest items in scrapbooking today are microscope slides. The technique in the Sisters layout (p.98) demonstrates the beauty and versatility achieved when mini glass collages are created with photos, patterned paper and silver foil tape. Glass is the ideal medium to help you attain aesthetic beauty and harmony on your next scrapbook page.

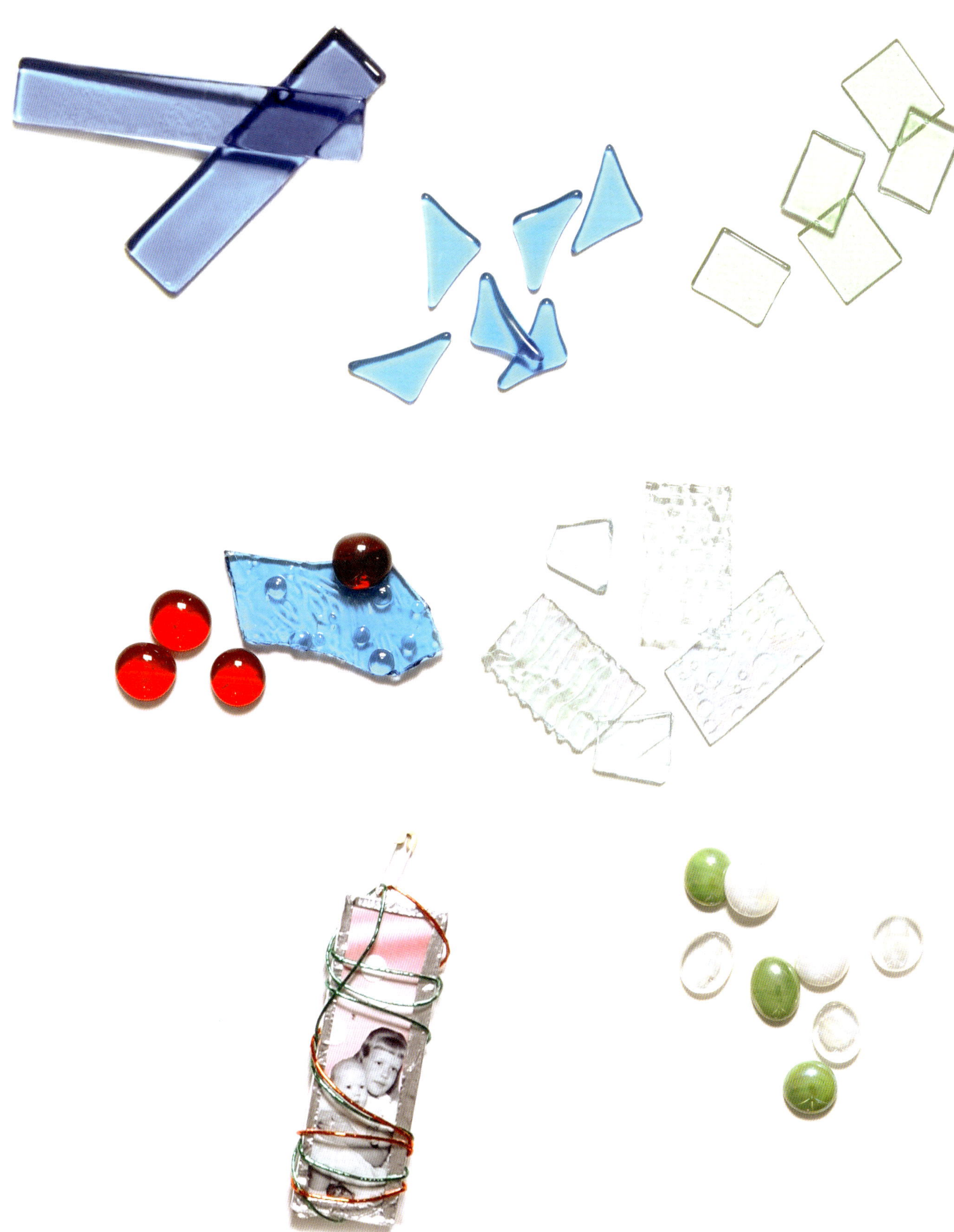

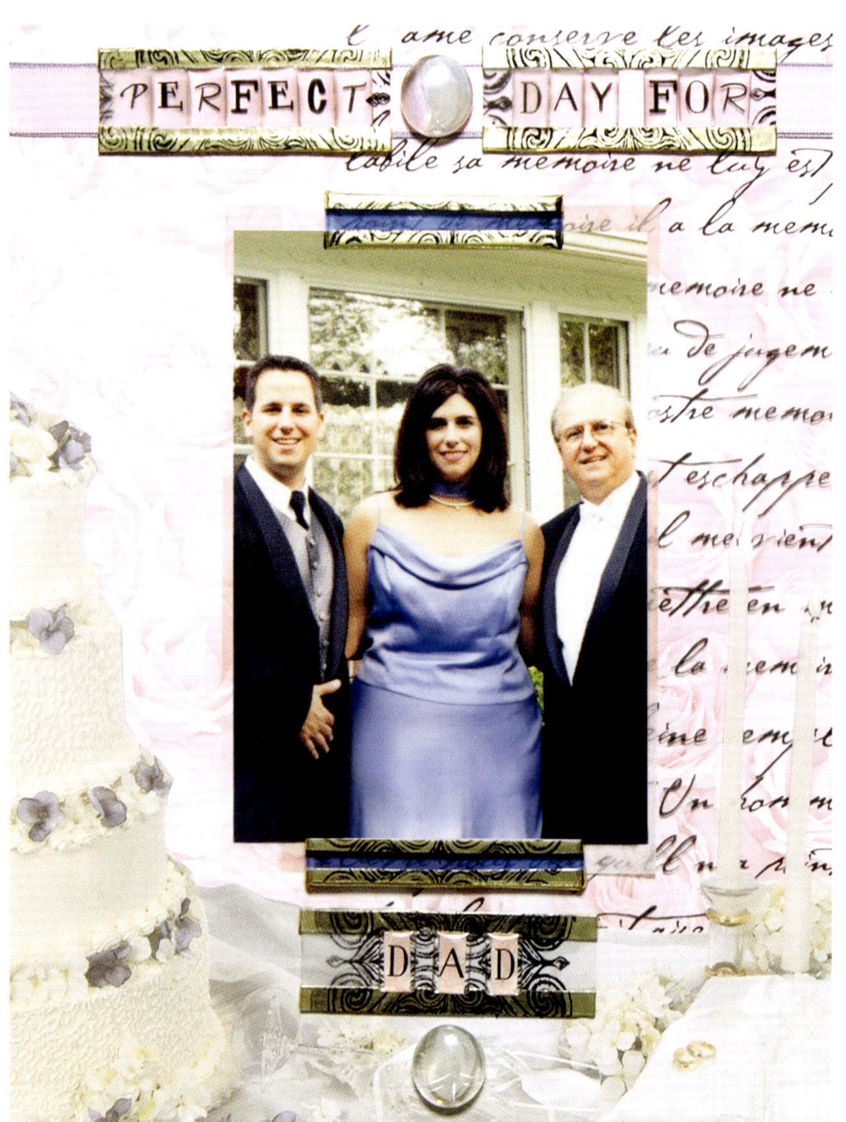

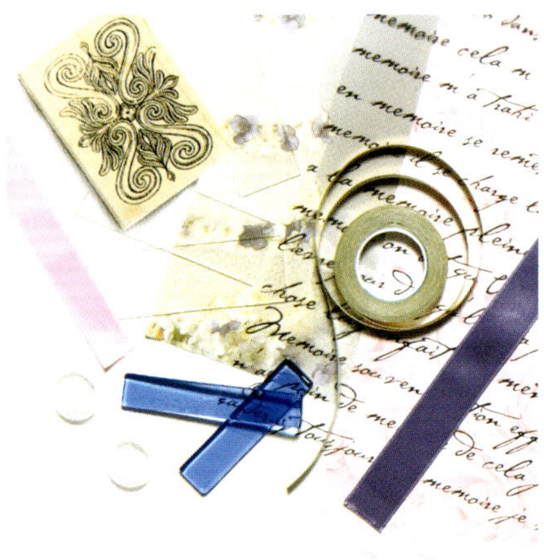

MATERIALS

Patterned Paper *Paper Pizazz*
Patterned Vellum *The C-Thru Ruler Company*
Transparency Sheet *Creative Imaginations, Inc.*
Black Solvent Ink Pad *StāzOn*
Rubber Stamp *Inkadinkado*
Satin Ribbon *Anna Griffin*
Gold Foil Tape *Metalworks™*
Glass Rods *Available from Stampington & Company*
Microscope Slide *Hobbylinc.com*
Flat Marbles *Mega Marbles*
Bubble Letters *Li'l Davis Designs™*

TECHNIQUE HINT

When stamping glass with solvent ink, press glass down gently on the stamp pad to avoid smearing.

Glass Rods, Microscope Slides and Flat Glass Marbles

My children Christa and Michael make a perfect day memorable as we all pose for a picture after my wedding ceremony. For the background select a sheet of 12 x 12-inch patterned paper. Slice transparency sheet 4.5-inches wide and place on right hand side of page. Select a sheet of wedding patterned paper, silhouette cake and candles and mount. Mount photo on patterned vellum; leave a 1/4-inch border and center on the page. Wrap glass rod with gold foil tape and imprint on stamp. Adhere on top and bottom of photo. Double mount two layers of ribbon. Wrap two microscope slides with foil tape and imprint on stamp. Place bubble letter words "Perfect Day For" and adhere to ribbon. Wrap another microscope slide with foil tape and imprint stamp on both sides of slide. Glue bubble letter word "Dad" on patterned paper and adhere to slide. Accent with flat glass marbles. Being blessed with great children is the perfect part of every dad's day.

HOW-TO STEPS

perfect day for dad

glass rods and microscope slides

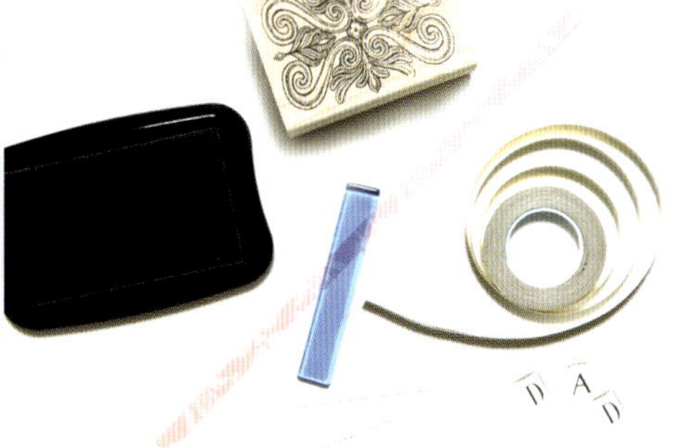

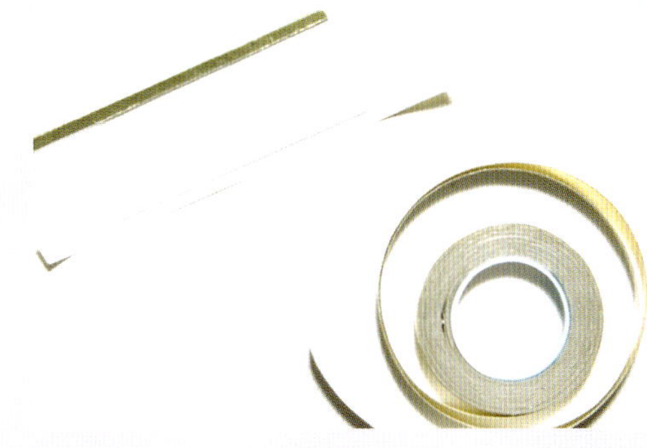

STEP 1

Cut a piece of foil tape and lay microscope slide evenly along edge. Wrap around edge tightly.

MATERIALS

- Microscope Slides
- Glass Rods
- Rubber Stamp
- Black Solvent Ink Pad
- Gold Foil Tape
- Patterned Paper
- Bubble Letters

STEP 2

Imprint wrapped slide with rubber stamp design in black ink. Press glass carefully on ink stamp.

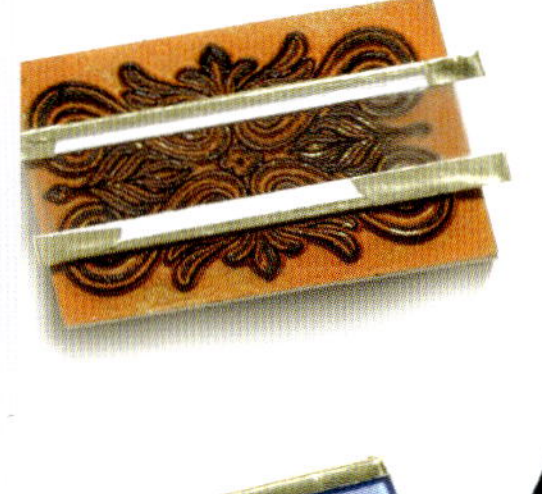

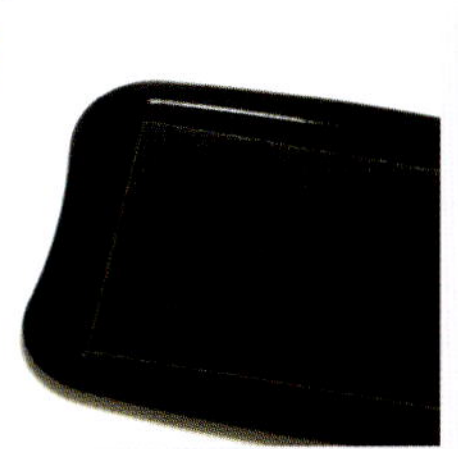

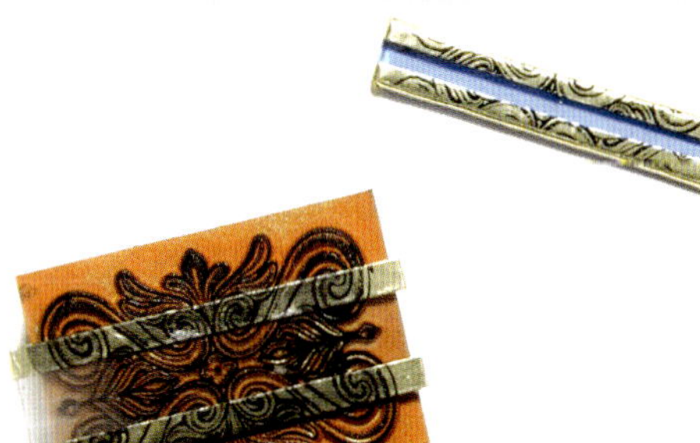

STEP 3

Turn slide over, place in same position and imprint glass in ink stamp.

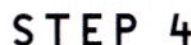

STEP 4

Cut patterned paper in strips and add bubble letters. Glue to slide.

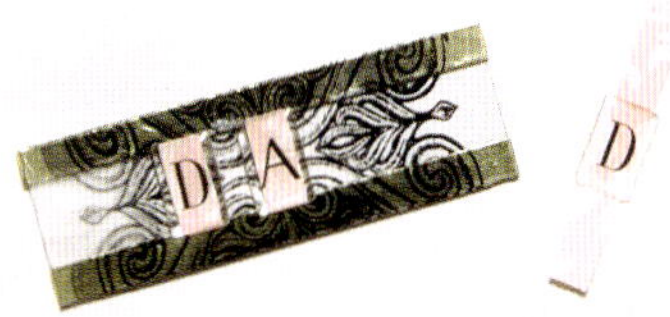

Glass Photo Corners

A father and mother's beaming smile reflects the pride and happiness they both share on their daughter's wedding day. Begin with a 12 x12-inch sheet of solid blue paper. Trim embossed paper 1/2-inch on two sides and center on solid paper. Place a 12-inch piece of ribbon vertically on the left side. Trim photos, mount on embossed paper with Victorian rotary cutter or scissors, and leave a 1/4-inch border. Add blue glass photo corners and adhere flower stickers. Print "The Rainbows In My Life," "Mom" and "Dad" in Lucida Handwriting computer font and print on blue vellum. Trim with deckle rotary cutter or scissors and mount. Glue blue glass rods above and below title. As parents share this special day together with their daughter, they remember and cherish the special love and memories of a lifetime.

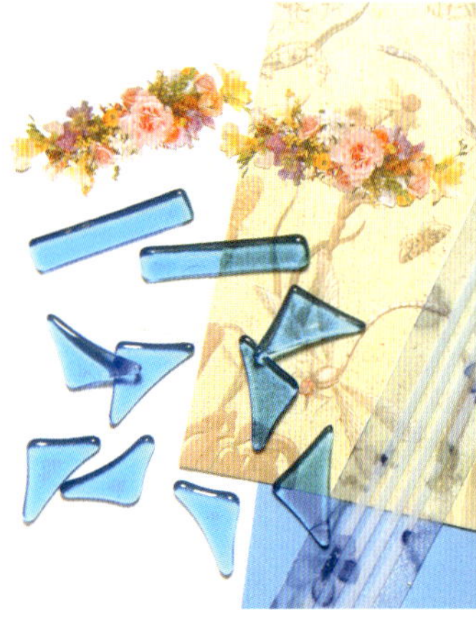

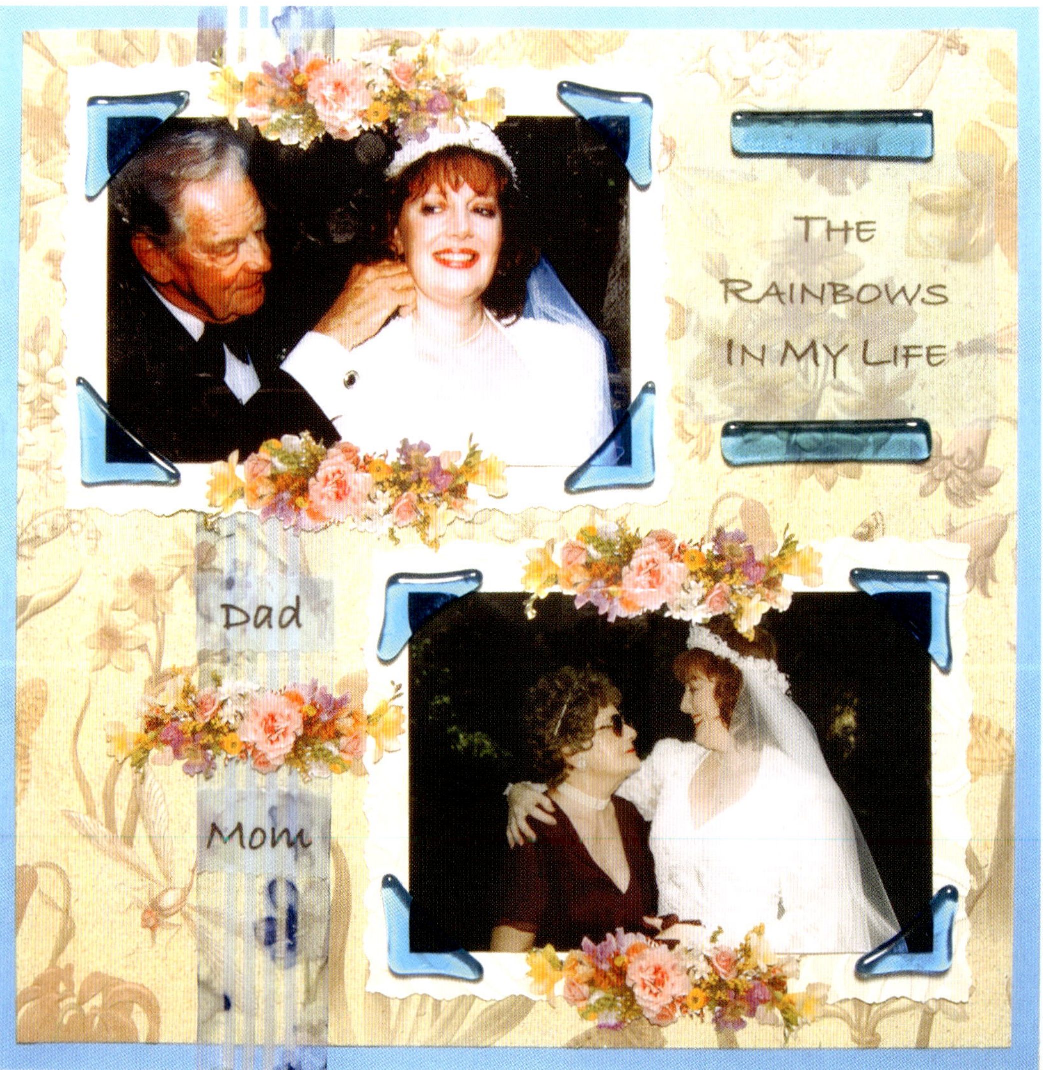

MATERIALS

Solid Paper *Making Memories*

Embossed Patterned Paper *K&Company*

Vellum *The Paper Company*

Flower Stickers *Mrs. Grossmans*

Ribbon *Offray Ribbon*

Glass Photo Corners *Available from Stampington & Company*

Glass Rods *Available from Stampington & Company*

Computer Font *Lucida Handwriting*

TECHNIQUE HINT

Use transparent drying glue with the glass photo corners. For best visibility, place in corner overlapping photo and mat.

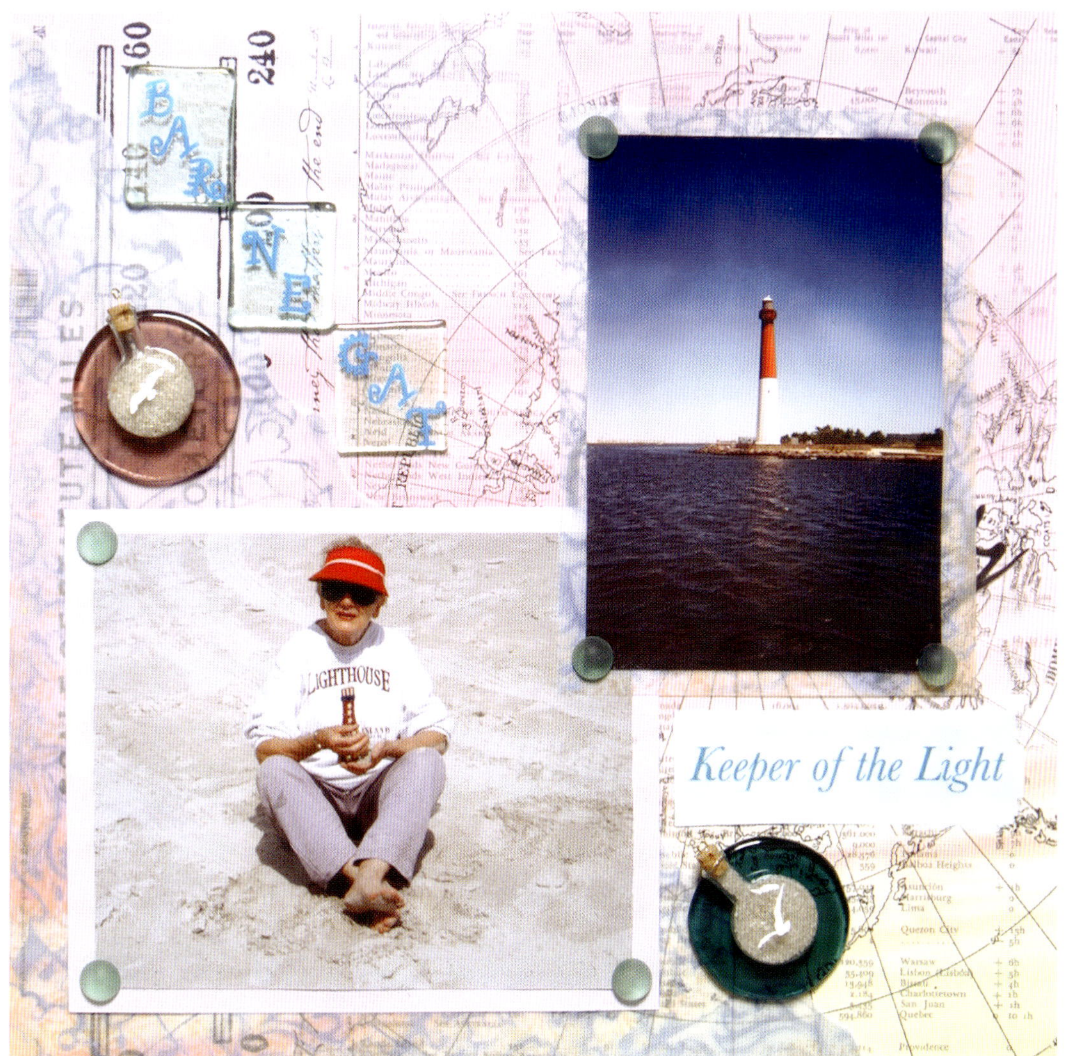

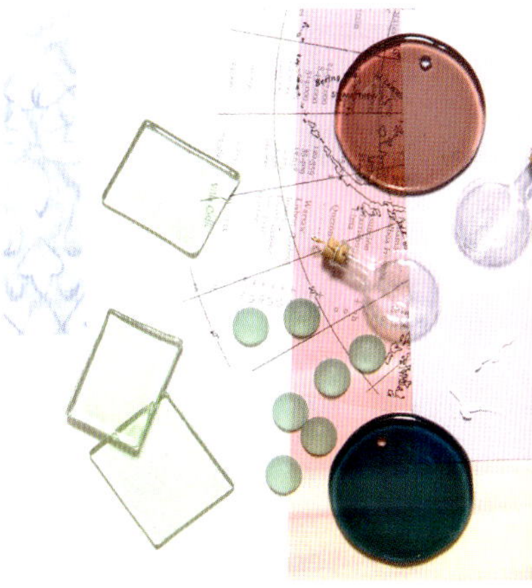

barnegat-keeper of the light

Glass Squares and Message Bottles

The Barnegat lighthouse is mom's favorite place. For the background, select a sheet of 12 x 12-inch patterned paper and mount transparency sheet on top. Tear a piece of vellum and secure on the left hand side of the page. Mount photo on solid lavender paper leaving a 1/4-inch border. Adhere on lower left hand corner of the vellum. Next, mount the lighthouse photo on patterned vellum and leave a 1/4-inch border. Glue mosaic pieces in each corner of the photos. Arrange glass squares diagonally and place sticker letters with the word "Barnegat." Fill message bottles with sand and adhere miniature seagull die cuts. Print title in Times computer font. The towering Barnegat Bay lighthouse invokes fond memories of our climbs to the top.

MATERIALS

Patterned Vellum *Colorbök*

Patterned Paper *The Paper Company*

Glass Squares *Available from Stampington & Company*

Message Bottles *Available from Stampington & Company*

Mosaic Pieces *The Beadery*

Glass Tags *Available from Stampington & Company*

Sticker Letters *Making Memories*

Seagull Die Cuts *Die Cuts With A View*

Computer Font *Times*

TECHNIQUE HINT

To create a frosted effect, lightly rub glass square surface with 300 grit sand paper.

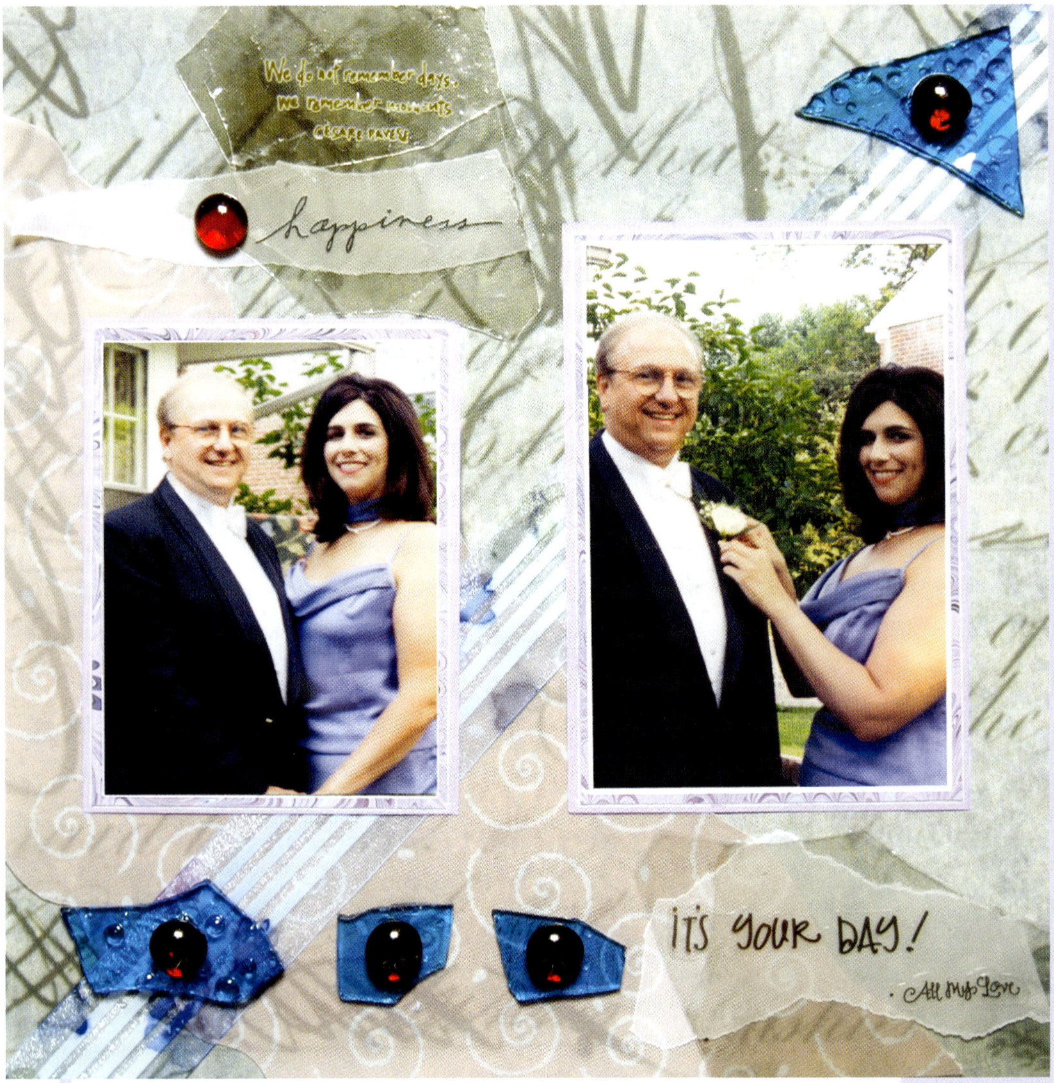

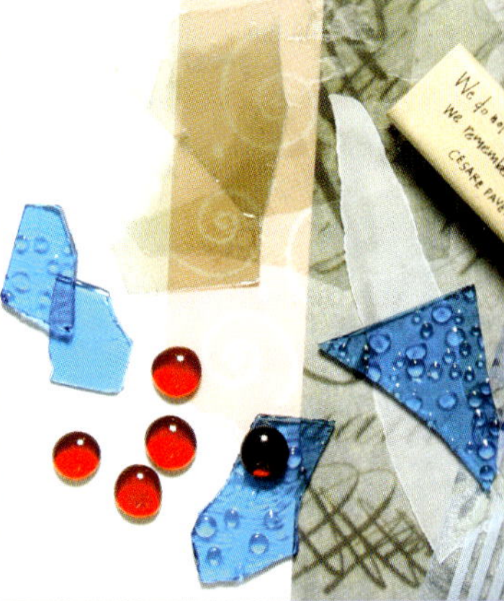

MATERIALS

Patterned Paper *K&Company / Paper Pizazz*
Solid Paper *Making Memories*
Patterned Vellum *Colorbök*
Stained Glass *Optimum Art Glass, Inc.*
Simply Stated Rub-on Words *Making Memories*
Adhesive Lettering *The C-Thru Ruler Company*
Ribbon *Offray Ribbon*
Mica Tile Sheets *Available from Stampington & Company*
Red Marbles *Plaid Enterprises, Inc.*
Ink Pad *Color Box*
Rubber Stamp Quote *Inkadinkado*
Silver Zig Pen *Kuretake, Co. Ltd.*

TECHNIQUE HINT

Mica tiles are multi-sheets of micro thin layers. Peel away layers to alter the shade.

happiness

Mica Tiles and Stained Glass Pieces

Christa and I never looked happier than on this memorable day. Sharing good times brings us closer together. Select a sheet of 12 x 12-inch patterned paper for the base. Using a sharp craft knife, cut a piece of spiral vellum on a diagonal making a wavy edge. Mount on patterned paper with transparent drying glue. Trim a piece of blue flowered ribbon; adhere diagonally across the page, and accent with blue stained glass pieces. Double mat photos on solid purple paper and patterned paper leaving a 1/8-inch border. Outline the photographs and the patterned paper border with a silver marker pen. Stamp quotation on mica with gold colored ink. Rub down the word "happiness" on a sheet of mica; place a piece of torn vellum underneath, and accent with a red marble. Place the words "It's Your Day!" and "All My Love" on a piece of thin mica and highlight with stained glass pieces and red marbles. Happiness is celebrating a special day with my daughter.

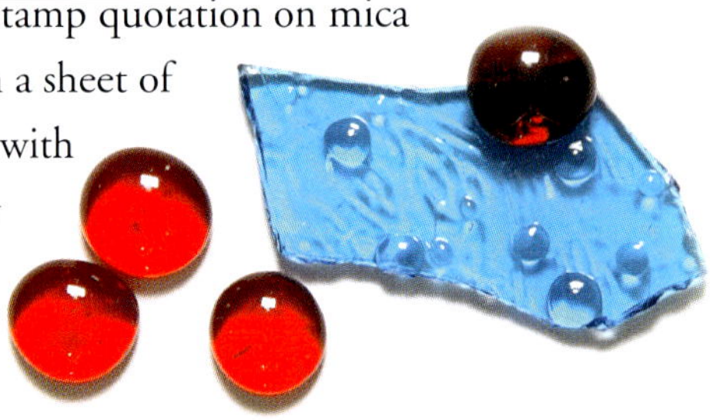

HOW-TO STEPS

happiness

mica tiles and stained glass pieces

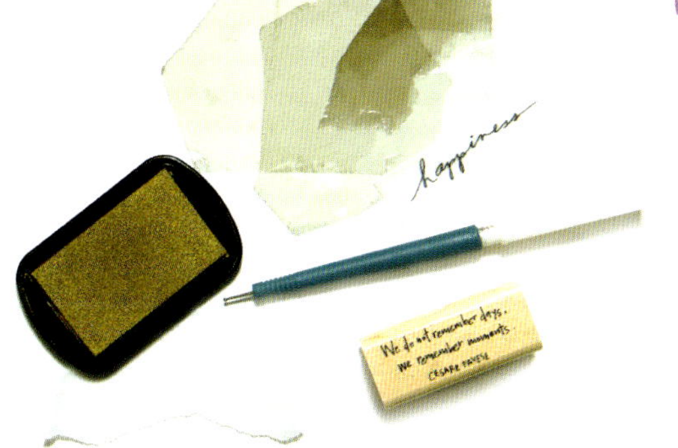

MATERIALS

Mica Tile Sheets
Rubber Stamp
Gold Ink Pad
Rub-on Lettering
Vellum

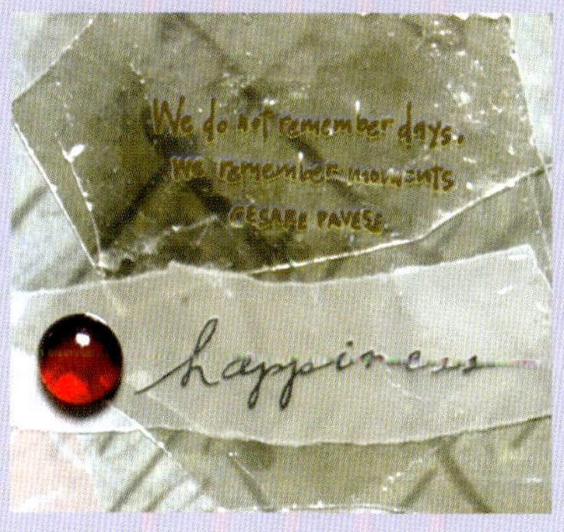

STEP 1

Peel away several mica sheets to obtain a warmer tone. Tear in an irregular shape.

STEP 2

Imprint rubber stamp quotation in gold ink.

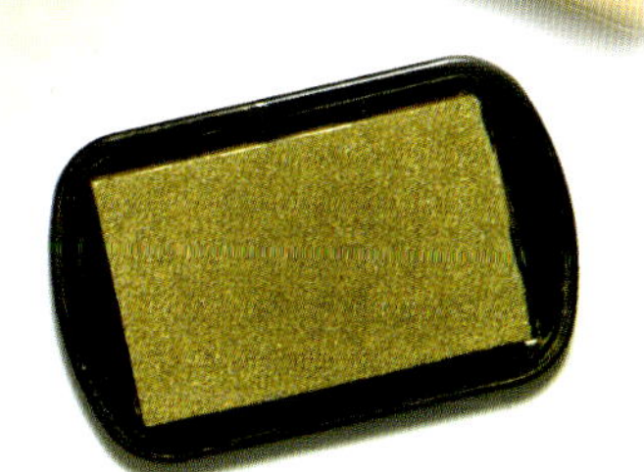

STEP 3

Rub down the word "happiness" on a sheet of mica. To make word legible, place a piece of torn vellum underneath.

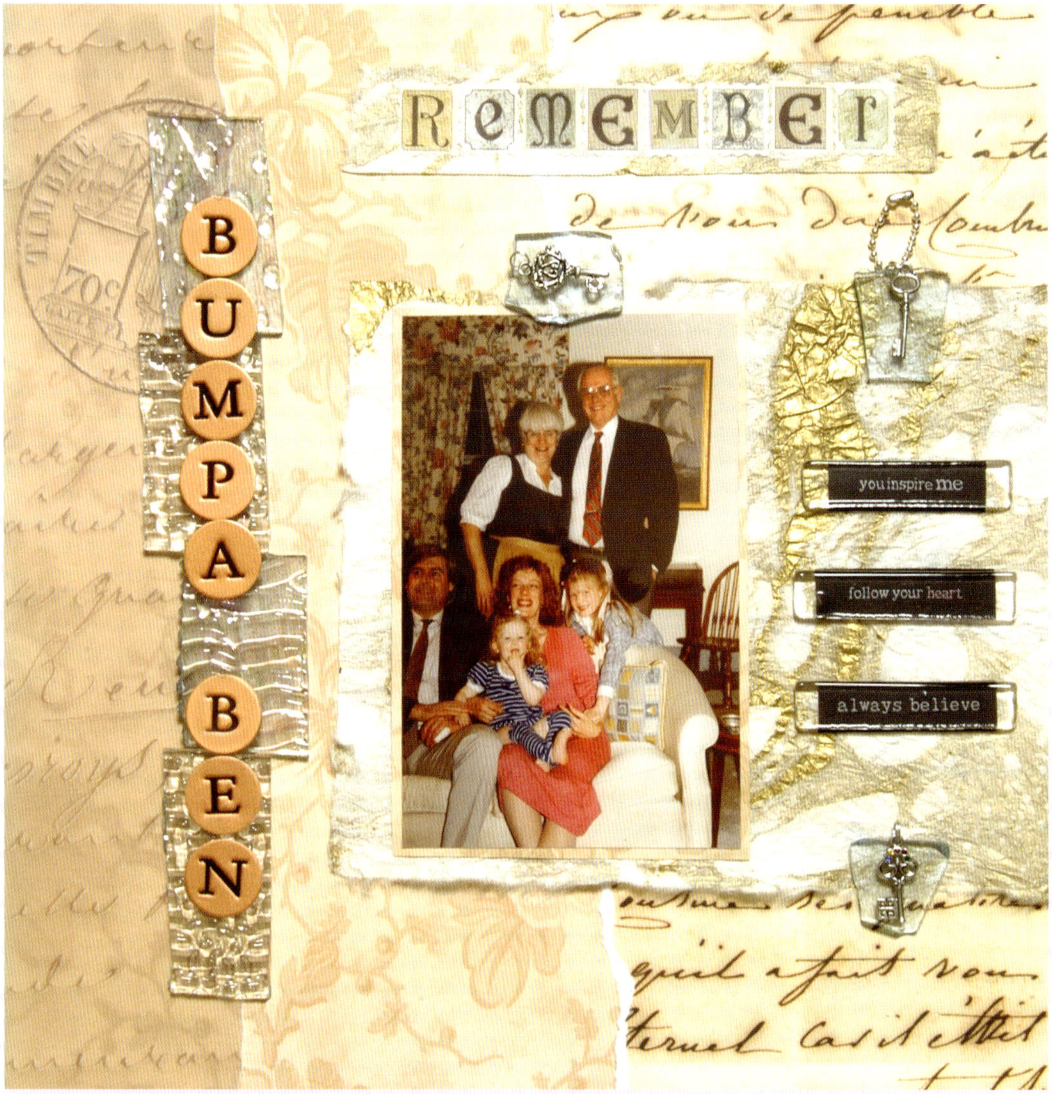

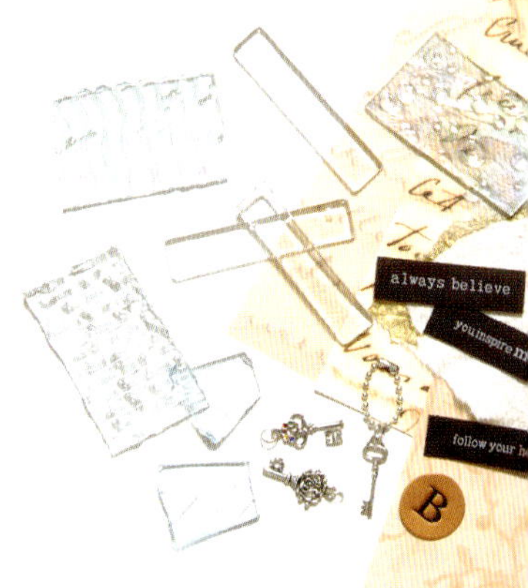

MATERIALS

- Patterned Paper *K&Company*
- Patterned Vellum *K&Company*
- Gold Rice Paper *Black Ink*
- Transparent Glass *Cobbs*
- Clear Glass Bars *Available from Stampington & Company*
- Woven Labels *Me & My Big Ideas*
- Key Charms *The Card Connection*
- Metal Stickers *Sticko*
- Sonnets Scrapbook Letters *Creative Imaginations, Inc.*

TECHNIQUE HINT

Choose clear or iridescent glass pieces that have surface texture imbedded in the glass such as lines, air bubbles or shapes.

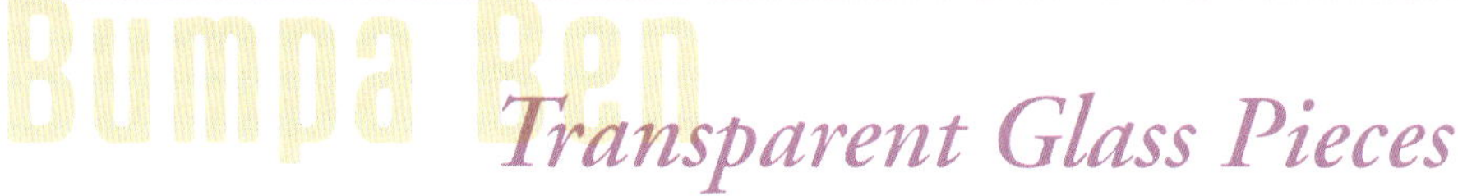

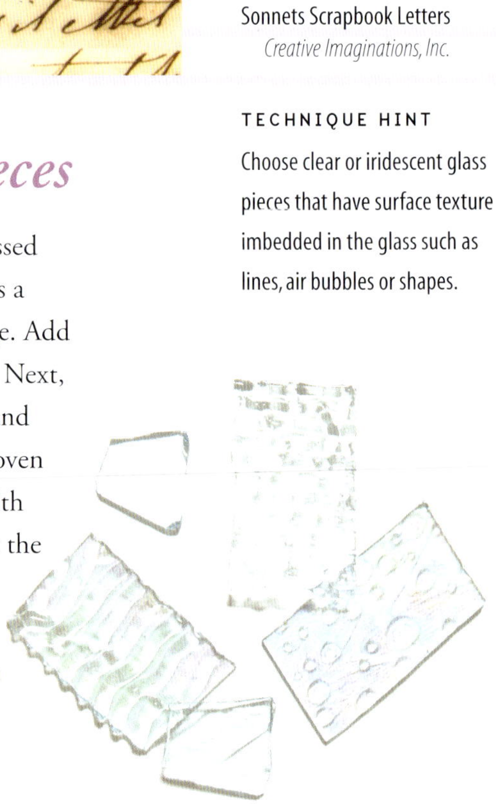

Transparent Glass Pieces

Grandfathers are a special part of every family and Bumpa Ben is truly missed by everyone in the family. Select a piece of 12 x 12-inch patterned paper as a background. Adhere a torn strip of vellum on the left hand side of the page. Add a 5-inch strip of script patterned paper and mount on the right hand side. Next, tear a piece of 8 x 6.5-inch gold rice paper and mount horizontally. Trim and mount photograph on patterned paper leaving a 1/8-inch border. Place woven inspirational labels beneath clear glass bars and glue in position. Accent with clear glass pieces and key charms. Place a row of glass pieces vertically over the vellum paper and attach the metal letter stickers with the name "Bumpa Ben." To complete the page, tear a strip of gold rice paper and attach postage stamp letters. All grandchildren love their grandfather and Bumpa Ben is the key to our hearts.

discover spectacular beauty

Flat Marbles and Vintage Optical Lens

Baby Julia is the picture of innocence and serenity as she sleeps cuddled in her mother's arms. Begin with a 12 x 12-inch piece of lavender embossed paper. Tear a piece of green embossed paper on a diagonal and mount leaving a 1/4-inch border. Next, mount photograph on green mesh leaving a 1/2-inch border. Place mounted photo on a piece of blue patterned paper and accent with flat marbles. Place a glass capsule filled with sand in the upper right hand corner of the photo. Stamp vintage optical lens with a butterfly stamp, emboss edge with blue embossing powder and adhere to the page. Tear two pieces of swirled vellum, position above and below the photo and rub down the words "Discover Spectacular Beauty" on the vellum. Cut a 12-inch piece of 1.5-inch wide ribbon and mount on left hand page. Finish with a row of flat marbles and add a dimensional butterfly sticker. Discovering motherhood is a beautiful and memorable moment.

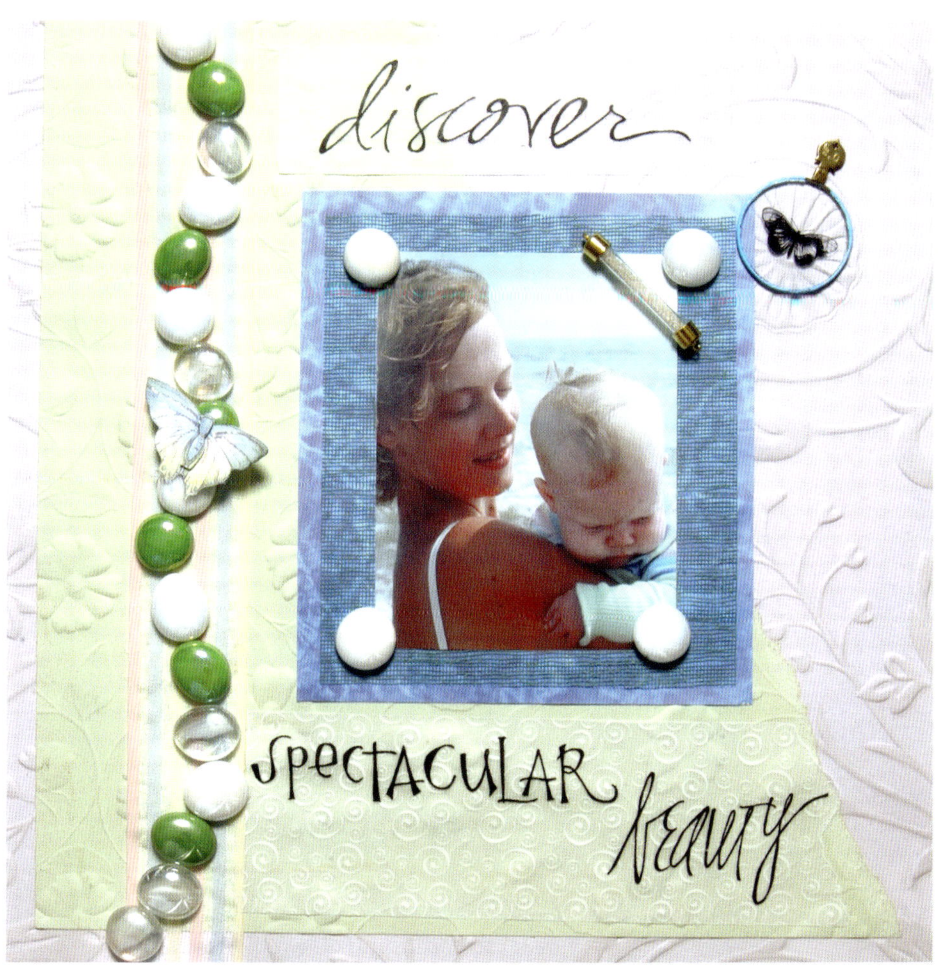

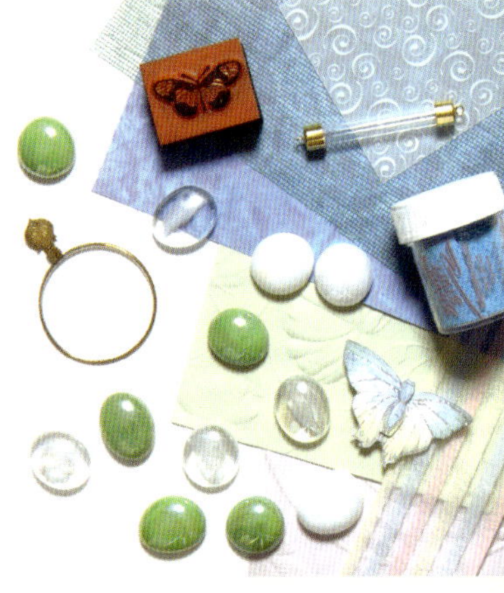

MATERIALS

Embossed Paper *K&Company*

Patterned Paper *The Paper Company*

Vellum Swirl Paper *Paper Pizazz*

Green Mesh *Aitoh*

Flat Marbles *Mega Marbles*

Butterfly Dimensional Sticker *K&Company*

Striped Ribbon *Michaels Stores, Inc.*

Butterfly Stamp *Inkadinkado*

Glass Capsule *7 Gypsies*

Vintage Optical Lens *Available from Stampington & Company*

Simply Stated Rub-on Words *Making Memories*

Black Ink Pad *Color Box*

Blue Embossing Powder *Stamp-n Stuff*

TECHNIQUE HINT

When mounting an optical lens, glue the stamped-side down to prevent smearing.

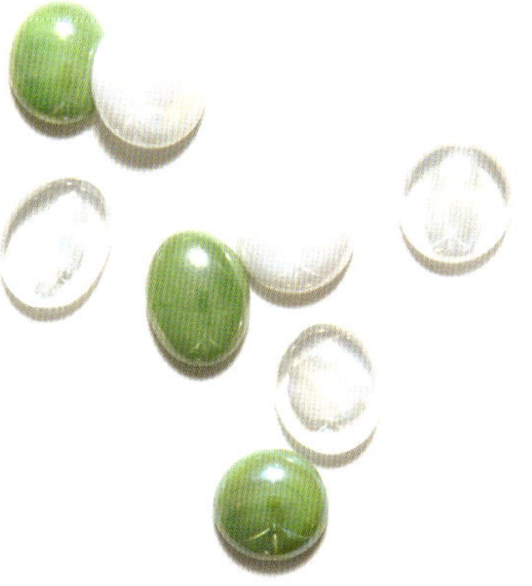

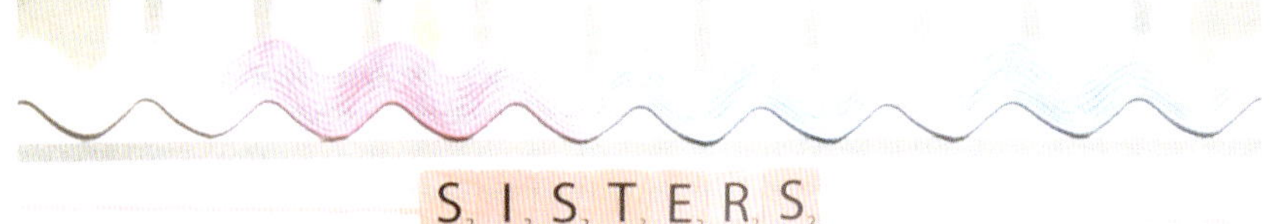

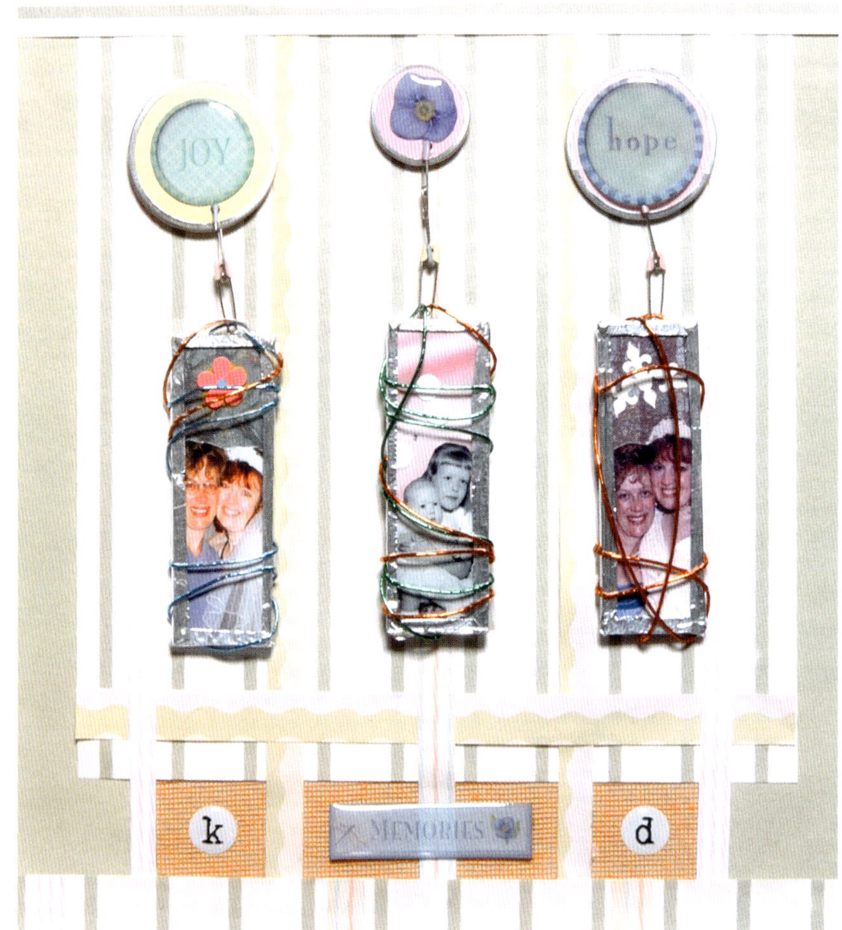

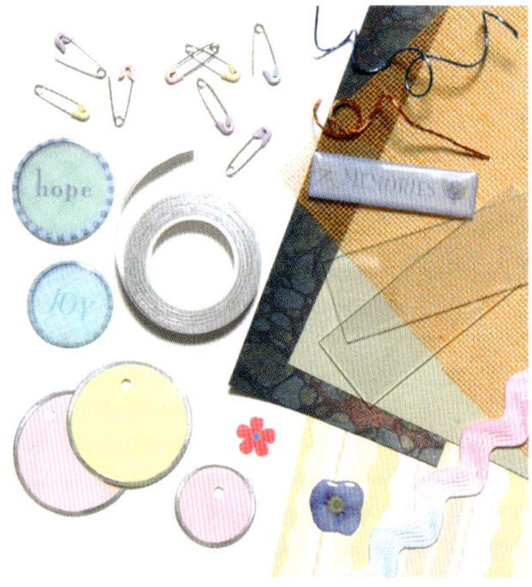

MATERIALS

Patterned Papers *K&Company*
Microscope Slides *Hobbylinc.com*
Safety Pins *Making Memories*
Silver Foil Tape *Metalworks™*
Hang Tags *Treasured Memories*
Bubble Letters *Li'l Davis Designs™*
24 Gauge Jewelry Wire *Nicole*
Dimensional Dome Resin Stickers *K&Company*

TECHNIQUE HINT

Microscope collages can be created using different color foil tape, wires, beads or rubber stamps.

sisters

Microscope Slides

The relationship between sisters is very close and cherished. This page is dedicated to that loving friendship. Cut patterned paper in strips and glue on top of striped paper. Glue a border of ric rac trim across the top of the page. Create a mini collage with photographs and patterned paper; insert between microscope slides and seal with foil tape. Wrap colorful metallic wire diagonally around the slide assemblage and attach baby safety pins. Pin to metal hang tags and add dome resin stickers. For the bottom border, mount mesh screen, add "Memories" dome sticker and bubble letters. Although we live far apart, this scrapbook page reminds us of the special love we share as sisters.

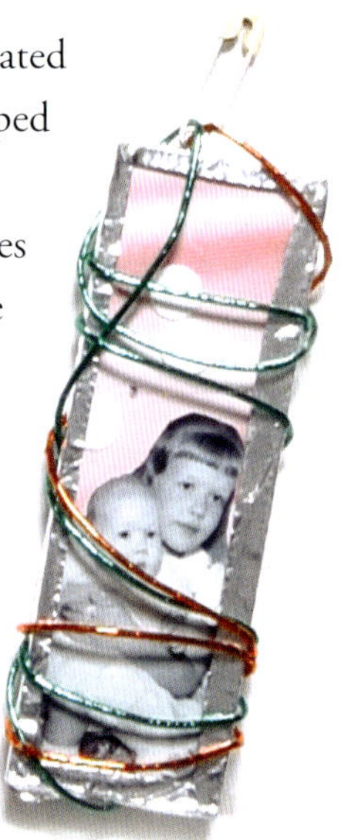

HOW-TO STEPS

microscope slides

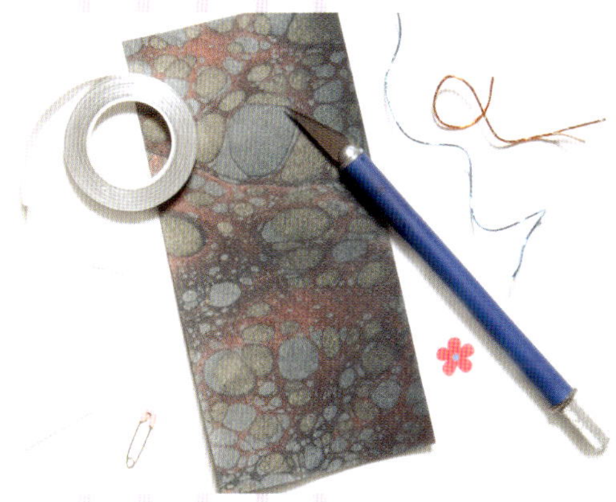

MATERIALS

Patterned Paper
Microscope Slides
Silver Foil Tape
24 Gauge Jewelry Wire
Craft Knife

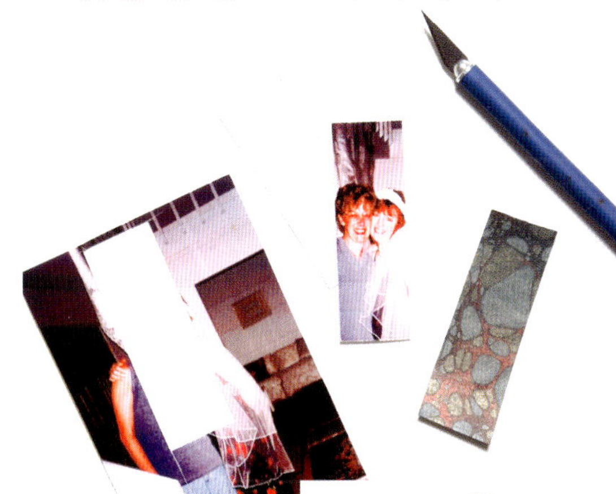

STEP 1
Use a microscope slide as a template to cut photos and patterned paper.

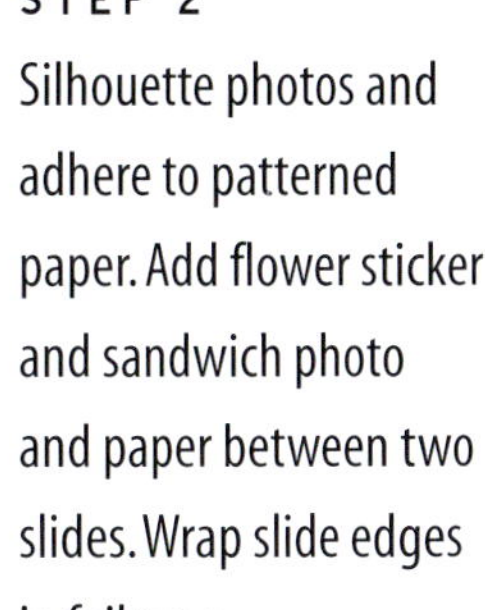

STEP 2
Silhouette photos and adhere to patterned paper. Add flower sticker and sandwich photo and paper between two slides. Wrap slide edges in foil tape.

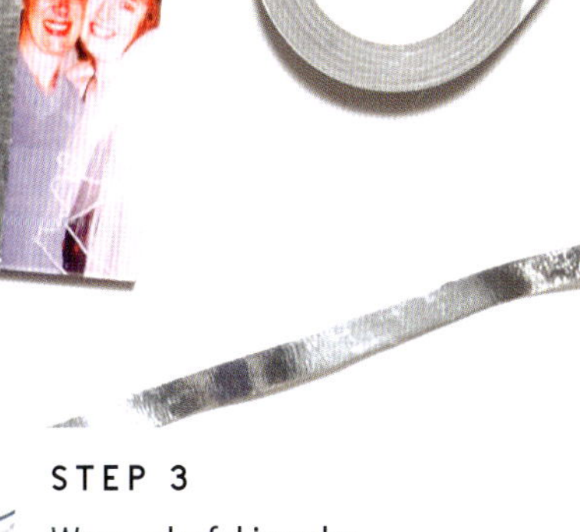

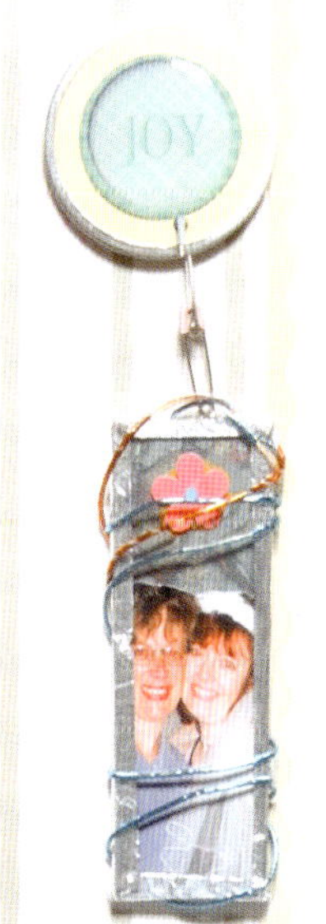

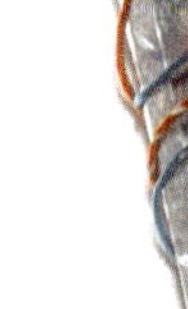

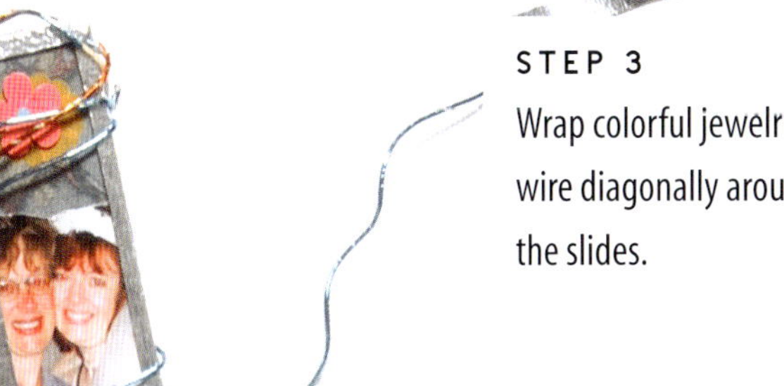

STEP 3
Wrap colorful jewelry wire diagonally around the slides.

Eclectic

Altered Designs

What's old is definitely new again! How about adding zippers or bottle caps to your scrapbook layouts! Like the altered book phenomenon, altered scrapbooking is the in vogue alternative to creating traditional scrapbook pages. Create retro, vintage or eclectic themes with new scrapbook materials including—real zipper stickers, vintage optical lenses, typewriter key stickers, faux postage stamp stickers, bottle caps,—and much more. Use your personal ephemera including foreign currency, bingo cards, game pieces, dominos and even old ticket stubs. Altered scrapbooking is the ultimate form of artistic experimentation. Juxtapose any texture, any medium, and any material to reach your desired results. There are no rules, no patterns and no set formulas. There's no right way, no wrong way, there's only your way. This new-found freedom gives scrapbookers the license to use every imaginative or whimsical approach without fearing the wrath of the scrapbooking gods.

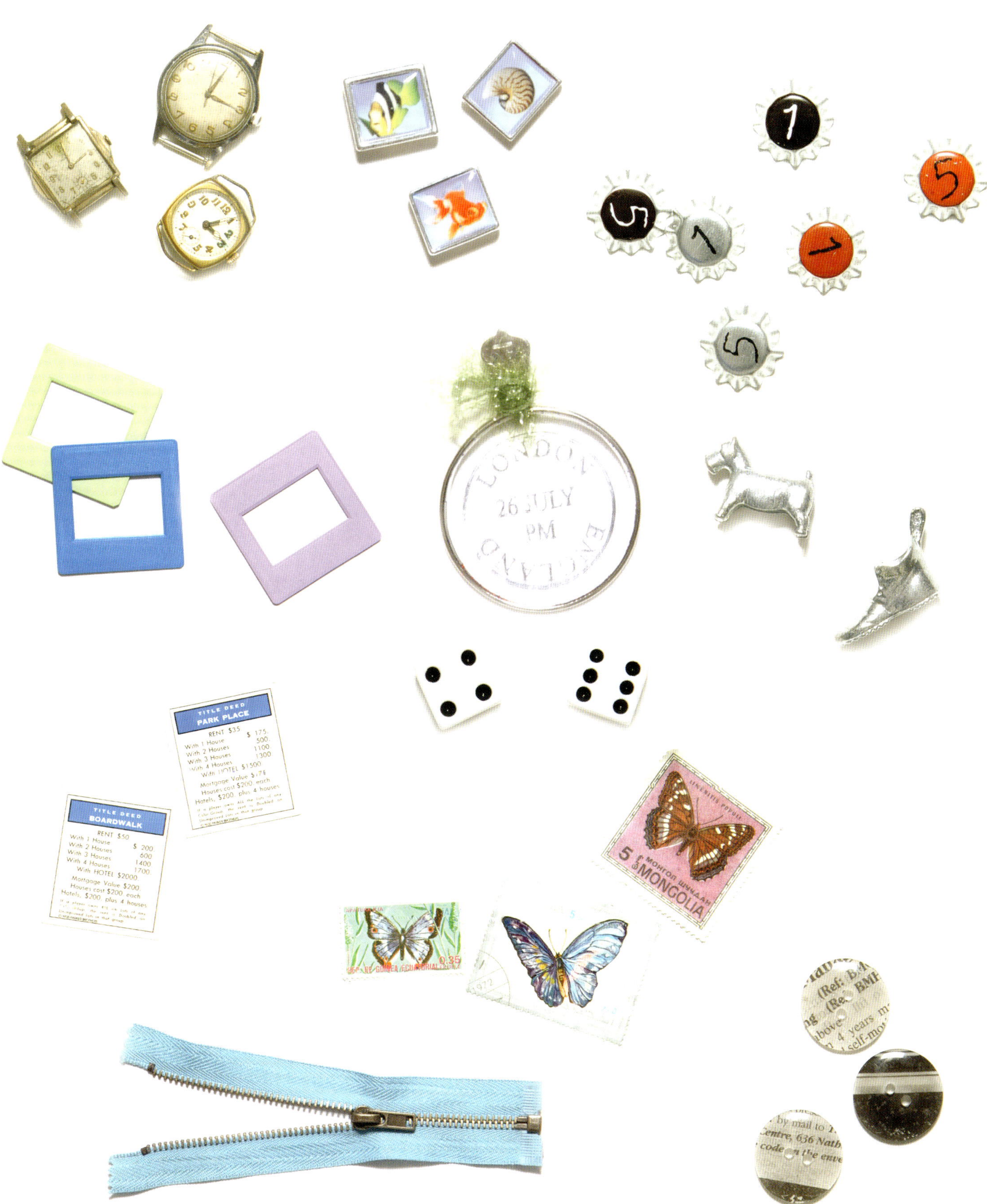
LONDON
26 JULY
PM
ENGLAND
TITLE DEED
PARK PLACE
RENT $35
With 1 House $ 175
With 2 Houses 500
With 3 Houses 1100
With 4 Houses 1300
With HOTEL $1500
Mortgage Value $175
Houses cost $200 each
Hotels, $200 plus 4 houses
TITLE DEED
BOARDWALK
RENT $50
With 1 House $ 200
With 2 Houses 600
With 3 Houses 1400
With 4 Houses 1700
With HOTEL $2000
Mortgage Value $200
Houses cost $200 each
Hotels, $200 plus 4 houses
5
MONGOLIA
0.35

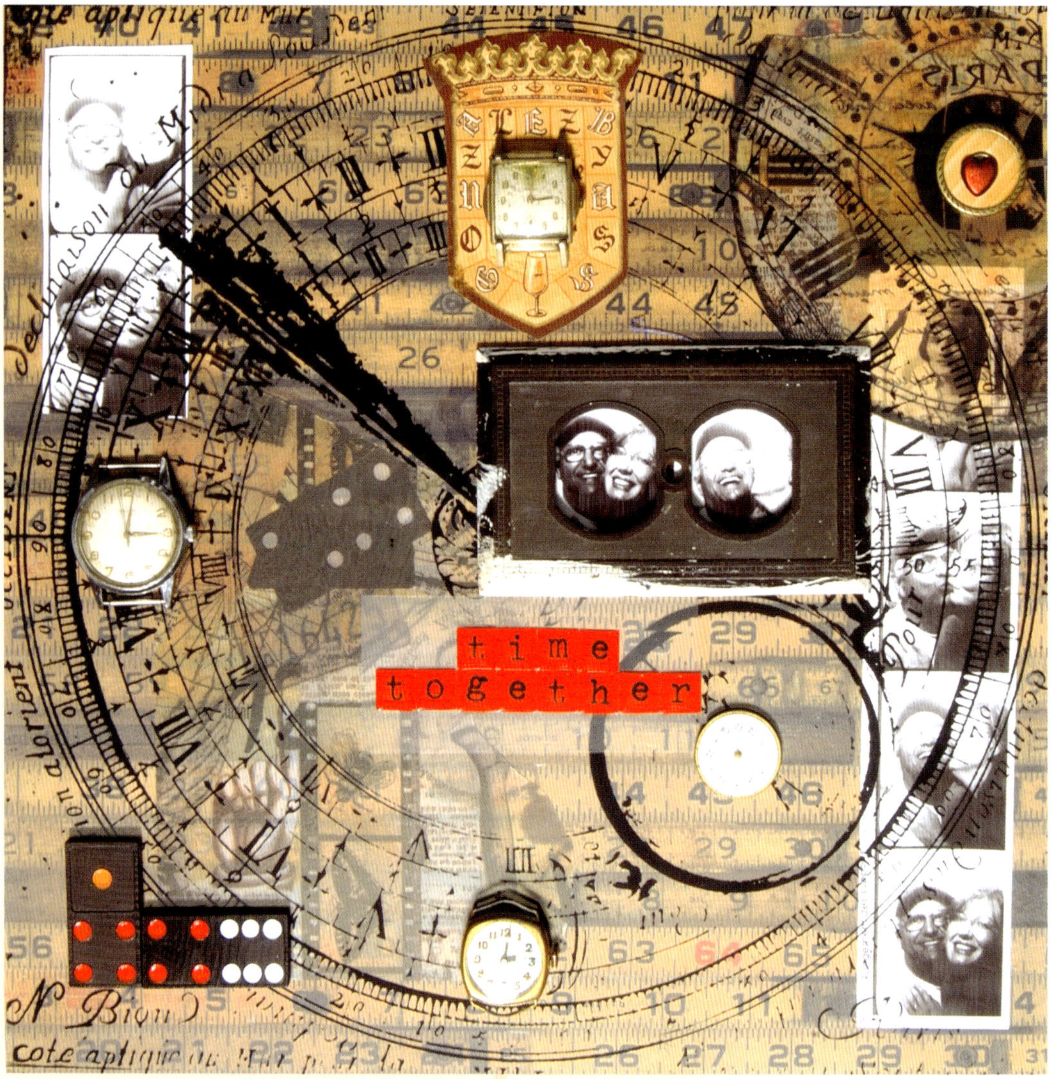

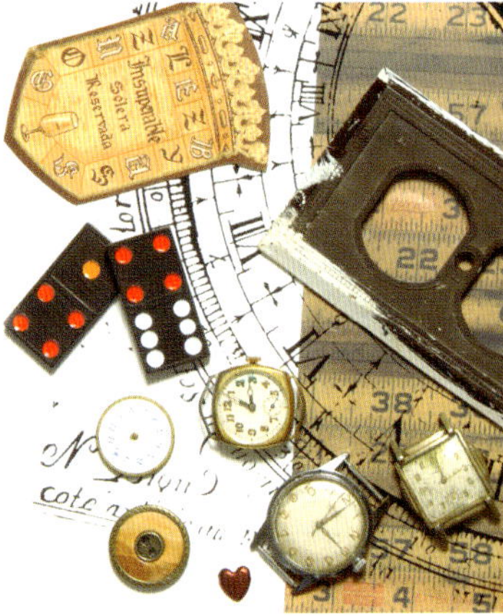

MATERIALS

Patterned Paper *K&Company*

Printed Acetate *K&Company*

Patterned Vellum *DMD*

Watches *Personal Collection*

Vintage Button and Outlet Plate *Antique Shop*

Dominos *Personal Collection*

Heart Brad *Treasured Memories*

Wine Label *Personal Collection*

Bubble Letters *Li'l Davis Designs™*

TECHNIQUE HINT

Make your own printed transparency by copying patterned paper onto acetate.

Watch Faces and Dominos

Sharing precious time working together is a luxury we both enjoy immensely. Choose a sheet of 12 x12-inch altered ruler paper. Cut pieces of patterned vellum and mount on top. Copy and trim photo-booth pictures, and mount them vertically in opposite corners. Adhere a piece of 12 x12-inch printed acetate over the entire page. Cut two photos, insert headshots behind the outlet plate and adhere to transparency layer. Remove watchbands from antique watches; bond watch faces to page, and fasten wine label behind watch face. Spell "Time Together" title with red bubble letters. Insert a red heart brad through a vintage button; position in upper right corner, and accent with multicolored dominos. Each day we spend together adds another happy page to our married life experiences.

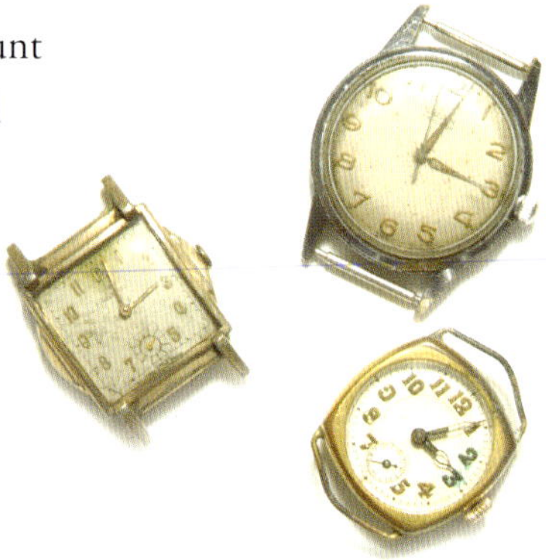

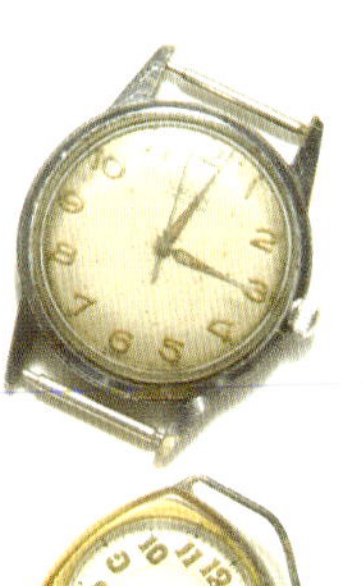

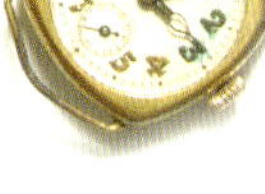

water polo Life Photo Tiles

Our niece was the only female player on the Amherst water polo team. Select a sheet of 12 x 12-inch patterned paper. Trim photo 8 x 5-inches and adhere to patterned paper. Cut a figure from the Antiquities collection transparency sheet and adhere in the upper corner of the photo. Select two images from the blue Winter collection transparency sheet and adhere under the photo. Glue clear glass rods next to the blue transparency pieces; slide marine life photo tiles on rods and center. Rub down the "My Life" lettering words and imprint rubber stamp decorative urn. Adhere "Water Polo" bubble letters on the blue patterned paper. Water polo is a very demanding physical sport. Catherine's ability to play water polo on the men's team demonstrates her innate competitive skills.

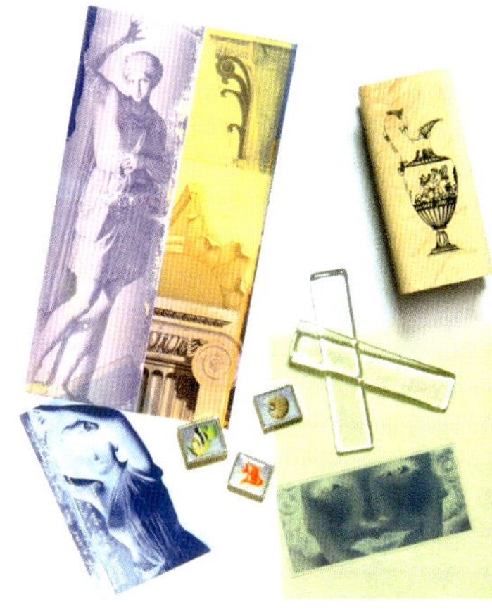

MATERIALS

Patterned Paper *K&Company*

Transparency Sheets *Available from Stampington & Company*

Marine Life Photo Tiles *Boxer Scrapbook Productions, LLC*

Clear Glass Rods *Available from Stampington & Company*

Simply Stated Rub-on Words *Making Memories*

Decorative Urn Rubber Stamp *Inkadinkado*

Bubble Letters *Li'l Davis Designs™*

TECHNIQUE HINT

An easy way to align bubble letters is to place them on acetate over lined paper. Here, they can easily be repositioned and straightened.

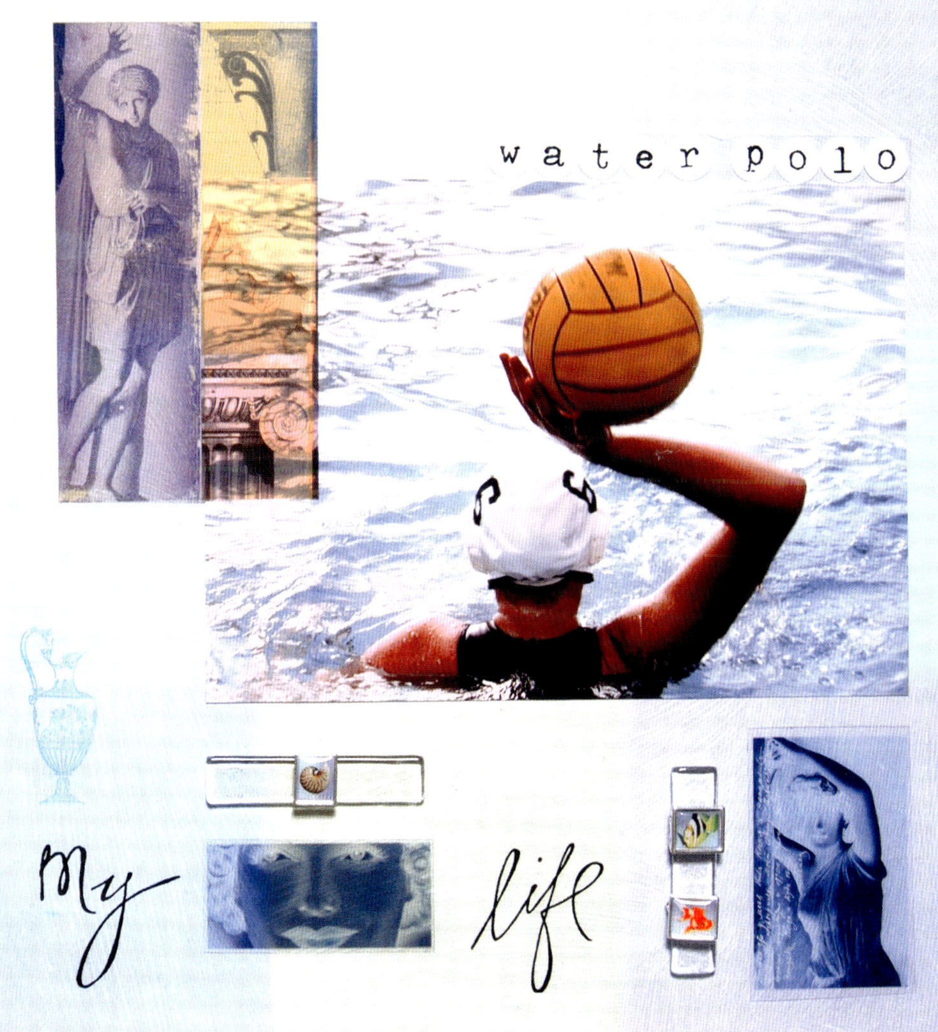

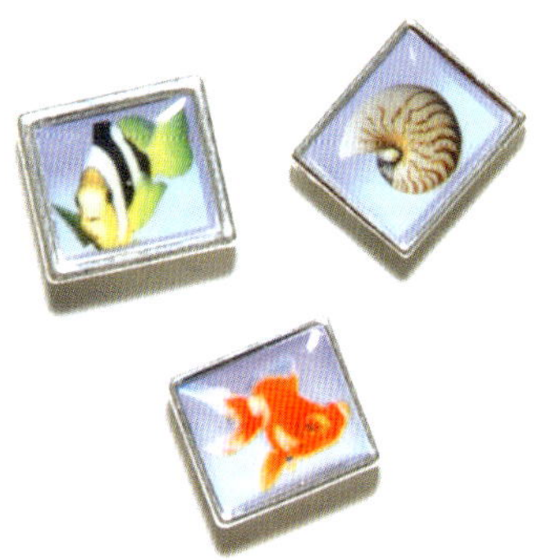

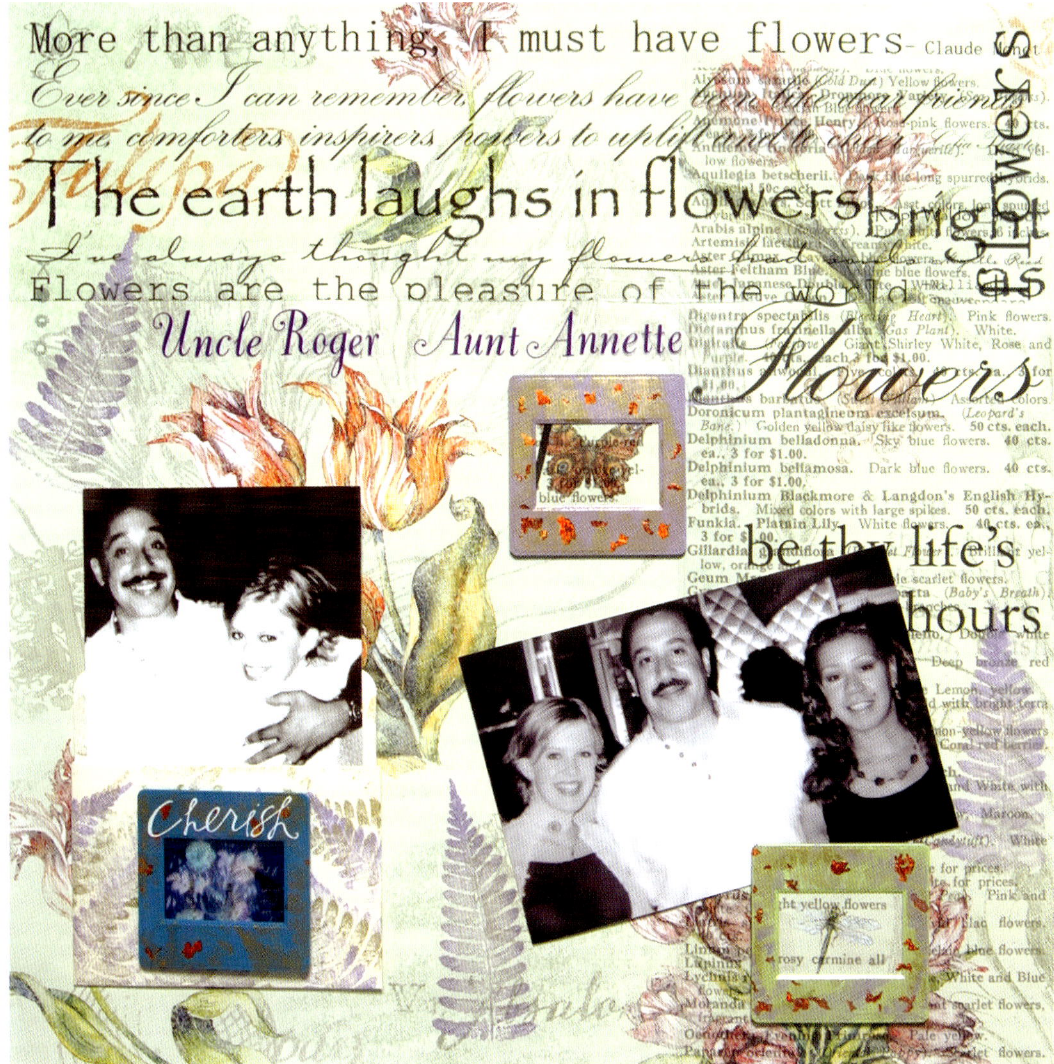

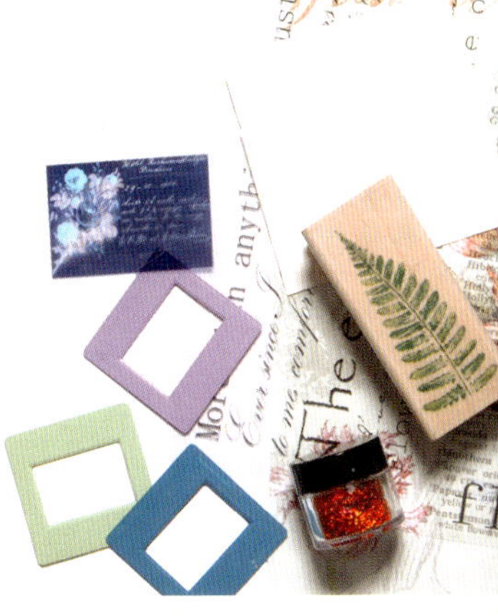

Slide Mounts and Transparency Sheets

Although they live in Seattle, Uncle Roger and Aunt Annette stay in close contact with Julia and her family. Begin with a piece of 12 x 12-inch patterned paper. Slice a sheet of transparency paper in thirds; lay one piece across the top of your layout page, and place a second piece down the right hand side. Next, stamp a book pocket with a fern rubber stamp and insert photo. Rubber stamp each slide with a fern stamp; insert a transparency inside the slide mounts, and decorate slide with gilding leaf. Adhere second photo next to the book pocket to balance the page. Use rub-on type to write the word "Cherish," and apply letter stickers for "Uncle Roger" and "Aunt Annette." Julia enjoys spending a large amount of quality time with her godfather Roger and Aunt Annette.

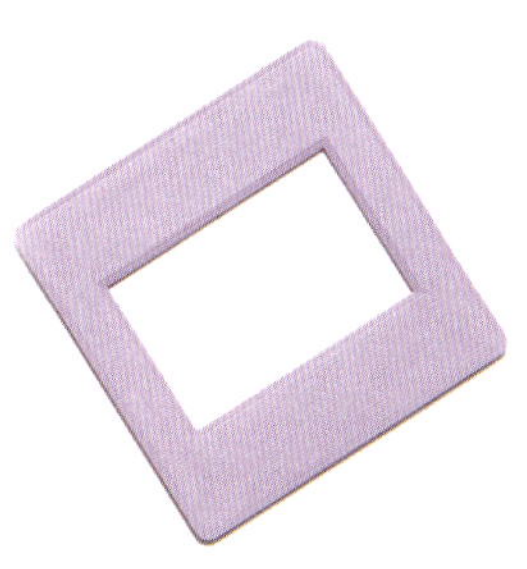

MATERIALS

Patterned Paper *PSX Papers for Creativity*

Transparency Sheet *Creative Imaginations, Inc.*

Book Pocket *Boxer Scrapbook Productions, LLC*

Rubber Stamp *Rubber Stampede*

Metallic Gilding Leaf *US Art Quest, Inc.*

Simply Stated Rub-on Words *Making Memories*

Slide Mounts *Boxer Scrapbook Productions, LLC*

Purple and Gold Solvent Ink Pad *StāzOn*

Letter Stickers *Sandy Lion*

TECHNIQUE HINT

Re-stamp slide mounts after applying the metallic gilding leaf.

HOW-TO STEPS

slide mounts

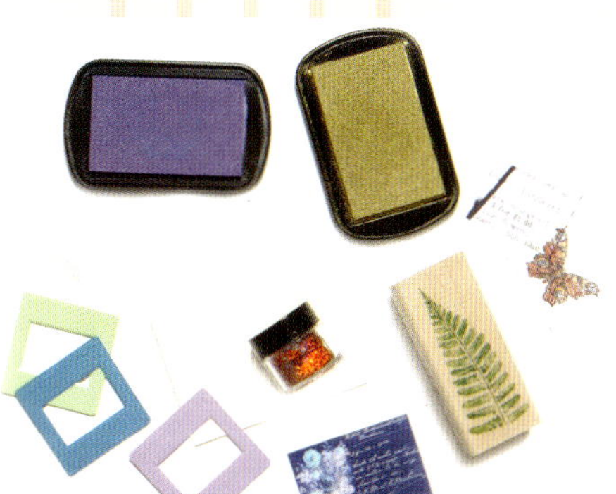

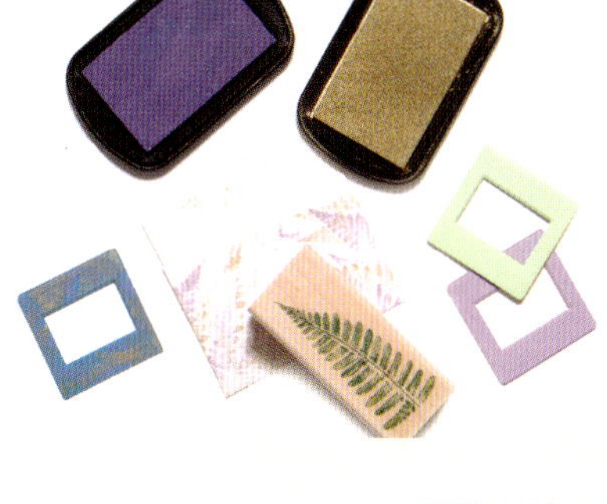

STEP 1

Rubber stamp book pocket and slide mounts with purple and gold solvent ink pad.

MATERIALS

Patterned Paper
Transparency Sheet
Book Pocket
Rubber Stamp
Purple and Gold Solvent Ink Pad
Metallic Gilding Leaf
Simply Stated Rub-on Words
Slide Mounts

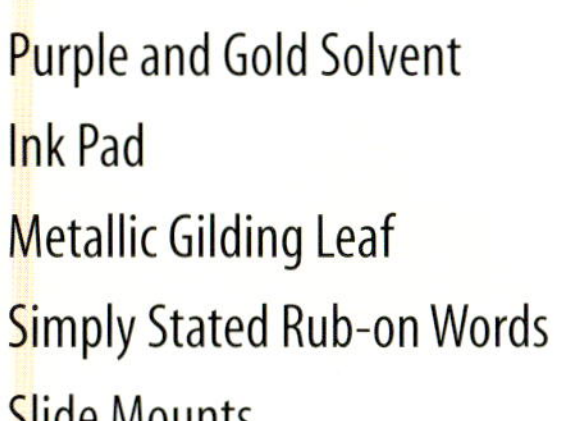

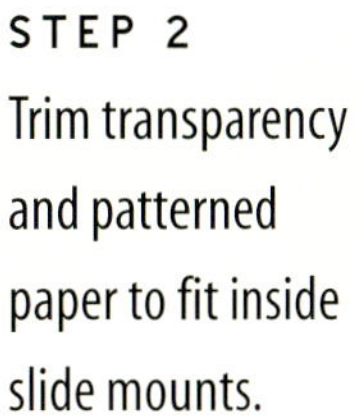

STEP 2

Trim transparency and patterned paper to fit inside slide mounts.

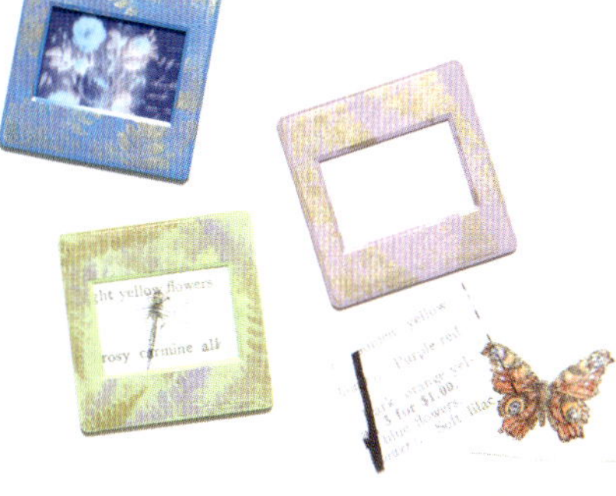

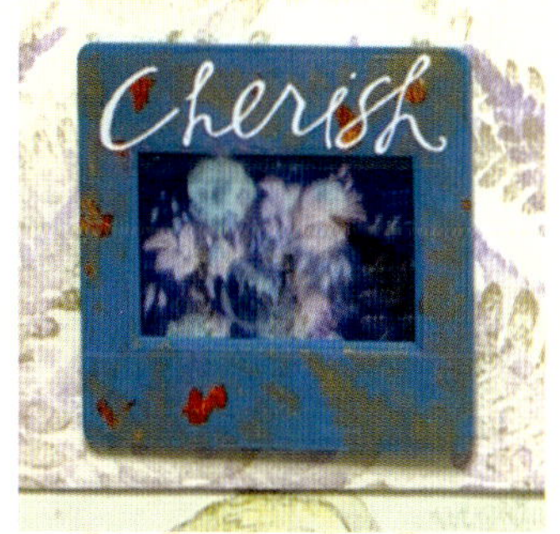

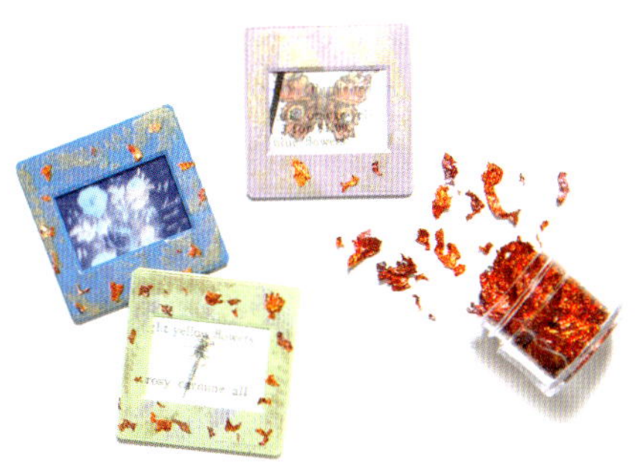

STEP 3

Adhere tiny pieces of metallic gilding leaf to slide mounts.

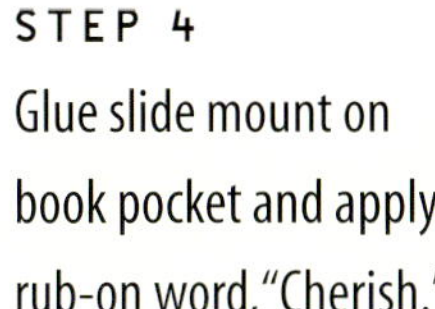

STEP 4

Glue slide mount on book pocket and apply rub-on word, "Cherish."

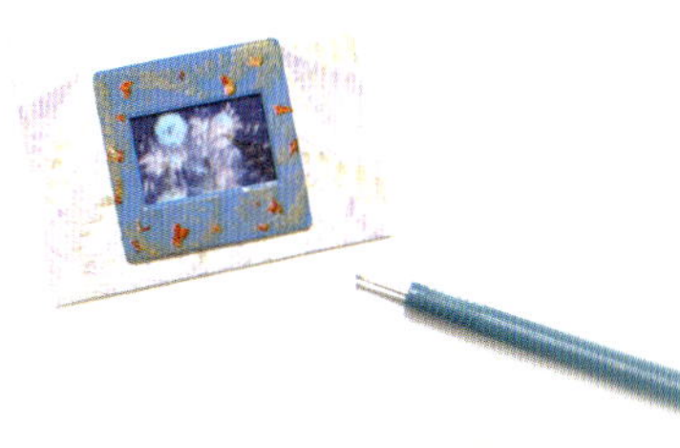

christa

Postage Stamps

Precious pictures of Christa as a little girl are great reminders of a happy childhood. Select a sheet of 12 x 12-inch solid purple paper as a foundation. Cut a piece of 8.5 x 10-inch vellum butterfly paper and place on top of solid paper. Add a sheet of 9 x 7.5-inch patterned paper. Place a small piece of vellum in the lower left hand corner. Trim photo and mount with a butterfly postage stamp. Next, mount small photo on round playing card and accent with a blue transparency sheet butterfly. Rubber stamp tag with a butterfly and accent page with newspaper buttons and butterfly playing card. Create the name "Christa" with selected lettering from your collection. It's wonderful preserving lasting memories of a precious little girl.

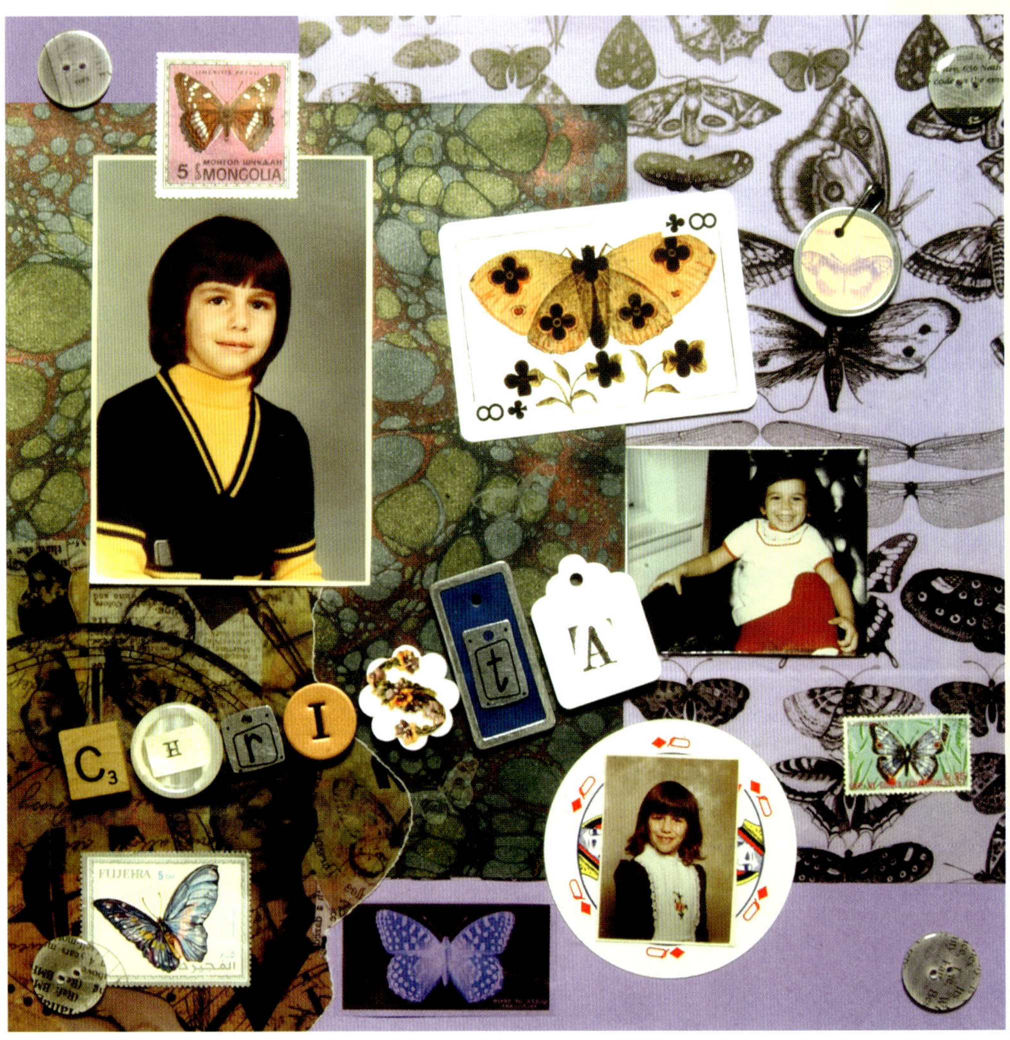

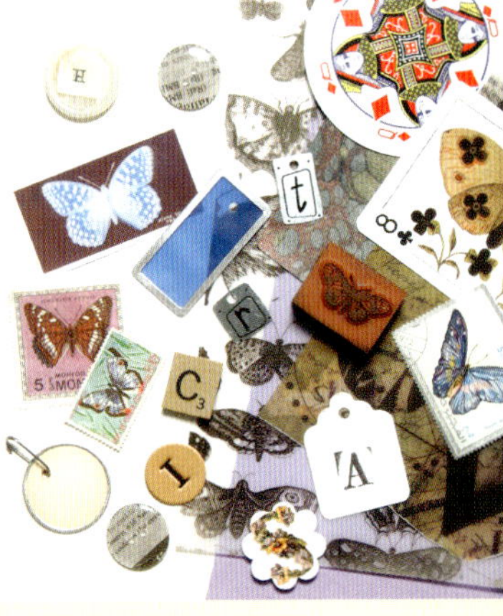

MATERIALS

Patterned Paper *Black Ink*
Solid Paper *Making Memories*
Vellum Butterfly Paper *DMD*
Round Playing Cards *Toy Store*
Butterfly Postage Stamps *Personal Collection*
Card Collage Pack *Available from Stampington & Company*
Transparency Sheet *Available from Stampington & Company*
Newspaper Buttons *Available from Stampington & Company*
Butterfly Rubber Stamp *Inkadinkado*
Letter C Wood Letter *Scrabble®*
Letter H Sticker *Sticko*
Letter R Alphabet Tagz *Provo Craft*
Letter I Metal Letter *Sticko*
Letter S Sticker Letter *The Gifted Line*
Letter T Alphabet Tagz *Provo Craft*
Letter A Rubber Stamp Letter *Brenda Walter*

TECHNIQUE HINT

It's fun creating letters from different scrapbook elements. Find and clip lettering from magazines, newspapers and advertisements.

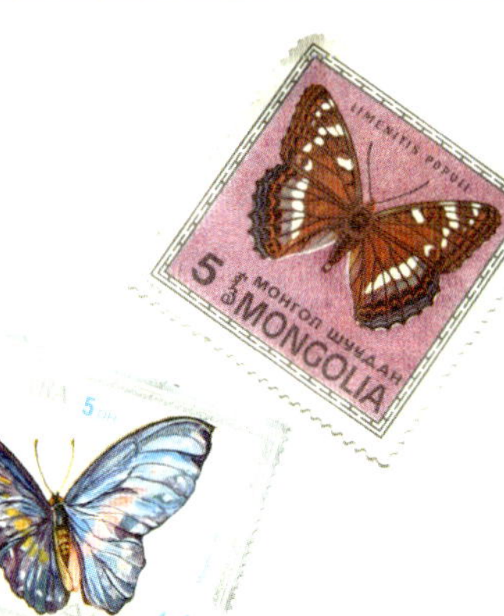

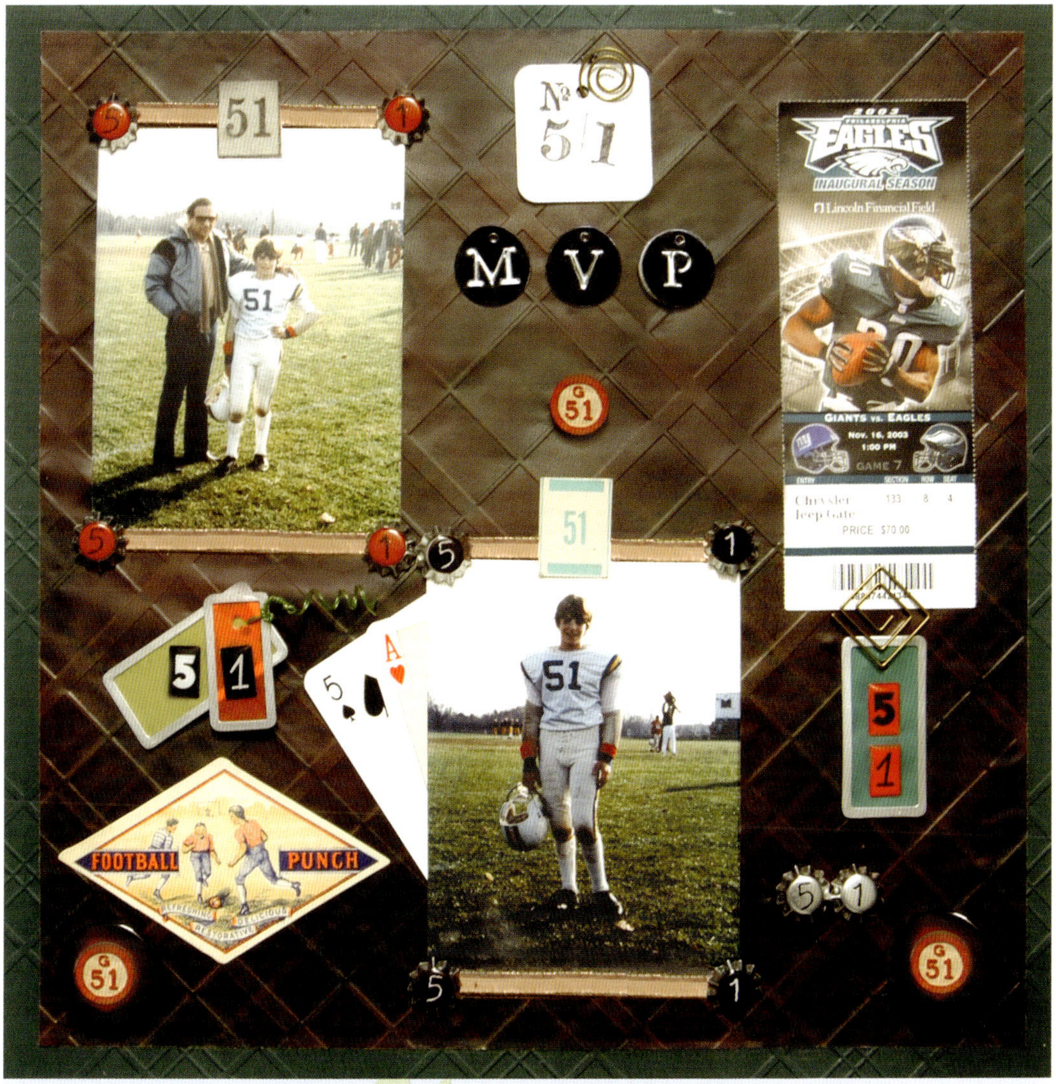

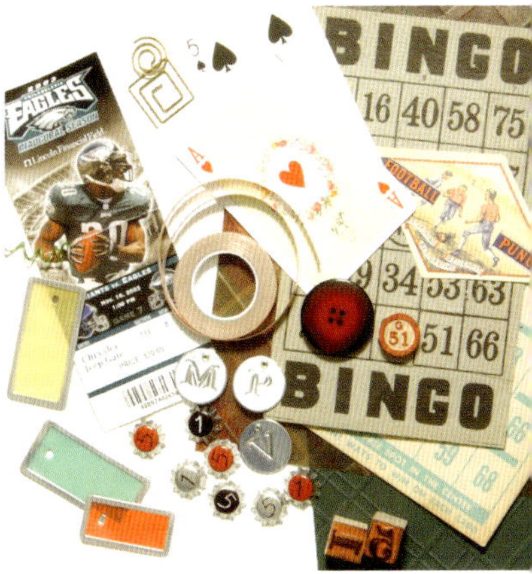

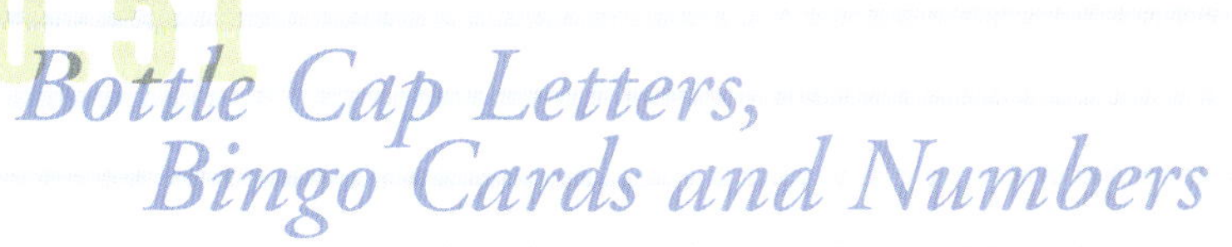

Bottle Cap Letters, Bingo Cards and Numbers

As a young boy, my son Michael enjoyed many exciting fall weekends playing football on his neighborhood team. For the base, begin with a sheet of 12 x12-inch embossed paper. Trim embossed vellum 1/2-inch on two sides and center on base paper. Attach copper foil tape on top and bottom edge of each photograph and mount. Insert playing cards under the photograph. Cut the number 51 from bingo cards and glue on the top metal strip of each photo. Using foam spacers, adhere bottle cap numbers 5 and 1 to each corner of the photos. Loop wire and metal clip through vellum tags and attach bubble numbers. Mount football ticket stub and ephemera sticker in opposite corners, and place G51 Bingo numbers on vintage circular buttons. Stamp No. 51 on white tag and attach a circular clip. Finally, dip MVP metal letters in black ink and adhere to page. As an adult, Michael continues pursuing his love of football as a passionate fan of the Philadelphia Eagles.

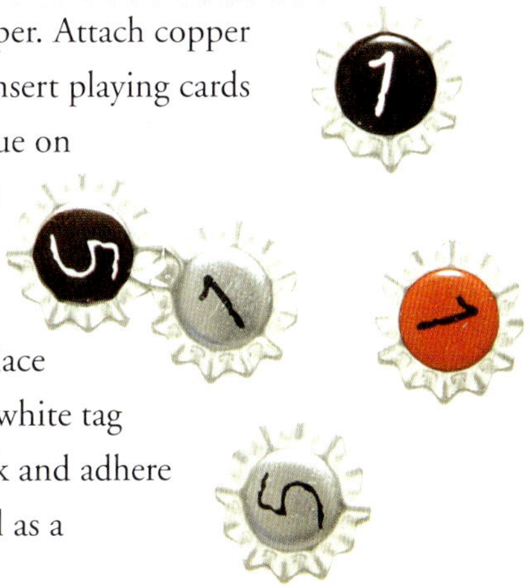

MATERIALS

- Embossed Paper *K&Company*
- Embossed Vellum *K&Company*
- Metal Letter Stickers *Sticko*
- Vintage Buttons *Antique Shop*
- Vellum Tags *Making Memories*
- Ephemera Sticker *Scrappychic™*
- Rubber Number Stamp *Brenda Walter*
- Card Collage Pack *Available from Stampington & Company*
- Copper Foil Tape *Metalworks™*
- Bingo Cards *Personal Collection*
- Eagles' Ticket Stub *Personal Collection*
- Black Solvent Ink *StāzOn*
- Digi Bottle Caps *Li'l Davis Designs™*
- Shaped Clips *Making Memories*
- Bubble Numbers *Li'l Davis Designs™*
- Jewelry Wire *Nicole*

TECHNIQUE HINT

If you are unable to find miniature scrapbook bottle caps, use real bottle caps and paint them.

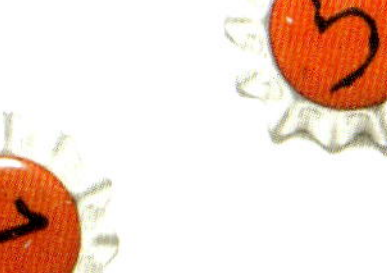

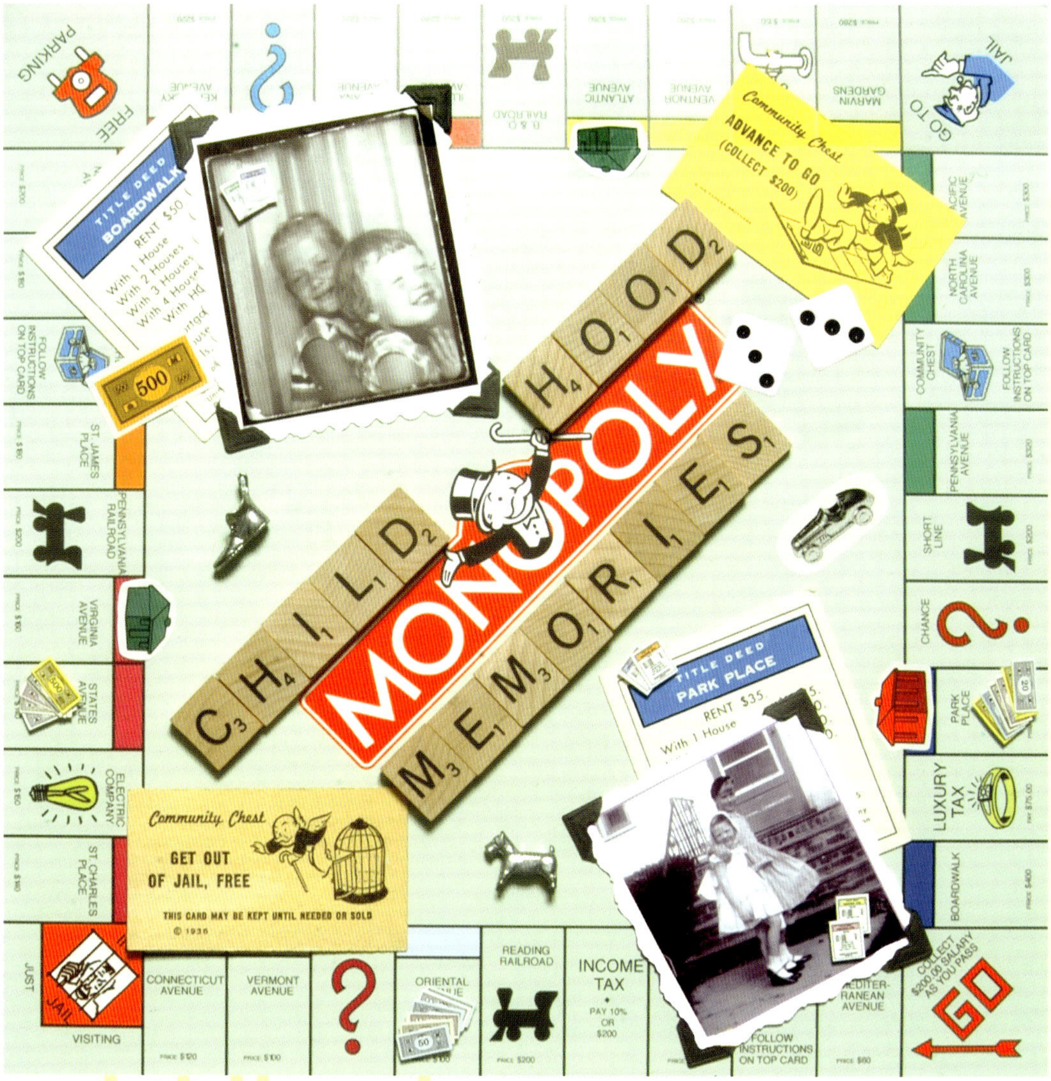

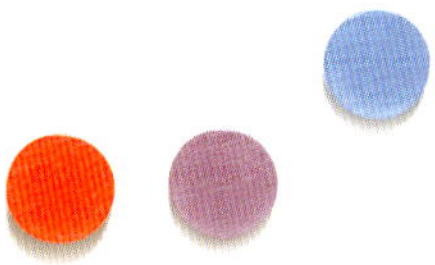

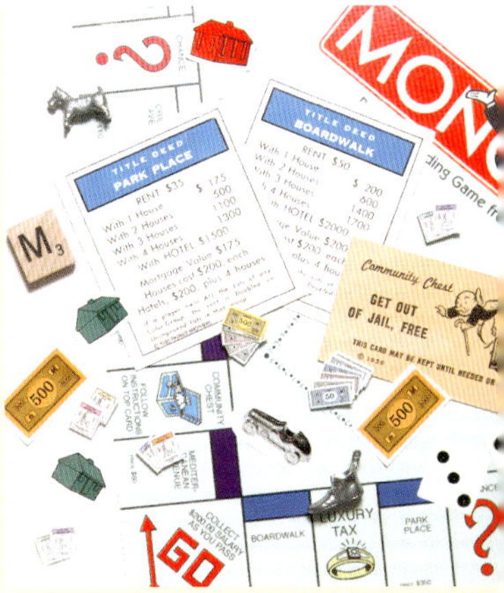

childhood memories

Board Game Monopoly™

As children, my sister Deborah and I spent many happy hours playing our favorite board game in the attic of our home on Edgewood Avenue. Select a 12 x 12-inch sheet of scrapbook Monopoly paper for your game page foundation. Trim black and white photos with deckle or scallop scissors and insert photo corners. Mount photos on Boardwalk and Park Place Monopoly game cards. Select two Community Chest cards and adhere in opposite corners. Photocopy game dice, cut out and glue to scrapbook page layout. Select Scrabble letters and create the title, "Childhood Memories." To complete, glue original pieces from Monopoly game on scrapbook page, and accent page with Monopoly scrapbook stickers. Today as adults, we continue to enjoy getting out of jail free and buying green plastic homes and red hotels.

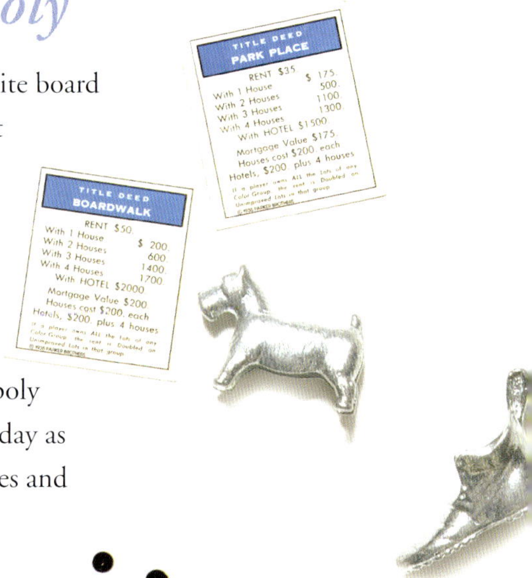

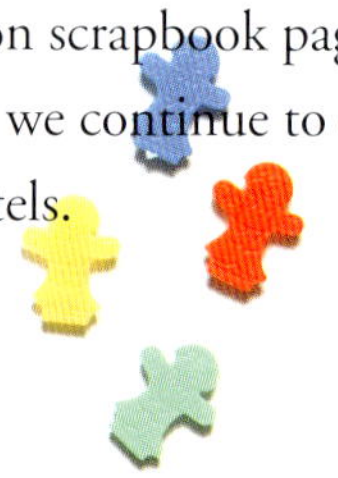

MATERIALS

Monopoly™ Game Board Paper *EK Success*
Monopoly™ Vintage Game Pieces *Hasbro*
Monopoly™ Sticker Collage *Jolee's Boutique*
Photo Corners *Canson*
Lettering *Scrabble®*
Game Dice *Hasbro*
Monopoly™ Stickers *Trend Enterprises*

TECHNIQUE HINT

Photocopy game dice, cut out and adhere to page layout.

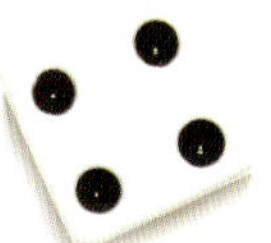

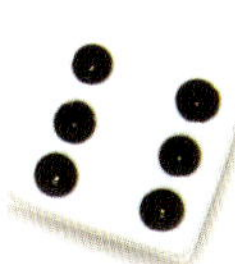

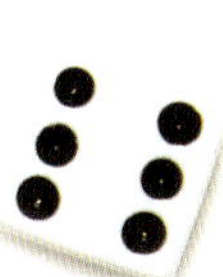

HOW-TO IDEAS

childhood memories board games

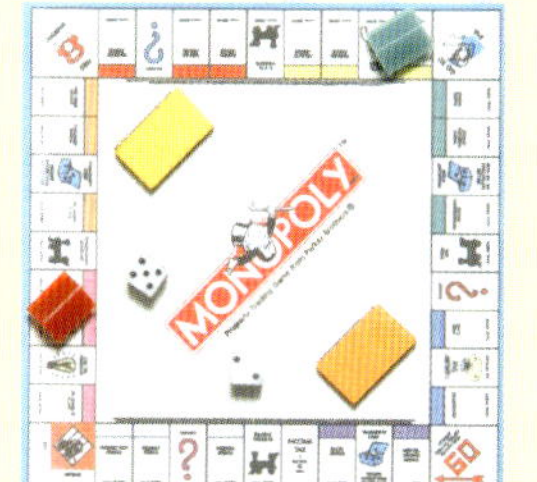

Scrapbook game boards are a great reminder of the fun we had as children.

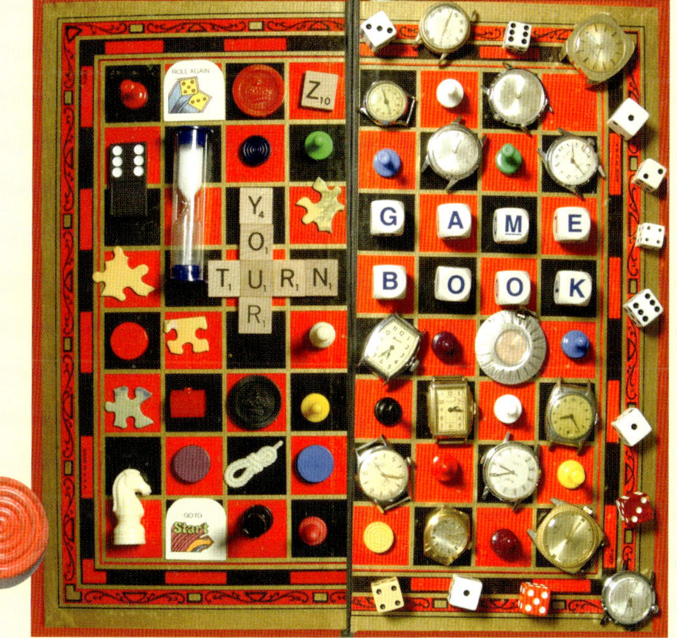

CHECKERS

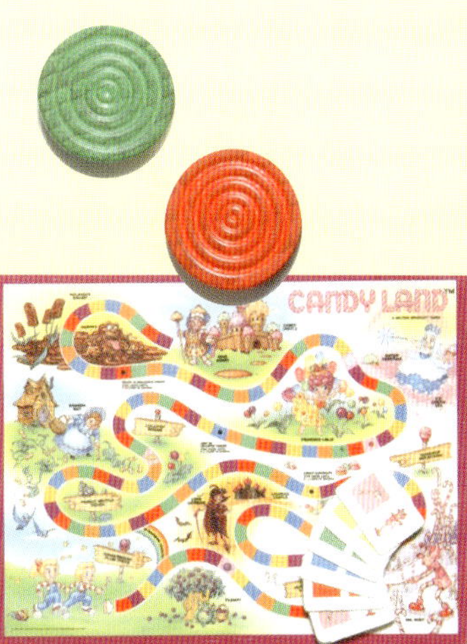

MATERIALS

Game Board	Puzzle Pieces
Paper	Cards
Game Board	Dominos
Stickers	Checkers
Game Pieces	Dice
Scrabble Letters	Watch Faces

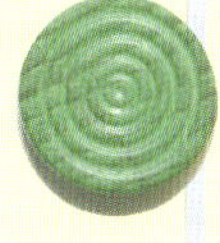

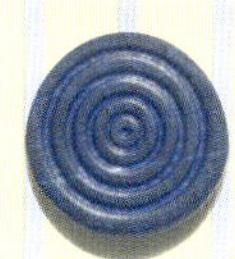

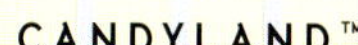

SCRABBLE®

CANDYLAND™

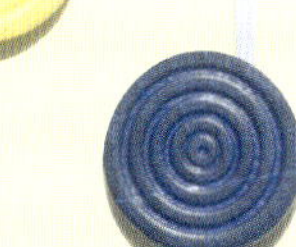

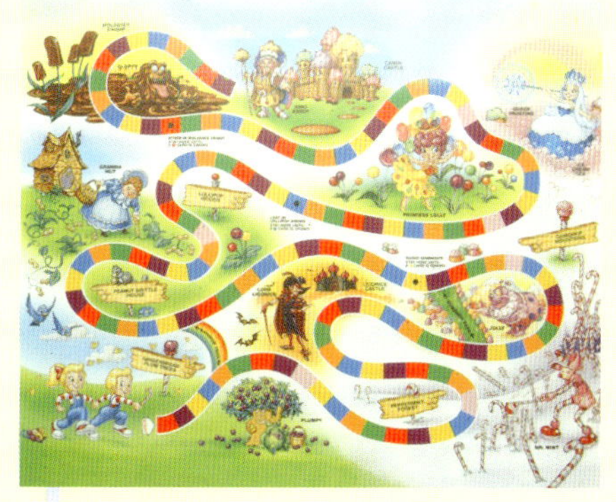

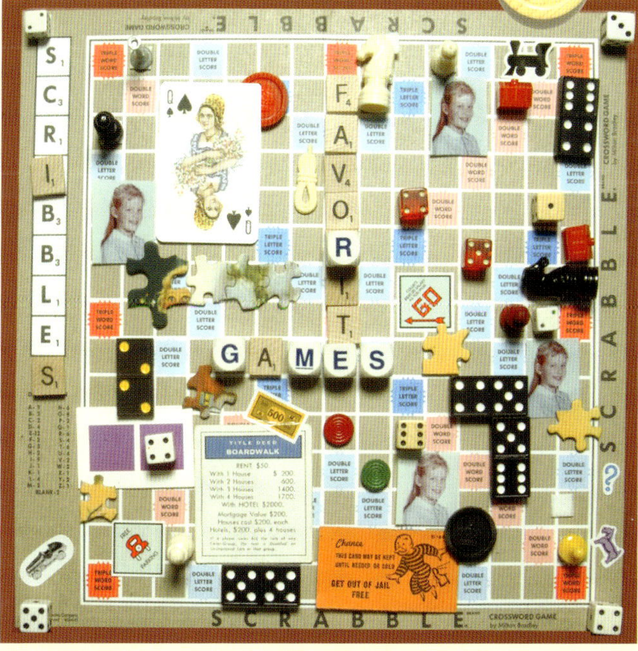

Newspaper Buttons and Transparency Sheets

Each year millions of tourists visit the famous landmark to see the forecourt with its hand and footprints of the stars. To begin, select a 12 x 12-inch sheet of button patterned paper and mount photos on an angle overlapping each other. Trim a torso image from a transparency sheet and mount. Select and trim transparencies of vintage Hollywood faces, adhere to lace stickies and mount on scrapbook layout page. Accent each corner with newspaper buttons and add handprint stickers. Complete the page with the words "Hollywood Dream" using bubble letters. Mom reminisces at the famous Grauman's Chinese Theater by placing her palms in the handprints of her favorite Hollywood stars.

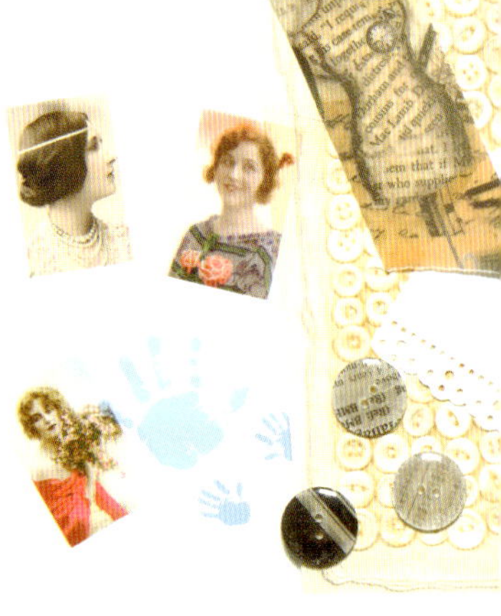

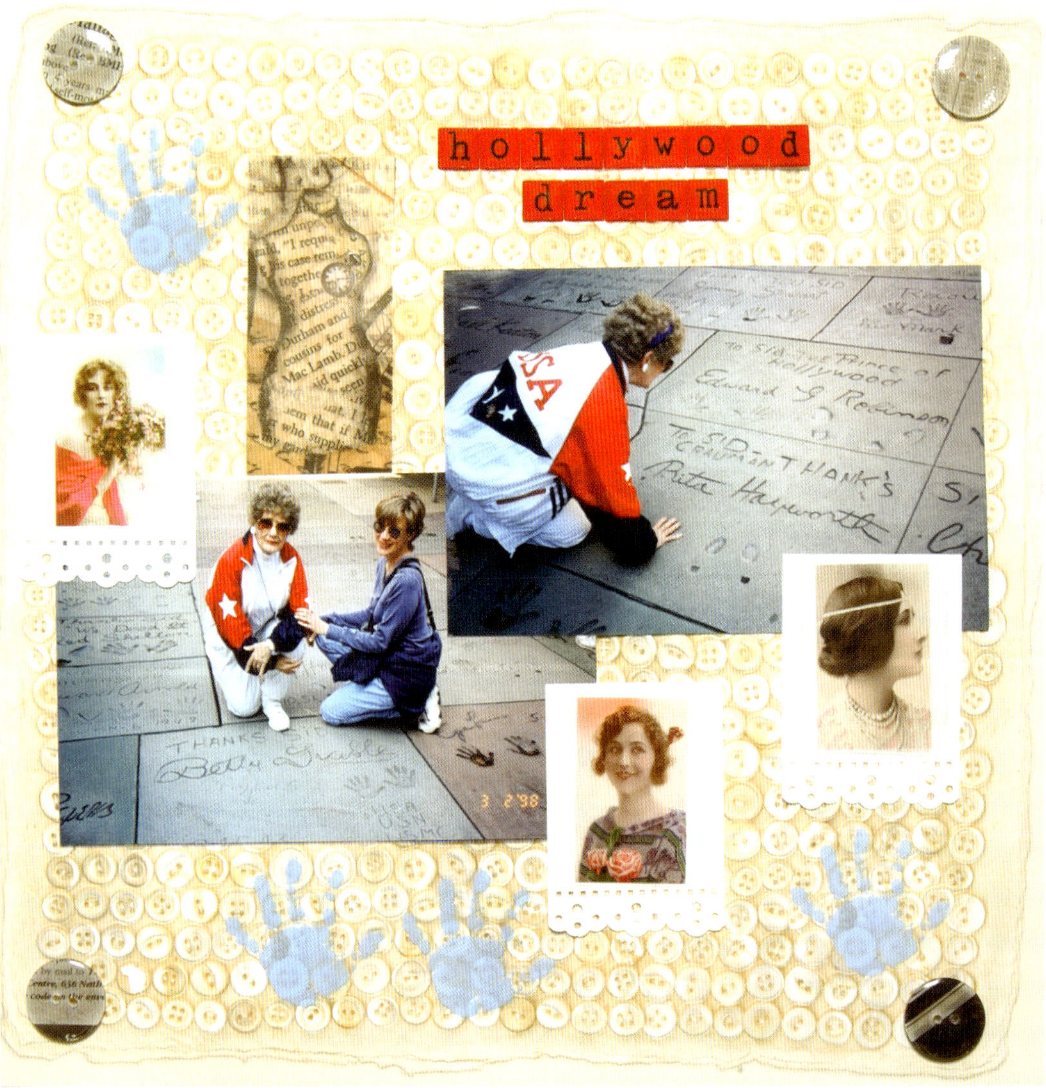

MATERIALS

Patterned Paper *K&Company*
Printed Vellum *DMD*
Transparency Sheet *Available from Stampington & Company*
Handprint Stickers *PSX Design*
Lace Stickies *Available from Stampington & Company*
Newspaper Buttons *Available from Stampington & Company*
Bubble Letters *Li'l Davis Designs™*

TECHNIQUE HINT

Attach transparencies to the back of lace stickies for easy positioning and adhere to page.

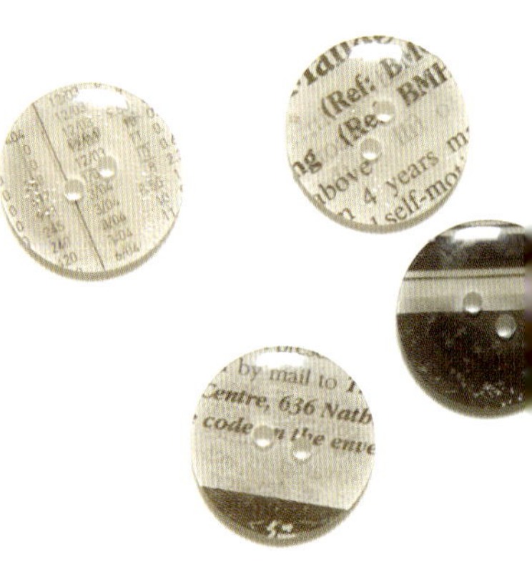

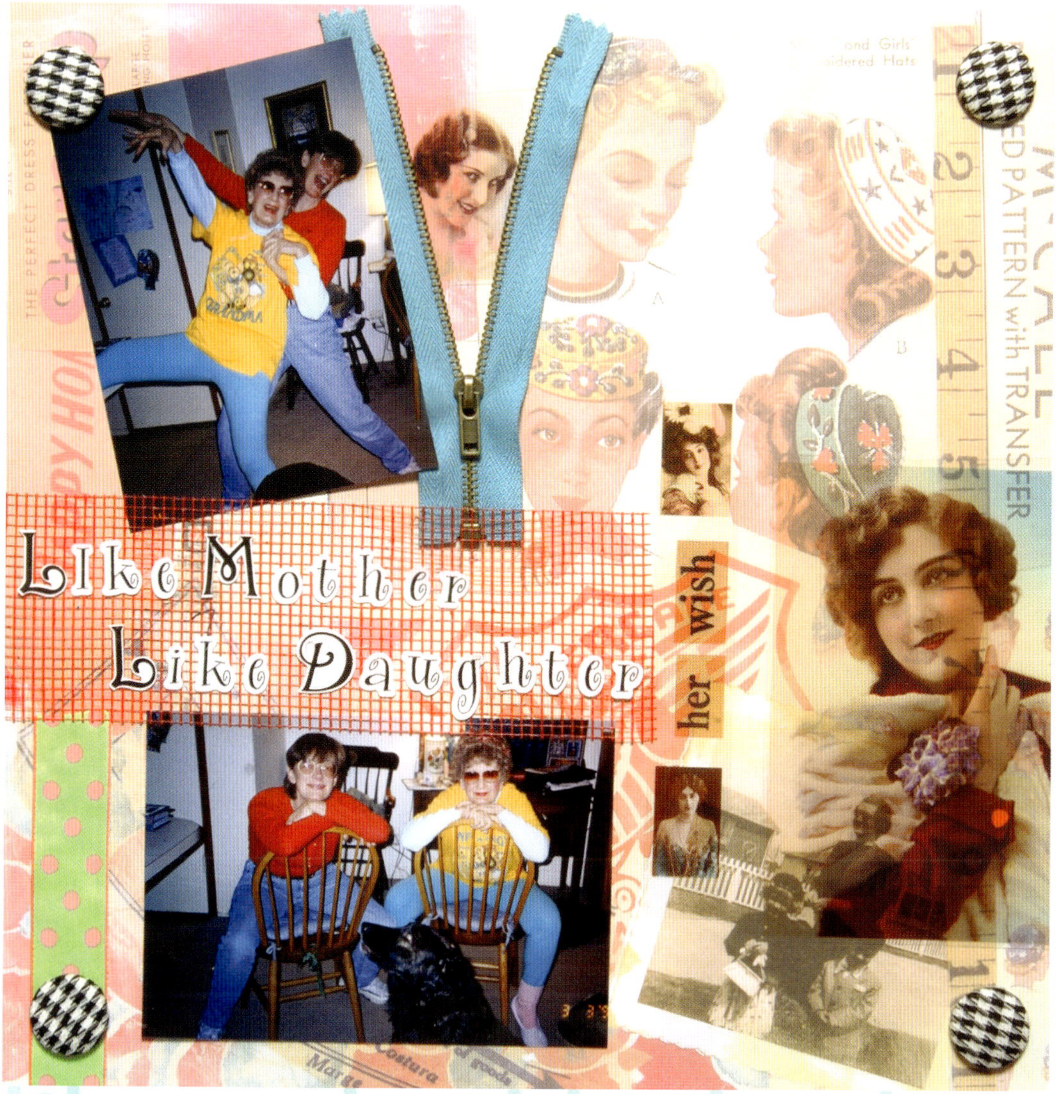

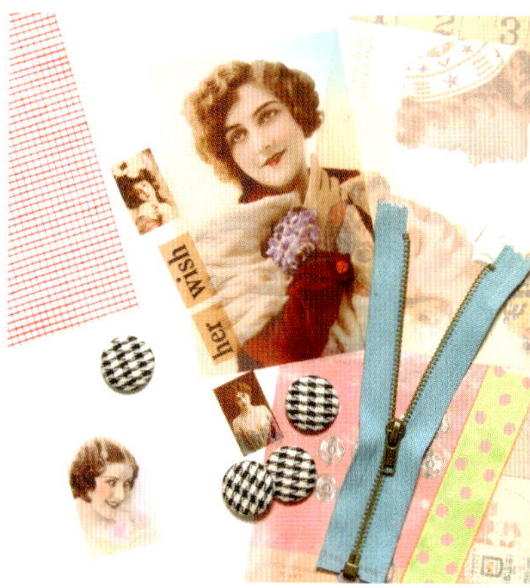

MATERIALS

Patterned Paper *Design Originals*
Mesh Screen *Making Memories*
Transparency Sheets *Available from Stampington & Company*
Adhesive Zipper *Junkitz™*
Ribbon *Michaels Stores, Inc.*
Vintage Buttons *Antique Shop*
Lettering *Me & My Big Ideas*

TECHNIQUE HINT

It's fun to open and fill a zipper with photos or elements. Trim and position everything in place before gluing.

like mother like daughter

Zipper and Vintage Buttons

My sister and mother share many common interests, especially in front of a camera. Select a piece of 12 x 12-inch retro patterned paper as a background. Open zipper halfway, peel off adhesive backing and position on page. Trim vertical photograph to fit zipper length and mount. Mount photograph horizontally on lower part of scrapbook page. Cut a 7-inch piece of red mesh and adhere to photos and zipper. Place lettering "Like Mother Like Daughter" on red mesh screen. Trim images from a transparency sheet; fasten on page with clear drying glue, and insert a small transparency inside V-shaped zipper opening. Cut a 5-inch piece of ribbon and mount under mesh. To complete layout, accent page with black and white herringbone vintage buttons. Whether silly or serene, mother and daughter are two of a kind.

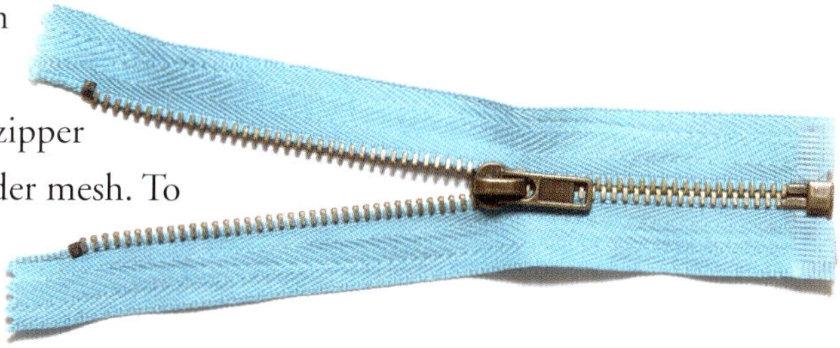

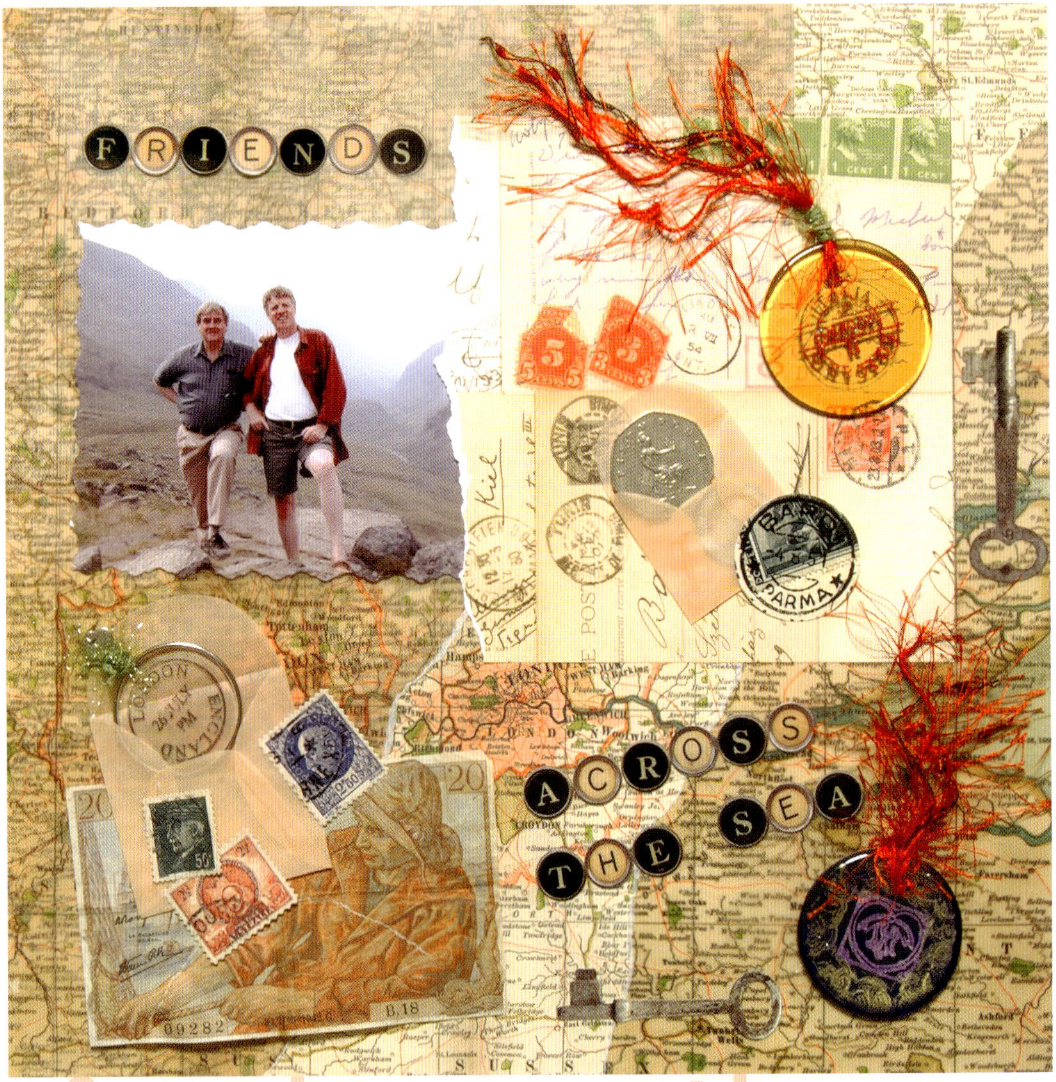

friends across the sea

Vintage Optical Lens, Stamp and Typewriter Stickers

Although separated by the Atlantic Ocean, best friends always find a way to spend quality time together. Select a 12 x 12-inch sheet of patterned map paper for your foundation. Tear a sheet of vellum map paper in two pieces and mount on patterned paper. Take a 6 x 6-inch piece of patterned paper and tear manually leaving a white edge. Trim photograph with deckle rotary cutter or scissors and mount under torn patterned paper. Next, attach a small vellum envelope to patterned paper; insert a foreign coin, and accent with a stamp sticker. Stamp and emboss yellow glass tag with postage imprint and tie with fibers. Stamp vintage optical lens with postage imprint; attach fibers, and place in vellum envelope. Mount lens on foreign currency and accent with stamp stickers. Emboss blue glass tag with gold design; add fibers and adhere to page. Use typewriter stickers to create title and accent with antique silver key stickers. Close friends share a camaraderie that distance can never tarnish.

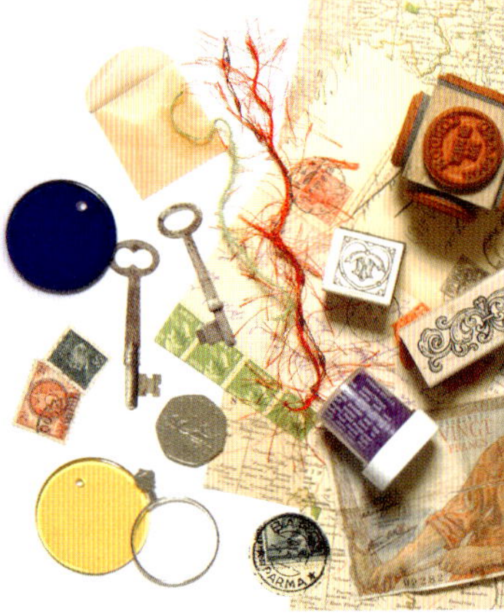

MATERIALS

- Patterned Paper *K&Company*
- Patterned Vellum *K&Company*
- Nostalgiques™ Stamp Stickers *Sticko*
- Nostalgiques™ Antique Key Stickers *Sticko*
- Rubber Stamps *Inkadinkado*
- Black and Gold Solvent Ink Pads *StāzOn*
- Embossing Powder *Stamp-n Stuff*
- Fibers *EK Success*
- Round Glass Tags *Available from Stampington & Company*
- Vintage Optical Lens *Available from Stampington & Company*
- Vellum Envelopes *The C-Thru Ruler Company*
- Foreign Currency *Personal Collection*
- Nostalgiques™ Typewriter Lettering *Sticko*

TECHNIQUE HINT

Use stamp stickers or copies of colorful foreign stamps printed on adhesive paper.

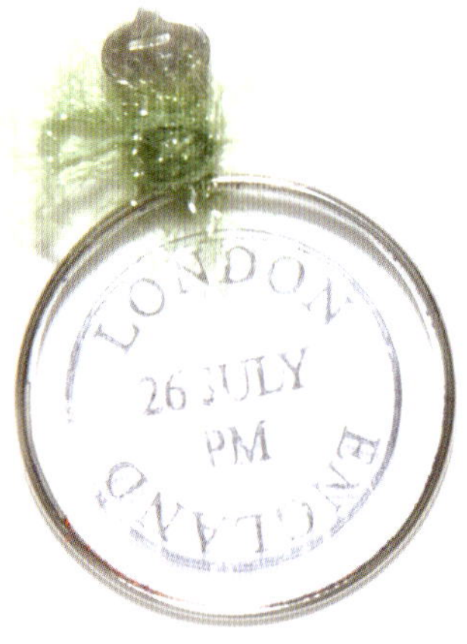

HOW-TO STEPS

Friends across the sea

stamped glass tags

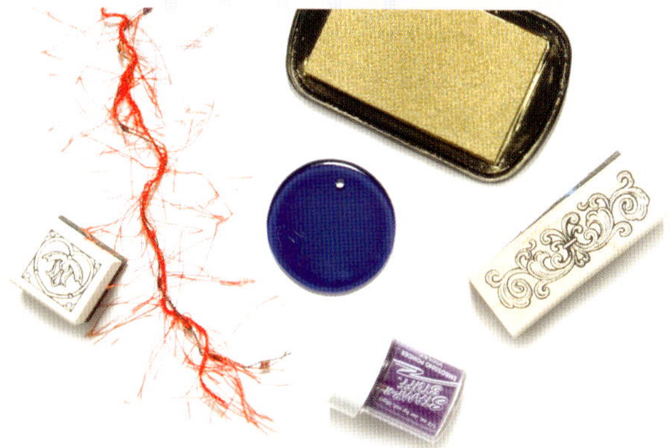

MATERIALS

Round Blue Glass Tag
Gold Solvent Ink Pad
Rubber Stamps
Embossing Powder
Fibers

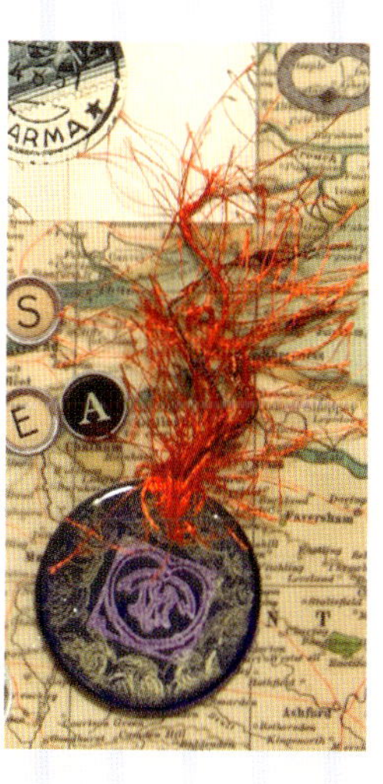

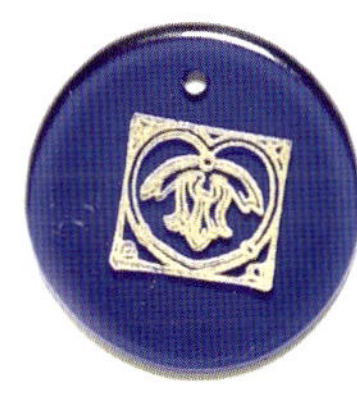

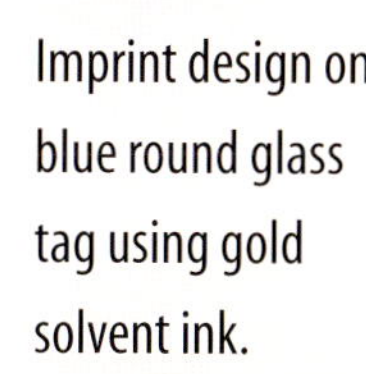

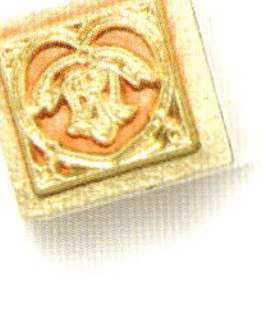

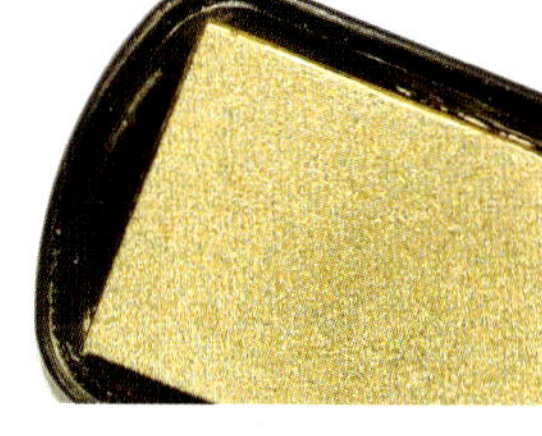

STEP 1

Imprint design on blue round glass tag using gold solvent ink.

STEP 2

Sprinkle purple embossing powder on moist imprint. Pour off excess and heat emboss.

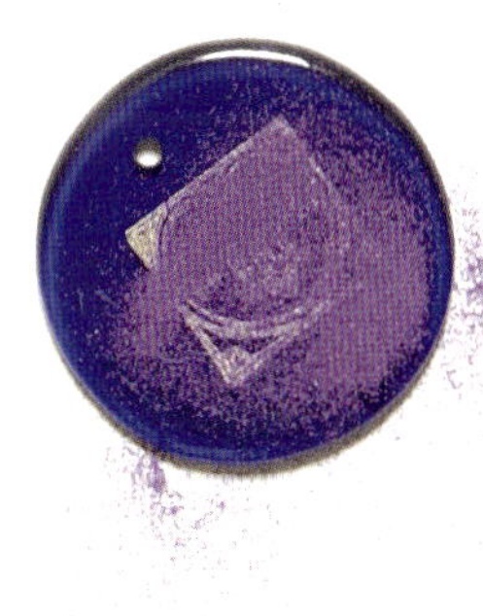

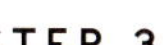

STEP 3

Imprint design on blue round glass tag along the outer edges using gold solvent ink. Cut a length of fiber, fold in half and loop through hole.

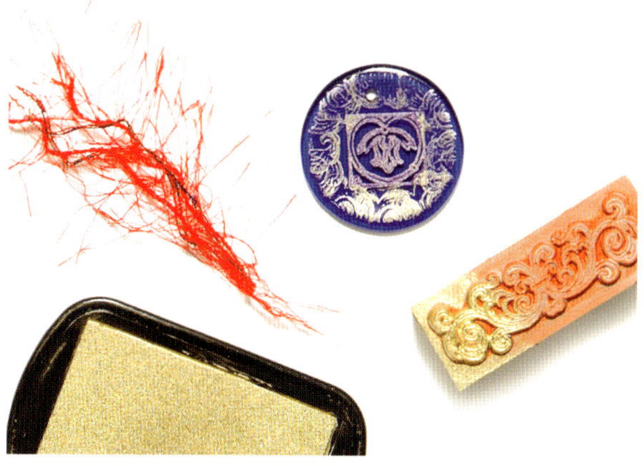

Computer

Digital Designs

Are you finally ready to get into digital scrapbooking? Our new techniques take the fear out of creating digitally mastered scrapbook layouts. Using your computer for journaling has never been easier. The popularity of computer fonts for scrapbooking has multiplied significantly during recent years. More scrapbookers are turning to their keyboard than ever before. This chapter explains how to create scrapbooking pages using Microsoft® Word and Adobe® Photoshop. Techniques include—digital mats, picture effects, clip art, curved text, digital sticker effects and titling and journaling on photographs,—to name a few. We have searched the Internet for you and have compiled a list of websites featuring downloadable scrapbook fonts from the best foundries in the business. (p.124) Use journal handwriting, applied to vellum, paper and photographs for quick, perfect text every time. Enhance and expand your journaling potential. *Scrapbooking Plus!* features more than fifteen versatile fonts to get you started. Digital scrapbooking is here to stay!—Have fun and enjoy!

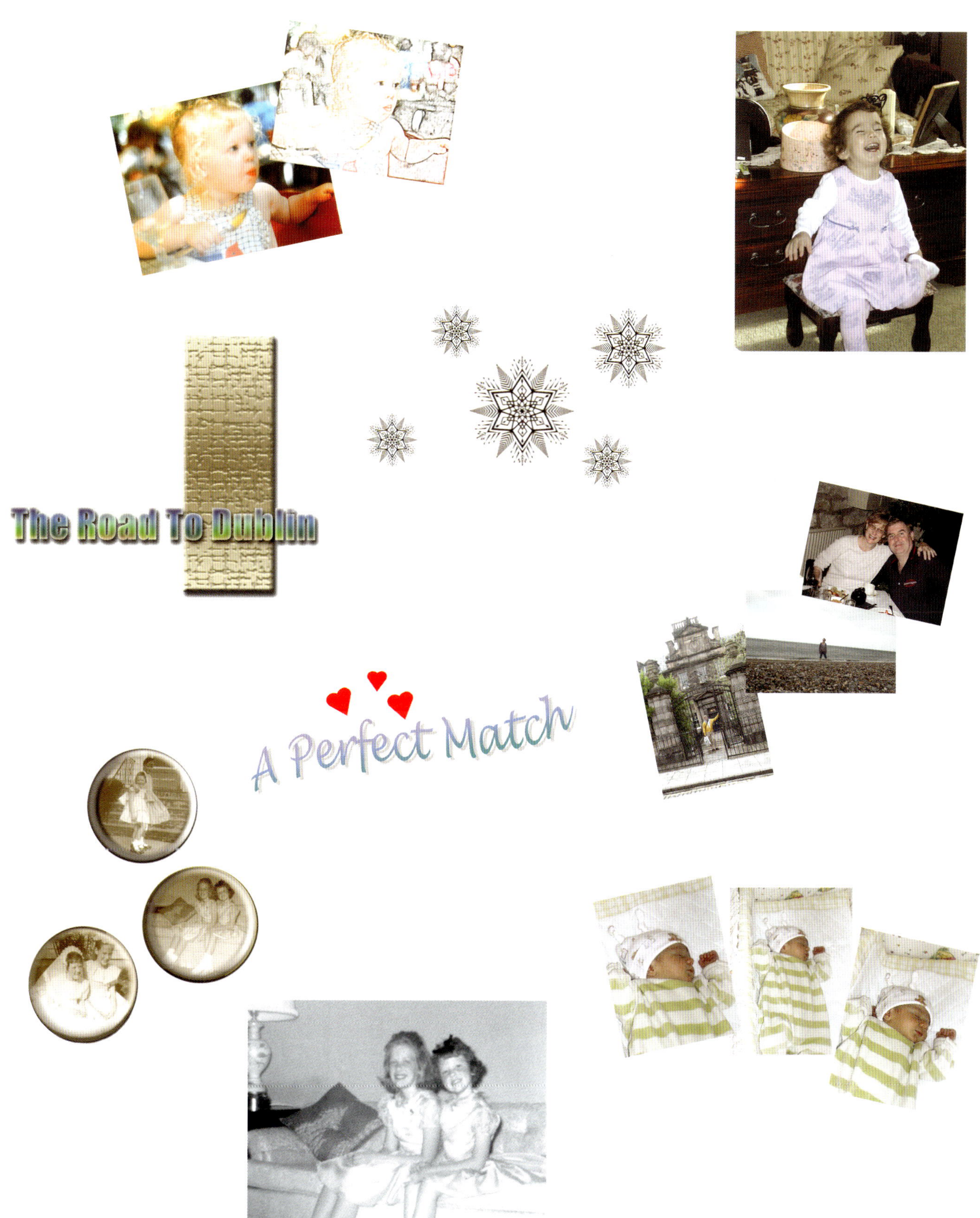
The Road To Dublin
A Perfect Match

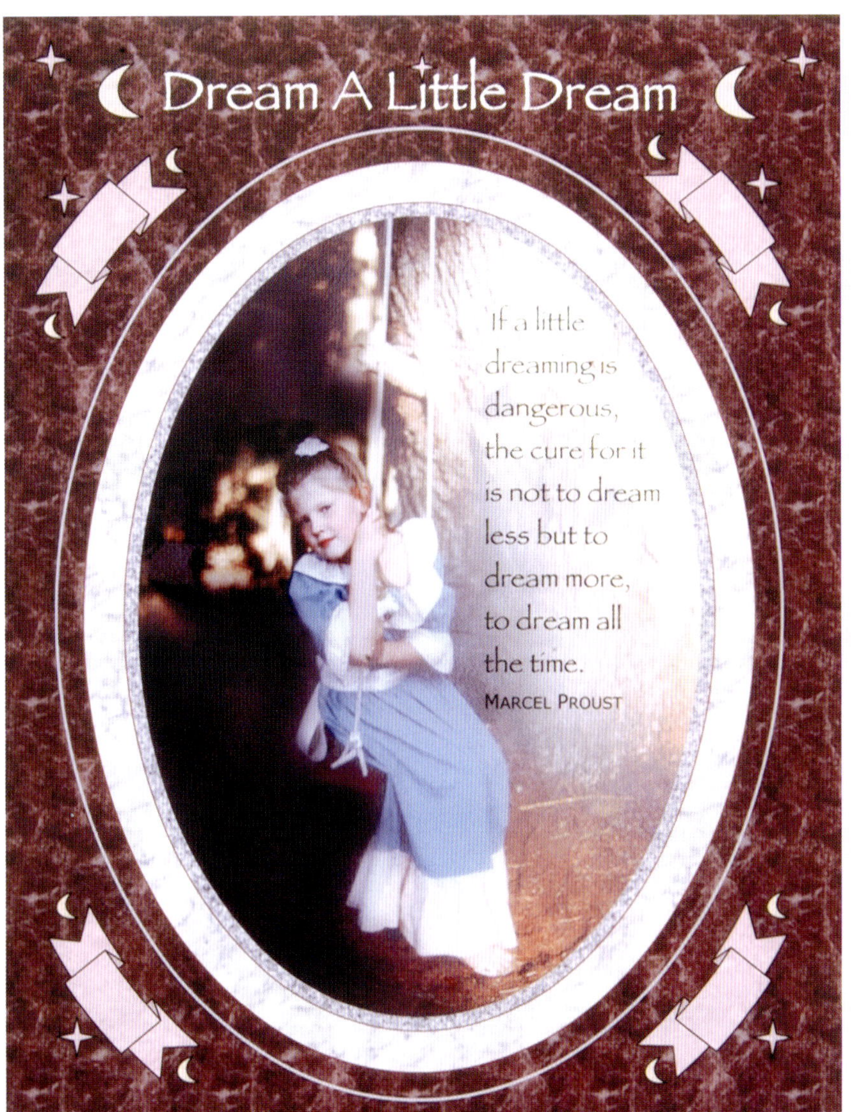

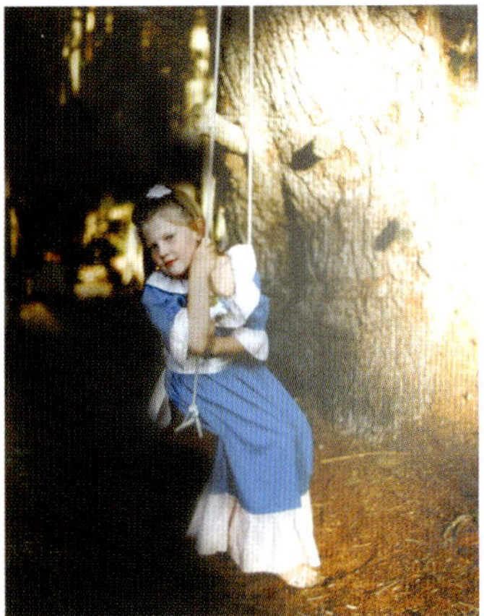

MATERIALS

Software *Microsoft® Word*

Glossy Photo Paper *Epson*

Computer Font *Papyrus*

TECHNIQUE HINT

To make journaling poem legible over the tree background, airbrush photograph in iPhoto.

dream a little dream

Digital Oval Mats

A little girl's dream for the future is beautifully reflected in this angelic photo as she floats carelessly on her fairytale swing. This scrapbook page was designed entirely in Microsoft® Word. Draw an 8 x10.5-inch box and change the color to brown marble. Create a 1 pt. oval and make it 50% gray. Reduce oval to fit inside original, increase width to 75 pt. and fill with white marble. Reduce oval to fit inside, decrease width to 35 pt. and change fill to granite. Insert the photograph from your file into a separate document. Use the oval marquee to select the area of the photograph, and then cut. Paste oval photograph into your original design and center. Type journaling poem in white Papyrus font and add banners, stars and crescent shapes. Apply Pink Tissue Paper texture for banners and stars, and Stationery texture for moons. Print on glossy photo paper. Dreams come true for those who trust in the magical powers of make-believe.

Picture Effects and Overlay Type

The excitement of a happy child enjoying her favorite dessert is captured beautifully in Julia's sun bathed face. Draw an 8 x10.5-inch box in Microsoft® Word and use fill effects to apply an orange gradient. Center the photo and change the size to 8-inches wide with a 50% gray shadow. Re-insert the photo and reduce size to 4-inches. To create a hand-drawn effect, apply colored pencil picture effects. Create a 1 pt. gray line around the perimeter of the small hand-drawn picture. Type "Cute and Adorable" on five lines and change black text to 25% gray. Type journaling double-spaced in Zapfino font. Type the title in Edwardian Script font over the bottom edge of the large photo and print on glossy photo paper. Cut and glue a thin strip of vellum over the photo and adhere the name "JULIA." Enjoying a dish of ice cream is a cool way to spend a hot summer afternoon.

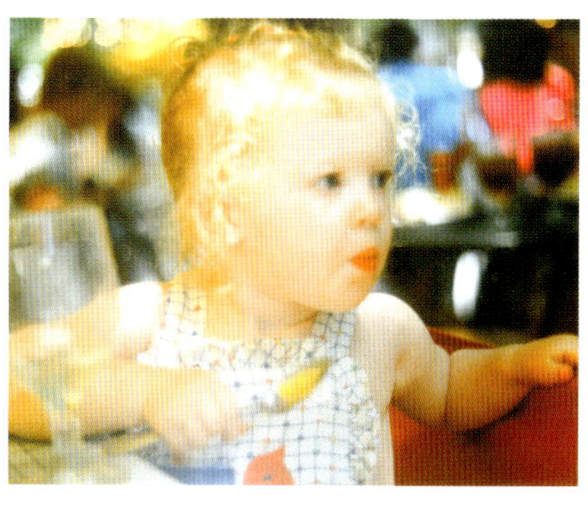

MATERIALS

Software *Microsoft® Word*

Vellum *The Paper Company*

Alphabet Eyelets *Making Memories*

Glossy Photo Paper *Epson*

Computer Fonts *Edwardian Script and Zapfino*

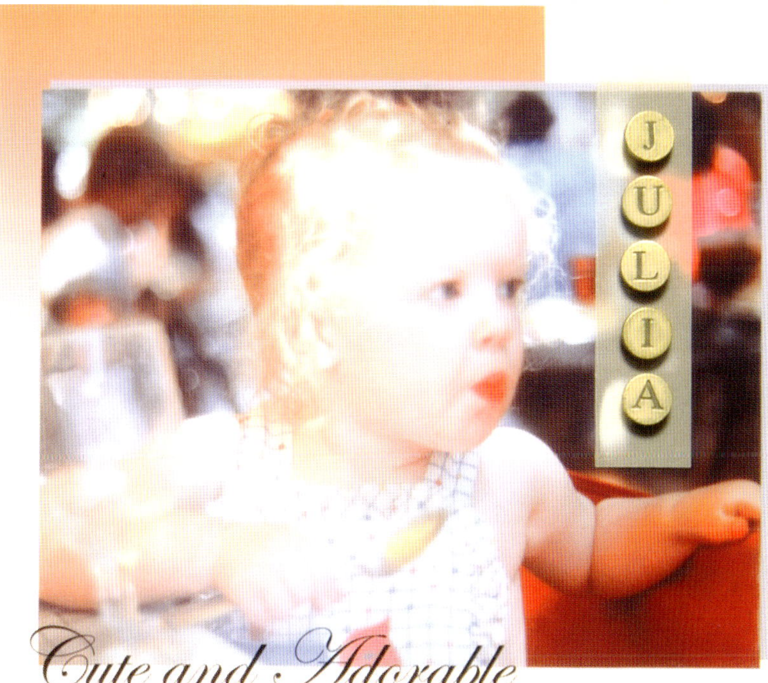

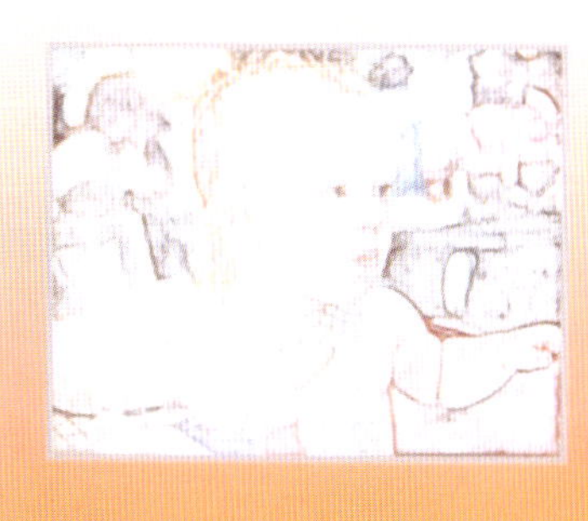

TECHNIQUE HINT

There are several Picture Effects in Microsoft® Word. Have fun experimenting with different ones on your photograph.

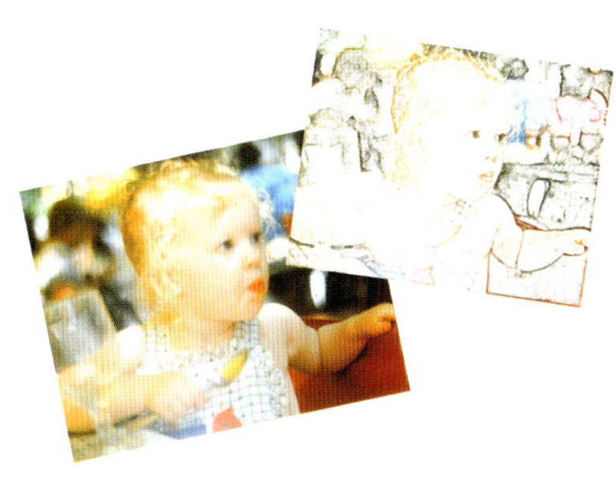

Clip Art

Setting out each Christmas in search of the perfect tree is a tradition enjoyed by everyone in the family. This page is easy to create and takes little time to design on your computer. Insert the photo on the page in Microsoft® Word and change size to 5.5 x 5-inches. Change the line to 10 pt. lime dots and create a variety of snowflakes in the seasons clip art gallery. Use the green Apple Chancery font and type journaling under the photo. Select a blue-green chalk banner from the clip art and place on top and bottom of the page. Type the words, "The Perfect Christmas Tree" using the Times Italic font and change the text to white. Print on glossy photo paper. This tall, beautiful Christmas tree sets the tone for all our holiday festivities.

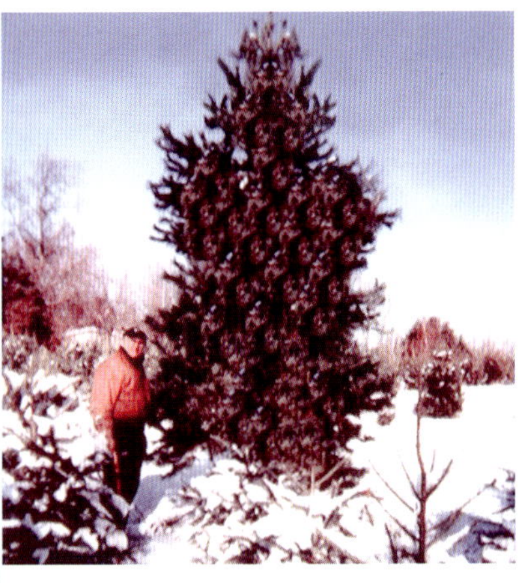

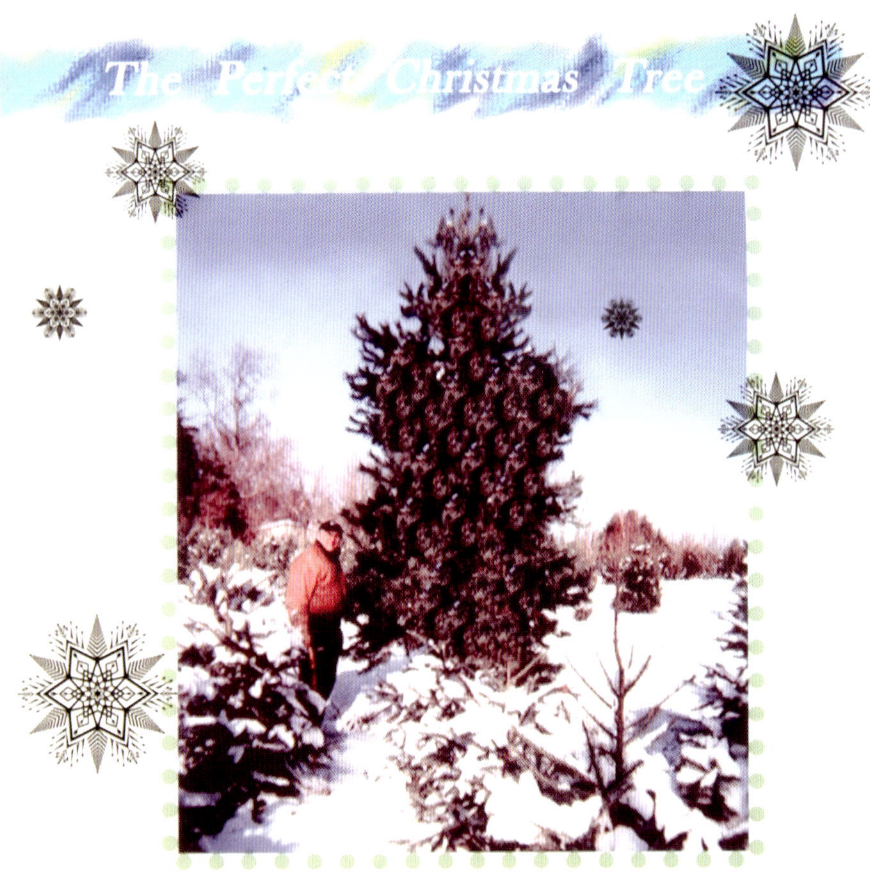

We have a large entrance in our foyer and every year we try to find the perfect tree from the local Christmas tree farm. My husband is about 6 ft so you can see this tree is quite tall. Towering 15 ft this enormous tree graced our home for the holidays.

MATERIALS

Software *Microsoft® Word*

Glossy Photo Paper *Epson*

Computer Fonts *Apple Chancery and Times*

TECHNIQUE HINT

To make text legible, adjust the brightness of the banner under the white type.

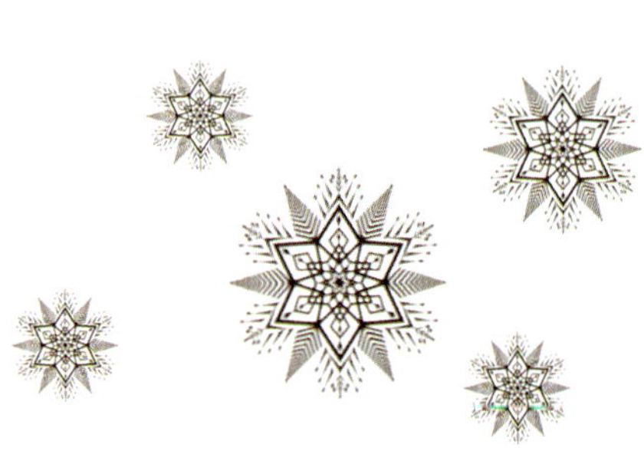

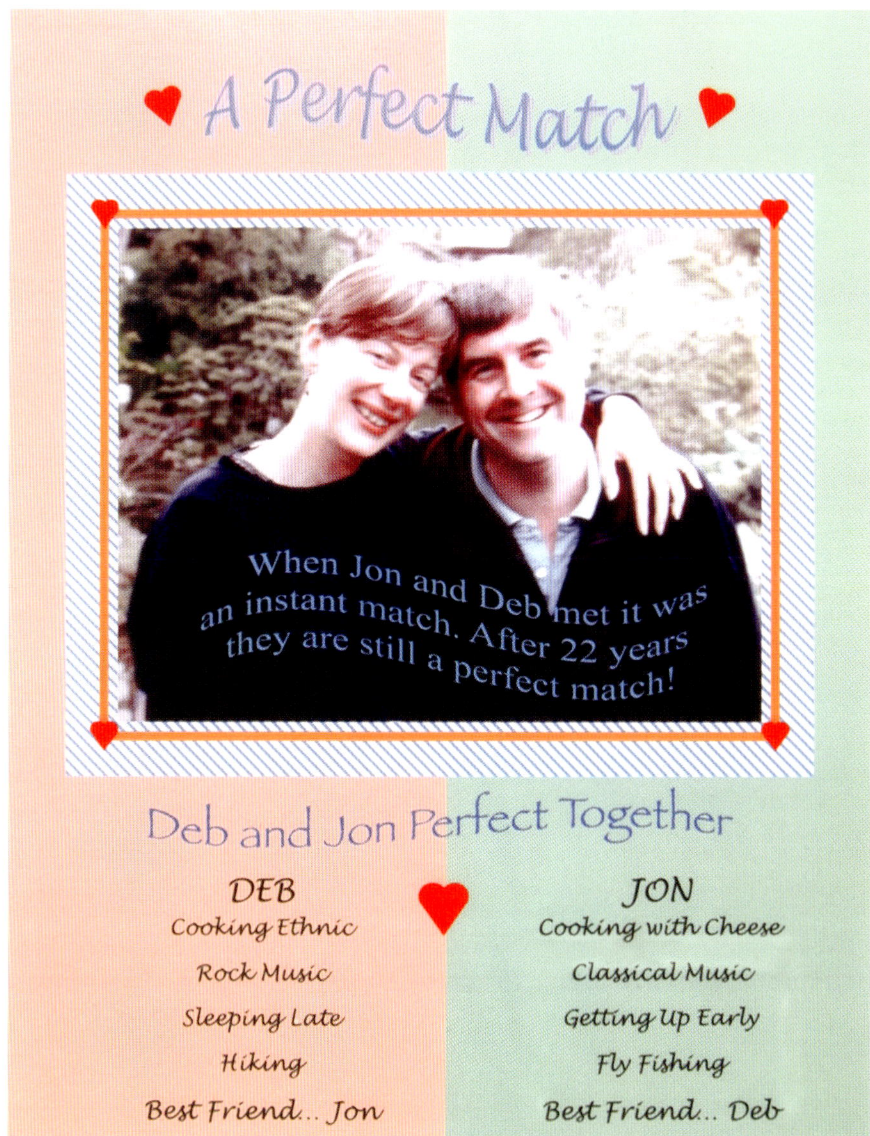

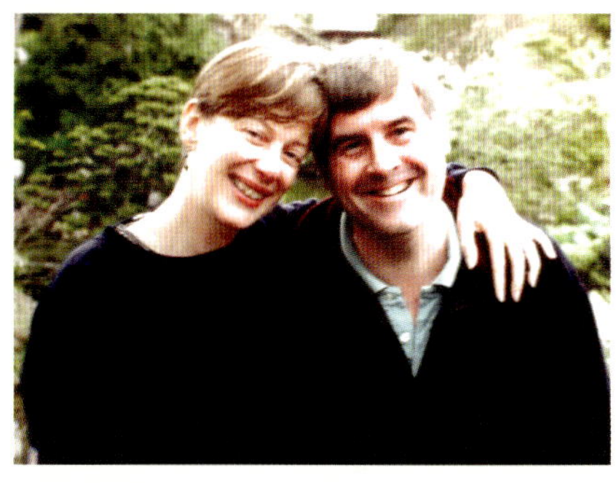

MATERIALS

Software *Microsoft® Word*

Glossy Photo Paper *Epson*

Computer Font *Papyrus*

TECHNIQUE HINT

To maintain a uniform size when using Auto Shapes tools, create one shape in the size and color desired then copy and paste in position.

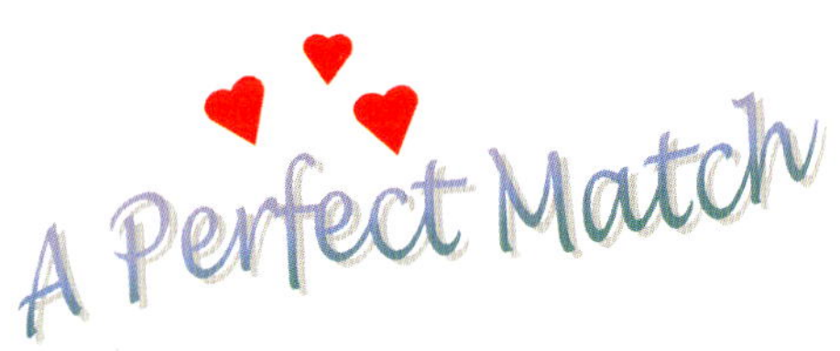

a perfect match

Curved Journaling and Title Text

Still happy after all these years is a wonderful way to describe my sister and her husband. Make two vertical 10 x 4.5-inch rectangular boxes in Microsoft® Word and apply rose and lime fill color to each box. Insert the photo on the page and change size to 6-inches wide. To create the illusion of a wide mat on the photograph, create a 35 pt. line with a wide downward diagonal blue pattern. Create another thin mat with a rectangle and make a 2 pt. line in orange. Use Basic Shapes to create red hearts. Apply a red color fill and copy and paste in each corner. To make large hearts, copy and paste then size to 1/2-inch. Make the title from WordArt in the Papyrus font and size, accordingly. In the WordArt toolbar, edit shape to Wave 1 and adjust color. Repeat Wave 1 for journaling on picture and subtitle. Create straight journaling text in Papyrus font and print on glossy photo paper. It's difficult to find a perfect match in life, but oh so much fun when you do.

live-love-laugh

Computer Font Titling Over a Photograph

A child's laughter is contagious. Her smiling face brings joy to everyone. Insert the photo into a Microsoft® Word document. Adjust size to 8 x 10.5-inches and change color to grayscale. Type the word "Laughing" in Edwardian Script font, center across the top of the photograph and print on glossy photo paper. Type journaling text double-spaced with the Lucida Handwriting font, print on pink vellum and attach with clear adhesive. Mount photo on 8.5 x 11-inch violet patterned paper then mount on 12 x 12-inch red embossed paper. Punch and set small flower eyelets in each corner. Cut three squares from another sheet of violet paper and mount lavender ribbon on top. Type the words, "Live-Love-Laugh" in the Lucida Handwriting font, print on adhesive matte vellum and adhere to vellum metal tags. Set red flower eyelets in the tags and glue on ribbon. Living, loving and laughing are three words that fill every moment of a little girl's happy life.

MATERIALS

Software *Microsoft® Word*
Embossed Paper *K&Company*
Patterned Paper *Paper Pizazz*
Vellum Paper *The Paper Company*
Vellum Metal Tags *Making Memories*
Ribbon *Offray Ribbon*
Flower Eyelets *Making Memories*
Glossy Photo Paper *Epson*
Computer Fonts *Lucida Handwriting and Edwardian Script*

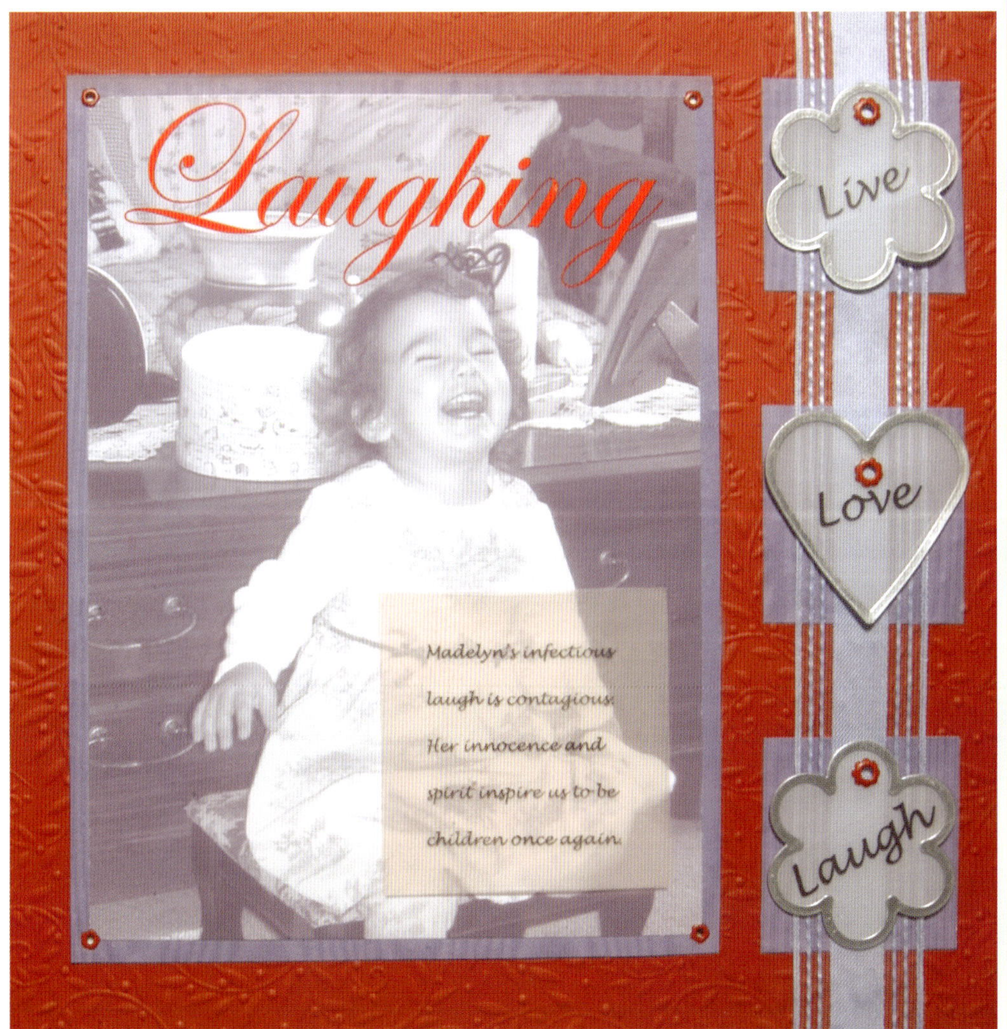

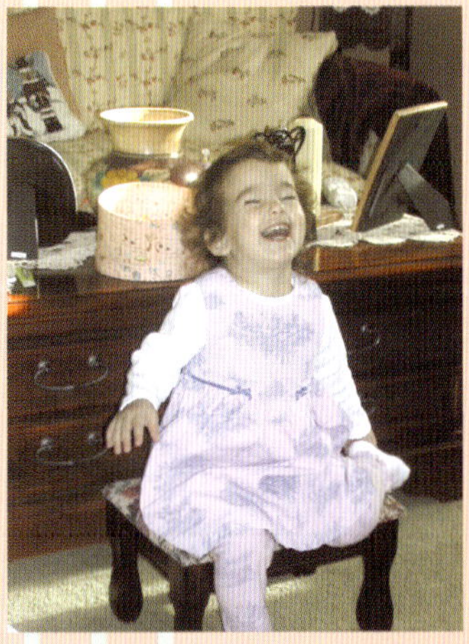

TECHNIQUE HINT

After positioning title words over the photograph, adjust the brightness of the picture to ensure text is legible.

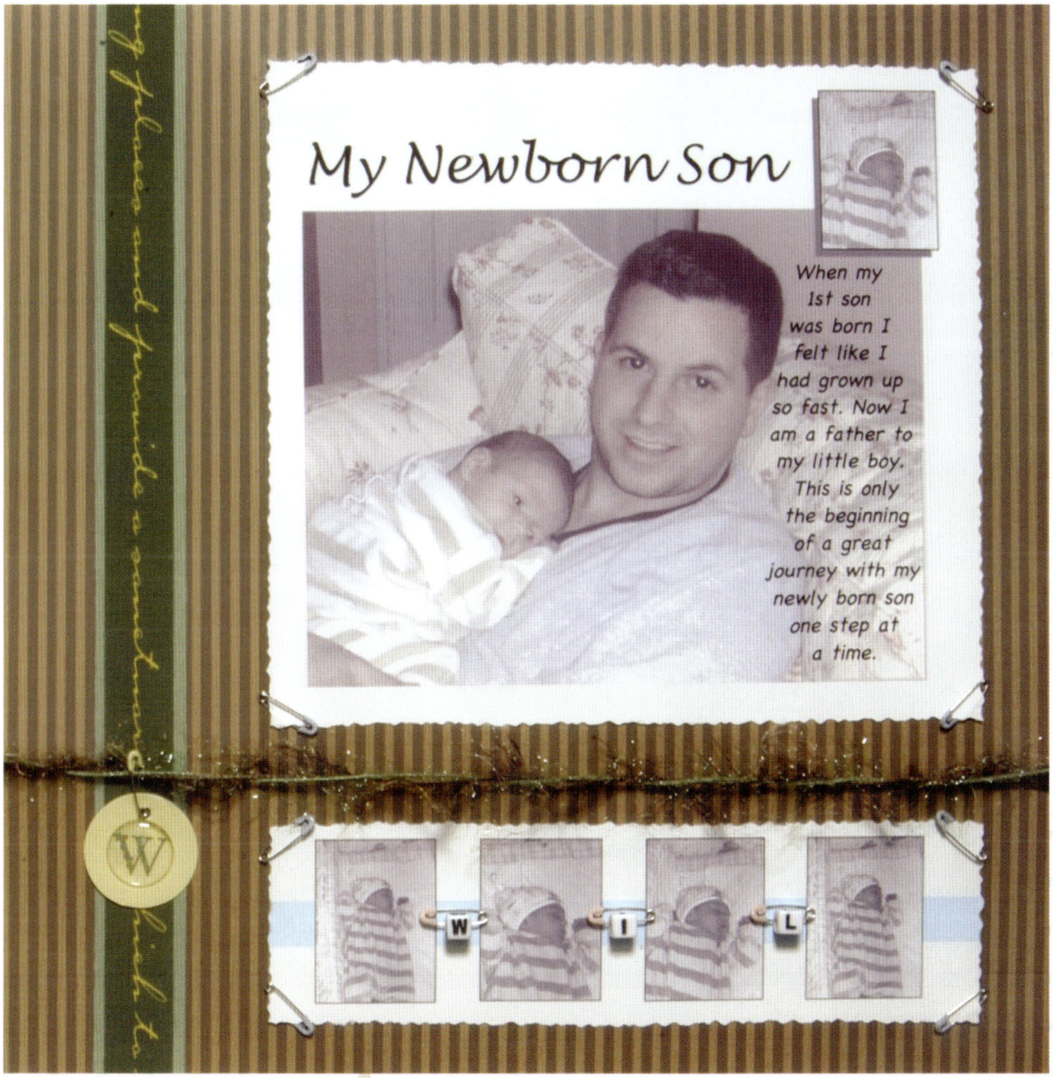

My Newborn Son

When my 1st son was born I felt like I had grown up so fast. Now I am a father to my little boy. This is only the beginning of a great journey with my newly born son one step at a time.

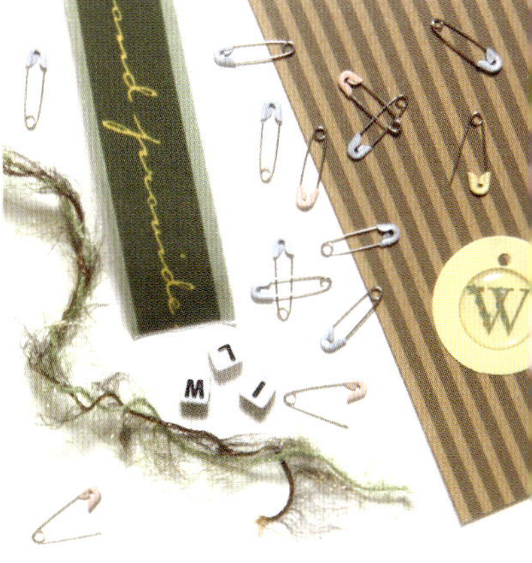

MATERIALS

Software *Microsoft® Word*
Patterned Paper *K&Company*
Peel 'n' Stick Fabric Trim *FabriCraft*
Green and Brown Fibers *EK Success*
Alpha Beads 7mm *Nicole*
Baby Pins *Making Memories*
Paper Tags *Making Memories*
Clearly Yours Alphabet *K&Company*
Computer Font *Lucida Handwriting*
Glossy Photo Paper *Epson*

TECHNIQUE HINT

To make text legible, insert text boxes over background areas away from the face. For best results, explore different text colors.

my newborn son

Digital Journaling on a Photograph

A proud father's first photos of his newborn son reflect the love shared by everyone in the family. Insert photo into the Microsoft® Word document. Adjust size to 8-inches wide. Type journaling double-spaced in Lucida Handwriting font and place in a narrow vertical text box.

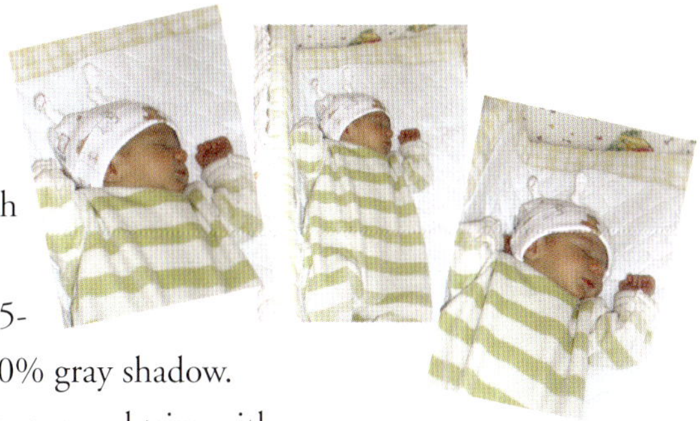

Adjust the brightness of the photo to make text legible. Type "My Newborn Son" and position on top of photo. Insert small photograph of infant in upper right hand corner and adjust size to 1.75-inches high. Change to grayscale and add 50% gray shadow. Insert four 1.75-inch infant photographs equally spaced at bottom of page and add 50% gray shadow. Create a horizontal blue band behind photos, print on glossy photo paper and trim with deckle rotary cutter. Mount on the right side on patterned paper and place fabric trim vertically on the left side. Attach fibers with baby pins on paper tag with clear "W" sticker. Insert alpha beads through baby pins and glue in-between photos. Complete with blue baby pins in each corner. Baby Wil seems very content in the arms of his loving dad.

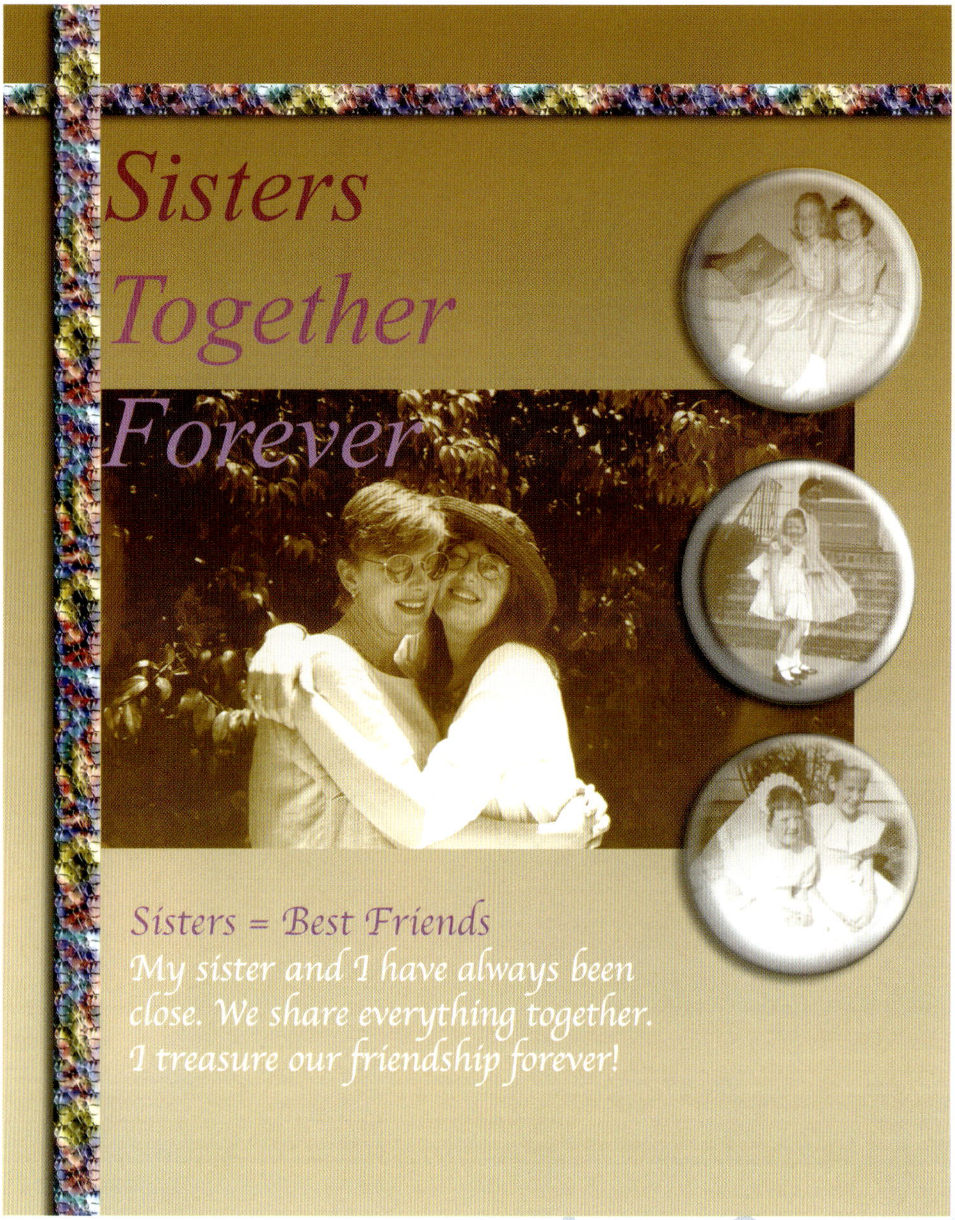

Sisters
Together
Forever

Sisters = Best Friends
My sister and I have always been close. We share everything together. I treasure our friendship forever!

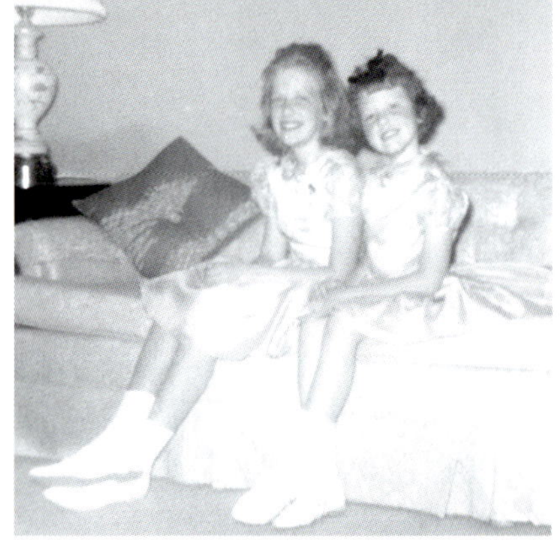

MATERIALS

Software *Adobe® Photoshop*

Glossy Photo Paper *Epson*

Computer Fonts *Times and Apple Chancery*

TECHNIQUE HINT

Create digital sticker effects in any shape using the geometry tools.

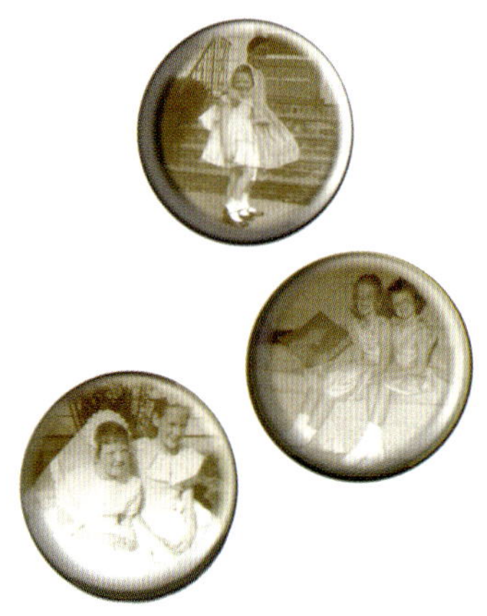

sisters together forever

Digital Sticker Effects

The deep love between two sisters is beautifully reflected in the photos taken from early childhood to the present. Insert the photo on an 8.5 x 11-inch page in Adobe® Photoshop and change size to 4 x 6-inches. Adjust the photo to a sun faded photo effect in the Styles window and apply a gradient overlay. Open three photographs and change mode to grayscale. Use the marquee tool to select a circular area on each of the photos and copy and paste on sun faded page. Space the photos evenly in a vertical line. In the Photoshop layer apply drop shadow, outer glow, inner glow, beveled edge and gradient to create a digital sticker effect. Make a dimensional ribbon border by drawing a thin box and applying a nebula style with a drop shadow, inner shadow, beveled edge, gradient and pattern. Type title in Times font, set journaling text in Apple Chancery and print on glossy photo paper. As sisters, we share a special bond that has nurtured and deepened over many loving years spent together.

Dimensional Titles and Textures

On their last trip to Ireland, my sister and her husband shared a remarkable adventure visiting the castles and pubs of this lush and beautiful country. Insert the photo on a page in Adobe® Photoshop and change size to 8.5 x 11-inches. Draw a vertical box along the right edge of the page. Change to ancient stone in the styles window. Open the layers, apply 70% opacity and add a drop shadow, beveled edges, color overlay, gradient overlay and pattern overlay. Insert three small photos and size to 1 x 1.5-inches. Apply drop shadow and beveled edges. Create captions in Times font and center. Design the main title in Impact font and color with tie-dyed effect from the styles window. Apply drop shadow, inner glow, beveled edges and pattern overlay. Print on glossy photo paper. The seaport city of Dublin, on the Irish Sea, is an ideal location to enjoy the beauty of Ireland and experience the legendary warmth and generosity of the Irish people.

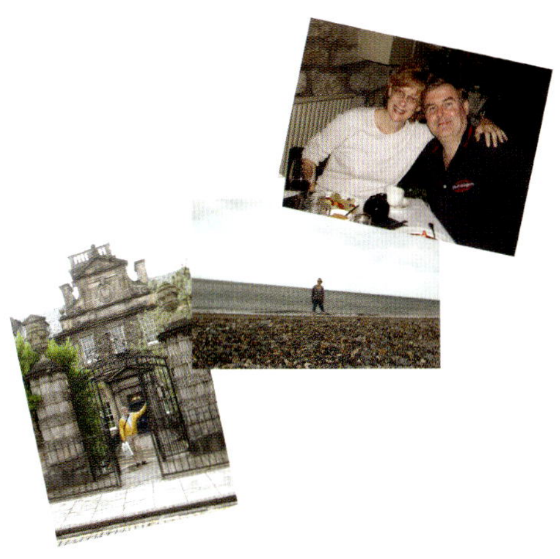

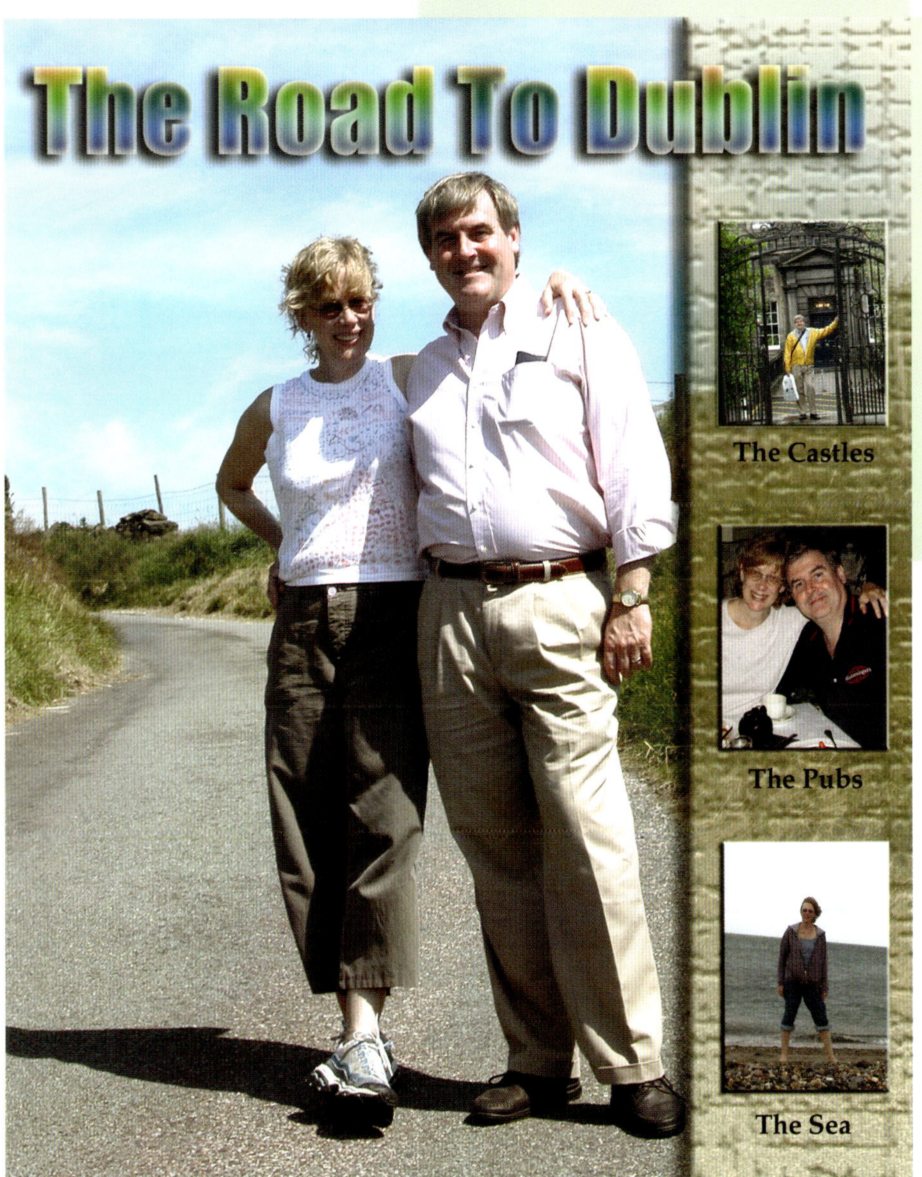

MATERIALS

Software *Adobe® Photoshop*
Glossy Photo Paper *Epson*
Computer Fonts *Impact and Times*

TECHNIQUE HINT

Experiment with the Styles window to create a variety of different fonts combined with color textures and effects.

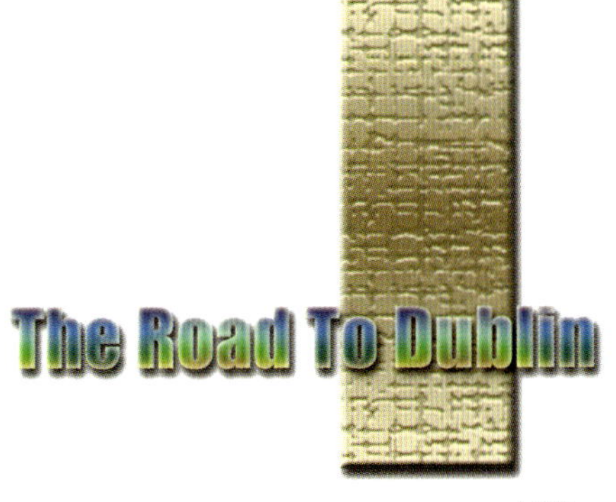

Free Fonts

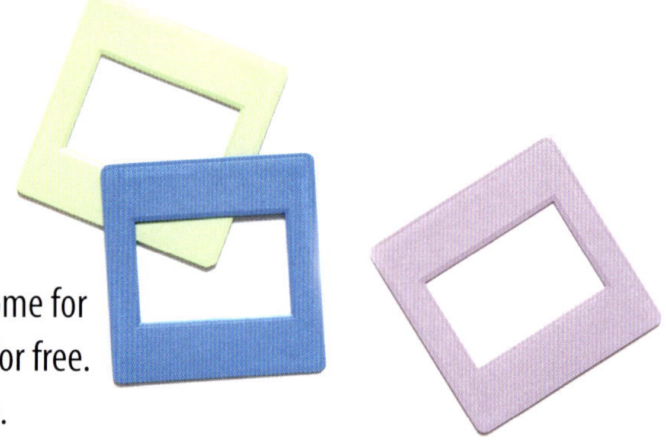

These websites feature free fonts. There are some for sale as well; find the links to download fonts for free. Most are Windows and Macintosh compatible.

L'ABÉCÉDARIENNE'S FONTS
WWW.ABECEDARIENNE.COM

ASTIGMATIC ONE EYE
WWW.ASTIGMATIC.COM

BLAMBOT
WWW.BLAMBOT.COM

COOLARCHIVE
WWW.COOLARCHIVE.COM

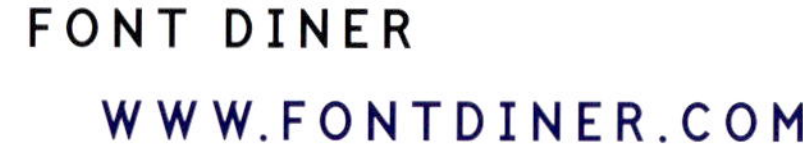

FONT DINER
WWW.FONTDINER.COM

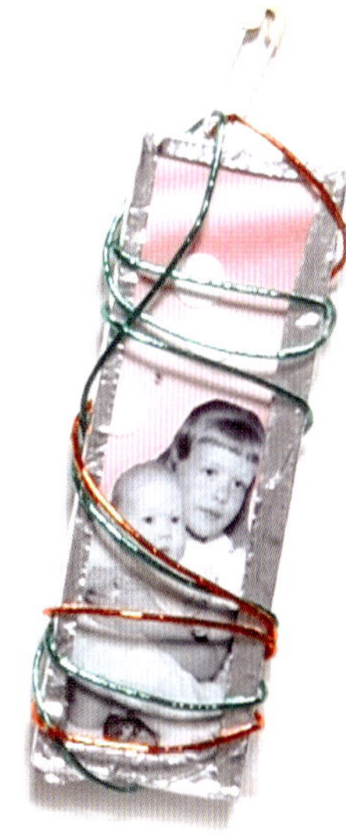

FONTALICIOUS
WWW.FONTALICIOUS.COM

TWO PEAS IN A BUCKET
WWW.TWOPEASINABUCKET.COM/FREEFONTS.ASP

TYPOASIS
WWW.MOORSTATION.ORG/TYPOASIS/THEMES.HTM

Contributors

K&Company
8500 N.W. River Park Dr. Pillar #136
Parkville, MO 64152
888.244.2083
kandcompany.com

Kay Stanley and Curt Seymour founded K&Company in August 1996 with the development of a unique personalized system called Frame a Name®. Today K&Company employs 110 people and operates out of its fifth location, a 130,000 square foot underground facility in the small historic town of Parkville, Missouri. K&Company also designs and manufactures scrapbook papers, stickers, albums, collegiate and military gifts.

Lil Davis Group
17835 Sky Park Circle / Suite C
Irvine, TX 92614
949.838.0344
info@lildavisdesigns.com

Tricia Barrett's love of scrapbooking led her and her husband Brian to open Li'l Davis Designs in January 2002. Best known for their laser shapes, the company's product line has expanded to include a complete embellishment line "Li'l Trinkets and Treasures," printed paper, templates, idea books and tools.

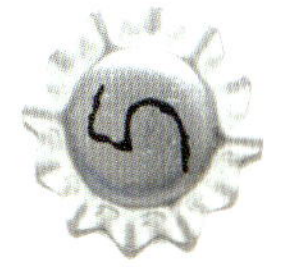

Making Memories
1168 West 500 North
Centerville, UT 84014
801.294.0430
makingmemories.com

Since its inception in 1997, Making Memories has become one of the nation's fastest growing manufacturers of craft and scrapbooking supplies. The privately held company boasts more than 4,500 products. Making Memories attributes its phenomenal growth to creating innovative products, close customer relationships, and providing an unending supply of inspirational ideas. For more information about Making Memories, visit www.makingmemories.com.

Contributors

Stampington & Company
22992 Mill Creek, Suite B
Laguna Hills, CA 92653
877-STAMPER (U.S. Toll-free)
stampington.com

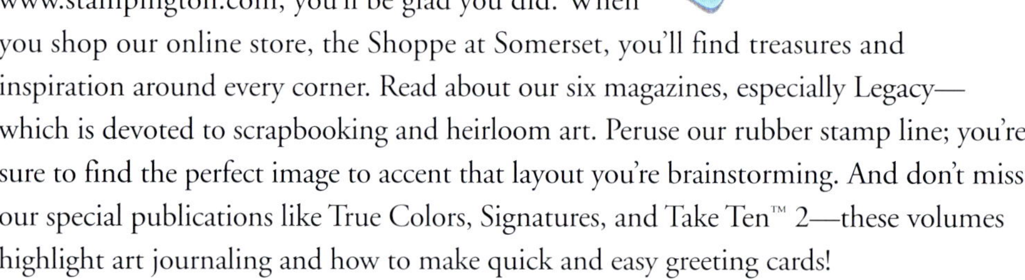

Glass tags and corners by Stacy Dorr.

Stampington & Company is the ultimate resource for paper artists everywhere! Visit our website at www.stampington.com, you'll be glad you did. When you shop our online store, the Shoppe at Somerset, you'll find treasures and inspiration around every corner. Read about our six magazines, especially Legacy—which is devoted to scrapbooking and heirloom art. Peruse our rubber stamp line; you're sure to find the perfect image to accent that layout you're brainstorming. And don't miss our special publications like True Colors, Signatures, and Take Ten™ 2—these volumes highlight art journaling and how to make quick and easy greeting cards!

The C-Thru® Ruler Company
6 Britton Drive
Bloomfield, CT 06002
800.243.8419
cthruruler.com

Since pioneering the manufacture of transparent plastic rulers in the United States in 1939, C-Thru's reputation as a cutting edge innovator and an international leader in the production of measurements and art materials has been unparalleled. Our commitment to meticulous quality, value-pricing and extraordinary customer service is the cornerstone of all our customer relationships.

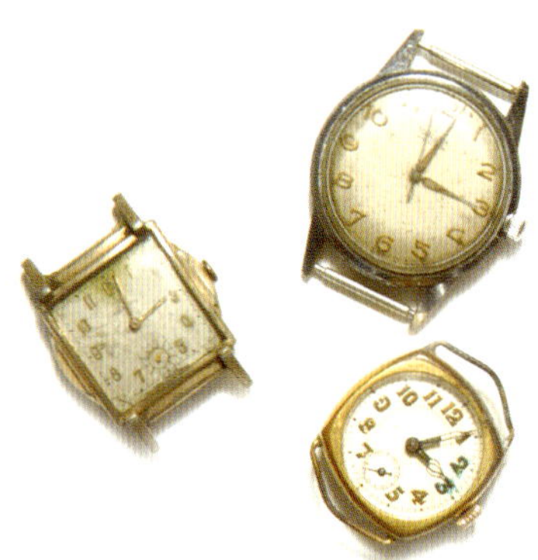

Resources

The following companies manufacture the materials featured in *Scrapbooking Plus!* Products may be purchased in local scrapbook retail stores or online.

Anna Griffin
888.817.8170
annagriffin.com

Berroco, Inc.
508.278.2527
Berroco.com

Boxer Scrapbook Productions, LLC
503.625.0455
boxerscrapbooks.com

*C-Thru Ruler Company, The
800.243.8419
cthruruler.com

Colorbök™ Inc.
800.366.4660
colorbok.com

Creative Imaginations, Inc.
800.942.6487
cigift.com

Die Cuts With A View
801.224.6766
diecutswithaview.com

Dress It Up
Fax: 610.435.8149
jessejamesbutton@rcn.com

EK Success
800.524.1349
eksuccess.com

Frances Meyer, Inc.
800.372.6237
francesmeyer.com

Halcraft
212.367.1580
halcraft.com

Hobbylinc
770.466.2667
hobbylinc.com

Inkadinkado
781.938.6100
Inkadinkado.com

Jacquard Products
800.442.0455
jacquardproducts.com

Jolee's Boutique
joleesboutique.com
phone unavailable

Junkitz
212.944.4250
junkitz.com

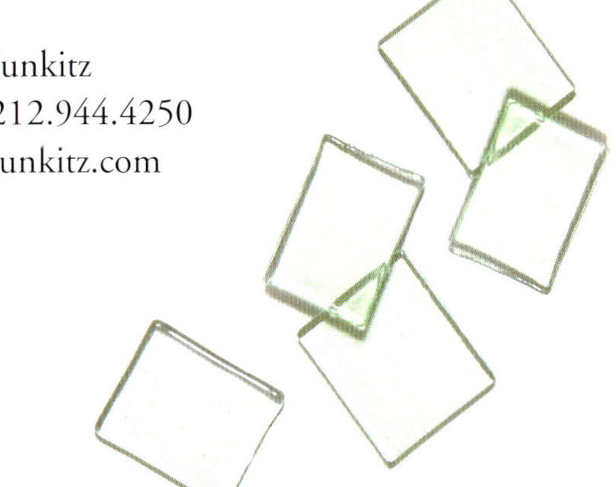

*K&Company
888.244.2083
kandcompany.com

*Li'l Davis Designs™
949.838.0344
info@lildavisdesigns.com

*Making Memories
801.294.0430
makingmemories.com

Marvy® Uchida
800.541.5877
uchida.com

Me & My Big Ideas
949.589.4607
meandmybigideas.com

Mega Marbles
800.846.4228
marketing@megamarbles.com

Metalworks™
505.598.5322
monsterslayer.com

Michaels Stores, Inc.
800.642.4235
michaels.com

Mrs. Grossmans
800.429.4549
mrsgrossmans.com

Paper Company, The
800.426.8989
thepaperco.com

Paper Pizazz
888.300.3406
paperpizazz.com

Provo Craft®
888.577.3545
provocraft.com

PSX Designs for Creativity
800.782.6748
info@psxdesign.com

Rubber Stampede
800.423.4135
rubberstampede.com

Sandy Lion
800.552.4707
sandylion.com

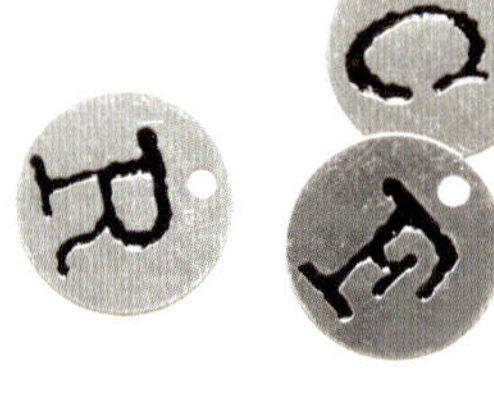

Simple Sets
800.333.3279
shopsei.com

*Stampington & Company, LLC
877.STAMPER (U.S. Toll-Free)
stampington.com

US Art Quest, Inc.
800.200.7848
usartquest.com

*Contributor

Photo Credits: Per Brandin: page 119. Anna Bressi: page 73. Deanna Finch Cohen: pages 26, 46, 65 and 66. Deborah Davis: pages 25, 30, 33, 40, 50, 52, 55, 59, 72, 74, 80, 81, 85, 92, 94, 103, 104 and 112. Jonathan Davis: page 111. Helen Frank: page 45. Kathleen Greco: pages 24, 29, 42, 54, 56, 58, 70, 84, 96, 107 and 118. Melissa Greco: pages 41, 44, 66, 82, 120 and 121. Michael Greco: page 64. Nick Greco: pages 28 and 36. Jonathan Reid: page 123. Ann Ziegler: pages 37, 38, 51, 56, 60, 68, 69, 94, 97, 98, 108, 116, 117 and 122. Robert Ziegler: pages 22, 86, 93 and 110.